MOSQUITO MAYHEM

MOSQUITO MAYHEM

de Havilland's Wooden Wonder
in Action in WWII

Martin W. Bowman

Pen & Sword
AVIATION

Dedication

Herbert 'Ed' Boulter DFC   5 April 1923 to 9 April 2010
Tommy Broom DFC**   22 January 1914 to 18 May 2010

First Published in Great Britain in 2010 and reprinted in this format in 2021 by
Pen & Sword Aviation
an imprint of
Pen & Sword Books Ltd
47 Church Street, Barnsley, South Yorkshire S70 2AS

Copyright © Martin W. Bowman, 2010, 2021

ISBN 978 1 39908 506 9

The right of Martin W. Bowman to be identified as author of this work
has been asserted by him in accordance with the Copyright,
Designs and Patents Act 1988.

A CIP catalogue record for this book is
available from the British Library.

All rights reserved. No part of this book may be reproduced or transmitted in
any form or by any means, electronic or mechanical including photocopying,
recording or by any information storage and retrieval system, without
permission from the Publisher in writing.

Typeset in 10/12pt Palatino by Concept, Huddersfield

Printed and bound in the UK by CPI Group (UK) Ltd, Croydon, CR0 4YY

Pen & Sword Books Ltd incorporates the Imprints of Pen & Sword Aviation,
Pen & Sword Maritime, Pen & Sword Military, Wharncliffe Local History, Pen
& Sword Select, Pen & Sword Military Classics, Leo Cooper,
Remember When, Seaforth Publishing and Frontline Publishing.

For a complete list of Pen & Sword titles please contact
PEN & SWORD BOOKS LIMITED
47 Church Street, Barnsley, South Yorkshire, S70 2AS, England
E-mail: enquiries@pen-and-sword.co.uk
Website: www.pen-and-sword.co.uk

Contents

Acknowledgements		vi
Chapter 1	The New Wooden Walls, by Bruce Sanders	1
Chapter 2	'Musical Mosquitoes'	17
Chapter 3	Defensive Night-Fighting	36
Chapter 4	Death In The Dark	62
Chapter 5	On The Defensive Again	84
Chapter 6	The 'Milk Run', Markers and 'Pampas'	118
Chapter 7	'Nuisance' Raiders	168
Chapter 8	The Enemy Within	190
Chapter 9	Jericho	218
Chapter 10	'Jane'	255
Index		267

Acknowledgements

I am most grateful to the following people for making it possible to include so much diverse information and anecdotes on Mosquito operations: Sidney Allinson; Philip Back DFC; Norman Bacon; H. Barker; Len Bartram; Tim Bates; Derek 'Taffy' Bellis DFC*; Air Vice-Marshal H. Bird-Wilson CBE DSO AFC; Philip J. Birtles; Barry Blunt BA (Hons); Dr Theo Boiten; Ed Boulter DFC; Tommy Broom DFC**; Jeff Carless; John Carnegie; Mike Carreck DFC; George Cash; Peter Celis; Mrs S.A. Chadderton; Dorothy Chaloner; Bob Collis; Hank Cooper DSO DFC; Patrick Corness; Luc Cox; Hans-Peter Dabrowski; Squadron Leader Mike Daniels; *Eastern Daily Press*; *Eastern Evening News*; Grenville Eaton; Leslie Fletcher; Mrs P. Jane Fox, *Legion* Magazine; J.D.S. Garratt DFC*; Rev. Nigel Gilson; Air Vice-Marshal Bill Gill DSO; Val Grimble; Ken Godfrey; Peter B. Gunn, author of *RAF Great Massingham*; Alan Hague; Leo Hall; G. Horsfield; Richard Howard; Squadron Leader Stephen J. Howard; M. Howland; Harry Jeffries; Bernard M. Job; *Legion* Magazine; *Lancashire Evening News*; E.W. Lawson; Wing Commander R.W. Leggett; Frank Leyland, Andrew Long; Squadron Leader George Lord; Sister Laurence May; G.F. Mahony; Captain Bill McCash AFM; Noelle Meredith, PRM, Royal Aeronautical Society; Denis Moore; Eric Mombeek; Wing Commander A.P. Morgan; F.G. Morris; Mosquito Aircrew Association; Wing Commander George Newby; J.A. Padilla; Wing Commander George Parry DSO DFC; Simon Parry, Air Research Publications; Squadron Leader Charles Patterson DSO DFC; Allan Pudsey; Ralph Ramm; John Rayner, G.Av.A; W.F. Rhodes; the late Peter Richard; Squadron Leader E.J. Saunderson; James F. 'Bill' Setchell Jr; Wing Commander Joe Singleton; Jerry Scutts; Group Captain E.M. Smith DFC* DFM; Colonel R. Smith; Derek Smith DFC*; Mrs Ann Solberg Clark;

Acknowledgements

Martin Staunton; Dr Robin Steel; C. Tarkowski; Geoff Thomas; Henk Van Baaren; John Vasco; Paddy Walker; Colin 'Ginger' Walsh; Peter Waxham; Alan B. Webb; Brian Williams; Phyllis and the late J. Ralph Wood; Squadron Leader R.G. 'Tim' Woodman DSO DFC; W.C. Woodruff CBE FRAeS; *Worcester Evening News*.

CHAPTER 1

The New Wooden Walls
Bruce Sanders

In July 1942 one of those unpredictable emergencies arose which even the widest and most comprehensive planning cannot insure against happening. It became a matter of great and vital urgency that certain papers should be flown to Russia and a reply received within the space of twenty-four hours. Search was made for a suitable plane and a highly trained and experienced crew to fly it. The crew selected was a pilot and observer[1] of Coastal Command, who had flown on many trips across the northern waters and knew the convoy routes. The plane they were given was one of the secret Mosquitoes, the all-wooden wonder being turned out by the de Havilland company and supplied to Bomber Command without any publicity in the home Press. The Mosquito was something the RAF was still keeping up its bright blue sleeve. It was a secret the enemy's Air Intelligence would have given a great deal to know about, a secret that was to cause him much operational grief before, more than four months later, the first story of the existence of the Mosquitoes was to be released – after the sensational and dramatic attack by these aircraft on the Gestapo Headquarters in Oslo in the broad light of day.

But in July, to the ordinary man and woman in the street, the mosquito was still a summer pest with a horrid appetite for sensitive skins, one of those lowly and thoroughly noisome creatures an incomprehensible Providence had allowed to multiply alarmingly in an already overcrowded world. Certainly never to be accorded the dignity of a capital M! However, as two Coastal Command men sat over their breakfast at six o'clock one bright July morning, a twin-engined plane, clean-cut in line, sprouting cannon,[2] was warming up ready for a take-off. For those two excited and very proud men the only mosquito in the world was the one on the runway whose engines purred with the rhythm of power. They did not dally over the meal.

The sun was beginning to find its real lustre when they climbed into the aircraft, settled themselves in their cockpits, quickly checked the instruments and radio and gave the ground staff the OK sign. The chocks were pulled away, the sleek length of the wooden frame shuddered slightly and the Mosquito moved forward. It rose off the airfield, circled once and then headed east. The highly confidential and urgent flight to an aerodrome in the north of Russia had begun.[3]

The pilot knew his stuff. He headed straight out across the North Sea, making for the Norwegian coast. He kept high and thrilled at the effortless ease with which his Rolls-Royce Merlins pulled the aircraft through the air. He kept glancing at the speed gauge, fascinated by what it revealed.

Making the Norwegian coast, he turned up it and headed due north, still keeping very high. Suddenly the oxygen supply failed. The observer placed his finger over a hole that had appeared in the oxygen tube, and the pilot put the plane's nose down into a sharp dive.

On that dive the needle of the speed gauge flickered on the 450 mark.

He pulled out of the dive suddenly and sent the Mosquito screaming away to the north-east. A glance below had revealed, spread over the surface of the sea, a fleet of German warships. He had been diving out of the clouds straight at them!

The Mosquito flattened out, twisted and zoomed. The flying skill of the pilot and the brilliant manoeuvrability of the aircraft warded off certain disaster.

'We had passed over them,' the pilot reported later, referring to the German warships, 'and into cloud in a matter of seconds – before they could open fire.'

The remainder of the flight to the aerodrome marked on the pilot's chart was made without incident. Landfall was made, and shortly before noon the British plane landed.

The two Coastal Command men received a hearty welcome from the Russian airmen, who eyed the aircraft that had made the flight with keen, appreciative eyes. The British flyers were taken into the Russian mess for lunch – and a rare lunch it proved for men who had been on rations.

There were mounds of pâté de foie gras, bottles of vodka, borsch, mountainous steaks of venison, piles of bright creamy butter, and the samovars worked overtime producing cup after cup of what the pilot described as 'the most perfect tea I have ever drunk'.

Lunch over, and smoking cigarettes, the Coastal Command men were shown over the aerodrome and generally entertained by their hosts.

At three o'clock they were back at the Mosquito in flying-kit, ready to take off.

Seven and a half hours later, with daylight still in the English sky, they dropped down over their own landing-field, having made an uneventful flight.

'We then had a late dinner', the pilot recounted later. 'Altogether we had been in the air eleven hours and fifty minutes. I was a bit cramped, since I couldn't leave my seat and had to wriggle my body to avoid stiffness.'

But the trip had been made. The papers were exchanged. The Mosquito had fully justified the faith placed in its design and production – and it was ready for more urgent work.

The urgent work was waiting. Work like the truly remarkable flight to Malta by way of France and Italy made by another Coastal Command crew flying a Mosquito. Here are the navigator's own words, describing the journey:

> We took off from England in fog and set course directly for Venice, climbing to 24,000 ft. The Alps were a breathtaking sight and visibility was now good. At 11.45 hours we sighted Venice, and after reconnoitring the city, harbour and aerodrome and clearly seeing a large battleship and a many-sided passenger liner, we flew over the shipbuilding yards at Monfalcone and then headed for Trieste. There were a number of naval vessels in the harbour. We noted these, set course for Fiume and flew over the small port of Pola on the southern tip of the Istrian peninsula.

It sounds very much like a peacetime tourist itinerary. These Mosquito airmen, flying in daylight, apparently wandered Italian skies as they wished. There is something about the complete success of the flight that smacks of covert nose thumbing, a quiet impertinence that is breathtaking.

> This job done [the navigator continues, in the same rich vein], we set course for Rome. The cloud thinned as we approached and, clearly showing amid the modern and well-planned streets of this ancient city, we saw the Colosseum. Final course was now set for Malta, a distance of 420 miles, with Sicily to cross. Soon the island loomed ahead, with Mount Etna easily visible to port. Losing height gradually, we spotted Luqa and made a perfect landing, little over six hours after leaving England.

The weather after their arrival turned unfavourable for flying, so for twenty-four hours these intrepid 'tourists' stayed on the island, but at six o'clock the following morning they were in the air again, the nose of their Mosquito turned south. They headed for the North African coastline.

> We then set course for Gibraltar [the narrative continues]. Malta to Gibraltar took just over five hours. Almost immediately after leaving Gibraltar we ran into heavy cloud and icing conditions, with the port engine missing occasionally, to keep us alive to the fact that we were not home yet.

But when they were over France the weather cleared and they crossed the Breton coast somewhere just south of the U-boat base of Lorient. When one recalls the many squadrons of German fighters kept in that sector to deal with intrepid raiders, it almost seems as though the two men were throwing the enemy a dare. A dare, anyway, that the Hun did not accept. They flew on and by radio pin-pointed their exact position when well above heavy cloud once more.

> At the right moment [the navigator concluded his account of the trip], we came below cloud and there was our base, right where it should have been. Never was there a more welcome sight. We had covered nearly four thousand miles since leaving England – and had forgotten to eat our grapes!

It is said that Coastal Command navigators are the finest in the world because they have to be. This trip offers nothing to discount the claim.

Among other things, it proved that the Mosquito craft were brilliant machines for the work for which they were designed. In the custody of carefully trained crews they would be a terrible weapon of war,

In the months that followed, Mosquito crews were trained for the part they were to take in the new offensive. The factories were urged to turn out more and more Mosquitoes. There was plenty of work waiting for them to do. They were to make daring daylight attacks that would upset the enemy's morale and give the lie to his vain propaganda about the inviolacy of the so-called European Fortress. That and various other pretty bubbles were to be pricked by the mosquitoes' long-reaching sting.

They opened their own particular offensive on 25 September 1942 when, in the middle of the afternoon, they pounced on the *Gestapo* Headquarters in Oslo.

The flight, consisting of four Mosquitoes, was led by Sqn Ldr D.A.G. Parry DFC and Bar.[4] They swooped down out of brilliant autumn sunshine, right over the centre of the Norwegian capital. Pin-pointing the skyscraper town hall, near the harbour, where the waters of the fiord sparkled, the old Akerhus fortress, the Royal Palace at one end of the main street and the high dome of the building housing the men who took orders from Heinrich Himmler was simple enough. Actually they had flown through cloud over the North Sea, but over the Skagerrak the sky cleared. To the south-east of the city was a low hill. The bombers passed behind that, keeping very low, and then with the city spread beneath them like a suddenly unrolled carpet of bright colours, they swept towards their objective.

However, they had been observed. A flight of Fw 190s shot up to intercept the raiders with the British 'target' on their wings, and as the Mosquitoes rounded the hill they attacked with blazing cannon.

One of the Mosquitoes went down, its port engine on fire, a Focke-Wulf close over its lifted tail. The other three pilots saw their comrade's aircraft crash into the waters of Oslo Fiord.[5] Another of the Mosquitoes took a cannon-shell right in the centre of its starboard airscrew, but it kept flying and did not lag behind. For thirty miles the Focke-Wulfs followed the others, but were unable to inflict any more damage. The Mosquitoes had the legs of them, and the *Luftwaffe* pilots must have been sorely puzzled by this appearance of British bombers, which were able to outpace the best fighters the *Luftwaffe* could put into the air.

The British crews had one hurried glimpse of people in the streets of Oslo as they tore over the house-tops at barely a hundred feet, and then the Nazi flag, with its centred swastika, was waving from the top of the domed building.

Down went the bombs, straddling the pile of red bricks, and debris and brick dust were hurled in the air in a cloud that had not dispersed when the crews took their last glance at the city falling away behind them.

On the night of Sunday the 27th, Sqn Ldr Parry went to the microphone and broadcast a personal description of the raid. He began:

> On Friday afternoon Quisling and I had an appointment in the same town. Quisling had a big crowd with him, I believe – it was one of his party rallies. I only had a little crowd – we were in four Mosquitoes – and they gave us very short notice. But we were punctual.

'We are punctual' would be a very good slogan for the Mosquito squadrons. In the following months they proved their punctuality time and again – not the least occasion being when they turned up in Berlin and prevented Goering from making a radio speech on schedule. But before that January afternoon they put in some good work over the Continent, striking at factories in the occupied countries working at full pressure for the German war machine. Putting back the Nazis' clock was a habit with the Mosquito crews.

One of the finest pilots and leaders in Bomber Command took Mosquitoes early in October[6] to make a low-level attack at dusk on a factory and power station near Hengelo, a hundred miles inland from the Dutch coast. This was Wg Cdr H.I. Edwards VC DFC,[7] and with him flew Sqn Ldr Parry, who had led the assault on Oslo. The only opposition the Mosquitoes met was a flight of birds. One of these flew straight into a Mosquito's window, smashing it, and the flying glass cut the crew badly about the face – so much so that the pilot was forced to turn back for home after momentarily losing control.

Edwards and another pilot placed their bombs in the centre of the factory; Parry did as good a job on the power station. The Mosquitoes then made for home, where they learned that other Mosquitoes had, earlier in the day, flown to attack targets in Western Germany.[8]

The new wooden walls of Britain were proving themselves masters of the air through which they flew.

Ten days later they were back over the Hengelo factory. This time they were not even opposed by a flight of birds.[9]

One of the important industrial targets working for the Nazis in Holland that the Mosquitoes attacked several times was the Eindhoven factory of Philips. It was the largest plant producing radio valves in Europe. But owing to the very nature and position of this vital target it was decided that there was only one way of attacking it without causing heavy casualties among the Dutch civilian population – in daylight from a low level. Early in December a Mosquito attack[10] was launched against this key factory. The attackers went over the target in waves, the first waves dropping HEs, the last, bombing from zero feet, mixing incendiaries with HEs fitted with short delayed-action fuses.

Sqn Ldr Brian Wheeler DFC,[11] who was in the last wave, remarked afterwards, 'It was the most magnificent bombing I have ever seen on any target', and he knew what he was talking about. Smoke rose more than three hundred feet in a wide column from the shattered buildings. The crews in the last wave had a genuine Mosquito's-eye view of the flame-shot picture. They saw the name 'Philips' beside the large clock, the hands of which pointed to 12.20, and one air gunner even caught the sheen of the sun on the buckle of a German anti-aircraft gunner's belt. Those German gunners on the roof remained firing even when the place was ablaze beneath them. The flak was hot, but it did not break up the attack, which was fierce and concentrated. A Maori gunner who went on the trip had his steel helmet knocked off by flak and two holes cut in his clothes, but he was not even scratched.

Wg Cdr R.H. Young AFC,[12] commenting on the raid later, said, 'We all felt that the attack had been well planned, but we realized, however cleverly it had been worked out beforehand, we owed a lot to our navigators, who had to keep us on course from landmarks that flashed by in a second only a few feet below.' The Mosquito crews were becoming specialists in this furious, fast and concentrated type of daylight intruding.

Four months later, at the end of March 1943, the Air Ministry announced:

> Ever since squadrons of RAF bombers attacked the great Phillips [sic] works at Eindhoven and left them very badly damaged, the Germans have been feverishly working to try to get the factory going again. Skilled Dutchmen have been pressed into service and under the eyes of experts from Germany have been made to labour day and night to repair the damage.

The labour was in vain, none the less. The radio valves so badly wanted by the U-boat constructors and the German aircraft factories, the *Reichswehr*'s radio-location stations and the shops and plants assembling tanks and Panzers, were not forthcoming from Eindhoven. The men flying Bomber Command's wooden walls saw to that.

When the Philips factory was about ready to start full production again, Wg Cdr W.P. Shand DFC led another formation of Mosquitoes to upset things.[13] The Mosquitoes switch-backed over Holland, dodging flocks of seagulls over the Zuider Zee and tearing over Eindhoven once more at 'zero' feet.

Plt Off T.M. Mitchell, who brought up the rear of the formation, saw the full effect of the strafing as he banked to turn for base.

> As we came in to attack [he reported later], I saw the wing commander's bombs, which were fused to go off a short time after impact, fall into the buildings, as we skimmed over the roof-tops. Then I let our own bombs go right into the middle of the factory. As I circled after the attack I saw the whole building become enveloped in smoke, with huge red flashes as the bombs exploded.

A South African, Plt Off Hay, from Pretoria, saw V-signs flashing from some of the Dutch houses in the failing light. The people of the Netherlands welcomed the cancellation of their months of labour.

One of the most ingenious pieces of Mosquito work was the bombing of a railway tunnel, on 9 December 1942, some forty miles north-west of Paris, by an ace pilot of Bomber Command, Sqn Ldr J.R.G. Ralston DSO DFM. His navigator, Flt Lt S. Clayton DFC DFM, cleverly directed the aircraft along the double railway track, and with split-second timing Ralston released a bomb with delayed-action fuse, right in the tunnel mouth on the Paris–Soissons line. Clayton saw the bomb for one brief moment actually skidding along the tracks into the tunnel. Then Ralston had pulled back the stick and they were skimming over the target.

Ralston made a couple of dummy runs and then released another bomb. This ricocheted on to the stonework at the tunnel entrance. Ralston again lifted his aircraft, flew to the opposite end of the tunnel and dived as a train entered. He placed another bomb accurately on the tracks, then went back to the other entrance, ready for the train when it reappeared – if it did. It did not. Those first bombs had done their work.

That is bombing raised to a fine art.

Ten days later,[14] targets in north-west Germany were feeling the sting of Bomber Command's Mosquitoes. One Mosquito came down so low that the crew read the name *Fritz* on a river-tug. The bombers swept over men working on a new barracks. 'They were near the end of the work,' was how the pilot reported the incident later, 'and we finished it off for them.' Another Mosquito peeled off to attack a gasholder near the coast and took a German cannon-shell in the nose, which made the aircraft lurch drunkenly, but the pilot, Sqn Ldr Reginald Reynolds DFC of Cheltenham, got the plane on to an even keel again. However, the anti-freeze mixture was pouring from the radiator and the cockpit filled with cordite fumes. WO Arthur Noseda, from Western Australia, moved the bomber he was piloting in close to Reynolds, and together the Mosquitoes recrossed the German coast near Wilhelmshaven. Coastal batteries opened up at them and the guns of a warship joined in. Fountains of water rose on each side of the aircraft, which were 'down on the deck'.

But the wooden walls were as sturdy as the old-time oaken ships that won the freedom of the seas, as today the RAF is winning the freedom of the skies. Noseda's help was not wanted. Reynolds did not come down in the North Sea. His crippled aircraft made a safe landing at base.[15]

In the New Year the Mosquitoes stepped up the tempo of their stinging attacks. Just before dusk on 27 January, Wg Cdr Edwards, who had attacked the factory at Hengelo, led a brilliant swoop on the submarine diesel shops and shipbuilding yards of Burmeister and Wain at Copenhagen. The success of the cleverly planned and executed attack caused the German-controlled Danish Press and radio to offer loud protests about the many Danes who had stood waving in the streets of the capital to the 'harbingers of spring and liberty' and those others who sent large wreaths and bunches of flowers to the funeral of the crew of the one Mosquito that was brought down in Denmark.[16]

The Germans were getting fidgety about the daring of the Mosquito crews. Their fidgetiness attained the dimensions of a paroxysm when, three days later, Bomber Command staged its most 'impudent' raid of the war to date – the attack on Berlin led by Sqn Ldr Reynolds at eleven o'clock in the morning, the hour *Reichsmarschall* Goering was timed to orate over the radio. The oration was put back a full hour and the Mosquitoes got home without loss, apparently an encouragement to those others who returned and were over Berlin at four in the afternoon the time when Dr Goebbels rose to speak in the Sports Palast.[17]

The Berlin performance brought the following message from Sir Arthur Harris to the air officer commanding the Mosquito group:

Please convey to all concerned and particularly to the crews of the aircraft, my warmest congratulations on the magnificent daylight attack carried out on Berlin by your Mosquitoes. Their bombs coincided with an attempt by Goering to broadcast to the German people on the tenth anniversary of Hitler's usurpation of power and cannot have failed to cause consternation in Germany and encouragement to the oppressed peoples of Europe.

In the following weeks the Mosquitoes spread their wings and dropped their bomb-loads over the large railway workshops at Tours,[18] the workers of which had been press-ganged by the Germans, and the German naval stores depot and marshalling-yards outside Rennes, some hundred miles south of Cherbourg.[19] Flt Lt Clayton was again on this latter exploit.[20] They also returned to Norway, on 3 March, this time to a mountain slope above a tiny lake. Their target was a small concrete building housing the crushing, grinding and washing plant of the Knaben molybdenum mines, where hundreds of Norwegian workers were forced to labour under practically slave conditions.

Wg Cdr Shand led the attack, and the navigational work was a nightmare. The Mosquitoes crossed four hundred miles of sea to make the exact spot on the Norwegian coast pencilled on their briefing-maps. The navigators found the ground snow-covered – it was early in March – and it was well-nigh impossible to pick out landmarks. At one stage the formation had to fly for a distance of some ten miles over the bright blue water at the bottom of a crevasse, with the snow-mantled rocks rising to five hundred feet on each side. The narrowness of the crevasse caused them to fly in single file. The tiniest variation from the central line of flight would have brought disaster.

But the Mosquitoes arrived over their target and pranged it thoroughly.[21]

After the heavy strafing of the Renault works at Billancourt, the salvaged plant was taken to a subsidiary plant near Le Mans. Mosquitoes in one afternoon[22] swoop wiped that off the enemy's list of assets. Led by Sqn Ldr Reynolds and Sqn Ldr J.V. Berggren, they also drew a line through the name of Cockerill, the vast armament works near Liège, when they bombed it in waves.[23] Paderborn, which is the centre of a triangle formed by the German townships of Münster, Hannover and Kassel, and was in the heart of a heavily defended industrial area, had its railway workshops blasted by Mosquitoes on 16 March. They flew eight hundred miles in daylight to complete that job of work.[24] Locomotive works of the Compagnie Générale de Construction des Locomotives Batignolles-Chatillon, at St Joseph, two miles north-east of Nantes, also felt the weight of their lightning attack.[25] Again the Mosquito ace pilot, Wg Cdr Shand, was around to see the bombs fall in the right places.

Railway workshops seemed, somehow, to attract Mosquitoes. They turned up in daylight on 1 April, apparently to celebrate the twenty-fifth anniversary of the founding of the RAF over the vast machine-shops and plant at Trier, on the German side of the Luxembourg frontier.[26] Sqn Ldr Ralston was in charge of this task, and he had with him as navigator Flt Lt Clayton, who was out on his hundredth operational flight. To mark the uniqueness of the occasion, the Flight Lieutenant did an especially fine piece of work that day, and when he returned he was awarded the DSO.

Clayton had made more than seventy of his hundred flights in daylight, and he had flown with Ralston on nearly eighty occasions. They were both sergeants when they 'crewed up' together to fly Blenheims. In the RAF they had earned an enviable reputation as one of the most competent partnerships in light bombers. Each was an ace in his own right.[27]

The Mosquitoes provided a two-pronged attack that day. While Clayton was figuring navigational details, Sqn Ldr John V. Berggren, who flew with the party to Trier, went on as leader of another flight to bomb the marshalling-yards and depot at Ehrang.

When the crews returned, there was a party to celebrate Clayton's century and the RAF's jubilee. That was when, appropriately, he was informed that he had won the DSO, and there was a personal message of congratulation from Sir Arthur Harris to round off the tribute.

A few days later the Mosquitoes strafed more engine-sheds, this time at Ronet, a short distance from Namur. The work was done with customary skill and exactitude.

But bigger things were in the offing for the wide-roving twin-engined Mosquitoes. They were suddenly turned over to night bombing, and their prime target was the German capital. They were led on these occasions by Wg Cdr J. de L. Wooldridge DFC and Bar[28] and the man who had spoiled Goering's speech-making, Reynolds, who now had a DSO ribbon alongside his DFC, and the three bands of a wing commander round his cuffs. On 22 May the Air Ministry was able to announce, 'Mosquitoes of Bomber Command last night attacked Berlin for the third night running and on six out of the last eight nights.'[29]

The Happy Valley excursionists were not allowed to grab all the glory that was Bomber Command's. The Mosquitoes were very much in the picture. The Berlin night-fighters tried every trick they knew to discourage the intrepid light bombers: they pounced on them in the middle of flak bursts, they even tried colliding with them, but punctuality was always, as we have seen, a Mosquito's strong point.

At the same time they did not overlook the locomotive shops at such towns as Orléans, while they found time to seek out new-type targets, such as the Carl Zeiss instrument works and the Schott glassworks at

Jena, in Thuringia – a journey of well over a thousand miles. That was another piece of polished leadership by Reynolds.[30]

Flg Off E.D. Sismore DFC, who hails from Kettering, gave a brief picture when he returned of what the task was like:

> As soon as we picked out the tall chimneys of the Schott factory, the ground gunners began firing at us with all they had. We dropped our bombs on the factory building and almost at once we were hit by three 20 mm shells. A large piece was knocked out of our port airscrew and my pilot was hit in the hand and knee.

The fact that he was able to make that report tells its own story. The Mosquitoes are hard to bring down. Their thirty-six-ply hides of balsa wood are tougher than steel, enthusiasts maintain.[31]

They are tough enough, anyway, for Coastal Command – who flew some of the first, as we have seen – to ask for Mosquitoes to help in the Battle of the Bay of Biscay. They were given them, and good work they were soon doing, especially among the swooping Ju 88s.

Fighter Command also asked for Mosquitoes for fast Intruder work. They too were supplied. On 27 March, Fighter Command extended its daylight offensive eastwards into the Reich for the first time in the war. The plane was a lone Mosquito, which flew more than six hundred miles and played havoc with a number of targets. It was piloted by a Canadian whose grandparents were Polish.[32] His observer was Plt Off H. Ladbrook, a Londoner.[33]

The Mosquito, in its few tempestuous months of operational life, had become an all-commands aircraft.

There could be no finer tribute to the quality of Britain's new wooden walls.

Notes

1. Flt Lt K.H. Bayley and Plt Off Little.
2. W4061, an unarmed Mosquito PR.I armed only with cameras.
3. On 6 July 1942 Flt Lt Bayley and Plt Off Little took off from Leuchars and headed for Norway to try to photograph the *Tirpitz*.
4. Flt Lt D.A.G. 'George' Parry was a veteran of two tours on Blenheims. He was always known as 'George' because, like the autopilot of the same name, he always came home! The three other crews from 105 Squadron were Plt Off Pete W.T. Rowland and Plt Off Richard 'Dick' Reilly; Flg Off Alec Bristow and Plt Off Bernard Marshall; and Flt Sgt Gordon K. Carter and Sgt William S. Young.
5. Flt Sgt Gordon K. Carter and Sgt William S. Young crashed into Lake Engervannet near Sandvika.
6. On 6 October 1942.

7. Wg Cdr Hughie Idwal Edwards VC DFC, an Australian of Welsh ancestry from Freemantle, took command of 105 Squadron for the second time on 1 August. Edwards had been CO of 139 Squadron when he took command of 105 Squadron in May 1941 when the two squadrons were flying Blenheims on suicidal anti-shipping strikes in the North Sea. On 15 June 1941 Edwards led a formation of three Blenheims in a successful attack on a 4,000-ton merchantman, and on 1 July he was awarded the DFC for this daring low-level exploit. On 4 July 1941 a raid on Bremen (Operation Wreckage, as it was codenamed) was led by Edwards. Although four crews were lost, successful attacks were made on the docks, factories, a timber-yard and railways, and great damage was caused to the tankers and transports, which were loaded with vital supplies. All the aircraft were damaged. After the target Edwards proceeded to circle Bremen and strafed a stationary train that had opened up on them, before leading the formation out of Germany at low level. Edwards, his aircraft minus part of the port wing, the port aileron badly damaged, a cannon-shell in the radio rack and a length of telegraph wire wrapped round the tailwheel and trailing behind, reached Swanton Morley, where he put down safely. Operation Wreckage received considerable publicity, and on 21 July it was announced that Wg Cdr Hughie Edwards DFC had been awarded the Victoria Cross for courage and leadership displayed on the operation.
8. Two high-level attacks were made from 15,000 ft and 26,000 ft on Essen and Bremen respectively. A low-level dusk attack was also planned on the Stork diesel engine works at Hengelo by three Mosquitoes led by Edwards and 'Tubby' Cairns, while George Parry and his observer, Plt Off 'Robbie' Robson, were to attack the central power station at Twente on the edge of Hengelo. Edwards's formation attacked what they thought was the diesel engine works, but in fact dropped their bombs on a factory in Almelo, which turned out clothing for the German Army. The bombs had 11-second delay fuses, and the rear aircraft, flown by Parry, flew over them as they detonated, nearly blowing his Mosquito out of the sky. Parry was able to regain control and continued on to his target. (One crew did manage to reach the Stork works and drop three 500 lb bombs from 250 ft into the target.) Parry carried on to the power station and hit his target 'pin-point' and 'on the dot'. (Part of the power station had just been taken out of service, so the electricity supply was unaffected.) See *Mosquito Thunder: No. 105 Squadron RAF At War 1942–45*. Stuart R. Scott (Sutton Publishing, 1999).
9. On 15 October a successful dusk shallow-dive attack was made on the Stork factory at Hengelo by four Mosquitoes of 105 Squadron led by Flt Lt Roy Ralston with his navigator Syd Clayton, who dived on the factory from 4,000 ft. (Joseph Roy George Ralston and Sydney Clayton were posted to 105 Squadron in May 1942 after flying Blenheim IVs in 107 Squadron. Ralston, a Mancunian from Moss Side, had enlisted in the RAF in 1930 as a technical tradesman.) A total of 2,000 lb HE was dropped. Three civilians were killed when two houses near the factory were hit. The next day, the attack was repeated by five Mosquitoes of 105 Squadron led by Roy Ralston and a 139 Mosquito flown by Sqn Ldr

Jack E. Houlston AFC and his observer, WO J.L. Armitage DFC. This time, the attack was made at low level from 100 ft, and all claimed to have hit the target, but again some bombs fell on Almelo. In Hengelo, two factories, the Stork and the neighbouring Dikkers works, were hit, although the bombs that hit the Dikkers works failed to explode. See *Mosquito Thunder: No. 105 Squadron RAF At War 1942–45*. Stuart R. Scott (Sutton Publishing, 1999).

10. On Sunday 6 December 1942, ninety-three Bostons, Venturas and Mosquitoes of 2 Group attacked the Philips works. See *The Reich Intruders*. Martin W. Bowman (Pen & Sword, 2005).
11. A Ventura II pilot in 487 Squadron RNZAF.
12. The CO of 464 Squadron RAAF who was awarded the DSO.
13. On 30 March Wg Cdr Peter Shand DFC led ten Mosquitoes of 139 Squadron to Eindhoven.
14. On 20 December eleven Mosquitoes of 105 and 139 Squadrons, led by Sqn Ldr Reggie Reynolds with Ted Sismore, attacked railway targets in the Oldenburg-Bremen area in north-west Germany. Reynolds had flown a tour on Hampdens and a tour on Manchesters. Sismore had flown on Blenheims on 110 Squadron, and while at the Blenheim OTU at Bicester and the Whitley OTU at Honeybourne, had flown on two of the 1,000-bomber raids in 1942.
15. WO A. Raymond Noseda DFC and Sgt John Watson Urquhart of 105 Squadron were KIA on 9 January 1943.
16. Wg Cdr Hughie Edwards VC DSO DFC and Flg Off 'Tubby' Cairns DFC led nine Mosquitoes of 105 and 139 Squadrons in a round trip of more than 1,200 miles to the Burmeister and Wain diesel-engine works. On the return to Marham Sgt Richard Clare and Flg Off Edward Doyle of 139 Squadron hit a balloon cable and tree at East Dereham after the starboard engine failed, and were killed. Edwards landed with only fifteen gallons of fuel in his tanks, enough for about another six and a half miles.
17. On 30 January three crews in 105 Squadron, led by Sqn Ldr 'Reggie' W. Reynolds DFC and Plt Off E.B. 'Ted' Sismore, bombed Berlin that morning when *Reichsmarschall* Hermann Goering was due to speak. In the afternoon, three Mosquitoes of 139 Squadron arrived over Berlin at the time Dr Joseph Goebbels, Hitler's propaganda minister, was due to address the German nation at the Sports Palast. The three Mosquitoes arrived over Berlin at exactly 11.00 hours, and the explosion of their bombs severely disrupted the *Reichsmarschall*'s speech. That afternoon the three Mosquitoes of 139 Squadron arrived over Berlin at the time Goebbels was due to speak. They dropped their bombs right on cue. However, the earlier raid had alerted the defences, and flak brought down the Mosquito flown by Sqn Ldr Donald F.W. Darling DFC and Flg Off William Wright.
18. On the afternoon of 14 February, in what became known as the 'Great Tours Derby', six Mosquitoes of 139 Squadron attacked the engine sheds in the French city from low level.
19. On 14 February Hughie Edwards, who had been promoted group captain four days earlier, left 105 Squadron to take up a post at HQ Bomber Command prior to taking command of RAF Binbrook on the

18th. Edwards's successor was Wg Cdr Geoffrey P. Longfield, who on 26 February led an attack by twenty Mosquitoes of 105 and 139 Squadrons on the Rennes Naval Arsenal.
20. Canadian Flg Offs Spencer Kimmel and Harry Kirkland, who were formating on Longfield, sliced into their leader's tail, and Longfield went up into a loop and dived straight into the ground west of Rennes St Jacques. Kimmel lost height and disappeared below the trees at 300 mph. Longfield and his navigator, Flt Lt Roderick Milne, and Kimmel and Kirkland all died. On the way home a 139 Squadron Mosquito flown by Lt T.D.C. Moe and his observer, 2nd Lt O. Smedsaas, both RNAF, crashed, and the two Dutchmen were killed.
21. Wg Cdr Peter Shand DFC led ten Mosquitoes of 139 Squadron to the molybdenum mines at Knaben in south Norway. Bomb bursts accompanied by orange flashes and a red glow were seen on and around the target, which resulted in the plant being enveloped in clouds of white and brown smoke and debris being blown to a height of 1,000 ft. Four Fw 190s intercepted the Mosquitoes on the homeward journey, and Flg Off A.N. Bulpitt and his navigator, Sgt K.A. Amond, were last seen being pursued by two Fw 190s and crashing into the sea. Flg Off J.H. Brown's Mosquito was hit and badly damaged, but he made a successful crash-landing at Leuchars.
22. On 4 March Sqn Ldr Reggie Reynolds DSO DFC led a successful attack by six Mosquitoes at low level from 50 to 200 ft on the engine sheds and repair workshops at Le Mans.
23. On 12 March twelve Mosquitoes of 105 and 139 Squadrons, led by Sqn Ldr Reggie Reynolds and Plt Off Ted Sismore, were briefed to attack the John Cockerill steel and armament works in the centre of Liège. Bombing had to be carried out very accurately indeed to keep losses to a minimum, and this task was given to the shallow-dive section led by Sqn Ldr John V. Berggren of 139 Squadron, with his observer, Peter Wright. Berggren had by now completed almost sixty operations. In peacetime Wright was a 'serious-minded' schoolmaster. A total of 9.8 tons of bombs were dropped on the John Cockerill works. Sgt Robert McMurray Pace and Plt Off George Cook of 139 Squadron crashed into the Ooster Schelde off Woensdrecht.
24. Sixteen Mosquitoes led by Sqn Ldr John Bergrren made low-level and shallow-dive attacks on the roundhouses and engine sheds at Paderborn. One Mosquito, flown by Flt Sgt Peter J.D. McGeehan DFM and Flg Off Reginald C. Morris DFC, was lost.
25. On 23 March ten Mosquitoes of 139 Squadron led by Wg Cdr Peter Shand DFC, and five of 139 Squadron led by Flt Lt Bill Blessing DFC, attacked the works at low level. The raid was timed to perfection as factory workers finished work.
26. Six Mosquitoes of 105 Squadron led by Wg Cdr Roy Ralston, and four of 139 Squadron led by Sqn Ldr John V. Berggren, bombed the power station and railway yards at Trier and engine sheds at Ehrang respectively from 50 to 400 ft.
27. By March 1945 Roy Ralston was CO of 139 Squadron, and still managed to fly on operations. He had been awarded the DSO for 'outstanding

leadership and determination', and he was awarded a Bar to his DSO after his eighty-third operation, promoted to wing commander and given command of 1655 Mosquito Training Unit at Marham. At the end of the war Ralston was listed for a permanent commission, but a medical examination revealed that he had TB and he was invalided out of the RAF in 1946. Wg Cdr Ralston DSO* DFC DFM AFC died on 8 October 1996.

28. On Saturday 3 April, Acting Wg Cdr John 'Jack' de Lacey Wooldridge DFC* DFM RAFVR led his first 105 Squadron operation. Wooldridge had joined the RAF in 1938 and flew two tours (seventy-three operations) on heavy bombers prior to taking command of 105 Squadron on 17 March, including thirty-two ops on Manchesters. On 3 April eight Mosquitoes carried out *Rover* attacks on railway targets in Belgium and France. All three of 105 Squadron's Mosquitoes returned safely from attacks on locomotive repair shops at Malines and engine sheds at Namur, but a Mosquito of 139 Squadron was lost. Flg Off W.O. Peacock and his observer, Sgt R.C. Saunders, were shot down by *Oberfeldwebel* Wilhelm Mackenstedt of 6./JG26 three kilometres south of Beauvais for the German pilot's sixth and final victory.

29. On 19/20 May six Mosquitoes attacked Berlin; on 20/21, three attacked the German capital; and on 21/22 May four attacked Berlin – all without loss.

30. Late on 27 May the final large-scale daylight raid by the Mosquito IVs of 2 Group took place when fourteen Mosquitoes were given two targets deep in southern Germany. Six aircraft of 139 Squadron, led by Wg Cdr 'Reggie' W. Reynolds DSO DFC and Flt Lt Ted Sismore DFC, set out to attack the Schott glassworks at Jena. A few miles further on, eight Mosquitoes of 105 Squadron, led by Sqn Ldr Bill Blessing DFC and Flg Off G.K. Muirhead, were to bomb the Zeiss Optical factory, which at that time was almost entirely engaged on making periscopes for submarines.

31. Plt Off Ronald Massie and Sgt George Lister, who were last seen as the formation entered cloud prior to reaching the target, crashed near Diepholz and were killed. Returning over Norfolk, Flt Lt William S.D. 'Jock' Sutherland and Flg Off George Dean in a 139 Squadron Mosquito were killed when they crashed at Wroxham railway station. They had flown into high-voltage overhead electric lines when attempting to land at RAF Coltishall on their return. Flg Offs Alan Rae DFM and Kenneth Bush died when their Mosquito crashed while they tried to land at Marham on one engine.

32. Plt Off A.M. Cybulski. Cybulski's home was in Renfrew, Ontario, but his grandparents were Polish. Newspapers heralded the record flight, but the pilot's name had to be suppressed lest it bring reprisals upon his relatives in Poland.

33. Taking off at 14.15 hours on the afternoon of 27 April, Cybulski and Ladbrook struck across the North Sea to Vlieland. They turned south-east past Stavoren to Mepple, where they altered course eastwards and hedge-hopped across northern Holland to reach Meppen, just across the German border. Here they flew down to the Ems canal to Papenburg,

and then turned westward for home, where they landed at 17.27 hours after covering more than 600 miles. Flying down the canal and railway lines between Meppen and Papenburg, the Mosquito attacked five targets. First Cybulski damaged a tug and two barges, from which debris flew into the air, and then he riddled a locomotive and raked a line of six freight cars. Two military buses were shot up, and to end the strafe, pieces were shot off another locomotive, which was left wreathed in clouds of steam.

CHAPTER 2

'Musical Mosquitoes'

On 4 June 1943, 139 and 105 Squadrons in 2 Group at RAF Marham in Norfolk learned of a change in their role. They would do no more daylight ops. Instead the two squadrons joined Fighter Command and were the first Mosquito units to join the specialist Pathfinder Force (later No. 8 (PFF) Group). This had been formed from 3 Group using volunteer crews on 15 August 1942 under the direction of Gp Capt D.C.T. 'Don' Bennett, and was headquartered at Wyton. On 13 January 1943 the PFF became 8 (PFF) Group and 'Don' Bennett was promoted to air commodore (later air vice-marshal) to command it. The tough-talking Australian ex-Imperial Airways and Atlantic Ferry pilot wanted Mosquitoes for PFF and target-marking duties. In 8 Group 105 Squadron became the second OBOE squadron. On 4 July 139 Squadron left Marham for Wyton to begin a new career in 8 Group as high-level 'nuisance' raiders flying B.IX Mosquitoes. They would also be required to go in with the early markers and carry out diversionary attacks, acting as bait for the enemy fighters to keep them at bay during the main OBOE raids. At Wyton 139 Squadron swapped places with 109 Squadron,[1] commanded by Wg Cdr 'Hal' E. Bufton DFC AFC, which transferred its eighteen Mosquito IVs and six IXs to Marham, which now became home to the PFF OBOE-equipped Mosquito marking force.

OBOE was the codename for a high-level blind-bombing aid, which took its name from a radar-type pulse, which sounded rather like the musical instrument. OBOE was to become the most accurate form of blind bombing used in the Second World War, and in practice an average error of only 30 seconds was achieved.

Six Mosquitoes of 109 Squadron flew the squadron's first operation from Marham on the night of 8/9 July 1943, when the main force attacked Cologne for the third time in a week. Flt Lt Stevens and Sqn Ldr J.F.C. Gallacher DFC acted as primary marker. The OBOE sky-marking was accurate, and over 280 Lancasters of 1 and 5 Groups devastated the north-western and south-western sections of the city. Over 500 people were killed and 48,000 more were bombed out, bringing the total number of displaced inhabitants that week to 350,000. On the night of 9/10 July, 105 Squadron flew its first OBOE operation when Sqn Ldr Bill Blessing and his observer, Flg Off G.K. Muirhead, and Flg Off William E.G. 'Bill' Humphrey and his observer, Flt Sgt E. Moore, went to Gelsenkirchen. Both crews had spent a month of training at Wyton.[2] Twelve other 'Musical Mosquitoes' were flown on the Gelsenkirchen operation by 109 Squadron crews. The raid by over 400 Lancasters and Halifaxes was not successful. The OBOE equipment failed to operate in five of the Mosquitoes, and a sixth Mosquito dropped sky-markers in error ten miles to the north of the target. On the night of 13/14 July, 105 Squadron operated Mosquito IXs for the first time when two OBOE Mosquitoes carried out a diversion for the main attack on Aachen by dropping green TIs and a 500-pounder apiece over Cologne. Eleven other OBOE Mosquitoes went to Cologne ahead of the main force. Eight of the Musical Mosquitoes marked with red TIs and three others dropped their mixed bomb-loads of three 500-pounders and one 250 lb bomb. Mosquito IXs could carry six 500 lb bombs, including one under each wing, although for long-range operations these were frequently used to carry additional wing tanks.

Meanwhile, the training of OBOE marker crews continued at Marham, where 1655 Mosquito Training Unit was tasked with instructing the specialist Pathfinder Force. All pilots had to complete a laid-down syllabus of thirty hours' flying – ten in the Dual Flight and twenty in the Bomber Flight, the latter complete with navigator. No pilot was allowed to touch the controls of a Mosquito until he had 1,000 hours as first pilot under his belt and had been selected to fly Mosquitoes. One such was Flt Sgt Edwin R. Perry, who had been posted to 1655 MTU in April and teamed up with Flt Sgt V.J.C. 'Ginger' Myles, his observer. On completing his education in 1937, his first career choice was to follow his family as a dairy farmer. Even so, his father was a keen organist and he hoped that his son might follow suit, but neither he nor his two sisters had any interest or musical aptitude. Perry recalls:[3]

> Another seventeen joined us to make up ten crews who were to be taught to fly the Mark IV Mosquito. When we joined 1655 initially it was to continue low-level flying over the East Anglian countryside, initially using the Oxford. We were then formed into crews (Ginger and I stayed together for the rest of our 8 Group experiences), and commenced a programme of low-level cross-country exercises in the Mosquito, flying at around 250 knots. Low-level practice bombing

also featured on the Whittlesey range near Peterborough. After the change in emphasis in training we concentrated on night flying, which, with so many airfields in the country, each with its own red two-letter identification beacon within a few miles, was in many cases easier for the navigator to monitor his position than with day navigation. There were also white aerial lighthouses of fixed position, enabling accurate bearings to be made of these with a hand-bearing astro-compass. The aircraft was also being equipped with GEE, a piece of radar equipment which measured the distances from a master and two slave stations to give a very accurate position, but then limited in range up to 4° east longitude. GEE took up less room than the 1154/5 and was easier for the observer to use, but had the disadvantage that the positions on the GEE grid map had to be transferred to the Mercator projection used for navigation. It was also known that VHF voice radio could be heard for long distances, up to 200 or more miles, and there was therefore no loss in establishing position on approach home when high-altitude flying without MFDF or HFDF Morse code facilities.

After three weeks 1655 was detached to Finmere, where we were the only unit. However, we later flew back to Marham to complete the course, my pilot for that flight being Flying Officer Ivor Broom DFC (later AM Sir Ivor), who had made quite a name for himself in Malta. Normally his observer was an amiable warrant officer named Tommy Broom, and it was claimed when they went on operations they went on a 'sweep'. Tommy really enjoyed his beer and raw onions, which was the normal supper in the Marham sergeants' mess. He 'strained' the beer through a magnificent moustache, but after one splendid drinking session Tom went to bed and on awaking found some rogue (never identified) had removed one side while Tommy blissfully slumbered on. A side effect was that nobody recognized him when he turned up at the 'Flights' next morning! 1655 was a happy unit. When at Marham our free time was spent in King's Lynn, where the Duke of York was a favoured hostelry, or we might go up the coast to Hunstanton or Sandringham. And so, at the end of 22.5 months' service and 315.5 hours' flying (50.45 at night), I was considered to be suitably trained for operational duties as an observer in Bomber Command Mosquitoes of PFF's Light Night Striking Force. Victor Myles and I were posted to 139 (Jamaica) Squadron on 17 July 1943, and we stayed there until 16 December 1943 at the very comfortable pre-war Sir Edwin Lutyens-designed station, Wyton, about four miles from each of Huntingdon and St Ives, on the edge of the flat fen country.

We found that the crews came from all over. To name but a few of this truly Empire Force, Mike Hay was from South Africa; Tex Cooke, Texas; Tuddy Tudenhope, New Zealand; Symonds, Forsyth,

Peter Swan and 'Red' Helliere, Australia; D.C. Skene and 'Mac' McDonald, Canada; Ulric Cross, Tobago; Ken Rawlins, Jamaica; and Don Boa, Rhodesia. Morale was a bit wobbly initially due to the change from low-level day to high-level night operations, but with such a mix of personalities there were many 'on and off' camp parties, with the Oliver Cromwell in St Ives or the George in Huntingdon great favourites. Once the high-altitude bombing and navigational techniques had been mastered, any 'yen' for the more spectacular and much more dangerous low-level flying went, and a great spirit ensued. Ginger and I were allotted to 'B' Flight, whose Officer Commanding was Squadron Leader Dennis Braithwaite.

The nineteen targets we were sent to included Lübeck, where we were coned by searchlights for ten minutes (it seemed much longer), Hamburg twice, a position off the Danish coast where target indicators were dropped to assist the mainstream 'heavies' who were going to Hamburg on 29 July 1943 and where 'Window', narrow strips of foil to confuse the German radar, was employed for the first time. During this flight one piece of the window finished in the pitot head, and as a result we had to complete the trip without an airspeed indicator or reliable altimeter reading. For good measure we also avoided an attack by a fighter in the vicinity of the target. Seven attacks were made on Berlin – on 17 August 1943 we made a return on one engine from the target. The sortie was made as a diversion for the main force, which was obliterating the rocket research base of Peenemünde on the Baltic. An especially unpleasant experience arose when we were going to Cologne with a full 4 × 500-pound bomb-load. It was a night with many thunderstorms and we were at 32,000 ft to get over them. However, one especially large cumo-nimbus cloud inverted us. My pilot said, 'Get ready to jump', and that was the time the navigation board trapped me. Fortunately, by the time I had cleared it Ginger had got 'O' under control again. That was nasty!

Ginger's view, in the light of later experiences, when we often had to fly through these thunderclouds as part of a mission, was that in fact we were turned upside-down by a anti-aircraft shell bursting under a wing. However, whatever the cause, we were thankful to release our bombs and go home.

Searchlights and 'flak' were the norm, although at the heights at which we flew neither proved too troublesome, and our main anxieties were due to Fw 190 night-fighters coming in from behind the searchlights, which presented a blind spot to us.

The main problem I experienced was a lack of sleep while on operations. We had a week's leave every six weeks.[4] This was a period when a number of new devices appeared, including a modification of the GEE box called GEE-H, which was a very accurate piece of navigation equipment. I was one of the observers selected to operate the new system, doing training flights in a specially fitted-out Oxford; however, I was posted on before the Mossies could have used the new system installed.

At the end of nineteen ops, Dennis Braithwaite told us that we were to go to Oakington to replace one of the Met Flight crews, Curly Addis and John Sharpe [who on 3 December 1943 crashed at night half a mile south of Exeter airfield]. Curly and John were two of the people we trained with at 1655 MTU. We were sorry to leave our friends, but soon realized that we had been posted to an élite unit of the Pathfinder Force, and we were mollified by knowing that Dennis, who had earlier been a CO of the Met Flight, was clearly very well disposed to it and would not wish it any harm.

On the night of 24/25 July 1943, the Battle of Hamburg, which was to last until 3 August, began. The city was beyond OBOE range, so the Mosquitoes flew diversionary and nuisance raids to Bremen, Kiel, Lübeck and Duisburg. 'Window', which was dropped for the first time, helped keep bomber losses to a minimum. Just twelve aircraft – 1½ per cent of the force – failed to return. Essen, which was the target for over 700 aircraft on the night of 25/26 July, was not beyond the range of OBOE, and seven OBOE Mosquitoes of 109 Squadron and four of 105 Squadron successfully marked the target for the main force. Twenty-six aircraft were lost, but the raid was a success, with much damage to Essen's industrial areas in the eastern half of the city. Hamburg was bombed again on 27/28 July by over 780 aircraft, and the PFF marking was carried out by H_2S. This was the night of the firestorm, which killed approximately 40,000 people. Following the raid, about 1,200,000 people – two-thirds of Hamburg's population – fled the city in fear of further raids. By 6 August the battle ended and 75% of the city had been laid waste. On the night of 30/31 July three of 105 Squadron's Mosquito IXs and six of 109 Squadron, each carrying four red TIs, departed Marham to mark Remscheid on the southern edge of the Ruhr, which was the target for over 270 aircraft. Flg Off Kenneth Wolstenholme, with Sqn Ldr J.F.C. Gallacher DFC, flew one of the 105 Squadron Mosquitoes.[5] The OBOE ground marking and the bombing by the comparatively small main force were exceptionally accurate, and 83 per cent of the town was destroyed. This brought the Battle of the Ruhr to an end after 18,506 sorties in which 58,000 tons of bombs had been dropped for a loss of 872 aircraft. By the end of the month Marham Mosquito crews had flown thirty-two Mk IX sorties.

August 1943 proved a relatively quiet month for the Marham Mosquitoes, which operated a mix of target-marking and bombing operations on just four nights, while Bomber Command concentrated its main efforts on Italian targets at Milan, Genoa and Turin. On 22/23 August, when the

IG Farben factory at Leverkusen was the target for the main force, Marham dispatched thirteen Mosquitoes. One of the six 105 Squadron Mosquitoes had a 'technical failure' and was unable to bomb, so Flg Off Ken Wolstenholme took over and marked. Each Mosquito dropped two long-burn red TIs and two red TIs, but OBOE was not operating as well as it should and the main force bombing was directed against at least twelve other towns in and near the Ruhr instead. The IG Farben factory received only minor damage from the few bombs that did hit Leverkusen. At Brauweiler the other Musical Mosquitoes of 105 Squadron also had problems marking with OBOE, and two Mosquitoes returned early with engine trouble. The four other Mosquitoes unleashed their 2,000 lb bombloads visually.

On the following night, 23/24 August, when over 720 aircraft visited Berlin, Marham again provided the OBOE markers so necessary for the main force to do its work. Three of 105 Squadron's Mosquitoes and five of 109 Squadron were to mark the bombers' route by dropping red LB TIs between the Dutch towns of Westerbork and Zweeloo, and green TIs just over the German border at Georgsdorf, 270 miles west of Berlin, to keep the heavies on course. Despite reservations in some quarters, who feared it might alert enemy night-fighters, the object was to keep the bombers away from known flak areas and to achieve a heavy concentration of bombs at the target. Ken Wolstenholme and his observer, Sqn Ldr Gallacher, were forced to abort after take-off when a flock of birds smashed into their Mosquito, but the other Mosquitoes carried out their marking duties. The main force attack was partially successful, but fifty-seven bombers were shot down by a combination of night-fighters and flak. A few nights later, on the 29/30th, four OBOE Mosquitoes visited Cologne. Lt 'Bud' Fisher DFC USAAF, an American pilot from Pennsylvania, and Flt Lt Robert W. 'Bob' Bray DFC, in J-Jig, and three other 105 Squadron Mosquitoes, marked Duisburg. On 30/31 August 600 aircraft of the main force attacked Mönchengladbach and the neighbouring town of Rheydt. Marking by twelve OBOE Mosquitoes, four of 105 Squadron led by the new CO, Wg Cdr Henry John 'Butch' Cundall AFC,[6] with Sqn Ldr A.C. Douglas DFC and eight of 109 Squadron, was described as 'excellent', and in particular Cundall and Douglas had only a 40-yard error.

On the night of 31 August/1 September over 620 bombers visited the 'Big City' again. Three Mosquitoes of 105 Squadron and six of 109 Squadron route-marked for the heavies by dropping red TIs near Damvillers in north-east France and green TIs near Luxembourg. Bombing was carried out using H_2S equipment and TIs, but the latter were dropped to the south of Berlin, while the main bombing was up to thirty miles away and was unsuccessful. The enemy used 'fighter flares' to decoy the bombers away from the target, and about two-thirds of the forty-seven aircraft lost were shot down over Berlin by night-fighters. In a separate operation thirty OTU Wellingtons and six OBOE Mosquitoes and five Halifaxes of the Pathfinders bombed an ammunition dump in the Forêt de Hesdin in northern France. All of Marham's Mosquitoes returned safely from the night's operations. During early September the OBOE Mosquitoes marked more 'special targets'. On the night of 2/3 September, thirty OTU Wellingtons and six OBOE Mosquitoes and five Lancasters of the Pathfinders were dispatched to ammunition dumps in the Forêt de Mormal near Englefontaine in France, about forty kilometres south-east of Valenciennes. Flg Off Don C. Dixon, an Australian from Brisbane, and Flt Lt Tommy W. Horton DFC of 105 Squadron, carrying two red LB TIs and two red TIs, and four 109 Squadron Mosquitoes marked successfully. Crews dropped their TIs from 26,000 ft and the heavies' bombs fell squarely on the dumps. The following evening six OBOE Mosquitoes carried out a similar operation in the Forêt de Raismes ten kilometres north-west of Valenciennes for thirty OTU Wellingtons and six Halifaxes. Flt Lt Tommy W. Horton DFC and Lieutenant 'Bud' Fisher of 105 Squadron, and the four Mosquitoes of 109 Squadron, again marked with two red LB TIs and two red TIs. On 8/9 September, when 257 bombers, including five American B-17 Flying Fortresses, attacked the German long-range gun batteries near Boulogne, the OBOE Mosquitoes marked the target with green LB TIs and red TIs. The marking and bombing was poor and the gun batteries were largely untouched.

Knowing that the Mk I version of OBOE would soon be jammed, trials were begun with OBOE Mk II (codenamed 'Penwiper') on 11 September by Wg Cdr H.J. 'Butch' Cundall AFC with Flt Lt C.F. Westerman in attacks on Aachen. (Aachen was the target for OBOE II trials again on 3 and 7 October.)

On 22/23 September, twelve OBOE Mosquitoes visited Emden as a diversion for the main force attacking Hannover. Most of the Mosquitoes bombed on DR after the OBOE system failed. On 23/24 September the OBOE Mosquitoes were dispatched to Aachen as the main force went to Mannheim. Two of 105 Squadron's Mosquitoes route-marked at a point near the Belgian-German border near Simmerath for six more Mosquitoes that successfully bombed the town. On 29/30 September four OBOE crews dropped 500 lb and 250 lb bombs on Gelsenkirchen, and nine OBOE Mosquitoes set out to mark Bochum with red TIs for 352 heavies. Many bombs fell accurately in the old part of the town. The Mosquito flown by Lt 'Bud' Fisher DFC and Flt Sgt Leslie Hogan DFM crashed one mile north-west of RAF West Raynham, killing both crewmembers. Bad weather returning from Gelsenkirchen forced Sqn Ldr Peter Channer DFC and WO Kenneth Gordon to land at RAF Coltishall.

In October the OBOE Mosquitoes flew operationally on twelve nights during the month, 109 Squadron flying 101 sorties and 105 Squadron seventy-six. On 1/2 October a steelworks at Witten, north-west of Hagen, was ground-marked with red TIs by twelve OBOE Mosquitoes for training purposes. Eight of the Mosquitoes bombed at Witten, and two whose OBOE system failed dropped their bombs on the fires at Hagen created earlier by 240 Lancasters and eight Mosquitoes of 1, 5 and 8 Groups. On 3/4 October twelve OBOE Mosquitoes attacked the Goldenbergwerke power station and Knapsack power station near Cologne, and four others carried out Mk II OBOE trials to Aachen. Knapsack was attacked again on 4/5 and 20/21 October, and again on the 22nd, when twelve Mosquitoes of 105 and 109 Squadrons set out in the early evening. Flt Lt Gordon Sweeney DFC and Flt Lt William George Wood of 105 Squadron failed to return. On 24/25 October raids were made on Rheinhausen and Büderich, and on 31 October Oberhausen was bombed.

On the night of 3/4 November twelve OBOE Mosquitoes ground-marked Düsseldorf for 589 heavies, and thirteen other OBOE Mosquitoes, each carrying three 500 lb MC and a 250 lb GP bomb, set out to attack the Krupp factory at Rheinhausen. Twelve Mosquitoes bombed successfully, while the unlucky thirteenth aircraft returned with two 500-pounders hung up in the bomb bay. On nights when the main force was not operating, the OBOE Mosquitoes were dispatched to keep the enemy defences alert. On 4/5 November twenty-four Mosquitoes attacked a chemical works at Leverkusen and four Mosquitoes visited Aachen again, all returning without loss. On 5/6 November twenty-six Mosquitoes carried out small-scale raids on Bochum, Dortmund, Düsseldorf, Hamburg and Hannover. Flt Lt John 'Flash' Gordon DFC and Flg Off Ralph Gamble Hayes DFM in a 105 Squadron Mosquito were returning over Norfolk. They tried to land at Hardwick, an American Liberator base, when, at 21.10 hours, they crashed into a field at Road Green Farm, Hempnall, about ten miles south of Norwich. Both men were killed.

With no major raids planned for the main force, the OBOE Mosquitoes spent most of November dropping their bomb-loads of six 500 lb MC bombs on Dortmund, Bochum, Essen, Duisburg, Krefeld and Düsseldorf, using DR when OBOE failed. The operation to Essen on the night of 7/8 November was typical of the non-main force nights. Apart from thirty-five aircraft minelaying off the French coast and a handful of OTU sorties, the only Bomber Command aircraft that were airborne were six OBOE Mosquitoes from Marham. The OBOE equipment failed because one of the ground stations was not in operation, and the Mosquitoes were sent a recall signal. Two of the OBOE aircraft received the signal and returned, but the other four continued to the target and dropped their twenty-four 500 lb MC bombs from 32,000 to 35,000 ft on a DR run from the last GEE fix. Two of these Mosquitoes returned home on one engine, and one of them put down at RAF Coltishall.

On the night of 9/10 November eighteen OBOE Mosquitoes attacked blast furnaces at Bochum and a steelworks at Duisburg. The Mosquito flown by Plt Off R.E. Leigh and Plt Off J. Henderson of 109 Squadron was hit by flak at the target, and they crash-landed at Wyton on return. As the

Mosquito touched down, the tail assembly broke away from the fuselage, but both men escaped uninjured. On 11/12 November Cannes was the target of the main force, while twenty-nine Mosquitoes raided Berlin, Hannover and the Ruhr. Marham dispatched twelve OBOE Mosquitoes to Düsseldorf. One of the four Mosquitoes of 105 Squadron, each carrying four 500 lb MC bombs, was flown by Plt Off Angus Caesar-Gordon DFM and his second tour navigator, Flg Off R.A. 'Dick' Strachan, who were on their first Mosquito operation. Strachan recalled:[7]

> The flak started about four or five minutes before the target, and immediately it was apparent that it was intense and extremely accurate. OBOE entailed the pilot flying dead straight and level for ten minutes on the attack run. Suddenly a tremendous flash lit up the sky about fifty yards ahead of our nose and exactly at our altitude. Within a tenth of a second we were through the cloud of dirty yellowish-brown smoke and into the blackness beyond. I shall never forget the spontaneous reaction of both my pilot and myself. We turned our heads slowly and looked long and deep into one another's eyes – no word was spoken – no words were needed. Despite continued heavy flak, we completed our attack run and dropped our bomb-load on the release signal, within a quarter of a mile of the aiming point and, with luck, some damage to a German factory. Turning for home and mighty glad to be out of the flak, I glanced out of the window at the starboard engine and immediately noticed a shower of sparks coming from the starboard engine cowling. A quick glance at the oil temperature gauge showed that it was going off the clock. Only one thing for it, and the pilot pressed the extinguisher button and then feathered the engine. The sparking ceased but we now had 300 miles to go and only one engine to do it on. I remember thinking this wasn't much of a do for our first operation. But at least we had a good deal of altitude and still had a fair amount of speed, even with just one engine. The danger was interception by a German night-fighter, and I spent a lot of time craning my neck around to check the skies about our tail. The other thing I remember was a terrible consciousness of our own weight, sitting as I was on the starboard side. However, this feeling wore off and the remainder of the flight home to base was uneventful. Then came the strain of a night landing on one engine – again that awful awareness of how heavy I was – but after one anti-clockwise circuit, a superb approach and magnificent landing. I recall the great feeling of relief as the wheels touched the runway. I also remember the urgent desire to get my hands round a jug of beer to relieve the dryness in my throat and to celebrate a safe return from what was to prove my worst experience on Mosquitoes. Needless to say, the beer was not long in forthcoming.

On 12/13 November seven Mosquitoes attacked Düsseldorf, Essen and Krefeld, and the night following, eight OBOE Mosquitoes attacked the blast furnaces at Bochum again. Both raids were flown without loss. On the night of 15/16 November ten OBOE Mosquitoes attacked the Rheinmetall Borsig AG ironworks at Düsseldorf and two others bombed Bonn. The Mosquito flown by Flt Lt J.R. Hampson and Plt Off H.W.E. Hammond DFC RCAF was shot down. Both men survived and they were later sent to *Stalag Luft III*. A flak shell exploded a few feet under Flt Lt Humphrey's Mosquito and turned the aircraft upside-down, and Humphrey was hit in the foot and leg. The Mosquito went into a spin but the crew managed to make it home, and Humphrey landed at Hardwick, whereupon one of his engines stopped.

On 17/18 November eighty-three heavies attacked Ludwigshafen. Twenty-one Mosquitoes visited Berlin and Bonn and the August Thyssen AG foundry in Duisburg and the semi-finished products of the Bochumer Verein in Bochum. None of the Mosquitoes was lost. On the night of 18/19 November the main Battle of Berlin began with a raid on the 'Big City' by 440 Lancasters, while another bomber force visited Mannheim and Ludwigshafen. Ten Mosquitoes went to Essen, and six each went to Aachen and Frankfurt. While returning from Aachen Flt Lt R.B. Castle and Plt Off J. Griffiths in a 105 Squadron Mosquito overshot the landing area at Marham and crashed at 23.31 hours. They were not seriously injured, but the Mosquito was a write-off. On the next raid on the IG Farbenindustrie AG chemical works at Leverkusen on 19/20 November, failure of equipment prevented most of the OBOE marking being carried out, and the bad weather prevented other PFF aircraft from marking the target properly. As a result bombing was widely scattered, and twenty-seven towns, mostly well to the north, were bombed. On 22/23 November, when the main force raided Berlin, twelve OBOE Mosquitoes set out for Leverkusen again. Berlin was again the target for the main force attack on 23/24 November, when six OBOE Mosquitoes braved the flak and searchlight defences protecting the Goldenbergwerke power station at Knapsack near Cologne again. Plt Off Eric Wade BEM and his observer, Plt Off Alfred Gerald Fleet, died when their Mosquito crashed at 19.50 hours five miles north-west of Swaffham at Contract Farm, Narborough. Throughout the rest of November the OBOE squadrons bombed familiar targets such as the Krupp foundry at Essen, the Rheinmetall Borsig AG ironworks at Düsseldorf and the steel producer Vereinigte Stahlwerke AG at Bochum.

On 3 December, Marshal of the Royal Air Force Lord Trenchard made a lunchtime visit to Marham and congratulated the squadron on the excellent work it had done leading the main force in the Battle of the Ruhr. He also praised its current role of precision attacks on special targets. The OBOE Mosquitoes were operational on fifteen nights during December, with return visits to targets such as Hamborn, Leverkusen,

Krefeld, Düsseldorf, Liège, Aachen and Bochum. Usually the operations were flown without loss, but there were early losses. On the night of 2/3 December Flg Off L.F. Bickley and Flg Off J.H. Jackson of 109 Squadron failed to return from a raid by six OBOE Mosquitoes on Bochum. Both men evaded. Then, on the night of the 12/13th, Plt Off Benjamin Frank Reynolds and Plt Off John Douglas Phillips of 105 Squadron were killed when they crashed at Herwijnen in Holland on the north bank of the Waal River. They had probably been hit by flak towards the end of the attack on the Krupp works at Essen. On the night of the 16/17th, when Berlin was the main target for the heavies, thirty-five Stirlings and Lancasters and twelve OBOE Mosquitoes were dispatched to bomb two V-1 flying-bomb sites near Abbeville in northern France, at Tilley-le-Haut and in a wood at Flixecourt.[8] Neither raid was successful. The attack on Tilley-le-Haut by twenty-six Stirlings failed because the six OBOE Mosquito markers of 105 and 109 Squadrons could not get their green and yellow TIs closer than 450 yards from the tiny target. At Flixecourt the nine Lancasters of 617 (Dam Busters) Squadron dropped their 12,000 lb Tallboy bombs accurately on the green TIs and LB TIs placed by Sqn Ldr Bill Blessing and Wg Cdr F.A. Green DFC. But the markers were 350 yards from the V-1 site and none of the Lancasters' bombs were more than a hundred yards from the markers.[9] Five more raids on V-bomb construction sites were flown during the rest of the month, two each on 22nd/23rd and 30th/31st and one on the night of 29/30 December, and only one site was bombed accurately.

Crew discipline and navigational accuracy were put to the test on the night of 23/24 December when twelve OBOE Mosquitoes were sent to raid Aachen and then to carry on to a second site to route-mark Berlin for 379 heavies heading for the 'Big City'. Sixteen Lancasters were lost, and the losses would have been higher had it not been for the cloud covering the Berlin area, which grounded many German night-fighters and the diversion raid at Leipzig by seven Mosquitoes. There were no bombing raids on Christmas Eve, and only a few Mosquitoes were airborne on 28/29 December when operations resumed again after a period of bad weather. A raid took place by over 700 aircraft on Berlin on the night of 29/30 December, with small numbers of Mosquitoes being sent to a number of targets in Germany and France without loss. This was followed on 30/31 December by the last raid of the year, when twenty-one OBOE Mosquitoes were dispatched to targets in Cologne, Duisburg and the Vereinigte Stahlwerke AG steelworks at Bochum again. A further attempt was also made to mark a V-l flying-bomb site at Cherbourg that had been missed on the earlier raid. Unfortunately, the markers were placed 200 yards from the target. All the bombs dropped by the ten Lancasters of 617 Squadron, though well grouped, and four 500-pounders dropped through 3/10th low cloud by Flg Off Bill

Humphrey and his observer Plt Off L.C. Poll of 105 Squadron, missed the site completely.

In January 1944 the OBOE Mosquitoes were operational on nineteen nights, with 105 and 109 Squadrons flying sorties on eleven nights during the period up to the 14/15th. It was much the same routine as in 1943, with area marking and attacks on industrial targets such as the Ruhrstahl AG steel works at Witten and J.A. Henckels Zwillingwerke AG at Solingen, the Krupp AG works at Essen, the Verstahlwerke at Duisburg and the Deutsche Edalstahlwerke AG at Krefeld. The Krupp Stahl AG works at Rheinhausen and the Rheinmetall Borsig AG ironworks at Düsseldorf and the Mannesmannröhrenwerke AG iron and steel tube plant at Untererthal were also bombed, as were the Gutehoffnungshütte AG foundry at Obershausen and the Chemische Werke industrial chemicals plant at Hüls. No fewer than twenty-one V-1 rocket-sites were also visited by the OBOE Mosquitoes during January. Losses at night remained at a thankfully relatively low rate. Returning from a raid on Duisburg by five Mosquitoes on the night of 7/8 January, a 109 Squadron Mosquito flown by Flg Off C.R.G. Grant RAAF and Flg Off K.F. Hynes hit a tree returning to Marham and crash-landed at Narborough. Grant scrambled to safety, but a crane was needed to move wreckage to allow Hynes to be freed. On the night of the 13/14th, Flg Off P.Y. Stead DFC and WO A.H. Flett DFM of 109 Squadron failed to return from the night's operations when they were shot down at 26,000 ft by *Oberleutnant* Dietrich Schmidt of *III./NJG1*, flying a Bf 110. Flett was killed but Stead survived and was taken prisoner.[10] Sqn Ldr J. Comer and his observer, Plt Off P. Jenkins DFM, of 105 Squadron were just setting out for Düsseldorf on the night of 20/21 January when at 2043 hours their Mosquito became uncontrollable and they baled out over Norfolk. The aircraft crashed three miles east of King's Lynn at Waveland Farm, Grimston. Returning home from their target on the night of 23 January, Flt Lt Kenneth Wolstenholme and Plt Off V.P. Piper crash-landed at RAF Manston after their Mosquito lost elevator control.

By way of a change, on the night of 25/26 January fourteen Mosquitoes of 105 Squadron were dispatched to bomb the Nazi HQ at Aachen, while 109 Squadron attacked four V-1 sites in northern France. Eleven of the OBOE Mosquitoes of 105 Squadron identified the target at Aachen, and amid light and accurate flak forty 500 lb bombs were released through cloud. A number of hits were scored. Two days later the OBOE Mosquitoes returned to Aachen and dropped 'spoof' green TI route markers just north of the town without loss, although Flt Lt J.W. Jordan landed at RAF Manston with an overheating starboard engine. On the night of 28/29 January, while 677 aircraft headed for Berlin, twenty-three OBOE Mosquitoes took off from Marham to bomb German night-fighter airfields in Holland. Six Mosquitoes of 109 Squadron were sent to attack

Leeuwarden and four more to raid Deelen, while 105 Squadron dispatched five to Gilze-Rijen. Six more went to Venlo and two visited Deelen.

On the night of 30/31 January, twenty-two OBOE Mosquitoes attacked the G&I Jager GmbH ball-bearing factory at Elberfeld when over 530 aircraft visited Berlin again. WO I.B. McPherson's Mosquito received several flak hits in the port engine and Flt Lt A.W. Raybould had the nose of his Mosquito shattered, but all aircraft returned safely. In February the ball-bearing factory at Elberfeld was attacked on no fewer than eight more nights. Just before the third attack by eight OBOE Mosquitoes on 4/5 February, Flt Lt John Fosbroke Slatter and his observer, Plt Off Peter Oscar Hedges, of 105 Squadron were killed on their NFT (night flying test). During the late afternoon they were involved in a collision with a Boeing B-17G 42-97480 of the 337th Bomb Squadron, 96th Bombardment Group from Snetterton, Norfolk. The Mosquito came down at Colne Field Farm near St Ives, Huntingdonshire. Slatter and Hedges were killed, while the Fortress landed safely with minor damage.[11]

On 9/10 February Flg Off R.G. Leigh RNZAF and Flt Lt M.R. Breed RNZAF of 109 Squadron were shot down over Holland. In the early hours of the 26th, Flg Off Taylor and Plt Off Mander of 1655 MTU crashed at Fincham, both crew being killed. Much of February was spent bombing airfields at Gilze Rijen, Deelen, Volkel, St Trond, Twente, Venlo and Leeuwarden, all without loss, and V-l sites in northern France. On the night of 23/24 February, when seventeen OBOE Mosquitoes raided Düsseldorf, the Mosquito flown by Plt Off L. Holiday DFM was hit in the fuselage, and his observer, Flg Off C.L. French, was wounded in the thigh. They continued to Düsseldorf, none the less, and bombed the target.

During the first five days of March, two of 109 Squadron's OBOE Mosquitoes acted as 'formation leaders' for bomber units of the 2nd Tactical Air Force (2nd TAF) attacking flying-bomb sites in northern France. The formation bombed as soon as it saw the bombs of the OBOE Mosquitoes being released. Altogether eight of these daylight operations were flown, the first being to Conches on 1 March. That same night an operation to Stuttgart by over 550 aircraft of the main force was supported by eighteen OBOE Mosquitoes, which bombed German night-fighter airfields at Deelen, Volkel, Florennes, St Trond and Venlo. The operations were flown without cloud cover over Holland and only broken cloud to the west. It was on this night that 109 Squadron dispatched its first Mosquito XVI sortie, to Deelen. Deliveries of the pressurized Mosquito B.XVI, an adaptation of the Mk IX and powered by the more powerful two-stage 1,680 hp Merlin 77/73 engines, had begun on 19 December when two of the aircraft were received by 109 Squadron. The XVI also had bulged bomb doors to permit a 4,000 lb 'Cookie' bomb to be carried.[12] All the airfields except Florennes, where OBOE failed, were bombed and all the Mosquitoes returned safely, but a heavy snowstorm over Norfolk made landings very difficult.

Flg Off Grenville Eaton, a 105 Squadron pilot, flew his first Mosquito operation on 1/2 March, in 'A-Apple', an OBOE-equipped B.IV. His observer was WO J.E. 'Jack' Fox, who had flown a first tour on bombers. Eaton recalls:

> Venlo, the target, was a German fighter aerodrome on the Dutch border near Aachen. (The first few trips were usually to 'less difficult' targets, but they were certainly no less important in countering the threat of fighters). With a full load of bombs, four 500-pounders and of petrol, it took, perhaps, one hour following carefully planned and timed legs all over East Anglia until setting course from Orfordness to the Dutch coast. Then, at the operational height of 28,000 ft, we flew towards the waiting point [where the track to the target extended backwards for a further five minutes], and there, at the precise appointed time [to hear the call-in signal in Morse], we switched on OBOE.

The navigator worked out the flight plan and calculated the time to set course in order to reach the target at the correct time. On marking sorties it was important that TIs were dropped at the correct time in order not to compromise the main force. Having worked out the time to set course, navigators actually did this with six minutes in hand to allow for any errors to the forecast wind, etc. Having settled into the flight and arrived at the ETA for the waiting point, crews usually had to make some sort of correction. If the full six minutes had to be lost, the pilot did a 360-degree orbit, and most pilots became expert in achieving this in the six minutes. Shorter times to be lost were accomplished by making a dog-leg. Grenville Eaton now had to find the beam and keep on it for perhaps ten to fifteen minutes to the target.

> Thanks to GEE, Jack Fox's navigation was spot on and we had a good run to target. His signals gave him our distance to target and finally, the bomb release signal, like the BBC time signal, five pips then the sixth, a dash, to press to release the bombs. We had a clear run. Holding steady for some seconds after bomb release to photograph the bomb explosions, we turned smartly onto the planned course home, keeping our eyes skinned for fighters, flak and searchlights, around 360° above and below. A gentle, slow dive at top speed, and we arrived at the Dutch coast at around 20,000 ft and the English coast at 12,000 ft. We landed at 0330 hours. So, Jack's 31st and my first 'op', took 3 hours 25 minutes. A simmering feeling of incipient fear throughout had been kept in check by being fully occupied. Now, home, we felt a tremendous feeling of relief and achievement, especially when we were told at debriefing that we

had achieved a 'Nil' target error on this, out first OBOE trip. Finally, a heavenly operational aircrew breakfast of bacon, eggs, toast, rum and coffee. Smashing!

Weather conditions improved, and the next night, 2/3 March, 105 Squadron flew its first Mosquito XVI sortie when six OBOE Mosquitoes formed part of the raid by 117 Halifaxes of 4 and 6 Groups on the aircraft assembly factory of SNCA du Nord at Meulan-Les Mureaux. The factory, about fifteen miles north-west of Paris, originally turned out Potez aircraft for the French Air Force and was now producing about fifteen Messerschmitt Me 108s each month, as well as components for Bf 109s and Dornier Do 24s. Wg Cdr H.J. 'Butch' Cundall AFC and his navigator Sqn Ldr I.E. Tamango flew the XVI (ML938), and they led four other Mosquito IXs of 105 and two of 109 Squadron. As usual the OBOE markers were to go in first and ground-mark the target with red and green LB TIs for the Halifaxes. Unfortunately, OBOE failed and Cundall relinquished primary marker duties to Flt Lt E.M. Hunter with Flt Lt Crabb and Flt Lt Jacobs and Flt Lt Tipton of 109 Squadron, who each dropped four red LB TIs. Two 105 Squadron Mosquitoes flown by Sqn Ldr L.F. Austin DFC with Sqn Ldr C.F. Westerman DFC and Flg Off Don C. Dixon and his navigator Flg Off W.A. Christensen, a fellow Australian from New South Wales, failed to drop their four green LB TIs. The reserve aircraft flown by Flt Lt Ken Wolstenholme with his observer, Flt Lt V.E.R. Piper, dropped four red LB TIs. The raid was successful and the Halifaxes caused considerable damage to the main assembly shops, the factory testing hangars and the seaplane base, while other parts of the plant were 'extremely severely damaged'.

On 5/6 March four OBOE Mosquitoes set out to mark Duisburg for three Mosquitoes carrying 4,000 lb 'Cookies'. Sqn Ldr Peter J. Channer DFC was forced to abort before the target when his OBOE equipment blew up, though he managed to return safely to Marham. The other Mosquitoes encountered slight but accurate flak on the run-in to the target. Flt Lt C.P. Gibbons's Mosquito of 109 Squadron was hit at 30,000 ft, but he was able to carry on. Flt Lt G.W. Harding of 105 Squadron reported a cloud of smoke and a red flare hanging over the target. Meanwhile, plans unveiled on 4 March in preparation for the Overlord invasion planned for that summer had put in motion precision bombing attacks on railway networks and marshalling yards, ammunition dumps and airfields in France. Seven rail targets at Trappes, Aulnoye, Le Mans, Amiens, Courtrai, Laon and Vaires-sur-Marne were selected for all-out attacks, which began on the night of 6/7 March, when Trappes was marked by OBOE Mosquitoes to enable 261 Halifaxes of 4 and 6 Groups to bomb. Photo reconnaissance later revealed that the engine shed had been destroyed, and six wrecked locomotives were seen lying in the almost demolished building. The water tower was completely destroyed, and throughout the yards there was a heavy concentration of craters affecting tracks, and all the internal lines were blocked. There was also considerable destruction and derailment of tenders and rolling stock. Seventeen direct hits on the main Paris–Chartres lines had put all but one line out of action. Attacks on Le Mans and also the road and rail junction at Aachen followed on 7/8 March. The Aachen operation was the second for Flg Off Grenville Eaton and WO Jack Fox, as Eaton recalls:

> The target was Aachen, an important road and rail junction just inside Germany. I was feeling more confident. Crossing Holland at 28,000 ft, with a clear sky, we could see the distant Zuider Zee. We switched on OBOE, found we were early, so guided by the navigator I wasted a precise number of minutes and seconds until finding and settling into the beam towards the target, about fifteen minutes' flying time away. We noticed we were leaving long white contrails behind us – frozen water vapour crystals in the exhaust of each engine. Suddenly streams of cannon shells and tracers enveloped us from the rear, hitting us in numerous places, but luckily missing Jack and me and the engines. I immediately dived to port, then up to starboard several times, then resumed height and regained the beam. The only protection was a sheet of steel behind my seat. Most instruments seemed to work, so we continued. Half a minute later, a second and noisier attack from the rear, so again I took evasive action, more violent and longer, and again regained height and beam. Now there was considerable damage to dashboard, hydraulics and fuselage. Shells had missed us, truly by inches. However, engines and OBOE still worked, so being so near we had to continue to target, deliver the load and turn for home, changing course and height frequently and assessing the damage as far as we could. Certainly, hydraulics, flaps, brakes, ASI and various other instruments were smashed – but we were okay.
>
> At Marham, landing in pitch darkness was a problem, but for safety I landed on the grass, by feel I suppose, at about 150 knots with no brakes. We hurtled across the aerodrome, just missing two huge armament dumps, straight on through hedges and violently into a ditch. Jack was out of the emergency exit like a flash. I could not move, could not undo the safety belt. Jack leapt back, released me and we scampered away to a safe distance in case of exploding petrol tanks, and the emergency services were quickly there. Debriefing was interesting, as not only was our run 'seen' on the CRT, but our bombing error was precisely calculated and we wondered whether all operations were to be like this one! Incidentally, we never saw the attacking fighter. Our aircraft was a write-off.[13]

On 11 March HRH the Duke of Gloucester, accompanied by AVM D.C.T. Bennett CB CBE DSO, AOC 8 Group, visited the station and HRH inspected the aircrew who were presented to him by Wg Cdr H.J. 'Butch' Cundall DFC AFC. On 10/11 March three Mosquitoes of 105 Squadron attacked Duisburg again. Flt Lt Ken Wolstenholme's Mosquito suffered flak damage to the starboard undercarriage door and starboard flap, but he returned safely to Marham.

Much of March 1944 was then spent bombing French marshalling yards and Trappes, Le Mans and Amiens. Diversionary attacks on Dutch airfields at St Trond, Venlo and Deelen were flown in support of main-force operations to Stuttgart on the night of 15/16 March. Many of the heavies' bombs fell in open country south-west of the city due to poor marking. Amiens marshalling yards were the main target for the OBOE Mosquitoes that night. Two aircraft were detailed to mark with four red LB TIs and two 500 lb MC bombs, but Flt Lt Almond returned early with generator problems. Technical failures prevented both Flt Lt Ken Wolstenholme and Flg Off Holland from attacking, but Flt Lt Bill Humphrey was able to make two runs, dropping two TIs each time with excellent results. There was some cloud and very thick haze over the target, and as only four sets of TIs went down at very irregular intervals it is doubtful whether much success was achieved. Some 132 Halifaxes and Stirlings were dispatched, and 105 heavies claimed to have dropped 605 tons of bombs. Little concentration of bombing was reported by the Mosquito crews, which in view of the poor marking was not surprising, but some of the main force were bombing to the north-east of the target before zero hour. Numerous searchlights were in operation and many fighter flares were seen. A subsequent Bomber Command report claimed that several parts of the north-east and southern areas of the yards were badly damaged, while railway workshops, storage buildings, tracks, sidings, rolling-stock, a road bridge, roundhouse, engine sheds and lines under construction were all hit severely. Two Halifaxes and a Stirling failed to return, and in Amiens eighteen French civilians were killed.

Further support operations were flown for raids on 18/19 March, when Frankfurt was raided, and St Trond, Volkel and Venlo were again attacked. On the 22/23rd it was the turn of Leeuwarden, Venlo, Deelen and Juliandorp, and Marham dispatched ten OBOE Mosquitoes. Nine of the aircraft carried six 500 lb MC bombs, while Sqn Ldr F.R. Bird and Flt Lt Norman Clayes DFC carried three 500 lb MC bombs and one white TI.[14] There was 10/10ths cloud at Leeuwarden, but four aircraft success-fully attacked the airfield, with good results. Bombs were seen to burst and the TIs were seen to cascade as markers for Fighter Command Intruders. Three Mosquitoes attacked Venlo with excellent results through small amounts of cloud, but Flt Lt J.H. Ford and his observer, Flt Lt L.W. Millett, had a wing-bomb hang up. They returned safely to Marham. Sqn Ldr Wills and Flt Lt Castle attacked Deelen through

5/10ths cloud with excellent results. But the Mosquito flown by Flt Lt Charles Frank Boxall and Flt Lt T.W. 'Robby' Robinson DFC also suffered a wing-mounted bomb hung up when the grease from the bomb release froze and the 500 lb MC bomb refused to drop. Boxall was forced to return with it to Marham, where at 2250 hours, on landing, the bomb freed itself and exploded. The wing disintegrated and Boxall died in the flaming aircraft. Robinson was injured but he survived and was taken to the RAF Hospital at Ely, suffering from shock and severe burns to his left foot and minor burns on the right foot. He also had a fractured left clavicle and facial abrasions.

The OBOE Mosquitoes were now carrying 'Cookie' bombs on a regular basis, and this bomb was known to be notoriously unstable. Also, the bomb-bay doors were prone to creep, and if not fully open before the release point the bomb would take the doors with it. Not surprisingly, crews preferred Graveley's hard runway to Marham's grass airfield for 'Cookie'-carrying operations. A decision had been taken to close Marham and begin the construction of three concrete runways and bring the airfield up to the standard for heavy bombers. It was a massive undertaking that would involve eighteen months' work and a cost of £1,740,000. On 7 March 1655 MTU departed for Warboys, and two weeks later 105 Squadron began the move to Bourn in Cambridgeshire, while in early April 109 Squadron began moving to Little Staughton. While the OBOE squadrons famously carried on their good work, Marham was placed under the custody of the Clerk of Works, from which it would finally emerge in early 1946, long after the Second World War had finished.

Notes

1. 109 Squadron was the premier marking squadron in the RAF, carrying out the most raids and flying the most sorties in 8 Group, which it joined on 1 June 1943.
2. On 26 July, during a night-flying test, Flg Off Bill Humphrey and Flt Sgt E. Moore experienced an engine failure on take-off, and the Mosquito crashed at Fincham.
3. MAA *The Mossie* Vol.13, April 1996.
4. 'On two of which I enjoyed Lord Nuffield's hospitality at the Tregenna Castle Hotel, St Ives, Cornwall and Lake Vyrnwy Hotel, North Wales – without letting on to my mother when I next saw her why I had not had a home leave for three months.'
5. Wolstenholme (who became famous after the war as a BBC sports commentator) flew Blenheims on 107 Squadron earlier in the war. On 21 May 1941 he made it back to Massingham with his observer, Sgt J.C. 'Polly' Wilson RNZAF, dead in his seat after their Blenheim was hit by flak on the operation to Heligoland. Wilson was laid to rest in the lovely country churchyard at Little Massingham, close by the airfield.
6. Later Gp Capt Cundall CBE DSO DFC AFC.

7. *Mosquito at War*. Chaz Bowyer. (Ian Allan, 1984) and *Mosquito Thunder*. Stuart R. Scott. (Sutton Publishing, 1999)
8. Plt Off R.A. Hosking in a PR Mosquito had photographed a V-1 site at Bois Carré, ten miles north-east of Abbeville, on 28 October 1942. This was the first V-1 flying-bomb launching site in France to be analysed on photographs, and the buildings shown were meant for storage of flying-bomb components. The *Vergelrungswaffe* I (Revenge Weapon No. 1) was a small, pilotless aircraft with a 1,870 lb HE warhead that detonated on impact. On 5 December 1943 the bombing of the V-1, or *Noball* sites, became part of the Operation Crossbow offensive. By 12 June 1944, sixty weapons sites had been identified. Hitler's 'rocker blitz' began on 13 June, when ten V-1s, or 'Doodlebugs', as they became known, were launched against London from sites in north-eastern France.
9. Sqn Ldr Blessing DSO DFC RAAF was KIA on 7 July 1944 on a PFF marking sortie over Caen.
10. Stead had joined 58 Squadron in July 1941, and he flew six sorties in 1941 as co-pilot to Leonard Cheshire VC before returning to 58 Squadron. He was posted to 196 Squadron, completed his first tour in June and began his second in October 1943. *Hauptmann* Dietrich Schmidt scored forty night victories in *NJG1*. He was awarded the *Ritterkreuz* and survived the war.
11. B-17G 42-97480 and Lieutenant Otto H. Brandau's crew failed to return from a raid on Germany on 13 April 1944. Four crew were KIA and six were taken prisoner.
12. The Mk IV Mosquito with a 'Cookie' on board was 'just' capable of a take-off on a main runway with favourable wind, and once in the air the aircraft handled sluggishly until 'bomb gone', when the altimeter unwound itself at an alarming rate. At take-off time many a fitter and rigger could be seen sheltering as soon as the aircraft taxied out for take-off. Aircrews learned that the safety height to fly when 4,000 lb bombs were exploding was a minimum of 4,000 ft.
13. Eaton's immediate award of the DFC for this operation was announced on 17 April 1944. He went on to complete ninety operations by 18 March 1945. On 7/8 March also Flt Lt Angus Caesar-Gordon DFM dropped 105 Squadron's first 4,000 lb 'Cookie', in the Duisburg area after the primary target at Hamborn could not be identified. (On 11/12 March a 105 Squadron Mosquito flown by Sqn Ldr J.S.W. Bignall and Flg Off G.F. Caldwell took off from Graveley in company with two Mosquitoes of 109 Squadron and dropped a 'Cookie' on the Verstahlwerke steel works at Hamborn). On 10 July 1944 Grenville Eaton and Jack Fox took off on their first daylight operation when the port engine blew up as they reached the end of the runway, an event that was usually fatal. Eaton somehow flew a circuit and landed safely on one engine, but when Fox dropped prematurely through the escape hatch the propeller killed him.
14. Flt Lt Norman Clayes DFC and his observer, Flg Off Frederick Ernest Deighton, were killed returning from an operation to Châteaudun on 12/13 May 1944 when a Very pistol was discharged in the Mosquito as they came into land.

CHAPTER 3

Defensive Night-Fighting

In the spring of 1942, following an attack by 234 RAF bombers on the old Hanseatic city of Lübeck, Hitler ordered a series of *Terrorangriff* (terror attacks) on England, mainly against cities of historic or aesthetic importance, but little strategic value. In Britain they became known as the Baedeker raids, after the German guidebooks of the same name. Despite its historical significance, the cathedral city of Norwich made a tempting target for *Luftwaffe* raiders ever since the first Baedeker raid on the Norfolk capital on the night of 27/28 April 1942. Nine Beaufighters, ten Spitfires and three AI V radar-equipped Mosquito NF.IIs of 157 Squadron based at Castle Camps met the twenty-eight *Luftwaffe* raiders. Meanwhile, twenty Ju 88s of *Kampfgeschwader* (*KG*) *30* laid mines off the coast. The enemy was picked up on radio at 2015 hours. Although radar contacts were made, the defending fighters failed to shoot down any of the raiders. From 2340 to 0045 hours the bombers rained down forty-one tonnes of high explosive and four tonnes of incendiaries onto the city of over 126,000 inhabitants, causing the deaths of 162 people, injuring 600 more and damaging thousands of buildings. Reports spoke of some of the bombers machine-gunning the streets. The raid was the first sortie by I./*KG2* since converting to the Do 217E. The '*Holzhammer*' unit, plus IV./*KG30* and II./*KG40*, all based in Holland, would venture to England many times over the next twelve months. 'Ack-ack' batteries were drafted into and around Norwich, and the fighter defences gradually improved. The Mosquitoes suffered particularly from problems with cannon flash and exhaust manifold and cowling burning.

'A' Flight in 151 Squadron at Wittering had received its first NF.II on 6 April ('B' Flight had to wait until later to replace its Defiants). No. 151 was commanded by Wg Cdr I.S. 'Black' Smith DFC, a New Zealander, and the station commander at this time was Gp Capt (later AVM, Sir) Basil Embry.[1] On the night of 1 May Wg Cdr Smith narrowly avoided a collision with a Dornier 217E-4. On 19 May a 157 Squadron Mosquito lost an engine and crashed at Castle Camps, killing both crew. No. 151 Squadron's first success came on the night of 29/30 May when Grimsby was attacked. Flt Lt Pennington intercepted a damaged Do 217E-4 in the very early morning. Attacking with cannon from 400 yards, he scored hits on the Dornier, which promptly took evasive action. When Pennington closed for a second attack from eighty yards, the enemy returned fire. The Mosquito was hit in the starboard wing and tail and the port engine. Pennington's fire hit the port wing and engine of the enemy aircraft, which dived away on fire into the haze above the sea, and contact was lost. The Mosquito flew 140 miles home on a single engine. Meanwhile, Plt Off John Alwyne Wain and Flt Sgt Thomas Steel Greenshields Grieve intercepted an incoming Do 217E-4 of *KG2* well out over the North Sea. Wain closed on the bomber and saw that it was carrying two large external bombs. He opened fire and the bomber immediately burst into flames and started to fall towards the sea. The crew claimed one 'possible' enemy aircraft destroyed. Both attacks took place over the North Sea while the bombers were *en route* to raid Great Yarmouth. On 30 May, another Dornier of *KG2* was almost certainly destroyed south of Dover by Sqn Ldr G. Ashfield in a 157 Squadron Mosquito from Castle Camps.

On 24/25 June Wg Cdr 'Black' Smith DFC and his navigator, Flt Lt Kernon-Sheppard, in W4097 intercepted three enemy aircraft off Great Yarmouth within thirty minutes. At 2330 an He 111 was intercepted at 8,000 ft. The New Zealander closed to 300 yards before opening fire, but the Heinkel dived away trailing fuel from its port tanks as a second approach was made. Ten minutes later he was vectored on to a Do 217-E4 of *II./KG40*. This time Smith approached unseen to a hundred yards before opening fire. Following a short burst of cannon fire, the Dornier dived abruptly into the sea and exploded. At 2348 radar contact was made on a Do 217E-4 of *I./KG2*, and on closing a long burst was fired from 200 yards. The shells hit both the Dornier's wing tanks, and the aircraft was engulfed in flames. Smith closed right in on the Dornier and fired a short burst into the stricken aircraft, which promptly went down into the sea.[2] Meanwhile Flt Lt Darling and Plt Off Wright engaged a Do 217 and a Ju 88, but both aircraft escaped without serious damage. The next night Plt Off John Wain and Flt Sgt Tom Grieve claimed an He 111H-6 over the North Sea.[3] On 26/27 June, when He 111 pathfinders, Ju 88s of *KüFlGr 506* and Do 217s of *I., II.* and *III./KG2* raided Norwich, Flt Lt Moody and Plt Off Marsh claimed a Do 217E-4 of *3./KG2* flown by *Feldwebel* Hans Schrödel about sixty to eighty miles from the east coast. It appeared to go down into the sea.

On 22/23 August 157 Squadron scored its first actual confirmed 'kill' when the CO, 29-year-old Wg Cdr Gordon Slade, and Plt Off Philip

V. Truscott destroyed a Do 217E-4 of *6./KG2* flown by 29-year-old ex-Lufthansa pilot *Oberleutnant* Hans Walter Wolff, Deputy *Staffelkapitan*, twenty miles from Castle Camps. August opened with bad weather, low cloud and poor visibility. No. 151 Squadron was detailed to intercept high-flying German night raiders, which were flying in over England on cloudy nights. Raiders coming in over the North Sea continued to be intercepted. In September 151 Squadron added two more Dornier Do 217E-4s to its 'kill' total. The first of these, on loan to *3./KG2* and piloted by *Feldwebel* Alfred Witting, was shot down by Ian McRitchie on 8/9 September when the *Luftwaffe* attacked Bedford. During a raid on King's Lynn on 17 September Flt Lt Henry E. Bodien DFC blasted a *7./KG2* Dornier piloted by *Feldwebel* Franz Elias. It crashed at Fring and all four crew were taken prisoner.[4] On 30 September 157 scored its first day-combat victory when Sqn Ldr Rupert F.H. Clerke, an Old Etonian and former PRU Mosquito pilot, downed a Ju 88A-4 off the Dutch coast.[5] It had been a particularly bad month for *KG2*, which on 19 August 1942, during the Dieppe operation, lost sixteen Do 217s and had seven damaged. By October 157 Squadron had added three more enemy victories

During 1942, some RAF night-fighter squadrons had re-equipped with the de Havilland Mosquito – 'a lethal brute with no vices' – and in October of the same year ACM Arthur 'Bomber' Harris, the AOC RAF Bomber Command, advocated that Mosquito fighters should be used in the bomber stream for raids on Germany. ACM Sir W. Sholto Douglas, AOC Fighter Command, loath to lose his Mosquito fighters, argued that the few available Mosquitoes were needed for home defence should the *Luftwaffe* renew its attacks on Britain.

On the night of 28 October 1942 Sgts Keith R. McCormick RCAF and W. 'Nick' Nixon MiD of 85 Squadron at Hunsdon, near Ware in Hertfordshire, were scrambled at 1505 hours to intercept and chase two bandits in their NF.II.[6] 'Nick' Nixon recalls:[7]

> Due to low cloud and poor visibility we were unable to make contact, and returned to Hunsdon. As we approached base the weather became worse and the field was almost closed in. During the approach we had to make two split-arse turns in order to see the end of the runway, and consequently lost forward speed and stalled in from about 50 ft. We hit the end of the runway and slewed off onto the grass, and eventually came to a halt after 300 to 400 yards, shedding bits of the aircraft on the way. We came to rest on the engine nacelles, and after getting out we were surprised to find that the rest of the aircraft, aft of the cockpit armour, did not exist and was strewn in our wake. We were later both commissioned and posted to 410 Squadron RCAF at Hunsdon in 1943. All the Canadian pilots were posted at the same time, taking with them their RAF

navigator/radar, as the Canadians did not have sufficient fully trained personnel.

No. 410 'Cougar' Squadron RCAF, which had been equipped with Beaufighter IIs, moved from Scorton in Yorkshire to Acklington in October 1942 to re-equip with Mosquito NF.IIs. Re-equipment boosted spirits, although conversion was slow and the process was only finally completed in December. During December 1942 to January 1943 the Cougars flew ninety-three sorties against the 'Jerry Weathermen' and 'milk train' patrols which proved to be fruitless. On 13 January Flt Sgt B.M. Haight and Sgt T. Kipling were vectored onto a raider, and they made a visual contact at 600 yards. Kipling identified it as a Do 217E from its silhouette against the clouds. One brief burst at a hundred yards' range produced a brilliant white flash on one engine. A second burst of seventy-five rounds from the Hispanos had no visible effect, but the Dornier disappeared into the clouds in a steep spiral dive, and contact was lost. The Royal Observer Corps, however, saw the aircraft dive into the sea with a brilliant white flash and explosion five miles off Hartlepool.

On 15/16 January 1943, 151 Squadron scored the first Mosquito 'kill' of the New Year, when Sgt E.A. Knight and Sgt W.I.L. Roberts shot down a Do 217E-4[8] during a raid on Lincoln. The Canadian Mosquito pilot aimed his first burst from quarter astern and hit the enemy's port engine. The pilot, *Leutnant* Gunther Wolf, dived and carried out evasive action. *Unteroffizier* Kurt Smelitschkj, the dorsal gunner, returned fire. Knight blasted the Dornier again and there was no more firing. His third burst caused pieces of the German bomber to fly off, and it crashed at Boothby Graffoe near Lincoln, killing everyone on board. On 17/18 January an NF.II of 85 Squadron, flown by the Canadian CO, Wg Cdr Gordon Raphael DFC*[9] and his navigator, WO W.N. Addison DFM, destroyed a Ju 88A-14, which fell over south-east England. No. 85 Squadron was a famous fighter squadron, and its badge, the mysterious hexagon, the origin of which no one could trace, had distinguished itself in the First World War. It had borne the brunt of much of the early fighting in France, and later it had won honours in the Battle of Britain. Converted to a night-fighter squadron, it was now stationed in the same North Weald sector from which the RAF had guarded the eastern approaches to London in the autumn of 1939. On 22 January a 410 Squadron RCAF Mosquito claimed a 'probable' Do 217E, and then there was a lull in the Mosquito 'kills'.

At the end of January 1943 Wg Cdr John 'Cats Eyes' Cunningham DSO* DFC*[10] assumed command of 85 Squadron at Hunsdon *vice* Wg Cdr Raphael – 'a vigorous young Canadian' who 'strongly disapproved of drinking' [which] 'had been weighing heavily upon the more light-hearted members of the squadron.'[11] Cunningham had shot down sixteen enemy aircraft while flying Beaufighters. This was due to a combination of flying skill and good shooting and airborne radar operated by his navigator, 39-year-old Flt Lt C.F. 'Jimmy' Rawnsley DFC DFM*.[12] Cunningham's miraculous night vision, the propagandists explained, was due to the fact that night-fighter pilots ate lots of carrots, because they were good for night vision. This had its origins in the half-truth that a deficiency of certain vitamins could cause night blindness. Not unnaturally, the public, who knew nothing about airborne radar, went along with it, but the Germans were not fooled for a moment, and Cunningham was saddled with the nickname 'Cat's Eyes', which he detested. In the late 1930s Rawnsley, a Londoner, had been 18-year-old Plt Off Cunningham's air gunner in the two-seater Demon biplane fighters that 604 Squadron, Auxiliary Air Force, flew. It was the beginning of what was to develop into a close association as a team that lasted throughout the years of the war. Known to all as the 'The Little Man', Rawnsley was appointed navigation leader at Hunsdon. Rawnsley's wife Micki had recently joined the ATS.

Cunningham's and Rawnsley's first concern after their introduction to the officers' mess in an old country house named 'Bonningtons' was to get to know all those in the squadron. Of these, the first was the adjutant, Flt Lt T.J. Molony, known as Tim, 'a massive and dignified man, urbane and very conscious of the niceties of decorum'. In civilian life he was a director of Ladbrooke's, the turf accountants; and he had been with the squadron since the early days in France. He also laid claim to being the last man to bowl underarm in first-class cricket, playing for Surrey. Because of this distinction, Tim described himself, using a happy phrase, as 'the last of the lobsters'. The engineering officer, Flt Lt J. Hoile, 'was a good-natured, hard-working old sweat of a Regular who knew his job thoroughly and in every detail from spinner to tailwheel'. The squadron intelligence officer was Flg Off E.A. Robertson, 'a wizened, dry old Scot'. Robbie was in the fishery business and lived in Hull. The senior flying control officer was Sqn Ldr M.H. Bradshaw-Jones, 'a tallish, gaunt, piratical figure of a man' who would often pack a revolver and wear thigh-length boots. In the mess one night 'Brad' quietly rode a solo motorcycle around the billiard table with four passengers on board. Before the war Brad, married and with two children, had been a keen amateur yachtsman. He had also raced in cars and on motorcycles. His business had been in manufacturing and wholesaling of fine silverware and in antiques. When war broke out he tried to join the RAF. Five times he was turned down on medical grounds; but he passed on the sixth try and went into Air-Sea Rescue, working with the high-speed launches. During the Battle of Britain he went through a dive-bombing attack one day while ashore at Gosport, and he was badly injured, his spine being stretched. But he still went on with his work with the launches until he was shot up in one after the bombing of a convoy. The Bembridge lifeboat rescued him from that.[13] One of Rawnsley's first duties was to assess the value of the navigators in relation to the positions they held in each aircrew:[14]

> Some had developed a patter that I could only describe as most extraordinary. It seemed to consist of a non-stop and bewildering stream of words somewhat like the chanting of a Dutch auctioneer trying to finish off the sale before closing time. It was not until I heard the retiring navigator leader in action that I discovered where it had all come from. He was a lively, vivacious man named C.P. Reed, a flight lieutenant. He was sharp featured and quick witted and a remarkably fast thinker. The words streamed out of him in a torrent, and I wondered how any pilot could ever take it all in. But the amazing thing was that it worked, and worked well. And what sort of argument could prevail against the unanswerable fact of success? All the same, I began with the newer navigators to use a more orthodox style, if only to simplify the interchangeability of crews. I had a pretty shrewd idea that Phil Reed owed his success more to his quick thinking than to his style.
> There were among the aircrews some well-matched teams. Many of them merged their own pronounced individualities in achieving this. Flight Lieutenant W.H. 'Bill' Maguire – who had been in the millinery business before the war – was a jovial, prosperous-looking man, an ex-instructor and a fine pilot. He had as his navigator a Welsh schoolmaster, Flying Officer W.D. Jones, a short, stocky man who was a great lover of music. Getting ready for a patrol always appeared to be an event with great relish in it for Bill Maguire, almost as if he were preparing for a feast, his eyes sparkling with anticipation, his bushy moustache bristling skyward. In his comfortable voice he would boom out, 'Now ... where's that Jonesy man?'
> In the quiet voice of Flying Officer George Irving, who came from Carlisle, there was just a hint of a border burr. His head of flaming hair naturally brought down upon him the nickname 'Red'. And there was always a suggestion of a smile in his twinkling, pale blue eyes, a smile always ready to break out in a flash of dazzling white teeth. He was navigator for Flight Lieutenant Geoffrey Howitt, a solid and imperturbable individual.[15]
> Squadron Leader Wilfrith. P. Green, 'A' Flight Commander,[16] had as his navigator a typical NCO of the best type, Flight Sergeant A.R. Grimstone. Known to everybody as 'Grimmy', he was, although unburdened by any unnecessary ambition, keen, quick witted and reliable. Peter Green was a slightly built, deceptively mild-mannered man, plagued with a nervous stammer, which, as I had noticed happened with other aircrew, was barely noticeable moments after he had left the ground. There was certainly no trace of nervousness about his flying. Another of the navigators, Sergeant Graham

Gilling-Lax, had only been with the squadron for a very short time when we arrived. He was an NCO of a very different type, and entirely different to the popular conception of what a sergeant was supposed to be. Greying hair topped a long, scholarly face, and he stooped slightly in a rather dignified manner. His voice was quiet and carefully and evenly modulated. I was not altogether surprised when I checked through the records to find that he had been a housemaster at Stowe. I seemed to have on my books an astonishing number of schoolmasters.

One of the more senior navigators – although young enough in years – was Flying Officer Frank Seymour Skelton.[17] I saw little of him, as he was just finishing his first tour of flying and was about to go on a rest; but what I did see of him made a lasting impression. He had been through the complete navigator's course, and at first he had been rather annoyed at having to specialize for night-fighters, as that was by no means the job of his choice. Known to everybody as Bill, he was tall and handsome with veiled eyes well set in a leonine head. A rather drawling, undergraduate voice tended to complete an impression that Bill was taking the whole business far too languidly ever to be much good at it. I should have known better, and subsequent events were to prove how wrong first impressions can sometimes be. In Bill Skelton, I felt, there could be more or less summed up the general standard of operating in the squadron: the basically fine material had been softened by prolonged and enforced inactivity. Most of them had got into the habit of doing only perfunctory night-flying tests, and their practice in the air was casual, even slapdash. It was the old and very sad story, all the result of a little too much of the playboy in their attitude towards things. I formed the impression that they were good, but not as good as they thought they were and by no means as good as they could be; and I became anxious to show up their shortcomings and my own, before the *Luftwaffe* did it for us.[18]

Early in February Cunningham and Rawnsley flew their first night flight in a Mosquito and eased themselves into their training regime. They decided that Rawnsley should control the interception during the early stages using their old and well-tried methods, and then, when they got close enough for any evasive action their quarry might take, Cunningham would take over. They carried out their first operational night interception in a Mosquito on 3 March when they flew I-Ink. Rawnsley picked up a contact in the London area and Cunningham closed to about 500 ft, but they were in dense cloud and they finally had to give up. They soon picked up another contact, however, and they followed it as it weaved its way outward bound between the swinging beams of searchlights. Cunningham looked up and saw a Dornier 217 twisting and turning ahead of them. They closed in for the attack, the twin fins of the Dornier standing out clearly. Rawnsley, whose faith in the AI had been quickly restored, had a perfect view of the enemy bomber. He realized that only the clear, wide panel of bullet-resisting glass of the windshield was all that was between them and the target and 'any hot tomatoes they might want to throw back at them'. But the Dornier crew did not see the Mosquito, and Cunningham attacked. However, when he pressed the gun-button nothing happened. He tried again, but still there was no response from the guns. And then somebody in the Dornier must have given the alarm. The long, slim bomber rolled right over to its left and plunged vertically downwards. Cunningham rammed I-Ink's nose over, and Rawnsley was lifted from his seat as the Mosquito fell away, but he forced his face into the visor of the AI Mk V set and just held on. The Dornier went plummeting down for several hundred feet, but they were still in contact. Then it levelled out and started to climb steeply, but the Mosquito was right behind it. A few minutes later Cunningham again had it in his gunsight. The Dornier was tantalizingly close, but again as he pressed the gun-button nothing happened! A moment later the Dornier peeled off and away again, straight on down in a long, high-speed dive that kept the Mosquito well behind, and finally he was lost in the ground echoes and Rawnsley could see nothing more of him on the AI. At Hunsdon a quick examination revealed that a severed lead had put the Mosquito's gun-firing circuit out of action. No. 85 Squadron had put up eighteen sorties and Cunningham and Rawnsley were the only crew to see a raider.

At Hunsdon in March Sqn Ldr Edward Crew DFC* joined 85 Squadron to take command of 'B' Flight.[19] He had as his navigator Flg Off Freddie French, who had never quite recovered from a Beaufighter crash at Middle Wallop in the winter of 1941/2, but he was determined to go on with his job. He had been flying with a pilot who had only recently joined 604 Squadron, and they had hit a hill near the aerodrome one night. The Beaufighter broke up and the pilot was killed, but Freddie was trapped in a part of the fuselage that had broken off. Badly injured, he lay there for some time before the rescue party arrived and hacked him out. Fortunately, the part of the aircraft that he was trapped in did not catch fire.

On 18/19 March *Fliegerkorps IX* set out to attack Norwich. Between 2255 and 2330 hours, twenty crews aimed 18 tonnes of high explosive and 19.2 tonnes of incendiaries on the part of the city that ran north and north-west of the large buildings in the city centre. In all, 3.3 tonnes actually fell on the streets, houses and factories. Thirteen junior crews, who were on the raid to gain combat experience, attacked harbour installations at Great Yarmouth. Mosquito and Beaufighter night-fighters had already taken off to intercept the bombers heading for Norwich. Flg Off G. Deakin and Plt Off de Costa of 157 Squadron took off from

Bradwell Bay at 2200 hours in their NF.II and were vectored out to sea by GCI at Trimley Heath. Sqn Ldr Kidd, the controller, directed the Mosquito crew towards an enemy aircraft approaching Orfordness. They got an AI contact with a Ju 88 at 9,000 ft range. (Deakin eventually obtained a visual sighting at 2,500 ft and recognized his prey.) The Ju 88 was climbing, so he opened up the throttles and climbed steeply behind him before opening fire with a long burst of four cannon and two Browning machine-guns at 600 ft dead astern. The Mosquito pilot continued firing while the Ju 88 'corkscrewed' in vain. Deakin carried on firing into the doomed bomber until all his ammunition was exhausted. The enemy raider flew straight and level, then disappeared, falling into the sea about four miles off Southwold.

A Coltishall-based 68 Squadron Beaufighter flown by Flg Off P.F. Allen DFC and Flg Off G.E. Bennett destroyed a Do 217E, a *6./KG2* machine flown by *Hauptmann* Hans Hansen. In the meantime an NF.II of 410 Squadron RCAF flown by Flg Off D. Williams and his navigator, Plt Off P. Dalton, had taken off from Coleby Grange at 2245 hours and was directed towards 'trade' in the King's Lynn area. Flt Lt Tuttle at Orby Control directed the two Canadians towards a 'bogey' three miles distant flying at 240 mph. Williams increased speed to 260 mph and Dalton picked up the contact at a range of two miles. Suddenly, another contact appeared at 1,000 yards, below and slightly to port. Williams put the nose down and at 8,000 ft made out the unmistakable form of a Do 217, flying along at 2,000 ft dead ahead. It was from *I./KG2* and was being flown by *Unteroffizier* Horst Toifel. The fear and shock aboard the Dornier at that instant can only be imagined. Toifel must have seen his pursuer because he immediately carried out a half-roll and tried to dive before his gunner, *Unteroffizier* Heinrich Peter, the radio operator, Ludwig Petzold, or the observer, *Obergefreiter* Georg Riedel, could even think about opening fire. Toifel was so preoccupied with trying to lose the Mosquito that he had no time to sight and fire his defensive armament. Williams followed the Dornier down and held his fire as he did so. At 1,800 ft the Mosquito pilot pulled out, and shortly afterwards a huge ball of crimson fire could be seen directly below, near Terrington St Clements. Williams could only think that the Dornier did not recover from its dive and therefore crashed.

On 28/29 March 1943 forty-seven bombers of *IX Fliegerkorps* bombed Norwich again. An NF.II of 157 Squadron flown by Flg Off J.R. Beckett RAAF and Flt Sgt Phillips took off from Bradwell Bay at 1940 hours and patrolled some thirty miles off Orfordness before it was vectored by HCI Trimley Heath onto an enemy aircraft approaching Lowestoft. Beckett had got contacts before on two of his previous twelve patrols, but so far had made no kills. After two momentary contacts, on a fighter crossing rapidly from starboard to port, another contact was obtained dead ahead on an aircraft flying west at 12,000 ft. It was changing course and height as it approached the coast. With some difficulty the NF.II closed in to 1,000 ft, where a visual sighting was obtained. Evasive tactics became more violent, which made the target difficult to identify, but from its exhaust system, which glowed orange-red, it appeared to be a Dornier 217.[20] Beckett wrote.

> The searchlights and ack-ack made identification difficult as we were also hit a few times. After we closed up to our firing position to identify the plane positively as an enemy one, their rear gunner fired at us, but missed, firing too high. I returned the fire at once with two bursts of cannon fire at 300–400 ft range lasting about two seconds each. After that I saw hits and sparks on the rear of the aircraft, and as a result the enemy fire stopped and the plane dived into the clouds a few hundred feet below us. Visual contact was lost, but AI contact was held by Phillips from 10,000 ft down to 5,000 ft with the Dornier turning hard to port. During that time we were constantly turning in left circles. Contact was lost when the enemy plane turned hard to port and left our screen.[21]

On 14/15 April 1943, during a raid on Chelmsford, Sqn Ldr Wilfrith Green and Flt Sgt A.R. 'Grimmy' Grimstone of 85 Squadron destroyed a Do 217E-4 of 4./KG40. Off Clacton Flt Lt Geoff Howitt and Flg Off George 'Red' Irving destroyed a Do 217E-4 of 6./KG2 flown by *Unteroffizier* Franz Tannenberger. This was Howitt's third victory of the war, having destroyed two He 111s while flying Havocs in 1941. Flt Lt James Gilles Benson DFC and his navigator Lewis Brandon DSO DFC of 157 Squadron intercepted a Dornier 217E-4 flown by *Unteroffizier* Walter Schmurr south-west of Colchester.[22] 'Ben' Benson gave the 6./KG2 machine a three-second burst at 200 yards with his four cannon from astern and above, but saw no results. He then fired a seven-second burst and saw strikes, first on the port engine and mainplane, which immediately burst into flames. These spread down the port side of the fuselage until the whole aircraft, including the tail, was ablaze. There was no return fire.[23] On 16/17 April Fw 190A-4/U8s of *Schnelles Kampfgeschwader* (SKG) 10 based in France took part in attacks on London. The fast fighter-bombers, each carrying a 250 kg or 500 kg bomb on its centreline, had first been employed in March against Eastbourne, Hastings and Ashford. To be better sited to meet the threat, 85 Squadron had, in May, moved from Hunsdon to West Malling, and 157 moved from Bradwell to take its place. The mainstay of the *Luftwaffe*'s raids on England at this time remained the Ju 88 and Do 217. On 24/25 April Flg Off John Peter Morley Lintott and Sgt Graham Gilling-Lax of 85 Squadron shot down a Ju 88A-14 of 8./KG6, and it disintegrated in the air and the wreckage fell in Bromley, Kent. In April 604 Squadron at Scorton converted to the

NF.XIII, and 256 Squadron began equipping with the NF.XII. They were followed, in May, by 29 Squadron, which did likewise.

Six German aircraft were shot down by Mosquito Intruders before May was out.[24] On the 13th, 85 Squadron moved from Hunsdon to West Malling aerodrome near the main London–Maidstone road, deep in the heart of the orchards and hop gardens of Kent, which was occupied by Typhoons of 3 Squadron. The move coincided with some terrific action, for during May 85 Squadron claimed eight aircraft. On the night of 16/17 May the Fw 190A-4/U8 fighter-bombers of *I./SKG10* came streaking in over the Straits of Dover. Much to the chagrin of 85 squadron, the Typhoons only were scrambled to meet them. The Mosquito crews waited almost an hour before they too were pitched into the fight after it was realized that the Typhoons, which did not have AI, were floundering. Sqn Ldr Peter Green and Flt Sgt A.R. 'Grimmy' Grimstone got off first and picked up an Fw 190 contact at three miles. The *I./SKG10* machine had dropped its centreline bomb and was on its way back to France. It never made it. Green shot it down into the sea off Dover. Geoff Howitt and 'Red' Irving shot down the second Fw 190 off Hastings. Flt Lt Bernard Thwaites, a quiet, pale young fighter pilot with a look of confidence in his eyes, and Plt Off Will Clemo DFM*, his older, former schoolmaster navigator, chased an Fw 190 all the way to the French coast before being recalled to West Malling. He and Clemo kept a close eye on the horizon as they headed back to base. Clemo was a thoughtful man who took his pleasure in solitary nature study rambles. On the ground he sported an enormous pipe with a deeply curved stem, and when he spoke, which was rarely, the words emerged reluctantly between puffs and in a gruff undertone. But there was a lively twinkle in his eyes that told of an alert brain working behind that dour façade, possibly savouring some secret joke.[25] In mid-Channel Clemo picked up a freelance contact crossing in front. Thwaites shot it down from fifty yards astern, collecting some of the debris in the air intake of one of his engines, but that did not prevent him from scoring three hits on another Fw 190, knocking a large piece off it, to claim it as a 'probable'.

Flg Off I.D. Shaw and Plt Off A.C. Lowton braved their own searchlights and brought down a fifth Fw 190 near Gravesend, returning to Hunsdon with their windscreen coated in soot and their rudder badly damaged.

Back at West Malling, to the accompaniment of *Yip I Addy 85*, Tim Molony ceremoniously presented the jackpot prize of bottles of whisky, champagne and gin and £5 in cash to Peter Green and 'Grimmy' Grimstone for being the first Mosquito crew to down an Fw 190 over Britain.[26] Sqn Ldr Bradshaw-Jones gave a silver Mosquito. Congratulatory signals were received from the sector commander, Gp Capt 'Sailor' Malan DSO* DFC*[27] and AVM H.W.L. 'Dingbat' Saunders at Group. There was soon more to celebrate. On the night of 19/20 May, Flg Off

John Lintott and Sgt Graham Gilling-Lax stalked an Fw 190A of 2./SKG10. Peering into his scope he guided Lintott onto the tail of the Fw 190, and his pilot shot it down. Their victory was celebrated at West Malling, where a dance was in progress, and the remains of the Fw 190A were auctioned off for £105 in aid of the 'Wings for Victory' appeal! On 21/22 May an Fw 190A was shot down into the sea twenty-five miles north-west of Hardelot by Sqn Ldr Edward Crew DFC* and Flg Off Freddie French. To complete a memorable month, on 29/30 May Lintott and Gilling-Lax shot down the first Ju 88S-1 to fall over England. It crashed at Isfield, Sussex.[28]

On 13/14 June Wg Cdr John Cunningham and Flt Lt C.F. 'Jimmy' Rawnsley of 85 Squadron pursued an Fw 190A-5 of 3./SKG10 over his own airfield and shot it down. Rawnsley wrote.

> It was an Fw 190 all right. The single exhaust flickered below the fuselage; the short, straight wings still had the drop-tanks hanging from the tips; the big, smooth bomb was still clutched fiercely to its belly ... John very briefly touched the trigger and the guns gave one short bark. The enemy aircraft reared straight up on its nose, flicking over and plunging vertically downwards. It all happened with an incredible speed. Standing up and pressing my face to the window, I watched the blue exhaust flame dwindle as the aircraft hurtled earthwards.[29]

The Fw 190, flown by *Leutnant* Ullrich, crashed at Nettlefold Farm, Borough Green, near Wrotham, but incredibly the pilot had been catapulted through the canopy in the death dive of the aircraft and was taken prisoner. Cunningham's seventeenth victory was his first on the Mosquito.[30]

On 21/22 June Flt Lt Bill Maguire and Flg Off W.D. Jones of 85 Squadron bagged an Fw 190 of 2./SKG10 in the River Medway. On 9 July Geoff Howitt and 'Red' Irving and Flt Lt John Lintott and Plt Off Graham Gilling-Lax, the two standby crews at Hunsdon, were scrambled to meet a wave of sneak raiders coming in under cover of the bad weather. The cloud seemed to be almost down to the ground, blotting out Wrotham Hill nearby, but both crews took off, and twenty minutes later crews at Hunsdon heard the sound of aircraft approaching, but now the notes of the engines varied, as if the pilots were jockeying for position. The Medway AA guns opened up, followed by a burst of machine-gun fire and the unmistakable throaty roar of cannon. Crews in the officers' mess at 'Bonningtons' rushed outside and strained their eyes, but they could see nothing in the driving rain that was now beating down around them. The note of the engines changed again and the drone rose to a howl, rising in pitch to a scream, and then it cut off abruptly with an ominous thump. There was silence as crews waited for news, and finally it came through on the telephone. A Dornier 217 had crashed near Detling. Lintott had obtained his fourth victory when he and Gilling-Lax shot down a Do 217K-1 piloted by *Oberleutnant* Hermann Zink of 6./KG2, which had just bombed East Grinstead high street and the Whitehall cinema, killing 108 people and injuring 235 more. Zink and his crew were all dead. The GCI controller who had put Lintott onto the raider saw two blips on his CRT merge and stay together for seven minutes: then they had faded. Geoff Howitt and Irving had crept in under the weather and had landed safely at Bradwell Bay across the other side of the Thames Estuary in Essex. Shortly afterwards word came that Lintott and Gilling-Lax had been found two miles from where the Dornier fell. They were dead in the wreckage of their Mosquito. Both men had just been awarded DFCs and Gilling-Lax had recently been given his commission. They were a bitter loss to the squadron.

Two months earlier, Flt Lt Edward Nigel Bunting, an experienced night-fighter pilot, had been one of the officers in 85 Squadron who operationally tested the high-altitude Mosquito NF.XV at Hunsdon. He attained a record altitude of 44,600 ft on 30 March 1943, but the project was abandoned after the demise of German high-altitude raiding.[31] Bunting, who was 27 years old and was from St John's, Worcester, had yet to score a confirmed victory. Flying a Havoc I in June 1941, he was awarded an He 111 'probable'. Flying a Mosquito II in October 1942, he had damaged a Ju 88. On 13/14 July, when KG2 headed for Cambridge, Bunting and Freddie French took off from the Somerfield wire-mesh runway at West Malling at 2300 hours in their NF.XII and patrolled the Straits of Dover in search of enemy activity. Flg Off Parr at Sandwich GCI station gave Bunting a vector towards a 'customer' some thirty-five miles away. The Mosquito soon narrowed the gap to three miles, and Bunting and French could see their prey well below them. French picked up another contact and Bunting pulled away, concerned that the red light he saw might be a decoy. French guided Bunting onto the higher, unlighted contact, which was at 25,000 ft. Climbing at full power, Bunting gave chase for fifteen minutes, opening and closing his radiator flaps to prevent overheating. When they were still at 7,000 ft range they could see the enemy's two bright exhausts. Eventually, a visual was obtained against the bright glow of the northern sky at a range of 1,800 ft. The Mosquito crew could make out the two engines trailing bright yellow exhaust flames with the narrow fuselage and twin barbettes bulging on either side. Rightly, they believed it to be an Me 410 *Hornisse* (Hornet). *Feldwebel* Franz Zwissler and *Oberfeldwebel* Leo Raida of 16./KG2 were flying it. Bunting closed to within 200 yards astern and worked his gunsight onto the target, but the Mosquito got caught in the Germans' slipstream and he could not aim his guns. Bunting dived below to recover and began easing up into position again before firing two short bursts. With flames streaming from the fuselage, the Me 410 rolled over on its back and dived vertically into the sea five miles off Felixstowe. It was the first Me 410 to be shot down over Britain.[32]

July 1943 was a month of high activity, thanks in considerable measure to enemy activity. On the 12/13th four Mosquitoes of 410 Squadron were scrambled from Coleby Grange to intercept an enemy raid on Hull and Grimsby. Sqn Ldr A.G. Lawrence DFC and Flt Sgt H.J. Wilmer intercepted a Do 217 over the mouth of the Humber, but after taking violent evasive action it got away after the crew had fired only one short burst at it. Flares, ack-ack and searchlight activity made it impossible to continue the chase. The crew was then vectored onto another Do 217, and following an AI contact and visual identification the enemy aircraft was given a short burst of cannon fire. This had no effect and a second burst was given. This caused a huge flash in the Dornier's starboard engine, followed by clouds of smoke. In a diving turn with the engine glowing brightly, the bomber went down, hitting the sea with a great splash. The enemy gunners had returned fire, but the streaks of red and white tracer passed under the Mossie's starboard wing. On the following night six crews were scrambled but no contacts were made.

On 15/16 July Flt Lt Bernard Thwaites and Plt Off Clemo DFM* of 85 Squadron shot down an Me 410 of *V./KG2* flown by *Hauptmann* Friederich-Wilhelm Methner and *Unteroffizier* Hubert Grube, which was heading for London, into the sea off Dunkirk. Flg Off Knowles of 605 Squadron shot down a Do 217M-1 flown by *Leutnant* Manfred Lieddert of *3./KG2* on 25/26 July, when the target was again Hull. South African Wg Cdr Geoffrey Park, CO of 256 Squadron, rounded off the month by shooting down *Oberleutnant* Helmut Biermann and *Unteroffizier* Willi Kroger in their Me 410A-1 on 29/30 July, when the target was Brighton. They fell into the sea twenty miles south of Beachy Head.

One of the heaviest losses to befall *KG2* in 1943 was on the night of 15/16 August, when it lost seven aircraft – six claimed by Mosquitoes – in a raid on Portsmouth.[33] On 17/18 August Flt Lt Edward Bunting of 85 Squadron damaged an Fw 190 off Eastbourne. On 22/23 August fellow squadron pilot Geoff Howitt, now Sqn Ldr DFC, and Plt Off J.C.O. Medworth, took off from West Malling at 2330 hours in their NF.XII and went on patrol. Off Harwich they zeroed in on *Feldwebel* Walter Hartmann and *Obergefreiter* Michael Meurer's Me 410A-1 of *15./KG2*. Howitt got a visual on the Messerschmitt's bright yellow exhaust emissions and closed in for the kill. It was difficult to get a sight of the silhouette, and at first Howitt thought his prey was a '210. Almost at once a stray searchlight beam illuminated the aircraft and he could quite easily see that it was a '410. With the German crosses easily visible, Howitt gave the Messerschmitt a short burst, and it immediately burst into flames with a brilliant flash. Showers of burning pieces flew past the Mosquito in all directions. The Me 410A-1 fell away, its entire starboard wing on fire, and crashed at Chemondiston. Meurer baled-out and came down at Stratton Hall, while Hartman's body was later found in a field, his parachute unopened.

On the night of 24/25 August an NF.XII flown by 85 Squadron's Norwegian pairing – Captain Johan Räd and radio operator Captain Leif Lövestad – took off to look for 'trade'. Räd and Lövestad searched the night sky for a 'kill'. Lövestad worked the AI VIII set and picked up a contact, a Messerschmitt 410. Räd fired four bursts into the enemy fighter, which exploded in a ball of fire. Blazing pieces broke off. Two explosions followed and a parachutist was spotted baling-out. The victory was officially shared with Wg Cdr R.E.X. Mack DFC of 29 Squadron, which claimed two more victories that night, their first Mosquito victories since converting from Beaufighters.[34] Tall and slim, Räd was a lively individual who had been an electrical engineering student and a pilot in the Norwegian Air Force Reserve when the Germans had invaded his country. He and fellow engineering student Per Bugge went into the Underground movement in Trondheim before setting sail six months later with eleven others for Britain. After nine days meandering around the North Sea and Atlantic Ocean, they had finally landed in Scotland. Lövestad, a man with massive hands and broad shoulders, a cheerful smile lighting a rugged, homely face, had started his career well before the war in the Norwegian Army, and had later changed over to the Air Force. He went through the air fighting in Norway, fighting as an observer in the Norwegian Air Force against the *Luftwaffe* until they had no aircraft left. Then he had gone underground, mapping and sketching the airfields the Germans were building, and taking documents out to the coast for friends to smuggle across to England. In August 1941 Lövestad and twenty-nine others set out for Britain across the North Sea in a small, dilapidated, old fishing-boat, following for reasons of safety the longest route from the Lofoten Islands to the Shetlands. The journey took them nine days. They missed the Shetlands and went sailing out into the Atlantic; but finally they decided to turn back and they landed near Scapa Flow on the north-east corner of Scotland. For two days they rested in the shelter of a small bay, and then they sailed on to Thurso, where they made their official landing. They even managed to sell the dilapidated boat to a Scottish fisherman, even though it was rotten all through![35]

For a time Lövestad and Räd were the only two Norwegian airmen in Britain who had some training as pilots, and they were allowed to complete their instruction in England rather than having to follow the usual course of going to Canada. Though he stood no more than shoulder high to Räd, Leif Lövestad had tremendous strength, and had been known to change with ease a car wheel without using a jack. Sometimes in the evenings he said, 'Now Johan ... you must be tired. Why don't you sit down?' and he would lift his pilot at arm's length as gently as a baby and deposit him on the counter of the bar. Using the same strength, Lövestad had battered his way through the side of their crashed Beaufighter at Middle Wallop and lifted the unconscious Johan clear of the wreckage as the flames sprang up around them. Soon they were joined at West Malling by three fellow countrymen: Claus Björn, Bugge's argumentative radio operator, who had reached England via Sweden, Russia, Japan and the USA, and Lieutenants P. Thoren and Tarald Weisteen. Björn was trained as an observer in Canada. Per Bugge was a flaxen-haired giant whose rare words emerged reluctantly in a series of scarcely audible grunts. He appeared to be unshakeable, and was always pleasant and most courteous. He soon made a name for himself as an exceptionally capable pilot. Weisteen was small, dark and slight of build. But his mind, like his features, was keen and taut. He had joined the Royal Norwegian Air Force before the war and was a regular officer. He had gone through the War Academy and was an established fighter pilot when hostilities broke out in Norway. It was said of him that he had had quite a time flying against the *Luftwaffe* in Gloster Gladiators until the Resistance was overwhelmed. And then he managed to escape to England.[36]

On 6 and 8 September 85 Squadron destroyed a total of five Fw 190A-5s. On 15/16 September Flg Off Jarris of 29 Squadron shot down *Oberfeldwebel* Horst Muller and *Unteroffizier* Wolfgang Dose's Me 410A-1 of *15./KG2* off Beachy Head during a raid on Cambridge. A *9./KG2* Do 217M-1 flown by *Oberfeldwebel* Erich Mosler was also shot down by Flt Lt Watts of 488 Squadron RNZAF into the sea south-east of Ramsgate. Flt Lt Edward Bunting destroyed a Ju 88A-14 of *II./KG6* for his second victory. Flg Off Edward Richard Hedgecoe, a 34-year-old former accountant officer who had remustered to aircrew, and Plt Off J.R. Witham of 85 Squadron destroyed a Ju 88A-14 of *6./KG6*. The nose of their Mosquito shattered as he fired and the crew baled-out, their aircraft crashing at Tenterden, Kent. They were uninjured, and on 2/3 November Hedgecoe scored his second victory, an Fw 190 near Gravesend, with Plt Off Norman Bamford DFC,* who was on his second tour, as his radar operator. In October the Norwegians of 85 Squadron had figured in two more victories. On 2/3 October Plt Off Tarald Weisteen and Freddie French destroyed two Do 217Ks during a raid on the Humber Estuary. On 7/8 October, when the *Luftwaffe* raided London and Norwich, Leif Lövestad was flying with Flt Lt Bill Maguire, whose usual radio operator, Flg Off W.D. Jones, was away on a navigator leader's course. Maguire, who sported a bushy moustache, was an ex-instructor and a fine pilot, who before the war had been a milliner. GCI control warned Maguire and Lövestad that two hostile aircraft were flying in line astern and a mile apart when they caught sight of an enemy aircraft in the moonlight showing reddish-yellow wingtip lights and a white tail light below its starboard quarter. At 2,000 ft distance *Feldwebel* Georg Slodczyk of *16./KG2* put his Me 410A into a tight turn. In the back seat, *Unteroffizier* Fritz Westrich must have known there was a Mosquito on their tail. For several minutes Slodczyk and Maguire weaved and manoeuvred violently. Maguire turned tighter each time and was able to identify their prey. He gave the '410 a short burst, using deflection, and flashes appeared all along the German aircraft's fuselage and wing. Slodczyk desperately pushed his nose down and dived at full speed for the cover of cloud below. Maguire dived after him and pumped another burst into the '410 from 300 yards, just as Slodczyk disappeared into the cloud. (Westrich's body was picked up off Dungeness on 13 October and buried at sea). Below, Sqn Ldr Bernard Thwaites DFC and Will Clemo DFM,*who shot down an Me 410A flown by *Feldwebel* Wilhelm Sohn and *Unteroffizier* Günther Keiser of *14./KG2* (which crashed at Ghent), saw Slodczyk and Westrich descend in flames into the sea and were able to confirm Maguire's 'kill'.

On 8/9 October 85 Squadron claimed its first Ju 88S-1 when ten Intruders flew in from Holland. Flg Off S.V. Holloway and WO Stanton shot their Ju 88S-1 of *8./KG6* down off Foulness. Flt Lt Edward Bunting shot down a Ju 88S-1 of *7./KG6* into the sea ten miles south of Dover at 2020 hours for his third victory. *Feldwebel* W. Kaltwasser, *Obergefreiter* J. Jakobsen and *Unteroffizier* J. Bartmuss were all killed. Summer and late 1943 had proved successful for the night-fighter crews of 85 Squadron, but they knew that they could rely on the *Luftwaffe* to step up its efforts as the autumn nights began to lengthen. The Germans had already begun mixing Ju 88s in with the Fw 190 fighter-bombers, and word was that they could expect to meet the Ju 188, a faster and more powerful version of the Ju 88, with pointed extensions to the wings to give a better rate of climb. On 15/16 October thirteen enemy aircraft started towards England. Only eight of them crossed the coast and of these three were destroyed. Maguire and Flg Off W.D. Jones, now returned from his navigator leader's course, shot down two Ju 188E-1s of *1./KG6* within the space of twelve minutes. One went into the sea off Clacton and the other crashed at Hemley, Suffolk, to become the first Ju 188 downed on land in the UK.[37] Flg Off Hugh Brian Thomas and WO C.B. Hamilton got the third Ju 188E-1, which crashed at Birchington, for their first victory. On the last night of the month they had added to their score, downing a Ju 88G-1 of *III./KG6* south of Shoreham.

On 17/18 October 1943 Flt Lt Edward Bunting and Flt Lt C.P. 'Phil' Reed shot down their second Me 410 and Bunting's fourth enemy aircraft overall when they destroyed the *15./KG2* raider in the Hornchurch area. Posted to 604 Squadron late in the year, Bunting was awarded the DFC. Another experienced pilot was lost when Geoff Howitt, who received a Bar to his DFC, was posted to 63 OTU, Honiley, having completed his second tour of flying.[38] 'Red' Irving, Howitt's navigator, became an instructor on the new AI Mk X. The radar war was hotting up. On 1 October a Wellington fitted-out as a flying classroom to train the

Mosquito radar operators on AI Mk X had arrived at Hunsdon. The presentation on the radar information on the new set was radically different from anything that had gone before, as Jimmy Rawnsley recalls:

> If the tube of our Mark VIII sets, so often infested with whirling spirals of light, might be likened to a slice of Swiss Roll, the new Mark X resembled more a piece of that sinister-looking cut cake, amber in hue and sparsely curranted, sold by the Naafi.[39]

Something also had to be done about the Mosquito XII's hard-driven engines, which were wearing out in the middle of chases against the fast, highly elusive fighter-bombers. Half-way through October, Flt Lt Branse Burbridge and Bill Skelton had a starboard engine pack up when they were 1,500 ft behind a hostile raider. A few days later Capt Johan Räd and radio operator Capt Leif Lövestad had an engine failure when they were only 1,200 feet behind an Me 410. The 23-year-old Bransome Arthur Burbridge, born in East Dulwich, South London, lived in Knebworth, Hertfordshire, when war broke out, at which time he was working for Royal Exchange Insurance. Burbridge and 'Bill' Skelton were deeply religious. Burbridge had been a Conscientious Objector on religious grounds for the first six months of the war before joining up. He had joined the RAF in September 1940 and had served individually on Havocs in 85 Squadron in October 1941 and January 1942 respectively. He and Skelton only crewed up on their second tour on the squadron in July 1943. A first-class team in every sense of the word, the two men were totally dedicated to their task.[40]

With November came the bad weather, but 85 Squadron morale remained high. Hedgecoe and Bamford's victory on 2/3 November was the squadron's fiftieth night victory.[41] On 7/8 November John Selway, who was returning to the squadron after a rest, and his old navigator, Plt Off Norman Bamford, shot down an Fw 190A south of Hastings. Shortly afterwards Bamford got another contact and then a visual. It was a Ju 188. At 1,000 ft range Selway tried desperately to slow up, but the German pilot suddenly throttled back, and as he did so his rear gunner fired at the pursuing Mosquito. A shell tore through the gap between the windscreen and the armour just below it, and smashed through the instrument panel, hitting Selway in the liver and causing him to momentarily lose control of the Mosquito. Soaked in blood and fighting off unconsciousness, he managed to regain control again and make it back to base, although his altimeter and airspeed indicator were now out of action. He walked unaided to the crewroom and drank a cup of tea, and it was only when he began undressing that the extent of his injuries was realized, and he was taken away to hospital, where he was on the danger list for some time. Selway's second tour had lasted but a few days.[42]

By the end of 1943 284 BMW-powered Ju 188E-1s were in service, and the first Junkers-engined A-2 version with water/methanol injection would enter production in January 1944. The outlook looked even gloomier with the knowledge that the Ju 188s and Me 410s were fitted with rearward-beamed radar, known as *Neptun Gerät,* which could only make the Mosquito crews' interceptions that much more difficult and dangerous. Although they should be able to cope with 188s with or without radar, the Messerschmitt 410 was a different matter, for it was just about on level terms with the Mosquito. With the tail warner they would have the advantage over the Mosquito when it came to trying to intercept them. Beginning in January 1944, the *Luftwaffe* was also ready to begin the first of a series of revenge raids against Britain at night.

Notes

1. On 27 May 1940 Embry had been shot down over France in a Blenheim and three times had been captured, but never made a PoW. On the second occasion, unarmed, he fought his way out; then, with a 'borrowed' German rifle, had killed three Germans and escaped to England.
2. He later became CO of 487 Squadron, which carried out the Amiens Prison raid. After the war he stayed in the RAF, retiring as a group captain in 1966.
3. On the night of 10 August Wain and Grieve took off in DD623 to make an interception. The aircraft crashed into the sea and the crew were lost. No report was made and the cause of the loss was not known.
4. This was Bodien's fourth victory. He had destroyed three aircraft flying Defiant Is on 151 Squadron in 1941, and had damaged a Do 217 near Clacton on the night of 8/9 September 1942. Sqn Ldr Bodien's fifth and final victory of the war came on a daylight sortie in a Mosquito II on 19 June 1943, when he shot down a Ju 88 in the Bay of Biscay.
5. Rupert Francis Henry Clerke, the stepson of ACM Sir Edgar Ludlow-Hewitt, was born on 13 April 1916 and educated at Eton College. He received a permanent commission in the RAF in July 1937, and a year later joined 32 Squadron. By 1940 he had become a flight commander in 79 Squadron flying Hurricane I fighters. He was awarded a one-third share in downing an He 111 off Sunderland on 9 August, and a one-fifth share for a Bf 110 and a Do 17 'probable' over the North Sea on 15 August. On 28 August he scored his first outright victory when he destroyed an He 59, and he was also awarded a Bf 109E 'probable'. In July 1941 he was posted to 1 PRU at RAF Benson, where, on their first sortie, on 16 September, the old Etonian and his navigator, 32-year-old Sgt Sowerbutts, a pre-war Margate barber, were forced to abandon the operation when they were pursued by three Bf 109s, but the PR.I easily outpaced them at 23,000 ft and returned safely. Clerke and Sowerbutts made the first successful Mosquito PR.I sortie the next day when they set out at 1130 hours for a daylight photo-reconnaissance of Brest, La Pallice and Bordeaux, before arriving back at Benson at 1745 hours. On 15 October Clerke undertook a record-breaking flight from Wick to

Benson, and on 4 November he made the first major overseas flight in the Mosquito, photographing targets in Italy *en route* and landing in Malta, where he remained for several days. Clerke returned to fighters early in 1942 and became a flight commander in 157 Squadron flying the Mosquito II. His second outright victory followed on 30 September, when he destroyed a Ju 88A-4 of I./KG6 off the Dutch coast. Two more victories followed in February and June 1943 when he was CO of 125 Squadron flying Beaufighter VIs. He was awarded the DFC in July. *Aces High: A Tribute to the Most Notable Fighter Pilots of the British and Commonwealth Forces in WWII.* Christopher Shores and Clive Williams (Grub Street, London, 1994).

6. DD741.
7. MAA *The Mossie* Vol.11, August 1995.
8. U5+KR of 7./KG2.
9. A teetotal non-smoker, Gordon Learmouth Raphael was born in Brantford, Ontario, on 25 August 1915, being educated in Quebec and then in Chelsea, London, where he attended the College of Aeronautical Engineers. He joined the RAFVR in September 1935, being commissioned in January 1936. Called up on the outbreak of war, he joined 77 Squadron in Bomber Command, flying Whitleys. Involved in the early leaflet raids over Germany, he became the first Canadian to be Mentioned in Dispatches, in February 1940. During May he was promoted to flight lieutenant and awarded the DFC. His aircraft was attacked while making for an oil refinery target at Hannover on the night of 18/19 May, one engine being set on fire, and Raphael was wounded in the foot. The rear gunner managed to claim the attacking Bf 110 shot down, but the Whitley had to be ditched in the sea. The destroyer HMS *Javelin* rescued the crew, and Raphael was hospitalized. On recovery in July he was posted to 10 Squadron, again on Whitleys. During the night of 16/17 August his bomber was again attacked by a Bf 110 during an attack on Jever, but once again this was claimed shot down by the rear gunner. In December 1940 he was posted as a flight commander to 96 Squadron as it was forming to become a night-fighter unit, but early in May he was moved to 85 Squadron, which had just re-equipped with Douglas Havocs. He was immediately successful, claiming four victories and a probable before the end of the year. He was awarded a Bar to his DFC in July after his third confirmed success, while in May 1942 he was promoted to command the squadron. He remained in command until January 1943, receiving a DSO the following month. He then commanded RAF Castle Camps and subsequently RAF Manston, from where during June 1944 he shot down two V-1 flying bombs. He was killed on 10 April 1945 when the Spitfire he was flying collided with a Dakota. *Aces High: A Tribute to the Most Notable Fighter Pilots of the British and Commonwealth Forces in WWII.* Christopher Shores and Clive Williams (Grub Street, London, 1994).
10. John Cunningham was born in South Croydon, Surrey, on 27 July 1917, where he lived with his widowed mother. Following education at the Whitgift School, he attended the de Havilland Technical School in 1935, which was staffed mainly by the school's students. In November that

same year he joined 604 Squadron, Auxiliary Air Force. Due to go onto the production side at de Havilland, instead, because of his Auxiliary training, he took over test flying from Geoffrey de Havilland and became No. 4 pilot in the test team during 1938. No. 604 Squadron was mobilized that year for two weeks at the time of the Munich Crisis, and in August 1939 was mobilized again, this time on a war-permanent basis. During May 1940 he was detached to Northolt to test the air-dropping of bombs on bomber formations, thereby missing the unit's day operations over Holland. The squadron then began night-fighter operations, and when the first Beaufighters began to arrive late in the year, he gained the first victory in one of these aircraft during the night of 19/20 November, with AC J.R. Phillipson as his radar operator. Thereafter he began to claim frequently during the winter months and spring of 1941. After his first three successes, Phillipson, now a sergeant (and later a warrant officer), was replaced by Sgt C.F. Rawnsley, who had been Cunningham's gunner when the unit had been equipped with Hawker Demons, but who had now trained as a radar operator. Thereafter successes mounted rapidly, including three He 111s in one night, 15/16 April 1941. On the night of 7/8 May Cunningham claimed an He 111 near Weston Zoyland while HM King George VI was in the operations room, listening to the engagement. By early June 1941 his total had reached 13. In August he became CO of the squadron, but only three more successes would be recorded by the end of May 1942, when he and Rawnsley, the latter now commissioned, were rested. Cunningham now became Wg Cdr Training at 81 Group, the Fighter Command Training Group at Aston Down. *Aces High: A Tribute to the Most Notable Fighter Pilots of the British and Commonwealth Forces in WWII*. Christopher Shores and Clive Williams (Grub Street, London, 1994).
11. *Night Fighter*. C.F. Rawnsley & Robert Wright (Elmfield Press, 1957).
12. Rawnsley was awarded the DSO in late 1944.
13. *Night Fighter*. C.F. Rawnsley & Robert Wright (Elmfield Press).
14. *Night Fighter*. C.F. Rawnsley & Robert Wright (Elmfield Press).
15. Geoffrey Leonard Howitt was born in Wallington, Surrey, on 29 January 1914, obtaining a private pilot's 'A' licence in 1933. He attended the College of Aeronautical Engineering in Chelsea and became a Class 'F' Reservist in September 1936, transferring to the RAFVR in October 1937 and training at Gatwick, Rochester and Hatfield. Called up in September 1939, he was posted to 245 Squadron as a sergeant in November, and was commissioned in April 1940. In October he was posted to 615 Squadron but had found air-firing by day difficult to master, and volunteered for night-flying, being posted to 85 Squadron in November. Now flying Havoc Is, he was able to claim two victories during summer 1941, only the failure of his guns preventing a third success to be achieved. In August he was posted to 51 OTU, Cranfield, as an instructor and promoted flight lieutenant, receiving a DFC the following month. He returned to 85 Squadron in April 1942 on Havocs and subsequently on Mosquitoes, but few hostile aircraft were to be found. In December 1942 he was sent on the CGS course at Sutton Bridge. *Aces High: A Tribute to the*

Most Notable Fighter Pilots of the British and Commonwealth Forces in WWII. Christopher Shores and Clive Williams (Grub Street, London, 1994).

16. Peter Green had joined 85 Squadron as a flight commander on 18 August 1942 from 277 Air-Sea Rescue Squadron.
17. Skelton was born at Pirbright, Surrey, on 26 August 1920. His father, a garden designer, died when Bill was 15, and relations financed the remainder of his time at Blundells. These included the Duke of Somerset, who carried the Sceptre at the Coronation of King George VI in 1937 and employed young Bill as a page to carry his coronet. By this time Skelton had left school and had started training as an accountant; he later claimed to have been one of only a handful of people who used public transport to attend the Coronation rehearsals. Skelton enlisted in the RAF in 1940 and he was commissioned the following year.
18. In February 1943 605 Squadron at Bradwell Bay began replacing its Bostons and Havocs with the NF.II. On 16 February 151 Squadron, which had equipped with the NF.II at Wittering in April 1942, began Night Intruder operations over France flying Mosquitoes fitted with Monica, a tail warning device. No. 151 continued to fly Night Ranger operations over the continent from May 1943 to April 1944 using NF.XIIs, attacking all targets. In August 85 Squadron finally began Intruder patrols with the NF.II. However, it would have to wait until October that year before getting its first scent of a kill – a Ju 88 damaged and a Do 217 probably destroyed.
19. Edward Dixon Crew was born in Higham Ferrers, Northamptonshire, on 24 December 1917. He was educated at Felstead School, Essex and Downing College, Cambridge, where he joined the University Air Squadron. Commissioned in the RAFVR in October 1939, he joined 604 Squadron in July 1940 on completion of training, to become a night-fighter pilot. Initially, he teamed up with Sgt Norman Guthrie as radar operator, and they claimed five victories together during the spring and summer of 1941. Crew was awarded a DFC on 29 July 1941, but at that point Guthrie was posted away. Flying now with Basil Duckett, he gained three further successes during spring 1942, becoming 'A' Flight commander during May. A Bar to his DFC was received in June. In October 1942 he was posted to command the Radio Development Flight, but returned to operations in March 1943 as a flight commander in 85 Squadron.
20. It was Do 217E-4 U5 + NM 4375 of *IV./KG2* flown by *Feldwebel* Paul Huth.
21. The Do 217 crashed a few minutes later in the sea off Horsey, at 2205 hours. Huth, Burschel, *Oberleutnant* Gottfried Thorley, the observer, and *Unteroffizier* Konrad Schuller, the radio operator, were all killed.. The victory was shared with a 68 Squadron Beaufighter piloted by Flg Off Vopalecky and Flt Sgt Husar; both Czech.
22. On 22 December 1940 Benson had claimed the first confirmed night victory for the Defiant, and his next three victories were on Beaufighter Ifs and Mosquito IIs with Brandon and his radar operator. Benson had been one of the replacements posted to 141 Squadron in July 1940 after the débâcle of 19 June when six Defiants were destroyed and one damaged by Bf 109s. He suffered a suspected fractured skull following a

crash in his Defiant during a night landing in January 1941, but fully recovered and had crewed up with Brandy Brandon to form another highly successful Mosquito night-fighter team.

23. *Unteroffizier* Franz Witte, the radio operator/gunner, was dead. The Dornier crashed at Layer Breton Heath, five miles south-west of Colchester. Schmurr, *Leutnant* Karl-Heinrich Hertam, the observer, and *Unteroffizier* Martin Sehwarz, the gunner, baled-out. Witte's body was found in the wreckage.

24. Night-fighter Mosquitoes of 157 Squadron shot down two Do 217E-4s of *KG2* piloted by *Leutnant* Stefan Szamek and *Leutnant* Gerd Strufe, on 13/14 May. A Do 217E-4 of *II./KG2* was intercepted by an NF.II of 157 Squadron from Hunsdon, flown by Sgt R.L. Watts and Sgt J. Whewell, and shot down after an exchange of fire. A fire started in the Dornier's starboard engine and it crashed about ten miles north-east of Colchester at 0207 hours. Near Norwich, a Do 217K-1 of *4./KG2* flown by *Unteroffizier* Erhard Corty was claimed at about 0250 hours.

25. *Night Fighter*. C.F. Rawnsley & Robert Wright (Elmfield Press).

26. Grimstone, who was awarded the DFM, and Green, the DFC, scored their third victory on 26/27 July when they destroyed a Ju 88 twenty-five miles east of Ramsgate. It was Peter Green's last victory with 85 Squadron, as he left in August to command the AI Beaufighter Flight at Drem. On 8/9 March 1945 Flt Lt Ian Dobie and WO A.R. 'Grimmy' Grimstone DFM of 85 Squadron destroyed a Ju 188 near Hamburg. Shortly afterwards, they were shot down by Allied flak near Koblenz. 'Grimmy' Grimstone had gone to 96 Squadron with Peter Green, but in August when his pilot had taken over command of 219 Squadron, 'Grimmy' had gone on a rest before returning to 85 Squadron. Dobie was thrown clear and came down safely on his parachute, and wandered into the American lines. Grimstone was found with his parachute open but burnt, still attached to his body, within fifty yards of the wreckage.

27. Adolph Gysbert 'Sailor' Malan, who was born in Wellington, South Africa, on 3 October 1910, was one of twenty-three South African pilots in the Battle of Britain. His nickname came about as a result of service as a Third Officer with the Union Castle Steamship Line. He commenced pilot training in England in 1936 and was posted to 74 Squadron in December that year. His DFC was awarded on 11 June 1940 for five victories, two confirmed and three unconfirmed. During the night of 19/20 June 1940, when the first major night raid by the *Luftwaffe* on England took place, in conditions of bright moonlight, he was able to claim two of the Intruders shot down, for which a Bar to his DFC followed in August. In action through July and August, he was promoted to command the squadron on 8 August. The unit was then withdrawn to Kirton-in-Lindsey to rest, and here he wrote his *Ten Rules of Air Fighting* which was produced and distributed throughout Fighter Command. In October the squadron returned to the south and received some of the first Spitfire IIs, seeing considerable action throughout the autumn. On Christmas Eve 1940 he received the award of a DSO, the citation crediting him with eighteen confirmed and six possible victories. On 10 March 1941 he was appointed as one of the first wing leaders for

the offensive operations planned for that year, leading the Biggin Hill Wing throughout the sweeps of May–July. A Bar to his DSO followed on 22 July, at that time recording his total as twenty-eight, plus twenty damaged or probables. In mid-August he was appointed CFI at 58 OTU, Grangemouth, by this time being listed as Fighter Command top scorer, with a total variously reported as thirty-two or thirty-five victories. In October he departed for the USA on a lecture tour and to liaise with the USAAC, together with five other leading RAF fighter pilots. While there he took part in the annual manouvres, flying P-38s and P-39s. Returning to the UK in December, he became commanding officer of the Central Gunnery School at Sutton Bridge, where he remained for a year, being promoted group captain in October 1942. In January 1943 he returned to Biggin Hill as commanding officer, remaining until October, when he took command of 19 Fighter Wing in the new 2nd TAF. *Aces High: A Tribute to the Most Notable Fighter Pilots of the British and Commonwealth Forces in WWII.* Christopher Shores and Clive Williams (Grub Street, London, 1994).

28. Only fifty of these very fast bombers were built. Most examples, which first entered service with I./KG66 at Chartres, were rebuilt versions of the A-4 with power-boosted BMW 801G-2 engines fitted with the GM-1 nitrous oxide injection system. Stripped of its ventral gondola and most of its armour, and reduced to just one MG13I machine-gun, the Ju 88S-1 was difficult to catch. Lintott had to climb to 29,000 ft in stages before he finally saw 3Z+SZ of I./KG66, his victim. A single hit in one of the three high-pressure nitrous oxide storage tanks in the rear bomb bay was enough to blow the aircraft to smithereens.

29. *Night Fighter.* C.F. Rawnsley & Robert Wright (Elmfield Press).

30. By January 1944 Cunningham had scored another three victories on 85 Squadron, which took his overall score to twenty destroyed. In March 1944 he handed over command of the squadron to Wg Cdr Charles Michael Miller DFC,** who was 24 years old and came from Curragh, County Kildare. The son of an Indian Army father; he attended Cambridge University, where he read mechanical engineering. He was called up in September 1939 and flew Wellington bombers from Malta before joining 29 Squadron, which flew Beaufighter IIs. He destroyed two Do 217s on 26/27 February 1943. His first victory on the Mosquito was on 18/19 April 1944, when he and Capt Leif Lövestad destroyed a Ju 88 near Dymchurch, and a second victory followed on 11/12 June when he and Flg Off Robert O. Symon destroyed a Bf 110 north-east of Melun airfield. Miller was awarded the DSO in November, but he had been diagnosed with diabetes and he was invalided out of the service in February 1945. *Aces High: A Tribute to the Most Notable Fighter Pilots of the British and Commonwealth Forces in WWII.* Christopher Shores and Clive Williams (Grub Street, London, 1994). See *Confounding the Reich.* Martin W. Bowman (Pen & Sword, 2004) and *100 Group (Bomber Support): RAF Bomber Command in World War II* (Pen & Sword, 2006).

31. Starting in March 1943, 'C' Flight in 85 Squadron was presented with five NF.XV high-altitude fighters, which had been pressed into service in response to the threat posed by the Ju 86 high-altitude bomber. The

prototype (MP469) was the first Mosquito with a pressurized cabin, and first flew on 8 August 1942, later being fitted with AI Mk VIII radar, as were the four NF.XVs built – all modified B.IVs with two-stage 1680 hp Merlin 72/73 or 1710 hp 76/77 engines driving three- or four-bladed airscrews. The NF.XV, which was capable of reaching heights of 43,000 ft+, was armed with four 0.303-inch machine-guns in an underbelly pack. In August the NF.XVs were reallocated to Farnborough for use in pressure cabin research.

32. Also on 13/14 July, a 410 Squadron RCAF Mosquito shot down *Unteroffizier* Willy Spielmann's Do 217M-l of *3./KG2* into the sea off the Humber Estuary. Flg Off Smart of 605 Squadron, flying an Intruder over Holland, shot down a Do 217M-1 of *2./KG2*, which that night had bombed Hull. *Unteroffizier* Hauck and his crew crashed in the vicinity of Eindhoven. Altogether, *KG2* lost four Dorniers that night.
33. Wg Cdr Geoffrey Park, CO of 256 Squadron, shot down *Unteroffizier* Karl Morgenstern and *Unteroffizier* Franz Bundgens' Do 217M-ls into the sea off Worthing. The wing commander then destroyed *Unteroffizier* Walter Kayser's Do 217M-l and damaged a third Dornier. Flt Sgt Brearley, also of 256 Squadron, shot down two Do 217Ms over France; *Feldwebel* Theodor Esslinger fell near Evreux, and *Leutnant* Franz Bosbach crashed near St André. Plt Off Rayne Dennis Schultz of 410 Squadron RCAF destroyed a Do 217 seventeen miles south of Beachy Head.
34. Two Me 410s were lost this night, one of which was an Me 410A-1 of *16./KG2*, flown by *Feldwebel* Werner Benner and *Unteroffizier* Hermann Reimers.
35. *Night Fighter*. C.F. Rawnsley & Robert Wright (Elmfield Press).
36. When Per Bugge finished his tour he was posted to a new unit in Scotland being operated by the Royal Norwegian Air Force, flying Lodestars on a run from Leuchars to Stockholm. After the war he joined John Cunningham's staff at de Havillands, working on the testing of the Comet airliner. Johan Räd joined a Mosquito pathfinder squadron, surviving a crash-landing one night with a 2,000 lb bomb-load on board after an engine failure on take-off. After the end of the war he returned to Norway and went into civil aviation. Claus Björn stayed on 85 Squadron with Leif Lövestad, and after the war returned to Norway. Björn died following an operation on a stomach disorder. *Night Fighter*. C.F. Rawnsley & Robert Wright (Elmfield Press).
37. On 8/9 November Maguire and Jones shot down an Me 410A of *15./KG2* near Eastbourne. *Major* Wilhelm Schmitter *Ritterkreuz und Eichenlaub* (Knight's Cross with Oak Leaves) and his *bordfunker*, *Unteroffizier* Felix Hainzinger, were killed when the aircraft crashed into Shinewater Marsh. Both Maguire and Jones were awarded DFCs at the end of 1943, and in July 1944 they were posted to the FIU. Maguire was to command this unit later in the year, and in late November he intercepted and shot down a V-1-carrying He 111. On 17 February 1945 he and his navigator, Dennis Lake, were carrying out rolling manoeuvres in a Mosquito to test a new altitude indicator when, on the second roll, the aircraft rapidly lost height, hit a house and disintegrated.

Defensive Night-Fighting

38. In April 1944 he commenced a third tour as 'A' Flight commander in 456 Squadron, RAAF, until December 1944, when he was promoted to command 125 Squadron on Mosquito XXXs. He was released in October 1945 and joined the Air Registration Board.
39. *Night Fighter*. C.F. Rawnsley & Robert Wright (Elmfield Press, 1957).
40. Their first victory was on 22 February 1944, when they destroyed an Me 410 off Dungeness, and this was followed on the night of 24/25 March by a Do 217 in the Dover Straits and a Ju 88 south of Sandgate. By the end of October 1944 Burbridge and Skelton had destroyed eleven enemy aircraft and three V-1s, and on the night of 4/5 November Sqn Ldr Branse Burbridge DSO* DFC* and Flt Lt Bill Skelton DSO* DFC* destroyed four enemy aircraft. Two more followed on the night of 21/22 November, and in December 1944 they destroyed a further three aircraft to take their score to double figures. On 2/3 January 1945 they destroyed their twenty-first and final enemy aircraft. Burbridge and Skelton finished the war as the top-scoring night-fighter crew in the RAF. Bob Braham also downed twenty-one enemy aircraft at night with three different observer/radar operators, and Wg Cdr John Cunningham destroyed nineteen enemy aircraft at night. Post-war, Burbridge became a lay preacher, while Skelton was ordained as a clergyman in the Church of England and became chaplain at Clare College, Cambridge. See *Confounding the Reich*. Martin W. Bowman (Pen & Sword, 2004) and *100 Group (Bomber Support): RAF Bomber Command in World War II* (Pen & Sword, 2006).
41. By December 1944 Sqn Ldr Hedgecoe DFC had scored a total of eight or nine victories, all except the one on 15/16 September with Bamford. After a short spell with the FIU, at the end of December 1944 Hedgecoe was posted as a flight commander to 151 Squadron, but on his first sortie with this unit on 1 January 1945 he crashed in bad weather and was killed. The award of a Bar to his DFC was gazetted in March, and a DSO in October.
42. *Night Fighter*. C.F. Rawnsley & Robert Wright (Elmfield Press, 1957).

CHAPTER 4

Death In The Dark[1]

By 1942 RAF bombers had begun to suffer increasing losses due to *Luftwaffe* night-fighter interceptions, and it was decided that RAF Intruder aircraft roving over enemy airfields in France and the Low Countries could alleviate some of the attacks on the bomber streams. Blenheim squadrons had pioneered offensive night-fighting in June 1940, in much the same vein as 151 Squadron, operating Sopwith Camels, had done in the First World War. In November 1939 600 Squadron had become one of the first squadrons to use AI (Airborne Interception) radar (604 followed suit in July 1940). When the *Luftwaffe* began operating at night from France in 1940, the opportunity of attacking German aircraft on French airfields arose, but the only suitable aircraft available were Hurricanes and Blenheims, and later Havocs and Bostons. The first major support of bombers by night-fighter squadrons was on the night of 30/31 May 1942 during the 1,000-bomber raid on Cologne, when Blenheims and Havocs and Boston IIIs of 23 and 418 (City of Edmonton) Squadron RCAF intruded over Holland.[2] No radar-equipped aircraft were used, as its operation over enemy territory was still banned. Mosquitoes were ideal for Intruder operations, and the FB.VI (in 1943) made possible Intruder sorties to as far afield as Austria and Czechoslovakia, but in 1942, squadrons re-equipping from other types had to soldier on with converted NF.IIs with increased fuel capacity and bereft of their Mk IV radar. There were few NF.IIs that could be spared, and any Mosquitoes that were available were welcome, whatever their pedigree. The same state of affairs concerning conversion to the NF.II persisted at Colerne, where, in May 1942, 264 (Madras Presidency) Squadron began its conversion. On 30/31 May Sqn Ldr C.A. Cook and Plt Off R.E. MacPherson scored the squadron's first Mosquito victory when they shot down a

Ju 88A-4 of *KüFlGr 106* at North Malvern Wells. In December 1942 what few NF.IIs were available carried out Night Rangers to airfields in France from Trebelzue, Cornwall. Rangers were low-level operations on moonlight nights, mainly against railway rolling stock and road transport, although one could shoot down enemy aircraft if they were encountered.[3]

On the night of 28/29 June an Intruder Mosquito of 264 Squadron from Colerne piloted by Flg Off Hodgkinson forced down *Unteroffizier* Rudolf Blankenburg over Creil as he made for home in a *KG2* Do 217E-2 after a raid on Weston-super-Mare. 264 Squadron had operated Defiant night-fighters since early 1942, and on 3 May had received its first Mosquito. The squadron flew its first operational sorties on the type on 13 June. A second Mosquito 'kill' occurred on the night of 30/31 July when a Ju 88A-4 was destroyed. During July and August *III./KG2*'s much reduced bomber force continued to send single aircraft on daylight low-level or cloud-cover 'pirate' sorties against selected targets in Britain. They also made several small-scale night raids, during which they began to encounter, in increasing numbers, the Mosquito night-fighter. Although 157 Squadron at Castle Camps had been the first to become operational on the NF.II, the enemy continued to elude it. To its chagrin, 151 Squadron Mosquitoes destroyed four more machines.[4] It brought 151 Squadron's claims by the end of the month to ten enemy aircraft destroyed.

In July 1942 23 Squadron, which had received a T.III for training on 7 June, began conversion to the NF.II at Ford, but these aircraft were at a premium because of the need to equip home defence squadrons. Eventually, twenty-five of the modified NF.IIs would be issued to 23 Squadron, but for a time the only one available for intruding was S-Sugar. Appropriately, the squadron's first NF.II Intruder sortie was flown in this aircraft on 5/6 July by the CO, the inimitable Wg Cdr Bertie Rex O'Bryen Hoare DSO DFC* and Plt Off Cornes.[5] 'Sammy', who sported a large handlebar moustache, 'six inches, wingtip to wingtip', was one of the leading Intruder pilots of his generation, having flown first Blenheims, then Havocs, on Intruder sorties over the Low Countries. Despite losing an eye before the war when a duck shattered the windscreen of his aircraft, Sammy Hoare became one of the foremost Intruder pilots in the RAF. A legend in his own time, he had done Heaven knows how many Intruder sorties both day and night from as early as 1941, during which he had destroyed and damaged eight more and left a trail of wrecked German aircraft on airfields in Germany and occupied territories. Most, if not all, of this was achieved with only one eye and without radar. He succinctly described Intruder operations thus: 'I should like to tell you not to measure the value of this night-fighter work over German aerodromes by the number of enemy aircraft destroyed. This is considerable, but our mere presence over the enemy's bases has caused the loss of German bombers without a shot being fired at them. Night-fighter pilots chosen for Intruder work were generally of a different type to the ordinary fighter pilot. They must like night-fighting to begin with, which is not everybody's meat. They must also have the technique for blind-flying, and when it comes to fighting, must use their own initiative and judgement, since they are cut off from all communications with their base and are left as freelances entirely to their own resources. Personally I love it. Once up, setting a course in the dark for enemy-occupied country, one gets a tremendous feeling of detachment from the world. And when the enemy's air base is reached there is no thrill – even in big-game shooting – quite the same. On goes the flare path, a bomber comes low – making a circuit of the landing-field – lights on and throttle shut. A mile or two away, in our stalking Havoc, we feel our hearts dance. The throttle is banged open, the stick thrust forward and the Havoc is tearing down in an irresistible rush. One short burst from the guns is usually sufficient. The bomber's glide turns to a dive – the last dive it is likely to make. Whether you get the Hun or miss him, he frequently piles up on the ground through making his landing in fright.[6]

Flt Lt Ronald 'Tim' Woodman, who flew Beaufighters and Mosquitoes on Intruder operations, adds.[7]

> Individually in the moonlight we crossed the Channel into France. The French Resistance informed us that the midnight passenger train out of Paris to Rouen was normally packed with German troops returning from leave. Shooting-up the engines resulted in the first passenger coaches also being hit. The Resistance then informed us that, because of this, the rear coaches were reserved for officers. So we shot up the engine (steam would spout out like hose-pipes and the engines would be put out of action and the lines blocked for some time), then came round again and shot-up the rear coaches. The cine film had large trees silhouetted against the moonlight.

During February 1943 NF.IIs of 410 Squadron RCAF, the third Canadian night-fighter squadron to be formed, had moved south from Acklington to Coleby Grange for Night and Day Rangers. The moon period of March came and went while the Night Rangers cursed the weather, which made it impossible for them to operate. Nine Day Ranger sorties were dispatched on the 26th, 27th and 30th, but eight were aborted at the Dutch coast because of unsuitable weather. The dangers appertaining to these operations was borne out on 6 April, when Flt Lt C.D. McCloskey – one of 410 Squadron's original members – and Plt Off J.G. Sullivan, were shot down and taken prisoner. Four days later Flg Off J.E. Leach and Flg Off R.M. Bull were killed in action over Friesland. Ranger operations began again when the moon period arrived in mid-April, and on the night of the 15th, the CO, Wg Cdr Frank W. Hillock, headed for the Ruhr. The weather was poor, and as the Mosquito skipped along at 300 ft over Holland, Hillock suddenly saw the eight radio masts of Apeldoorn station rushing towards him. There was no time to climb and no room to fly between them, so he threw the Mosquito on its side and ripped through the antennae, tearing away several wires. On his return to Coleby Grange it was found that one wingtip had been sliced off and the other wing had been cut through to the main spar before the wire had broken; about 300 ft of well-made ¼ in. copper cable was trailing behind the Mosquito! Despite this shaking experience, Hillock had coolly flown to his target before coming home.[8] Over the next four nights crews located a convoy off the Dutch coast suitable for a naval attack, strafed barges in Holland and a factory in Rees and strafed rail yards at Cleve. On 20 April Flt Sgt W.J. Reddie and Sgt Evans went missing. There then followed a week of poor weather, which made it unsuitable for Rangers. Operations resumed again on the 30th, and during the moon period in May 410 Squadron extended its sphere of operations to include France and Belgium.

No. 456 Squadron RAAF, which was largely equipped with Beaufighter VIfs, in February/March 1943 began to include some NF.II Ranger operations in addition to its day-fighting role, first from Middle Wallop and then from Colerne. From late May it was successfully employed on Intruder sorties over France, attacking railway rolling stock and intruding on French airfields. In May 1943, 60 OTU at High Ercall was expanded and made responsible for all Intruder training.[9]

On the night of 4/5 May 1943 the bulbous glass-nosed Dornier Do 217K-Is of *6./KG2* taxied out at Eindhoven. On board one of them, *Oberfeldwebel* Heinrich Meyer and his three crew prepared to take off and join the circuit. Their bomb bay normally held either four 500 kg high-explosive bombs or ABB500 incendiaries, and they were destined for Norwich. For the 4/5 May raid, *III./KG2* at Eindhoven had only recently returned from a sojourn to Carcassonne when the French fleet was on the point of defecting to the Allies. *KG2* and *II./KG40* would be joined on the Norwich raid by Ju 88As of *I* and *III./KG6* based in Belgium. Six Mosquito Night-Intruders were abroad that night and over Holland shortly after *KG2* took off. Near Hilversum, Meyer's Dornier was written off when it crashed. It was the start of a bad night for the famed 'Holzhammer' unit. The remaining forty-two Dorniers of *KG2* and *III./KG40* and thirty-six Ju 88s of *KG6*, including one aircraft that was to monitor the operation from Cromer, evaded their hunters and flew on low over the North Sea towards the Norfolk coast. Four of the Ju 88s had, at the same time, flown south to create a diversionary attack on the south coast of England. Over the North Sea the oncoming German bombers noticed about forty RAF bombers at the same height, these being among 596 RAF bombers that had attacked Dortmund. The Do 217s and Ju 88s approached eastern England hoping that the CHL (Chain Home Low) stations would interpret their blips on the radar screens as 'friendly' bombers. For a crucial period of time it seemed to have worked, because the German bombers carried on unmolested and then turned on a heading for Norwich, with their navigation lights on to further fool the defenders. *Oberst* Dietrich Peltz, 'Attack Leader England', intended to deliver upon Norwich its heaviest raid of the war. That it did not happen was due to a fault in the target illumination and guidance system. The showers of flares were released well enough; in fact John Searby, who was in one of the RAF bombers returning from Dortmund, diverted to look at the marker flares and was so impressed he 'wished we had some to equal them'. However, the parachute flares were dropped in the north-west of Norfolk, and the majority of the phosphorus and mixed incendiaries fell harmlessly in fields or did little damage.

Then the defences were alerted. Aboard Do 217K-1 U5 + AA,[10] *Leutnant* Ernst Andres sat in his contoured pilot's seat in close confinement with his crew: *Unteroffizier* August Drechsler, radio operator; *Obergefreiter* Wilhelm Schlagbaum, observer; and *Flieger* Werner Becker, gunner, who sat facing rearwards behind them in his dorsal turret. All four crew were keen to impress 31-year-old *Major* Walter Bradel, *Kommodore* of *KG2*, who was flying as an observer on the operation. Bradel had succeeded *Oberst* von Koppelow three months earlier, and was probably flying on the raid to help restore shattered morale after heavy losses in his *Gruppe*.[11]

Flg Off Brian 'Scruffy' Williams and his navigator, Plt Off Dougie Moore, in 605 Squadron, were complete opposites, but equally dedicated to their task. Moore was on his first tour, but the 21-year-old pilot had flown over thirty ops on Bostons in 418. Williams was an exceptional pilot. At 51 OTU, the CO, none other than Guy Gibson, had marked his course assessment 'Above Average', but had added: 'May get over-confident'.[12] Williams and Moore had taken off from Castle Camps about an hour and a half after the raid on Norwich and were stooging around Eindhoven when they chanced upon the returning Dorniers. The first aircraft could be seen circling the airfield with its red and green navigation lights on. Brian Williams recalls:

> It was bloody dark. There was no moon. I saw a Do 217. I fired but saw no strikes. Lost it! I'd probably frightened him to death! [The crew of *Leutnant* Alfons Schlander of 2/KG2 is also listed as being shot down near Eindhoven that night.] Then I saw a second one in the same circuit. It was a Do 217 and it also had its green and red navigation lights showing. I went in and made a beam attack. I fired my cannon and saw numerous strikes, but I didn't see it hit the deck so I later claimed a 'damaged'. I saw two more crossing in front of us but I didn't go after them because we had no chance of catching them, so I finished the patrol and flew home to base. While I was on home leave I received a phone call from the CO, Wing Commander C.D. Tomalin. He had rung to tell me that the Do 217 I had claimed as 'damaged' had crashed. Apparently, it had caused a furore in

the German newspapers, which said that the Dornier was the one carrying *Major* Bradel. He was killed in the crash [at Landsmere, near Amsterdam]. *Leutnant* Andres was seriously injured."[13]

For 410 Squadron June 1943 was a rather quiet and uneventful period as far as scrambles and Rangers were concerned. Coastal Command anti-submarine operations in the Bay of Biscay were being hampered by enemy counter air activity, and 410 Squadron was requested to supply fighter support. (Another 410 Intruder detachment was temporarily established at Hunsdon.) Four crews were detached to Predannack for Instep patrols in company with Polish crews from 307 Polish Squadron, who began flying Night Rangers, and 456 Squadron RAAF. The Cougar crews remained at Preddanack for a month and flew twenty patrols lasting between four and five hours. On the afternoon of the 13th Plt Off R.B. Harris and Sgt E.H. Skeel were accompanied by three other Mosquitoes of patrol, when south-west of Brest the formation intercepted four Ju 88s. Fw 190s then arrived on the scene, and three aircraft, including the 410 Squadron crew, were shot down. The next morning, Plt Offs J. Watt and E.H. Collis, with three Polish crews, sighted five U-boats in the bay. When the Mosquitoes were sighted they drew into a tight defensive circle. Two of the Mosquitoes attacked the U-boats, which sent up a considerable amount of flak. Strikes were made on the conning towers of the U-boats and one Mosquito was damaged by flak. All the aircraft returned safely to Predannack. On the 19th, on another patrol with 307 Squadron, Flg Offs E.A. Murray and P.R. Littlewood of 410 Squadron encountered a Bv 138 flying-boat as they zigzagged at low level over the Bay of Biscay. The Mosquitoes made two line-astern attacks on the Bv 138, which attempted to climb into cloud cover. On the first attack one engine was hit and began to smoke, and the aircraft, being unable to gain height, nosed down towards the sea. On the second attack the starboard engine was hit and caught fire. The aircraft then crashed into the sea. Three crew emerged and scrambled into a dinghy. The last action occurred on 21 June when Plt Off C.F. Green and Sgt E.G. White were members of a patrol that attacked two small armed merchant vessels or trawlers, both of which were damaged.

Early in July 1943 410 Squadron received six FB.VI bombers for use on Intruders and Ranger operations. Flt Lt Murray took charge of a special section formed to carry out these activities, the first sortie being made on the 15th. On a Night Ranger to France from Ford, on the 18th, Plt Off L.A. Wood and Flg Off D.J. Slaughter failed to return. Poor weather prevented any further ops until the night of the 25th, when two Cougar crews went on Flower sorties (Bomber Command support) to Deelen airfield, in Holland. The first crew, Norman and Hunt, saw visual Lorenz lit three times during their patrol, and noticed bombs fall on or near the aerodrome, starting fires. An hour later they were relieved by Murray and Littlewood. Approaching Deelen, after orbiting a dummy aerodrome for a few moments, the crew saw an aircraft come in and land. Thirty minutes later a second Hun appeared, flicking its navigation lights on and off. The FB.VI crew came in behind a Do 217 and fired a three-second burst at the aircraft. Searchlights coned the Mosquito, while the flak guns opened up. The port engine of the Dornier caught fire and, lit up by five searchlights, it veered to the left, crashed and exploded in flames on the airfield boundary. As the crew continued to circle the airfield, a third aircraft made a hurried landing, and on reaching the end of the runway the navigation lights were turned on. Murray came down in a sharp diving turn and fired a long burst at the aircraft, damaging it. The navigation lights were quickly doused and the enemy ground defences immediately came into action again.

Patrols were made on three nights between 28 and 30 July to Schleswig/Jegel, Gilze-Rijen and Venlo airfields, all without success. The Cougars suffered a severe blow on the 30th when Flt Lt E.A. Murray and Flg Off P.R. Littlewood were killed at Honiley, Warks., when flying an Oxford on a navigation flight. Murray, a native of Stelleraton, Nova Scotia, was deputy flight commander of 'B' Flight, while Littlewood came from Saanichton, Vancouver Island, BC.[14]

Another of the Mosquito crews rapidly making a name for themselves on offensive night-fighting patrols at this time was that of Flt Lt James Gillies Benson DFC and Flt Lt Lewis Brandon DSO DFC of 157 Squadron. On the night of 3/4 July 1943, flying an NF.II, they shot down a Do 217 over St Trond. On 13/14 July Flg Off Smart of 605 Squadron, flying an NF.II, destroyed a Do 217M-1 near Eindhoven. In July 456 and 605 Squadrons re-equipped with the FB.VI for intruding, and 418 Squadron flew the last of its Boston sorties and concentrated on Flower operations using the FB.VI.

In August 1943, when it was realized that the *Luftwaffe* was operating radar-equipped night-fighters against the 'heavies' of Bomber Command, some AI-equipped Beaufighters and Mosquito night-fighters were released over enemy territory on Mahmoud operations as bait for enemy night-fighters in their known assembly areas. With centimetric AI being used in Mosquitoes, it was necessary to fit Monica tail warning devices, as the later marks of AI did not scan to the rear. Mosquitoes pretending to be bombers were not successful, as the enemy soon recognized their speed difference. Nevertheless, on 15/16 August Flt Sgt Brearley of 256 Squadron, flying an NF.XII, destroyed two Do 217M-1s over France. Six FB.VIs and six NF.IIs with AI fighters were available to 410 Squadron for Flower operations in August, in addition to the squadron's usual defensive commitments. Twenty-five sorties, four by day, were made, mainly during the last half of the month. The first part of the month had poor weather, and much of this time was occupied with training.

On the night of 15/16 August two Rangers were made from Castle Camps to St Dizier airfield. Lawrence and Wilmer dropped two 250 lb bombs on the runway, and on the return flight attacked a train near Paris. Plt Off Rayne Dennis Schultz, who was 20 years old and came from Bashow, Alberta, and Flg Off V.A. Williams in FB.VI HP849 did not reach St Dizier. Instead they attacked three locomotives between Clermont and Poix and bombed a bridge. On their way home, some twenty miles off Beachy Head, they spotted another aircraft, and on closing, found it to be a Do 217M-1. The Do 217 was a *9./KG2* machine flown by the pilot's namesake, *Unteroffizier* Josef Schultes. The under-gunner opened accurate fire on the FB.VI, and Schultes tried to shake off the Mosquito. A long pursuit followed. Schultz's second burst hit the cockpit, where fires broke out and debris fell away. Three, perhaps four, of the crew were seen to bale out; then the Dornier turned for France in a shallow controlled dive. Schultz fired again, the starboard wing and engine broke away and, completely enveloped in flames, the bomber hit the sea, where it continued to burn brightly. After taking some cine films of the scene and reporting the position of the crew, Schultz headed for home to report their first victory.[15]

On 17/18 August Flt Lt David Henry Blomely DFC of 605 Squadron in a FB.VI destroyed a Bf 109 east of Schleswig, and on 22/23 August a 29 Squadron NF.XII crew in HK164 destroyed an Me 410A-1 north of Knocke. Blomely was credited with another victory on 21 September, when he destroyed two Ju 88s west of the Skaggerak. By September 605 Squadron were flying Intruder sorties over Denmark and Germany. That same month Sammy Hoare assumed command of the squadron, and he returned to combat operations on 27/28 September, whereupon he promptly dispatched a Do 217 at Dedelsdorf – his seventh confirmed air-to-air victory. (On 10/11 January 1944 Sammy Hoare scored the County of Warwick Squadron's 100th victory when he and Flg Off Robert C. Muir in an FB.VI shot down a Ju 188 four miles east of Chièvres. Sammy claimed a probable and damaged three aircraft in 1944, and shot down his ninth and final aircraft in March that year). Intruder victories were now hard to find, and in fact none were recorded until Flt Lt Blomely DFC destroyed a Bf 110 twenty-five miles west of Aalborg on 9 November. Wg Cdr Roderick A. Chisholm DFC and Flt Lt F.C. Clarke of the FIU[16] destroyed a Bf 110 at Mannheim on 18/19 November. In November 1943 a 307 Squadron detachment at Sumburgh, Scotland, carried out Rhubarbs over Norway, destroying two He 177s and a Ju 88. When they returned south they continued intruding, and later flew bomber support operations until March 1945.

For 410 Squadron at least the first three weeks of September were somewhat quieter than August. Ranger sorties were cancelled, but Flower ops continued. Fifteen sorties were made between the 3rd and the 16th, and attacks were made on St Michel and Loan airfields and against railway targets. Plt Off J.E. Fisher and Sgt D. Ridgeway failed to return from Melum on the 16th. Ranger and Flower ops ceased, and in their place Mahmoud, or offensive patrols over specific points in search of enemy aircraft, were made. Two specially-equipped NF.IIs were used for these activities. During the period 17–23 September only a number of fruitless scrambles were undertaken, and on the 24th 410 Squadron started Mahmoud operations, but these were not successful until the night of 27/28 September. Flt Lt M.A. Cybulski and Flg Off H.H. Ladbrook, flying NF.II D7757, made a Mahmoud patrol of the Zuider Zee and Meppen area from Coleby Grange. The ninety-minute patrol was unsuccessful, but on the way home an AI contact was made on a Do 217, which was then located flying east. The enemy pilot went into a steep climb, with the Mosquito closing rapidly. A three-second burst was fired and the enemy aircraft immediately exploded with a terrific flash and descended enveloped in flames. Burning petrol and oil flew back onto the NF.II, scorching the fuselage from nose to tail, the port wing inboard of the engine, the bottom of the starboard wing, the port tailplane and the rudder, from which the fabric was torn away. Pieces of the Dornier struck the port oil cooler, resulting in the loss of oil and making it necessary to shut down the engine. Cybulski was completely blinded and Ladbrook had to take control of the aircraft for about five minutes until the pilot regained normal vision. Course was set for base, and the seriously damaged aircraft completed a hazardous 250-mile single-engine return. The crew received immediate DFC awards. A further eight more Mahmouds were completed, all without incident, and between the 1st and 19th, twenty-six scrambles were made. Coleby Grange was made unserviceable one night by enemy bombing activity. No. 410 Squadron moved from its base to West Malling having completed a total of 286 sorties, of which 125 had been scrambles, seventy-eight Rangers, forty-nine Intruders and Flowers, twenty Insteps and twelve Mahmouds. Nine crews had been lost on operations and two in flying accidents. The squadron moved again, to Hunsdon in October 1943, and then Castle Camps, where regular patrols were flown in defence of southern England.

On 15 October 1943 Wg Cdr Cathcart M. Wight-Boycott DSO took command of 25 Squadron at Church Fenton, equipped with the NF.II.[17] Wight-Boycott, who was 33 years old and came from Wiveliscombe, Somerset, had attended Cambridge University in the 1930s and had joined the University Air Squadron. On graduation he had joined the civilian staff of the Metropolitan Police, and in 1937 had joined the RAFVR as a pilot officer. He recalls:

> 25 Squadron had been given the role of Intruder operations over western Europe using bombs, for which crews, trained for night defence of the UK using AI Mk IV, had no previous training or experience. Morale was not high. They had had a number of

casualties. 'A' Flight Commander, Squadron Leader Brind RNZAF, had been intercepted returning from a low-level sortie and ditched. He and his navigator were taken prisoner. Just before I arrived, a flight commander and his crew attempting a single-engined landing in bad weather had been killed. A few days later another flight commander, Squadron Leader Matthews and crew, failed to return from a sortie over the Low Countries. A month later, the most experienced squadron pilot, Flight Lieutenant Baillie and Flying Officer Simpson, on their last flight before going on rest, also failed to return from a night sortie. It was not surprising that morale among aircrews was not high, especially as intelligence could not give any clue as to how these experienced crews had got into trouble.

The Mahmoud[18] Mosquitoes were only with us for a month before 25 Squadron moved to Acklington to re-equip with NF.XVIIs, which were fitted with AI Mk X. During that time I flew two Mahmoud sorties. On the first one we were briefed to fly over the Low Countries and wait for a German night-fighter to get on our tail, and then turn 360 degrees to get ourselves in position to get behind the German night-fighter. This manoeuvre was quite unsuccessful. Although I tried it three times in all, the German night-fighter remained on my tail and I had to take some pretty drastic evasion tactics to avoid being shot down myself. Our intelligence were quite unaware of the very efficient German ground control in the Low Countries.

My next sortie was to fly a pin-point near Bonn at 20,000 ft, where I was told I would find a narrow vertical beam, around which there would be a German night-fighter orbiting, waiting to be ordered by ground control into a heavy bomber stream. Nobody explained how a defensive night-fighter crew could possibly find the vertical beam navigating by dead reckoning, no means of checking wind speed and direction and unable to see the ground. Moreover, the crew had only experience of positioning by ground control – the navigator was Navigator Radar on board just to work a radar set. If this wasn't enough, no information was in the briefing on our own bomber routes and heights, and we arrived in the midst of our own bomber stream and were lucky not to be shot down by unfriendly 'friendly' rear gunners. In our efforts to avoid the stream, we became more and more lost, and could never have got closer to our target than fifty miles. We decided optimistically to assume we were reasonably close to our target, and set course for home (Coltishall), and with relief recognized that we had reached the North Sea and would soon sight the Norfolk coast. We seemed to fly for hours and couldn't understand why we didn't reach the coast, unless there was a 90 mph head wind. We eventually had to break

R/T silence and get a 'steer' from Coltishall, which showed that we were so far south we were flying west down the English Channel, any moment about to start a transatlantic crossing! We had had no fix for over three hours. I was very relieved that shortly afterwards we left our Mahmoud operations behind.

In November 1943 100 (Special Duties) Group[19] was formed under the command of Air Cdre (later AVM) E.B. Addison. The group's task was two-fold: its heavy bomber squadrons were employed on radio counter-measures (RCM) and 'spoofing' operations, while its Mosquito squadrons (141, 239, 515, 169, 157, 85 and 23 Squadrons)[20] were used on loose escort duties for the main force, as well as Night Intruder operations over Germany and the Greater *Reich*.

Alf Rogers, a navigator who for a period of eleven months from July 1944 to June 1945 served with 515 Intruder Squadron at Little Snoring, recalls:

100 Group came into being with the purpose of reducing the losses of heavy bombers. They did this in various ways, one of which was Low-Level Night Intruding. For this Mosquitoes went out singly to *Luftwaffe* night-fighter bases and patrolled around them for an hour at low level while the heavy bombers passed by above. The Intruder would attack an active aerodrome, and any aircraft taking off risked an encounter with a Mosquito. So invariably when a Mosquito arrived the aerodrome switched off all lights and closed down. As a result the number of enemy aircraft destroyed was very low. The value of intruding was not so much that enemy night-fighters were destroyed but rather that they were persuaded to stay on the ground.

A typical Night-Intruder op began by crossing the North Sea at less than 500 ft. In this way they were too low to be detected by German radar. The Dutch coast was crossed at a point five miles north of the town of Egmond. From there on navigation was by map reading, which could be difficult on a dark night. Water features showed up quite well so these were used as pin-points. After crossing the coast the next turning point was the distinctive mouth of the Ijsell river on the eastern side of the Zuider Zee. Then on to the Dortmund–Ems Canal, next Dümmer Lake, then Steinhuder Lake. Depending on which aerodrome was being visited, the Intruder would turn off at one of these points and head for the target. If the target was in southern Germany the route would be via Belgium. This involved another problem as the Allied armies moved in. They created several 'Artillery Zones' where the gunners were free to fire on any aircraft flying lower than 10,000 ft. Intruders never flew higher than 2,000 ft, so they had to avoid these zones to avoid being shot down by our own guns. Sometimes the target was Lista in Norway. This involved a 500-mile sea crossing where GEE was not available. Then it was a matter of trusting that the Met officer had been accurate in forecasting the wind velocity and that the navigator had worked out his flight plan correctly.

Occasionally Intruders carried bombs, HE or incendiary, in which case the primary target was the *Luftwaffe* base. Failing that, any other 'legitimate' target that presented itself was attacked. So Low Level Night Intruders contributed to the safe return of many a bomber crew.

Although we had no illusions about the fact that we were involved in the serious business of war, it was nevertheless in many ways a happy time. We were privileged to be flying in the finest aircraft of that era – the incomparable Mossie. For this reason many other aircrew envied us. There was a lively sense of humour among the crews, which helped to make squadron life enjoyable. And there was a great spirit of comradeship, which was in itself a source of fun. Of course life was not all fun. It was not fun to wake up in a morning to see a friend's bed empty and then watch in silence as the squadron adjutant came into the hut to pack up your friend's kit and personal belongings and to know that you would never see him again. Then there were those times when we returned from an operational flight at perhaps three or four o'clock in a morning to hear that one of our aircraft was missing. A little later, having a meal in the mess, a few of us would sit around the table talking about the crew who were missing and hoping for the news that in our hearts we knew would not come. Then as the daily life of the aerodrome began we would face up to the fact that there was no use in waiting and hoping any longer, and we would make our weary way to bed. That wasn't fun either. Thankfully our casualty rate was not as high as that of the heavy bombers, but there was always an air of uncertainty about it. Two men had flown off into the night and had not returned. And we were left wondering what exactly had happened to them. There were a number of possibilities, but it didn't do to dwell on them too much. The same possibilities were involved in every operational flight, and we soon learned that we had to put those things behind us and get on with the job we had to do.

Two men who flew off into the night and did not return on the night of 27/28 May 1944 were Flg Off R.K. Bailey and his navigator, Flg Off J.F.M. White, on 239 Squadron at West Raynham. Bailey and White's Mosquito was one of six night-fighter crews detailed to arrive at Leeuwarden airfield in north Holland at a precise time. Intelligence had declared Leeuwarden to be the main reaction base of the German night-fighter force for operations that night. Bailey recalls:[21]

> We were detailed to arrive at Leeuwarden when the German fighters would be reacting to the radar indication of the approach of the main force of bombers (we crossed the North Sea at sea level to avoid detection). In addition to normal airborne interception radar, each Mosquito was equipped with 'Serrate', which picked up German night-fighter radar transmissions giving azimuth and elevation indications but not range, which had to be obtained from the AI radar. The plan of operations worked, for no sooner had we reached the Leeuwarden area than the navigator called, 'Serrate contact'. We followed this target in a climbing orbit to 11,000 ft, where in conditions of high haze and resultant poor visibility I sighted an Me 110 directly ahead and at very close range. Two bursts from the four 20 mm cannon resulted in an explosion and showers of debris, into which we flew. The navigator called out another Serrate contact, which I had to ignore, being engaged in feathering the propeller of the starboard engine, which had overheated and stopped. Assessing the situation, the navigator said he would give a course for our base in Norfolk. I asked him instead for a course to Calais and thence to Manston, Kent, to avoid a North Sea crossing in a damaged aircraft, the extent of which was unknown. Ten minutes later the port engine failed and I ordered, 'Bale out.'
>
> Within seconds the navigator was gone, and I made to follow, diving head first across the cockpit to the escape hatch. I had trimmed the rudder for asymmetric flying when the starboard engine failed, but I omitted to neutralize trim when the port engine failed. The result was a steep spiral dive. Meanwhile I was trapped, having caught the top section of the hatch. I was head and shoulders out in the slipstream with my legs and torso in the aircraft. I was almost reconciled to this situation when a stupid thought crossed my mind that when the aircraft struck the ground I would be sheared in two! This possibility brought about a frenzied new effort. Suddenly I was free from the whistling slipstream and falling in space. I pulled the ripcord and the parachute opened; I said a prayer of thanks. Some seconds later I made contact heavily with the ground. I took stock. I was somewhere in enemy-occupied territory, position unknown, a sprained ankle, blood issuing from a wound in the face, and the 'chute (which should be hidden) was caught up in barbed wire on the far side of a ditch. I needed help. It was approximately 1.45 a.m. I saw a chink of light from an upper window of a small farmhouse a short distance away, hardly likely to be billeting Germans. I made my way to the house and knocked at the door using the Morse 'V'.

Presently, after some muttering conversation, the door opened and a woman's voice said, 'Come here.' On getting to a small room she set about bathing the blood from my face. While this was being done I noticed the man leaving the house; gone for the police, I thought dejectedly. A short time later he returned, ushering a boy of about 15 years. This boy, his eyes ablaze with excitement, asked in good English what I wanted to do. 'Hide up for a few days', I replied. He then added he had the ideal hiding place – a hollowed-out haystack at his father's farm, which he had prepared for such an event as this.

We set out for the farm, but on the way we stopped to recover the tell-tale parachute. With the 'chute safely hidden, we set out for the farm and the sanctuary of the haystack. Lying in the restricted confines, I dwelt on events of the past few hours and the information that I was in a small village, Renswoude, in the province of Utrecht, under the care of the family Largereeij. The boy's Christian name was Kees. On reflection I don't know where I got the moral strength for the hours, days and weeks in my hiding-place. Uppermost in my thoughts was concern for my wife Jean, who was eight months pregnant on 29 May. How had she reacted to the news that I was 'missing', would Heaven protect her in the days leading to the birth?

There were two highlights. The first was 6 June when Kees came with the news of the Normandy Invasion and, 'It won't be long now.' The second, a few days later, with a visit by district Resistance leaders. They asked about my welfare and pointed out that since the invasion the Germans had tightened movement control, and it was unlikely that I could be moved south in the foreseeable future. In response to this disappointing forecast I said the thing I missed most of all was exercise. They replied that they would arrange some exercise for me.

True to their word, a few days later a number of men riding bicycles arrived at the farm with a spare machine for me. These men assembled for a meeting in the farmhouse. Plans for my exercise were soon made clear. The leader stated that with so many Dutchmen 'hiding up' to avoid forced labour in Germany, plus evading aircrew and Jews, it was necessary to augment supplies of ration cards and money. It had been learned that a post office in a neighbouring village had just received new supplies, and that was our target. We were each issued with a hand-gun and set forth on bicycles to the objective at a leisurely pace. I was quite enjoying the outing after some weeks in the haystack. I didn't dwell on the operation, naively thinking that the post office would co-operate willingly with members of the Dutch Resistance, but this was not the case! Instead they regarded us as 'Brigands and Robbers', and were most unco-operative. I had just taken my position at the front door, to allow free entry but to stop anyone leaving while the raid was under way. There was much shouting from our side and hysterical screaming from behind the counter. Suddenly two shots rang out and one of the workers, who had made to exit via a rear door, slumped to the floor. As one man we hastily left the scene of screaming women, ran to our bikes and set out at breakneck speed away from the scene. Fearful of pursuit while cycling along the main road, we set a furious pace. I have never before or since pedalled so hard, it was only after a few miles, when we turned onto a cycle track leading to the farm, that we were able to relax our furious pace and breathe easily.

My eventful day was not yet over, for when we reached the farm Kees came running to say there were two men wishing to meet me. They introduced themselves as Mr Van Den Topp from Stroe in Gelderland and 'Dick', a British agent. Dick questioned me for some time to establish that I was an evading RAF pilot. On being satisfied, they explained the purpose of their call. I was invited to Mr Van Den Topp's home to meet an American pilot who was being hidden there. I readily agreed because it seemed a face-saving way to sever my connections with the reckless Resistance band, my erstwhile comrades.

I met Bill Lalley, a Fortress pilot from Lowell, Michigan.[22] The new rendezvous lacked nothing in creature comforts, a bedroom of one's own, a huge bed and clean sheets; a luxurious bath washed away the grime of the past weeks. Alas, my good fortune did not last more than two days. There was also a young Jewish girl visiting the Van Der Topps' residence, and it was considered that the lack of breathing-space made the recess behind one of the wardrobes unsuitable for house searches that could last several hours. So I was to become the guest of Dr Dirk Eskes and his wife in a small house in wooded country not far from Stroe. While it was considered safe for me to have freedom of the grounds in daylight hours, at dusk I was lowered into a hiding-place like a grave, the trap-door was closed behind me and I lay on a mattress awaiting release at dawn. It was a pretty rugged lifestyle, demanding self-discipline. After a few weeks of this existence, about mid-July, word came from Stroe that our identity papers were now being prepared and I was to return to pick up Bill Lalley. My travelling-papers described me as a deaf and dumb basket maker, a most unlikely cover!

Next day Bill and I mounted a tandem, on which neither of us had previous experience, to follow a lone cyclist. We were taken to separate houses a few miles from Stroe to stay overnight prior to the next day's train journey to south Holland. Next day I was reunited with Bill and escorted by two guides, who sat in separate compartments. We travelled uneventfully to Arnhem, where, while waiting for some hours for a connection, we were housed with our two guides in the station-master's private apartment. Later that day we completed the journey to Breda without incident. I was taken to the home of Gerry and Arie Zanen at 8 Artillery Straat. Bill was taken elsewhere.

I spent approximately two weeks with the Zanens. Then, in the space of four days and with many changes of guide, I arrived at Turnhout in Belgium, where, with two guides, Bill and I completed the journey to Antwerp, lodged in a café bar and told to await our guide for the next step of the journey. Meanwhile, between Breda and Turnhout our party was augmented by a third member, Viv Connell, a Lancaster navigator, whose home was in Broken Hill, NSW, Australia. He had been hiding for some time in a convent.[23]

Eventually we met a new guide, an attractive young girl (late teens/early 20s); by this time it was early evening on 10 August. She led us on foot a short distance to a flat where we were to spend the night. She prepared a meal (egg and chips), showed us some bottles of wine and left the flat, saying we would be picked up the next day for the next stage. Viv Connell was the first to be collected, while Bill and I awaited our turn. Soon we were also collected and set out on foot along the streets of Antwerp, one guide leading the way, while the other followed a few paces behind. On glancing behind I could see he carried his hand in his right jacket pocket as though holding a hand-gun. Soon we entered a large office and we were taken to separate rooms for questioning. My questioner introduced himself as a leader of the Belgian Resistance. He said he could get us back to England in two days, and wondered why we had spent three months in Holland. He thought this resulted from poor organization, and he said he would be pleased to give advice on how to improve their procedures. He would of course need the names and addresses of where I had been. At this point alarm bells started ringing in my head. It was well-known practice in the Resistance never to divulge names and addresses. I stalled him with ignorance of names and addresses. Quickly his benevolent manner of a so-called Belgian Resistance leader changed to one of aggression. 'Do you know you are in the hands of the *Gestapo*? You were captured in plain clothes and carrying false papers, you are either a saboteur or a spy, not an airman.'

I took my identity discs from my jacket pocket and gave them to him, whereupon he threw them onto the floor, saying, 'You are on dangerous ground; no one knows where you are.'

The questioning ended, and I with Bill Lalley was bundled roughly down the stairs to a waiting car. They took adequate action to safeguard their prize. One guard in the front seat leaned over pointing a gun at us, while the two others squeezed into the rear on either side of us, also pointing guns. We were whisked at a furious pace to Antwerp Jail. There in Cell 42 we were reunited with Viv Connell [who had been captured at Antwerp on 7 August].[24] 'Pig's arse, am I glad to see you again!' He added that the straw palliasses were alive with bed bugs. We moved the bedding to one wall and laid a trail of water across the cell floor, hoping the water would isolate us, and set about sleeping on the cell floor. Alas, the bed bugs climbed the wall and down the other side of the water obstacle and came for a feast.

During my stay in Antwerp I was bitten so badly as to develop huge blisters on both legs. I used to go to a German sick-bay for treatment, which consisted of a rub with ammonia and paper-bandage dressing. During our stay of three weeks I was constantly harassed by bed bugs; and like many others, I was fearful of the fate awaiting us, following many direct threats of being shot. In this I was glad that I had not tried to ingratiate myself with the so-called Belgian Resistance leader by mentioning my part in the raid on the post office. I am sure, in retrospect, that execution would have been my fate.

During the remaining months of the war, 25, 68, 96, 125, 151, 307, 406 and 456 Squadrons, Fighter Command and the seven Mosquito squadrons in 100 Group, flew bomber support, 'Lure' and Intruder operations to pre-selected airfields on the other side of the 'bomb line'. Flg Off Basil McRae, a 25 Squadron NF.XXX pilot, explains:

On bomber support operations, the objective was to protect our bombers from attack by enemy fighters from airfields adjacent to the target area. By timing our arrival some ten minutes prior to the coloured TIs being dropped by the pathfinders and the subsequent arrival of the main bomber force, we would orbit allocated airfields. During the bombing we would continue to orbit the designated airfields, my navigator, Flying Officer Frank Sweet, keeping a watchful eye on the AI Mk X radar tube for any activity from below. The time spent over the target area, often without incident, could become rather tedious, and I would look for targets of opportunity on the way home. Roads and autobahns showed up well in moonlight, and vehicles could be seen quite distinctly from 500 ft.

Operation Lure was designed to intercept enemy fighters should they be following our bombers returning from the target. For this purpose we would join the rear of the stream, and by throttling back and lowering a few degrees of flap, we could simulate the bombers' speed. Equipped with rear-facing Monica, it was my navigator's function to watch for any unidentified aircraft approaching. In the event, it was open throttles, raise flaps, smart 180-degree turn, make contact with our Mk X radar and intercept, or perhaps I should say, investigate. Sometimes they turned out to be a crippled Lanc or a Halifax.

Our final operations were night intruding to strafe pre-selected airfields. Due to the rapid advance of the Allied armies, designated airfields for attack had to be 'cleared' just prior to briefing. On 22 April 1945 Frank Sweet and I were disappointed to learn that the airfield allocated had not been 'cleared'. The airfields that had been were being visited at hourly intervals, so I sought and got permission to attack Neuburg airfield half an hour later, when, hopefully, the element of surprise would he on our side. We lost GEE *en route* to the target, and as I recall we located the Danube and proceeded to navigate visually below the cloud base of around 1,500 ft. We located what appeared to be a marshalling yard, with many white wagons bearing the red cross. It was rumoured that much ammunition was transported this way, and having circled the area a couple of times, I was tempted to have a go! Frank was not in agreement, saying that they might be 'legit'. Ar this juncture a break in the cloud allowed bright moonlight, which revealed our target airfield, which we had been overflying while circling. Many parked aircraft were plainly visible. The instant I pressed the firing-button, intense fire was returned from all sides; tracer shells seemed to be everywhere. I managed to silence one gun position, but not before being hit, which caused an almighty shudder throughout the aircraft. It was then time to disengage and head rapidly for cloud cover and a worrying return to base, where, fortunately, the damage to the Mosquito was not very serious, the butts of the cannon having taken most of the impact. This proved to be our last operation of the war.

Despite the dangers Mosquito Intruders faced, night-fighting was the safest part of the war. You were the aggressor.

Notes

1. Motto of 410 'Cougar' Squadron RCAF.
2. In February 1943, 418 converted to the Mosquito.
3. Nightly 264 patrolled in the West Country and by day it operated in the Bay of Biscay and the Western Approaches. On 21 March 1943, during a Bay of Biscay patrol, two Ju 88s were destroyed, the second being the squadron's 100th German aircraft destroyed. On 29 March an He 111 was probably destroyed during an Intruder patrol. April added nothing to the score, but many locomotives and ground targets were damaged and destroyed. May saw the squadron at Predannack for Bay of Biscay patrols and Day Rangers (concentrating on Laon and Juvincourt), with fair success. June was excellent over the Bay. On the 13th an Fw 190 was damaged after an encounter with three of the single-engined fighters. On the 20th a Ju 88 was probably destroyed, and on the night of the

20th/21st 'a real picnic was enjoyed', as the squadron diarist wrote it, by Wg Cdr Allington, when three Blohm und Voss seaplanes were sighted. A BV 138 was destroyed in the air and two six-engined BV 222s were destroyed in the sea, with another BV 138 destroyed on the water. Another BV 222 was damaged and a minesweeper and hangars left in flames. Wg Cdr Allington was awarded a Bar to his DFC for leading the sortie. On 27/28 June a Do 217 was claimed as 'damaged', and on the 28/29th, Flg Off A.J. Hodgkinson forced down *Unteroffizier* Rudolf Blankenburg of *KG2* over Creil, as he made for home in a Do 217E-2 after a raid on Weston-super-Mare.
4. On 21/22 July Plt Off Fisher shot down a Do 217E-4 flown by *Oberfeldwebel* Heinrich Wolpers and his crew of *I/KG2* off Spurn Head. On 27/28 July Sqn Ldr Pennington and Plt Off Field each claimed a bomber destroyed. *Feldwebel* Richard Stumpf of *I./KG2* and *Leutnant* Hans-Joachim Mohring of *3./KG2* were their victims. On 29/30 July, when the *Luftwaffe* bombed Birmingham, Australian pilot Flg Off A.I. McRitchie and Flt Sgt E.S. James attacked a Do 217E-4 flown by *Oberfeldwebel* Artur Hartwig of *II./KG2* and it crashed into the sea.
5. Sammy Hoare's first successful Intruder in a Havoc was on the night of 3/4 May when he got an He 111 for sure and a Ju 88 as a probable.
6. Sammy Hoare's first NF.II sortie on 5/6 July proved somewhat uneventful in that no sightings were made, but the night following, 6/7 July, he and Plt Off Cornes dispatched a Dornier Do 217 sixteen miles east of Chartres with three short bursts of cannon fire. On 8/9 July Sqn Ldr K.H. Salisbury-Hughes, flying S-Sugar, destroyed a Do 217 over Etampes and an He 111 at Evreux. On 30/31 July Sammy Hoare in S-Sugar destroyed an unidentified enemy aircraft at Orléans. On 8/9 September three Mosquitoes were lost on Intruder sorties over the continent. Then, on 10/11 September, Sammy Hoare and J.F. Potter, flying B-Bertie, destroyed another UEA twelve miles south of Enschede. In December 1942 23 Squadron was posted to Malta for Intruder operations against the Axis. Sammy Hoare left 23 Squadron prior to its departure overseas to set up a specialized Intruder training 'school' at No. 51 OTU at Cranfield, Bedfordshire.
7. Tim' Woodman was born in Trowbridge, Wiltshire, on 3 June 1914, becoming an engineering apprentice at Hadens in Trowbridge until 1936, when he joined the Air Ministry's Mechanical and Electrical Design staff. He transferred to pilot training in 1940, being sent to Canada for much of this, and being commissioned in February 1941. In June he returned to the UK and attended 52 OTU on Hurricanes, then being posted to 410 Squadron RCAF on Defiants and then Beaufighter IIs. As a flight lieutenant he was seconded to Bristol Aircraft in June 1942 as a production test pilot on Beaufighters until August, when he rejoined 410. In December he was posted to 96 Squadron, where he remained until November 1943, when he went to 169 Squadron to undertake 100 Group bomber support operations on Mosquitoes.
8. Hillock completed his tour on 20 May and was succeeded by Wg Cdr G.H. Elms.

9. Predannack was also used by a detachment of 25 Squadron NF.IIs detached to 264 Squadron. 25 Squadron had received NF.IIs in October 1942 and had started freelance Ranger sweeps over the continent. In June Mosquitoes of 456 and 605 Squadrons began successful, albeit small-scale, bomber support Flower attacks on German night-fighter airfields during raids by main-force bombers. Flowers supported bombers by disrupting enemy flying control organizations. Long-range Intruder aircraft fitted with limited radar equipment were used, and these proceeded to the target at high altitude, diving down whenever they saw airfields illuminated. This type of operation, if correctly timed, prevented the enemy night-fighters, which were already short of petrol, from landing at their bases.
10. Werk Nr 4415.
11. Popular with his crews, Bradel was a former cavalry officer who had flown in the Spanish Civil War, first as a *Staffelkapitan*, later as a *Gruppen-Kommandeur* and, finally, as a *Geschwaderkommodore* in the Condor Legion. He held the Spanish War Medal and the Spanish Gold Cross with Swords. In Norway Bradel was employed as leader of a transport *Staffel*, bringing up supplies and equipment to the mountain troops near Narvik. He then took part as a bomber pilot in operations against England, and later in the Balkan campaign (he was said to have been the first to land and take possession of Athens airfield) and the operations against Crete. In the course of the latter he claimed to have sunk a British destroyer with bombs. On the Eastern front, his chief exploit seems to have been a low-level attack on 500 Soviet tanks in the battle for Grodno. On 17 September 1941 he was awarded the *Ritterkreuz* (Knight's Cross).
12. Late in 1942 Williams was sent to an Aircrew Refresher Course at Brighton, a euphemism for a 'bad boys school'. He was perplexed, and took his parachute and 'Mae West' with him. Instead, early-morning PT on the beach, drill all day and frequent haircuts awaited him. One of his fellow defaulters, a Pole, had been caught with a girl in his bed after he had left his shoes – and those of his lady friend – outside his door for his batman! After three weeks the 'bad boys' were returned to their units – if they had behaved. Williams stayed for ten weeks! Then he was posted to 605 Squadron at Castle Camps, where he flew his first Mosquito op on 10 March. They patrolled over the Dutch airfields to await the raiders' return. 605 and 418 (RCAF) Squadrons were the first Mosquito Night-Intruder squadrons sent to attack *Luftwaffe* airfields on the continent. The former had taken over 23 Squadron's Bostons and Havocs and had begun Intruder operations over French airfields in July 1942. In February 1943 605 began equipping with the Mosquito, and by May 1943, when 418 received its first Mosquito, the County of Warwick squadron was making its presence felt.
13. Bradel probably died of injuries he sustained because he had not been strapped in. *Flieger* Wernerker was also killed, although he may have died in the Mosquito attack, and the rest of the crew were injured. All recovered, Andres being promoted to *Oberleutnant* and receiving the *Ritterkreuz* on 20 April 1944. He was killed with *5./NJG4* on 11 February 1945.

14. Offensive patrols in July 1943 saw no combats. The first patrols of August 1943 included a successful attack on armed trawlers, one being destroyed. On the 7th 264 Squadron left for Fairwood Common, where it carried out Night Rangers and ASR cover patrols, and on the 18th 264 dropped its first bombs on Laon airfield. Bomber support patrols were carried out from Castle Camps. During September detachments were sent there and to Bradwell Bay, and for raids on enemy airfields Coltishall and Ford were sometimes used. In November 264 operations largely meant liaison with the Navy at Swansea and a move to Exeter for Day Rangers, and several trains were successfully attacked. On 17 November 264 Squadron moved again, this time to Coleby Grange in Lincolnshire, and Coltishall was used as a forward base for bomber patrols. In mid-December 1943 264 moved to Church Fenton to re-equip with Mk X AI equipment, which it retained until after the end of the war.
15. Ranger sorties were flown on the 16th, 17th, 18th, 23rd, 27th and 29th (daylight); Flg Offs G.B. MacLean and H. Plant were lost on the 18th over Germany. There were also a number of scrambles, the most significant being on the 31st when five crews were dispatched – only one contact was made. Flg Off F.W. Foster and Plt Off J.H. Grantham were hit by enemy cannon and machine-gun fire shortly after becoming airborne. Foster took immediate evasive action by climbing to 10,000 ft, and the contact was lost.
16. In NF.II HJ705.
17. Flt Lt Wight-Boycott had shot down a Heinkel He 111 on 20/21 September 1941, flying a 219 Squadron Beaufighter If. On 17/18 January 1943 Wg Cdr Wight-Boycott, flying a 29 Squadron Beaufighter, shot down two Ju 88s and a Do 217 and damaged another. On one remarkable night, 17/18 January 1943, he destroyed two Do 217s and a Ju 88 and damaged three other Dorniers. The following night he shot down two more Dornier 217s and a Ju 88.
18. Mahmoud was the codename for a special kind of operation that was devised after it was realized that the *Luftwaffe* was operating radar-equipped night-fighters against the 'heavies' of Bomber Command. In August 1943, this had led to a decision to release some Beaufighters with AI Mk IV radar over enemy territory as bait for enemy night-fighters in their known assembly areas. The British fighters flew individually over the continent to try and induce German night-fighters to intercept them. Mosquito night-fighters also flew Mahmoud operations, but were less successful at pretending to be bombers, as the Germans soon recognized the speed difference. AI Mk IV had an all-round scan, so it was possible for the radar observer to detect on his CRT (Cathode Ray Tube) an enemy night-fighter trying to intercept them from astern. The British pilot would then carry out a 360-degree turn to try and get on the tail of the enemy and shoot him down. With the more powerful centimetric AI being used in Mosquitoes it was necessary to add Monica tail warning devices, as these later marks of AI did not scan to the rear. Later in the war, when the RAF received details of the *Luftwaffe* night-fighter assembly-point beacons from the Resistance, Mahmoud sorties by single aircraft were also made against them.

19. From May 1944 100 (Bomber Support) Group. See *Confounding the Reich*. Martin W. Bowman (Pen & Sword, 2004) and *100 Group (Bomber Support): RAF Bomber Command in World War II* (Pen & Sword, 2006).
20. 192 Squadron was equipped with Mosquito IV, Halifax and Wellington X aircraft for the ELINT (Electronic Intelligence) role (monitoring German radio and radar).
21. MAA *The Mossie* Vol.17, August 1997.
22. 2nd Lt William J. Lalley was co-pilot of B-17 42-3513 of the 326th Bomb Squadron, 92nd Bomb Group flown by 2nd Lt Russell M. Munson, which was shot down on 29 April on the mission to Berlin and crashed at Millingen in Holland. Munson and the other eight members of the crew survived to become prisoners of war.
23. Flt Sgt Viv Connell was navigator of ND752, one of seven 75 Squadron RNZAF Lancasters that were shot down on 20/21 July 1944 on the raid on Homberg. Connell and one other man survived from Flg Off H.J. Burtt's crew. They had taken off from Mepal in Cambridgeshire at 2330 hours, and the Lancaster crashed at 0140 hours near Tilburg. *Royal Air Force Bomber Command Losses of the Second World War*. W.R. Chorley (six vols, Midland Counties, Leicester, 1992–98).
24. *Footprints On The Sands of Time: RAF Bomber Command PoWs in Germany 1939–45*. Oliver Clutton-Brock (Grub Street, 2003).

CHAPTER 5

On The Defensive Again

On the night of 21/22 January 1944, ninety-two German bombers headed for London in the first of a series of revenge raids on Britain code-named Operation *Steinbock* directed by *Generalmajor* Peltz, *Angriffsführer* (Attack Leader) England. Peltz had assembled a small fleet of all types of bombers and fighter-bombers for dive-bombing over England as retaliation for RAF heavy-bomber raids on German towns and cities. Each raid carried out by the *Kampfgeschwader* normally bore emotive code-names like *Munich* and *Hamburg* to remind the *Luftwaffe* crews that they were embarked on revenge raids for the round-the-clock bombing of centres of German population. As the *Luftwaffe* became short of aircraft, new types, like the Heinkel He 177 *Greif* (Griffon), were now employed on bombing raids against English cities. Pathfinders led the German bombers, including fifteen He 177A-3s of *I./KG100* to London, and *Düppel* (German 'Window') was scattered by the attacking force in an effort to confuse the radar defences. The first He 177 to be shot down over the British Isles, an He 177A-5 of *I./KG40*, fell to the guns of a Mosquito NF.XII flown by Flg Off H.K. Kemp and Flt Sgt J.R. Maidment of 151 Squadron from Colerne.[1] Altogether, the first *Steinbock* raid cost the *Luftwaffe* twenty-one aircraft.

German units were rested until the night of 28/29 January, when sixteen Me 410s and ten Fw 190 fighter-bombers raided East Anglia, Kent and Sussex again. One Me 410 was destroyed by a Mosquito, but one of the defending fighters was lost in action. The following night the *Luftwaffe* force also included He 177s of *3./KG100* and *I./KG40*. Some 130 of the 285 enemy aircraft tracks penetrated inland, thirty reaching London. Bombs were dropped in a wide swath across Hampshire, the Thames Estuary and Suffolk. A Mosquito of 410 Squadron RCAF flown by Lieutenant R.P. Cross RNVR and Sub-Lieutenant L.A. Wilde RNVR and equipped with AI VIII radar was just gaining height after taking off from Castle Camps at 2030 hours when they received a vector from Flt Lt Parr at GCI Control at Trimley Heath. A 'bogey' had been picked up on radar, and Parr told Cross to climb to 15,000 ft. Wilde picked up the 'bandit', a Ju 88, at 2039 hours, three miles distant (the AI VIII radar set had a range of 6½ miles straight ahead), flying west. Cross closed in behind the unsuspecting raider. A five-minute chase ensued and finished with Cross lifting his nose up and blasting the Junkers with two short bursts of 20 mm cannon fire. Cross and Wilde did not see any hits on the Ju 88 when firing. A Ju 88A of *3./KG54*, which crashed at Barham, Suffolk, at about this time, fell to a 68 Squadron Beaufighter.

On the night of 3/4 February 240 enemy aircraft operated in two phases over London and south-eastern England. Ninety-five went inland, seventeen reached London and fourteen were lost. Six squadrons of Mosquitoes met them. No. 410 Squadron RCAF got six NF.XIIIs off from Castle Camps. Canadians Flg Off E.S. Fox and Flg Off C.D. Sibbett took off at 0400 hours and were vectored by Sgt Burton at GCI Trimley, who gave them a 'bandit' crossing starboard to port. Sibbett worked his AI VIII radar set until he obtained a contact 3½ miles distant at 18,000 ft. Fox turned to port and closed to 2,000 ft. The German intruder was dropping *Düppel*, and Sibbett lost contact temporarily, as his screen became cluttered with pulses. He radioed control, but before they could respond, contact was regained and Fox set off in pursuit.

The Mosquito pilot closed to 200 ft, and the German, a Do 217, immediately began violent evasive action to shake off his pursuer. Fox gave the Dornier a one-second burst, but the shells missed as he peeled off to starboard. Fox turned right, then left, and regained contact. He stalked the enemy bomber for 10 miles and maintained visual contact despite continued violent evasive action on the part of the German pilot. The Canadian closed to 200 ft and gave him a two-second burst. A large piece flew off the enemy aircraft and it exploded. Fox orbited and watched the flaming wreckage hurtle down into the sea. It went in and exploded with such force that the tops of the clouds were illuminated over a wide area. (The only Do 217M-1 lost this night came from *8./KG2*, but crews of 85, 410 and 488 Squadrons each claimed one!)

Fellow Canadians Flg Off W.G. Dinsdale and his observer, Flt Sgt J.E. Dunn, also of 410 Squadron RCAF, picked up a radar contact and closed to 2,000 ft, slightly below the 'bandit', which was flying at 15,000 ft at about 220 mph near Stapleford Tawney. Dinsdale drew to the left to prevent overshooting his prey. It was a Ju 88 flying straight and level, seemingly oblivious to the Mosquito's presence. However, just as Dinsdale turned into an attacking position the Ju 88 peeled off violently to port and headed directly for them! It flew dangerously close underneath, and its fin or tailplane clipped the Mosquito's starboard propeller as it passed. Dinsdale temporarily lost control, regained it again and dived the aircraft to the left. Despite Dunn getting several more contacts, the enemy aircraft disappeared before the Canadians could attack again. They could only claim a 'damaged'.

An NF.XIII flown by Flg Off Hugh Brian Thomas and WO C.B. Hamilton of 85 Squadron at Biggin Hill was climbing to 20,000 ft when they received a vector from the Sandwich controller to intercept two contacts. One turned out to be a friendly fighter and the hunt was called off. Then another contact was obtained and the hunt was on again. This time it was a German bomber. At 1,500 ft distance the 'bandit' was made out to be a Do 217. Thomas closed from 300 to 100 yards before opening fire. In three very short bursts, each lasting just 2½ seconds, 120 20 mm rounds were pumped into the hapless Dornier. Thomas observed strikes, and with the third burst the Dornier exploded and the starboard engine erupted in flames. Thomas broke off, his windscreen covered in oil, and watched the German aircraft fall away, well alight. It hit the sea twenty miles east of the Naze and lit up the clouds with an orange glow. Thomas and Hamilton returned to Biggin and were told to orbit the station, as 'hostiles' had been reported overhead, but flying debris from the Dornier had penetrated the Mosquito's port engine, and five miles west of the base Thomas feathered the propeller and landed. Thomas ended his tour in the summer of 1944, having scored four victories and earning the DFC. He returned to the squadron in April 1945 as a flight lieutenant, and claimed his fifth victory west of Lutzkendorf, flying an NF.XXX.

The third 'kill' of the night went to Dutchman Flt Sgt Christian J. Vlotman and his navigator, Sgt John L. Wood, of 488 Squadron RNZAF at Bradwell Bay. On his AI VIII, Wood picked up a Do 217 gently weaving at 17,000 ft, 2½ miles distant. Vlotman was directed by ground control until he was able to make contact at about 1,000 yards. The Dutchman closed to 300 yards dead astern and let fly with his four 20 mm cannon. His port inner stopped, fouled by loose rounds, but the shells had done their work. The Dornier peeled off to port, its left side and engine aflame. Vlotman followed the stricken fighter-bomber down and gave it two more short bursts to make the 'kill' certain. It spun violently down, shedding pieces of debris. The enemy cockpit was well alight and no crew were seen to bale out as it went down over the North Sea, forty miles off Foulness Point, Essex.

On 4 February Keith R. McCormick RCAF and W. 'Nick' Nixon MiD of 410 Squadron took off from Hunsdon on an air test in Mosquito NF.XIII HK454. Nixon recalls:[2]

As we had a little engine trouble with the starboard engine, we went up to about 13,000 ft to give the engine a full run-up and test. Mac completed the test and he seemed satisfied with the result, as he then said to me, 'OK, Nick, that's fine; let's go home.' He then did a starboard wing over and put the nose down in the usual way of quickly losing height. After losing 2,000–3,000 ft, Mac pulled out of the dive; there was an almighty bang right under my backside and I was flung onto the floor. Mac immediately leaned over me and attempted to jettison the door, which was on the starboard side. Then the starboard wing outside of the engine collapsed, and I think it took out the side of the nose. The engine caught fire and we started to go down in a tight spiral. I saw my parachute roll over the floor towards the hole and I just managed to grab it. Clipping it on, I tried to get out through the hatch, but the centrifugal force of the spin held me for what appeared to be ages, but I suppose it was only for seconds. I then found myself in the air, conscious of the fact that the aircraft was falling above me, burning and raining bits down onto me. I do not really remember much after this, except that somehow I must have hung onto the parachute. It seemed that as soon as it opened, I hit the ground and the burning Mossie landed nearby, about a hundred yards away. I managed to get out of the harness and ran towards the aircraft, but someone got hold of me, kept me back until the accident and ambulance services arrived to whisk me away. On the way to hospital the 'Doc' told me that Mac hadn't made it. He had been trapped in the aircraft and did not survive. I discovered later that my parachute and harness had been recovered, and only one retaining hook was attached to the harness. The usual result of this happening was 'candling', and I was indeed lucky to escape with a few burns. Sadly I lost a friend and a mate.[3]

The fourth major *Steinbock* attack took place on the night of 13/14 February, and Mosquito crews were again triumphant. One of the victors was Flt Lt Rayne Schultz DFC of 410 Squadron, who took his score to five. On the night of 10/11 December 1943 he and Flg Off V.A. Williams had scored a hat trick of victories. They downed three Do 217s of *KG2*, for which they had received DFCs. Schultz's victory on 13/14 February was a Ju 188, which was shot down about twenty miles off East Anglia. Fellow Canadian, Sqn Ldr James Dean Somerville, of 410 Squadron RCAF, who was 25 years old and came from Esshaw, Alberta, destroyed a Ju 88S-1 of *Major* Helmut Schmidt's *I./KG66* pathfinder unit, and it fell at 2110 hours at Havering-Atte-Bower, Essex. Flt Lt Edward Bunting DFC and Phil Reed, now of 488 Squadron RNZAF, and a 96 Squadron pilot, scored a victory apiece to take the total to eight enemy aircraft that failed to return. Five Ju 88s from *KG6* went into the sea and a Ju 188 crashed in France on return. Altogether, the raiders attacked targets in Britain on eight nights in February, including a devastating raid on London on the 18th, whose success owed much to the Ju 88 pathfinders of *KG6* and *KG66*. Fortunately for British civilians, the intended wholesale use of V-1 flying-bombs had not materialized, and *Luftwaffe* morale was further sapped by the poor performance of the He 177.

On the night of 20/21 February, ninety-five German raiders crossed the English coast between Hythe and Harwich, heading for London.[4] Mosquitoes of 25 Squadron, which had arrived at RAF Coltishall near Norwich on 5 February, were alerted. At 2110 hours Plt Off J.R. Brockbank and his navigator-radio operator, Plt Off D. McCausland, took off in their NF.XVII, code-named Grampus 16. Flt Lt Joe Singleton DFC and his observer, Flg Off W.G. 'Geoff' Haslam, also took off at about the same time. Singleton, who was 27 years old and came from Leyland, Lancashire, had scored two victories flying the Beaufighter If in 1942 and the Mosquito II in 1943, and he had also damaged three others in the air. Both NF.XVIIs were equipped with AI X radar, and an NF.XVII had yet to shoot down an enemy aircraft at night. As soon as they cleared the circuit both aircraft were handed over to GCI at Neatishead, from where the controllers gave them their instructions. Grampus 16 was told to climb to 17,000 ft, while Singleton (Grampus 20) was ordered to climb to Angels 18 (18,000 ft). At 2143 hours he was passed on to the Chain Home Low (Radar) Station at Happisburgh, which gave him new vectors after they had picked up a 'bogey' going eastwards at Angels 10.

Meanwhile, at 2137 hours Brockbank and McCausland obtained a contact, at seven miles' range, on an aircraft crossing from left to right. Brockbank throttled to 2,650 revs at +4 boost and gained gradually on the target. His prey was a Ju 188E-1 flown by *Leutnant* Ewald Bohe of 5./KG2. Bohe weaved gently at first and then made more violent manoeuvres in an effort to shake off the Mosquito. Brockbank closed in several times to 1,000 ft, but he could not get a visual on the target and was forced to break off each time. McCausland lost contact but Neatishead restored it after a further vector. At this point a single searchlight pierced the gaps in the cloud and illuminated the fighter. Bohe 'corkscrewed' violently and tried to outdistance his pursuer, but Brockbank stuck doggedly to his task, chasing the German for twenty-five minutes, gradually closing the gap. At 600 ft he could make out the enemy's exhaust glows. The Ju 188E crossed gently from port to starboard, and as it was crossing back Brockbank fired two short bursts. Tenaciously, he closed to 75 ft and poured more rounds into the hapless German. It caught fire, flew straight and level for a few seconds and, blazing furiously, commenced a deep death-dive through the clouds to crash at Park Farm, Wickham St Paul, Essex. Both the artificial horizon and direction indicator aboard the Mosquito were put out of action after the cannon were fired, so Grampus 16 headed back to Coltishall, where the time of the 'kill', 2203 hours, was logged: the first 'kill' attributed to an NF.XVII.

Singleton, meanwhile, had pursued his enemy aircraft at 9,000 ft over the sea to fifty miles east of Lowestoft. Haslam used night binoculars to

The fighter prototype W4052 made its first flight on 15 May 1941 from Salisbury Hall in the capable hands of Geoffrey de Havilland. After trials with the A&AEE at Boscombe Down it joined the Fighter Interception Unit at Ford and was eventually scrapped on 28 January, 1946. *(RAF Museum)*

NF.IIs first equipped 157 Squadron on 13 December 1941. DD750, which served with 157, 25, 239 and 264 Squadrons, is fitted with AI.Mk.IV 'arrowhead' and wing mounted azimuth aerials. All four machine guns were deleted to make room for *Serrate* apparatus. The all-black scheme could slow the aircraft by up to 23mph. The first NF.IIs that 100 Group received in December 1943 had seen long service and the Merlin 21s were well used. Finally, in February 1944, all re-conditioned engines were called in and while stocks lasted, only Merlin 22s were installed. *(DH)*

FB.VI NS850 TH-M *'Black Rufe'* of 418 (City of Edmonton) Squadron RCAF crewed by S/L Robert Allan Kipp and F/L Peter Huletsky at Holmsley South in June 1941. As this impressive scoreboard shows Kipp and Huletsky claimed ten aircraft shot down and one shared destroyed, one shared probable, one damaged, seven destroyed on the ground and eight damaged on the ground, the bulk of these being scored during December 1943 to June 1944 in this aircraft. NS850 was written off in a landing accident at Hunsdon on 1 November 1944 when the fighter overshot the runway following an air test, its pilot having been forced to re-land with an engine feathered. *(Stephen M. Fochuk)*

Five B.IVs of 139 Squadron in echelon rear formation. Nearest aircraft is XD-G DZ421 flown by the CO, Wing Commander Peter Shand DSO DFC. Next is DZ407/R, which joined 139 Squadron from 105 Squadron on 22 December 1942 and which failed to return from the raid on Burmeister & Wain on 27 January 1943 when Sgt Richard Clare and F/O Edward Doyle hit a balloon cable and tree at East Dereham after the starboard engine failed.

DD737 an AI-equipped NF.II, was one of the first Mosquitoes issued to 85 Squadron when it converted to the de Havilland night fighter from the Havoc at Hunsdon in August 1942. DD737 was delivered to 30 MU (Maintenance Unit) on 29 August 1942 and then to 85 Squadron on 21 September. It was passed to 264 Squadron on 13 March 1943 and then returned to de Havillands on 6 May. After languishing in various MUs it joined the BSDU (Bomber Support Development Unit) on 14 October 1944, before passing to 54 OTU (Operational Training Unit) at Acklington, with whom it was lost on 6 December 1944 when it failed to return from a cross-country exercise. *(DH)*

B.IV DK338 which was delivered to 105 Squadron in September 1942 on a test flight from Hatfield. *(Charles E. Brown)*

Gary Herbert, a 105 Squadron Mosquito pilot, with his wife Jeanne outside Buckingham Palace after DFC investiture by King George VI on 27 July 1943.

F/O Ralph Gamble Hayes DFM (left), navigator and (right) his pilot, F/L John 'Flash' Gordon DFC of 105 Squadron who were killed on the night of 5/6 November 1943 over Norfolk. They tried to land at Hardwick, an American B-24 Liberator base used by the 93rd Bomb Group, when at 2110 hours, they crashed into a field at Road Green Farm, Hempnall, about 10 miles south of Norwich. (*RAF Marham*)

S/L Vernon R.G. Harcourt DFC RCAF and W/O J. Friendly DFM, a South African, on 139 Squadron who were KIA on 21 May 1943 during an operation to the locomotive sheds at Orleans. (*RAF Marham*)

B.IV Series ii DK296/G of 105 Squadron. When S/L Bill Blessing DSO DFC RAAF crash-landed *G-George* at Marham and broke its back the Mosquito was duly repaired and on 24 August 1943 it was placed in store with 10 MU at Hullavington. The following month it was issued to 305 Ferry Training Unit at Errol, in Scotland, where it was given Red Air Force markings and used to train Soviet crews who were converting onto Albermarles. On 20 April 1944 DK296 was ferried to the Soviet Union by a Russian crew, being officially accepted on 31 August 1944 and subsequently serving with the Red Air Force. Its ultimate fate is unknown. (*via GMS*)

W/C John de L. Wooldridge DFC* DFM CO, 105 Squadron, 17 March 1943-1944. Wooldridge joined the RAF in 1938 and flew two tours on heavy bombers prior to taking command of 105 Squadron, including thirty-two ops on Manchesters in 61, 207 and 106 Squadrons.

The navigator of a B.IV Mosquito demonstrates how the Mk.IV bombsight was used, just as in heavy bombers. (*Shuttleworth Collection*)

W/C Hughie Idwal Edwards VC DFC, an Australian of Welsh ancestry was 26 years old when he took command of 105 Squadron in August 1942. He was only the second Australian to receive the VC for his leadership on 4 July 1941 when he led nine Blenheims on the operation to Bremen. On 10 February 1943 Edwards was promoted G/C and he became station commander of Binbrook. By 1944 he had taken up an appointment in ACSEA and held the rank of Senior Air Staff Office until the end of 1945. Edwards was awarded the CBE in 1947 and in 1958 he was promoted to Air Commodore before retiring from the RAF in 1963. He returned to Australia, was knighted and in 1974 became Governor of West Australia. (*RAAF*)

Crews on 456 Squadron RAAF at Colerne on 23 September 1943. L–R: F/O M.N. Austin; W/O A.S. McEvoy; F/O Richard S. Williams; F/L Gordon 'Peter' Panitz DFC; P/O G. Gatenby; F/Sgt A.J. Keating (kneeling); P/O J.M. Fraser; F/O J.W. Newell; P/O A.M. Abbey and F/O S.D.P. Smith. On the night of 14/15 May 1944 F/O A.S. McEvoy and F/O M.N. Austin destroyed a Ju 188A2. As CO of 464 Squadron RAAF W/C Panitz was KIA on 31 August 1944 attacking targets in France. (*RAAF*)

Raid by 105 Squadron on Tours railway workshops on 18 March 1943.

Raid by 105 Squadron on Tours railway workshops on 18 March 1943.

NF.II DZ659 was built at Hatfield as a NF.II but was modified with a 'Universal' nose and fitted with SCR 720/729 *Eleanora* radar, also known as AI.Mk.10. The aerial for the SCR 720 radar can be seen beneath the fuselage behind the cannon ports as can the azimuth aerials at each wing-tip. DZ659 was delivered to the FIU at Ford on 1 April 1943, where it remained, apart from six months at Defford and was eventually SOC at 10 MU Hullavington on 28 January 1946. (*via Jerry Scutts*)

(*Bottom left*) F/L Johnny Downs DFC (left) with S/L Dennis Furse DFC who joined 604 'County of Middlesex' Squadron at Scorton in the winter of 1943 at Hurn airfield in May 1944. During his time on 406 ('Lynx') Squadron RCAF and 604 Squadrons S/L Furse claimed four victories.

(*Bottom right*) S/L Paul V. Davoud DSO DFC (pointing) and his navigator, F/L Douglas Alcorn DFC (above) of 418 (City of Edmonton) Squadron RCAF with S/L C.C. Moran DFC during a debriefing session after a successful Intruder operation. On 27/28 June 1943 S/L Moran had claimed a Ju 88 and a He 111 destroyed at Avord, the pilot also blasting a train and a radio mast during the same sortie. By the end of the summer he had earned a deserved reputation as a 'train-buster', his technique usually consisting of a strafing run to stop the locomotive, before finishing it off with bombs. Having attained wing commander rank, Paul Davoud led the squadron from June 1943 to January 1944. (*Stephen M. Fochuk*)

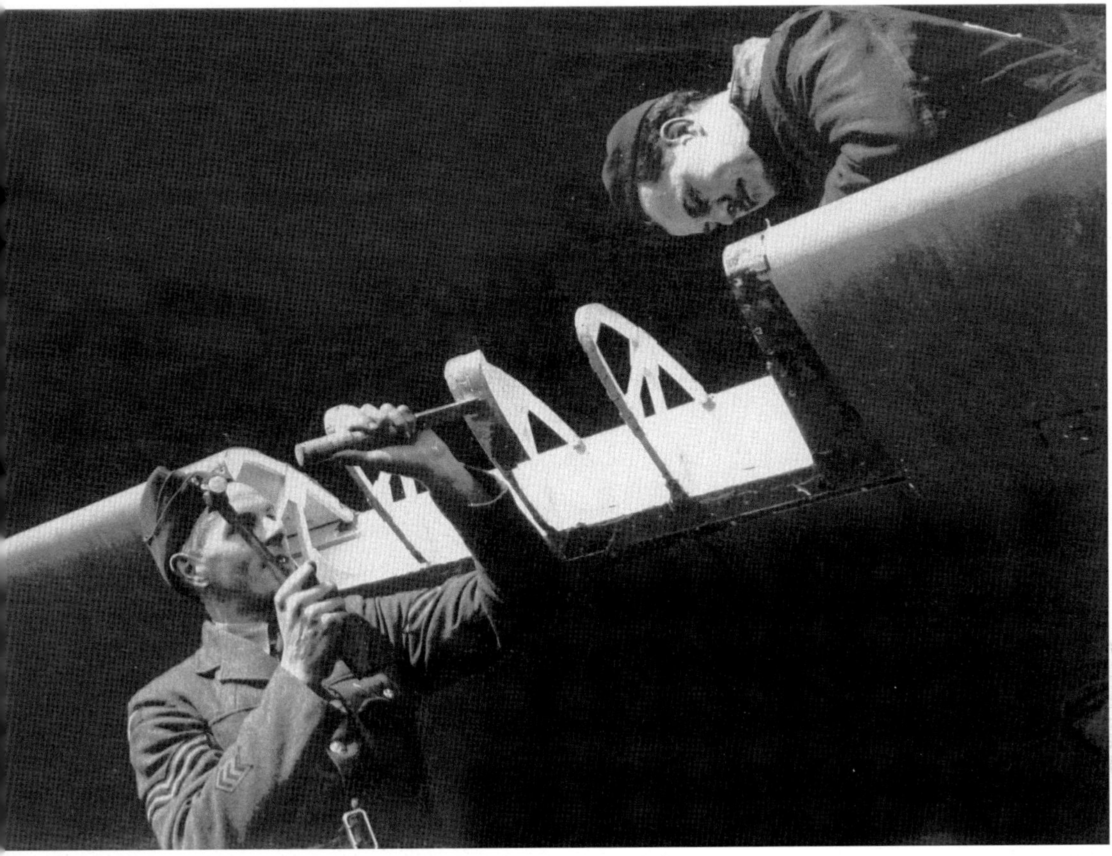

Naturally, anyone who knew or knows what a Mosquito was could tell you that it was affectionately known as the 'Wooden Wonder' but few apart from those who built them and a few RAF people, could have seen this. The picture, taken at Ford, shows where W/C Keith MacDermott Hampshire's chunk of engine landed and presented the 456 Squadron RAAF CO with his second victim in a minute on the night of 27/28 March 1944 when he destroyed a Ju 88 near Beer and a second at Brewer Isle. (*Ken Lowes*)

F/O John Barry (top) and F/O Guy Hopkins (below) showing how tricky it was getting into and out of the very small aircrew door into the close confines of the Mosquito cockpit. To bail out the pilot could only follow his navigator. On 7/8 June F/L Barry and Hopkins destroyed two Ju 188s to take the pilot's score to four. Barry and Hopkins died in a flying accident during a NFT while based at Hunsdon a few weeks after the invasion. (*Ken Lowes*)

4,000lb 'Cookie' bombs in train for loading aboard B.XXVIs of 692 Squadron at Graveley, formed there on 1 January 1944 with B.IVs and flying its first LNSF operation on 1/2 February, three B.IVs going to Berlin. By early 1944 suitably modified B.IVs were capable, just, of carrying a 4,000lb Blockbuster, although it was a tight squeeze in the bomb bay, which was strengthened and the bomb doors re-designed. No. 692 had the distinction of being the first Mosquito squadron to drop a 4,000lb bomb over Germany when DZ647, a modified B.IV, released one during a raid on Düsseldorf on 23/24 February 1944. B.XVIs were used from June 1944 until October 1945. (*via Tom Cushing*)

W/C Paul V. Davoud DSO DFC and F/O Keith Reynolds of 418 (City of Edmonton) Squadron RCAF. Davoud commanded the squadron from June 1943 to January 1944. (*MAA*)

F/L Ivor G. Broom and F/L (later S/L DFC**) Tommy Broom (note the crossed broomsticks on the nose!). Tommy and Ivor (no relation) flew fifty-eight operations (twenty-one to Berlin) with 571, 128 and 163 Squadrons in 8 Group Pathfinder Force. Ivor later became Air Marshal Sir Ivor Broom KCB CBE DSO DFC** AFC. (*via Rolls-Royce*)

F/L John Burt and F/L Ronald Curtis on 109 Squadron at Little Staughton in front of their Mosquito B.IX ML907 with their ground crew after completing the aircraft's 100th operational sortie late in 1944. (*Roy W. Edwards*)

Applying black and white invasion stripes to a Mosquito of 2nd TAF just prior to D-Day. (*British Newspaper Pool*)

On Tuesday 11 April 1944 six Mosquito FB VIs of 613 Squadron led by the CO, W/C R.N. 'Bob' Bateson DFC attacked the Dutch Central Population Registry in The Hague. The *Gestapo* building was completely destroyed in what an Air Ministry bulletin later described as 'probably the most brilliant feat of low-level precision bombing of the war'. (*BAe Hatfield*)

On 19 August 1944 613 Squadron Mosquito crews, led by S/L Charles Newman carried out a daring low level attack on a school building at Egletons, 50 miles SE of Limoges, believed to be in use as an SS troops barracks. Fourteen of the Mosquitoes located and bombed the target, scoring at least twenty direct hits and the target was almost completely destroyed. One Mosquito, crewed by F/L House and F/O Savill, was hit in the starboard engine over the target area and failed to return but the crew survived and returned to the squadron just five days later. (*Vic Hester*)

F/L Bert Willers (left) and F/L Les Bulmer of 21 Squadron supposedly going over the route while their FB.VI is warmed up behind in this staged photo taken by James Jarche for *Illustrated* magazine. Les Bulmer recalled that he did not seem to appreciate that crews did not get into a Mosquito with the engines running and he also had to borrow a pair of flying boots because apparently, he did not look the part of an intrepid aviator without them! 21 Squadron operated as part of 140 Wing, 2nd TAF, which gained a distinctive reputation for pinpoint bombing raids. On 6 February 1945, the squadron moved to Rosieres and remained on the continent until the end of the war. (*via Les Bulmer*)

F/L George Esmond 'Jamie' Jameson DFC RNZAF of 488 Squadron RNZAF, pilot of NF.XIII MM446 *R for Robert*, who with his navigator F/O A. Norman Crookes claimed eleven victories. Jameson returned to New Zealand and the award of a DSO followed. Crookes, who after the war became a teacher in Kent, received a bar to his DFC. Jamie's score made him the highest scoring New Zealand fighter pilot of the war. 'Jamie' Jameson died aged 76 in a bulldozer accident in 1998.

Mosquitoes of 409 ('Nighthawk') Squadron RCAF at Lille, France in 1944. The nearest aircraft is NF.XIII HK425 KP-R. (*Ross Finlayson*)

F/L J.A. 'Peter' Broadley DSO DFC DFM does up the harness straps for G/C Percy C. Pickard DSO DFC before the take off for the raid on Amiens Prison on 18 February 1944. (*via Jerry Scutts*)

On The Defensive Again

make a positive identification of the enemy aircraft. (It was a Do 217K-1 of *7./KG2*). At 2236 hours Singleton dispatched *Oberleutnant* Wolfgang Brendel and his crew into the sea with a two-second burst from dead astern. Brendel, *Feldwebel* Bruno Preker, *Oberfeldwebel* Bruno Schneider and *Unteroffizier* Heinz Grudssus, were all posted as 'Missing'. Then Singleton and Haslam picked up the chase again and pursued *Unteroffizier* Walter Schmidt's *KG2* Do 217M-1 to within twenty miles of the Dutch coast before they had to return to Coltishall, low on petrol. All in all, a successful night for the Battle of Britain station.

Two nights later, 22/23 February, He 177s of *I./KG100* based at Rheine, and *3./KG 100* from Châteaudun, were included in the all-out assault on England. Mosquito night-fighter teams like Flt Lt Bill Baillie and his navigator-radio operator, Flg Off Simpson, were always on the lookout for 'bogies' in their part of the sky. They had taken off from Coltishall at 2125 hours and had not been on patrol long when Flg Off Humphries, one of the controllers at the radar station at Happisburgh, told them that there was the possibility of 'trade' south-west, travelling west about twenty miles away. They were vectored to within three miles of the contact when the radar station said it could not give much more help. At three minutes after midnight Simpson picked up two blips on his AI X cathode-ray screen at two miles' range, 10–15° above at 17,000 ft. Baillie set off in hot pursuit and within minutes had narrowed the range to just 2,000 ft. He could see the exhausts and resins of the rear aircraft. At this point the rear blip veered away to the left and the other went slightly to the right as the enemy aircraft carried out mild evasive action. Had they picked up the Mosquito's presence? Baillie and Simpson peered ahead through the narrow windscreen of their fighter. Immediately they looked away, dazzled momentarily by groping searchlight beams, which bathed the Mosquito in bright light, before they were eventually extinguished.

Their night vision restored, Baillie and Simpson strained in the direction of where their quarry should be. Baillie narrowed the gap, closing to 400 yards from the blip. And there it was! At 14,000 ft they made out a rough outline against the night sky. The large black silhouette of fuselage and engines was ploughing along, intent on death and destruction. It motored on as if it owned the sky. Even the exhausts emitted no flames. They were at one with the black expanse and dark grey cloud shapes. Baillie stared intently. 'It's a Dornier Do 217', he reported, and closed to just 200 ft astern. In fact it was an He 177A-3 of *3./KG100* flown by *Oberfeldwebel* Wolfgang Ruppe. At just 23 minutes after midnight Baillie opened fire, sending the He 177 down in flames to fall in the vicinity of Wolsey House Farm, Yoxford. It lay scattered over an area about a quarter of a mile across. The only survivor was the rear gunner, Emil Imm, who floated down in his turret and lived to tell the tale. He was found next morning by workmen, who revived him with coffee from their flasks.

Oberfeldwebel Ruppe's He 177 was one of 150 *Luftwaffe* bombers which crossed East Anglia on the night of 22/23 February 1944. By and large they got through. Only two Me 410s were lost. One fell to Sqn Ldr G.L. Caldwell and Flg Off Rawling of 96 Squadron at Framfield, Sussex; the other to AA fire at Radnage, Buckinghamshire. Sqn Ldr C.A.S. Anderson and his observer, Flt Sgt G.P.I. Bodard, of 410 Squadron RCAF were on interception patrol at 20,000 ft in their NF.XIII from Castle Camps when they were vectored north by Trimley GCI. The two Canadians were told to climb to 23,000 ft to investigate a 'bogey' near Earls Colne. When Trimley told them to descend to 18,000 ft it was at this point that Anderson and Bodard made contact. A German raider was flying along two miles in the distance, well below the height of the approaching Mosquito. The Trimley controller had done his job well.

Anderson closed, but before he could line up his guns he had overshot the bomber. He orbited and Bodard picked up the 'bogey' on his screen again, range ½ mile, and still below. The same thing happened again! Anderson orbited a second time and Bodard made contact, range ¾ mile. Anderson closed slowly this time, to 50 ft, and obtained a visual. The twin-engined enemy machine began carrying out a wild evasive action and visual contact was lost several times until Bodard managed to hold the contact and Anderson could close to 50 ft. It was a Ju 88A-4 of 9./KG6, one that had taken off from Melsbroek to bomb London. Astern and below, Anderson lined up to fire. Just as he was about to launch a fusillade of 20 mm cannon and HEI rounds, the Ju 88 pilot peeled off violently to the left and spoiled his aim. However, Anderson managed to get in a short burst from 150 ft and he was pleased to see some of the rounds find their mark on the fuselage and starboard engine, which caught fire. The Junkers levelled out and Anderson attacked again, this time from 75 yards. The stricken bomber was hit further, and the German crew, impotent, it seemed, must have known they were doomed. The pilot refused to give up the struggle, however, and turned to the right as Anderson pumped more shells into the target. Small explosions danced on the Junkers' fuselage, and finally it burst into flames. It spun away into the night and broke up before plunging into the North Sea.

Bodard returned to Trimley GCI control. Flt Lt Carr calmly informed the Mosquito crew to go to 17,000 ft; he had picked up another 'bogey' over Essex. Range, three miles. Anderson closed in while climbing, but the enemy aircraft was too high and he undershot. Bodard lost contact and asked Trimley for help. Carr gave them a vector of 270° and Anderson closed on the enemy to 500 ft. A visual was obtained, but this 'kill' was not going to be any easier than the previous one, and the enemy pilot immediately carried out evasive action. Contact was maintained, however, and Anderson closed to 150 ft, keeping underneath and to one side, just to be on the safe side. The two Canadians made the bomber out to be a Ju 188E-1. Immediately, the German bomber dived to the left. Anderson gave a short burst from 50 yards and the rounds struck home on the side of the Junkers' fuselage and wings. The wounded machine took further violent evasive action and lost height, but the Mosquito crew would not be shaken from their stride. Anderson pumped more bursts into the Junkers, and a fusillade that struck the cockpit area seemed to signal the end of the German bomber. It dived steeply, levelled out momentarily and finally spun in, out of control. Anderson followed it down and pulled out at 6,000 ft when he recognized that the Junkers was finished.

With characteristic understatement, Britons by now called the Operation *Steinbock* raids the 'Baby Blitz'. Mosquito night-fighter crews encountered all manner of German bomber and fighter types, including Do 217s, Me 410s and even the occasional Fw 190 and He 177. On 23/24 February three enemy aircraft were lost and a Do 217 fell to AA fire. The following night Mosquito crews claimed three 'probables' and eight enemy aircraft shot down.[5] *Steinbock* raids continued over East Anglia and London throughout the remainder of February and into March. The 'Baby Blitz' showed no sign of easing up, and seventy aircraft attempted to bomb London on 1 March. Only ten managed to evade the defences and reach the capital, however.

On the night of 14/15 March, 140 German raiders crossed the coast of eastern England in four waves. Two-thirds of the force crossed between Cromer in Norfolk and Shoeburyness, Essex, while a smaller wave crossed over Sussex. Some of the bomber force used skill and daring to infiltrate British airspace under cover of returning Mosquitoes, and *Düppel* was dropped to complete their disguised approach. Most of the invading bombers crossed the coast between Great Yarmouth and Southwold at heights ranging from 14,000 to 24,000 ft before turning south for London and its environs. The incursions were met in some strength by a determined force of Mosquitoes. Seven of 410 Squadron RCAF at Castle Camps were scrambled to intercept. 1st Lt Archie A. Harrington and Sgt D.G. Tongue destroyed a Ju 88A-4 of 2./KG54,[6] which fell at Hildenborough, Kent. Harrington, who was 29 years old and came from Jamesville, Ohio, was a USAAF officer attached to the RCAF to gain night-fighting experience. (Over Germany on the night of 25/26 November they intercepted and shot down three Ju 88G nightfighters to take their score to seven). Sqn Ldr Peter Wilfrith Green DFC got a Ju 88 for his fourth victory of the war and his first since joining the Canadian squadron from 85 Squadron in the spring.[7] A Ju 188E-1 flown by *Leutnant* Horst Becker of 4./KG6 fell to the guns of Flt Lt Edward Bunting DFC and Phil Reed of 488 Squadron RNZAF. It broke up in the air and crashed in flames at White House Farm, Great Leighs, near Chelmsford.[8]

Meanwhile, Joe Singleton and his observer, Flg Off Geoff Haslam, of 25 Squadron had taken off from Coltishall at 2105 hours for a Bullseye exercise (when training aircraft from the bomber OTUs were engaged by the sector searchlights and subjected to dummy attacks by nightfighters). Singleton had just returned to the squadron after instructing, being promoted to flight lieutenant and receiving the DFC. Sector control passed them on to Neatishead GCI. At 18,000 ft Singleton asked his controller if there was any 'trade'. There were 'possibilities', came the reply, and a few minutes later, on a vector of 140°, Singleton and Haslam obtained a head-on contact at 4½ miles. Singleton went in pursuit, guided by Haslam, who was able to make contact and hold it. The enemy plane was at about 16,000 ft, flying along at approximately 240 mph. The two men observed that it was taking the normal 'corkscrew' evasive action. Singleton closed to 1,000 ft. Haslam raised his night binoculars to his eyes. 'It's a Ju 88!' he said. At this the Mosquito went in closer until Singleton was within 75 yards of his quarry. A three-second burst of 20 mm cannon – fewer than 120 rounds – produced a big explosion. Fire erupted on the left-hand side of the Junkers' fuselage, and Haslam and Singleton could quite clearly see the black crosses on the underside of the port wing as the stricken bomber toppled over and fell, burning fiercely. The leading edge of the Mosquito's starboard mainplane took some of the flying debris from the doomed 88 as it disappeared into 8/10ths cloud at 5,000 ft. Almost immediately, the clouds were illuminated by the blaze from the Junkers, which crashed into the North Sea five miles east of Southwold. (The Ju 88 was from *KG30*, which lost a second aircraft this night.)

On 19/20 March, Singleton and Haslam were among the aircrews at readiness in 25 Squadron at Coltishall who were alerted to intercept a force of about ninety bombers over the North Sea, heading for Hull. Singleton and Haslam had taken off from Coltishall at 2055 hours in NF.XVII HK255. Neatishead radar told them to 'hurry and climb to 16,000 ft', as a contact had been made. At about 8,000 ft the CHL station at Happisburgh gave them a vector towards twelve 'bandits' crossing up ahead of them. At 16,000 ft Haslam established contact on his American-made AI X radar at 8½ miles' range (the AI X set had a range of 8–10 miles in an arc at most altitudes). Singleton wrote later:

> We turned to port and followed, closed the range and obtained visual 10° above at 1,600 ft. We identified it as a Junkers and closed to about 100 yards. I gave him a 2½-second burst from dead astern. It exploded. As we were still closing we had to pull up steeply to avoid collision; debris from the enemy aircraft spattered our aircraft. We orbited and watched the enemy aircraft go down in a steep dive to port in flames. When it had dropped to about 5,000 ft it broke up

completely, and several burning pieces hit the sea and cast a glow over a wide area.

Their first victory of the night had gone down at 2120 hours, fifty-six miles north-north-east of Cromer. After fixing the position with Neatishead, Singleton and Haslam were given a vector by Happisburgh. Haslam got a contact at 4½ miles' range, crossing slowly from right to left. Singleton closed in behind and slightly below the intruder and obtained a visual at about 1,500 ft. The unsuspecting machine (Ju 88) was not making any evasive manoeuvres. At 2127 hours, Singleton took careful aim from 100 yards dead astern and fired a 2½-second burst. The centre of the Ju 88's fuselage exploded and the aircraft went down almost vertically before it fell into the Wash, where it continued to burn fiercely on the surface for a few seconds. Singleton orbited the scene and obtained a fix of the position from Neatishead, sixty-five miles north-north-east of Cromer.

Almost immediately, Haslam obtained a third contact, at four miles' range. He watched it crossing hard right to left on the scope of his AI X, and directed Singleton accordingly. The pilot made a hard turn left and followed the blip at 230 IAS and at a height of 16,000 ft. This Ju 88 put up a fight. It carried out a series of quite violent evasive manoeuvres and changed height several times as the Mosquito closed to 1,500 ft. At 2133 hours Singleton fired a 2½-second burst at 125 yards dead astern. The German's starboard engine emitted a myriad of sparks, which danced along the nacelle until it erupted in flames. The Ju 88 pilot fought frantically, but uselessly, with the controls as his aircraft dived like a shot pheasant. Singleton delivered the *coup de grâce* with a three-second burst at 500–600 yards' range, and the aircraft disintegrated into a blazing inferno. Burning debris flew off in all directions as it plummeted into the sea, sixty-three miles north-north-east of Cromer at 2133 hours. The water engulfed the flaming bomber and eventually snuffed out its flames and the lives of the crew – if they were not already dead.

Singleton levelled out, but both engines were running very roughly. The needle on the port radiator dial quivered on 140°, while the starboard indicated 120°. Singleton immediately throttled back, opened his radiator flaps and succeeded in cooling the engines slightly. Happisburgh were informed by radio that the 'Mossie' had engine trouble, and they responded quickly by giving the ailing night-fighter a vector and telling the crew to go over to GCI at Neatishead. They crossed the coast at 5,000 ft. By now the port engine was very hot and was emitting a succession of sparks, so Singleton feathered the prop. He flew on towards Coltishall with both engines throttled as far back as was practical without losing too much height. The radiator temperatures were by now reading 130–140°, and he told Haslam to get ready to bale out.

Singleton called Coltishall and asked for the aerodrome lighting to be switched on so that he could see the base from the coast and make a direct approach. Both engines were still running, but very roughly, and the aircraft was gradually losing height. Singleton had decided to land with wheels and flaps up. At about 1,000 ft the starboard engine seized and burst into flames. Haslam operated the starboard engine fire extinguisher, while Singleton switched on the port landing-light. He tried to get more power from the port engine, but this also seized. At 140 mph Singleton levelled out and suddenly felt the aircraft hit the ground. Haslam opened the top hatch and jumped out; Singleton followed a few seconds behind him. They ran about twenty-five yards from the wrecked Mosquito, which had come down at Sco Ruston, half a mile from Coltishall, and sat down.

Singleton saw that the engines were burning at the cylinder heads, and went back and climbed into the cockpit to switch off petrol and other switches and look for the fire extinguisher. He could not find it, so he clambered down and threw clods of earth onto the engines, and had extinguished the flames in the starboard Merlin by the time the fire tender and ambulance arrived. Singleton and Haslam were treated for slight head injuries. On examination, it was found that both glycol tanks, which had been holed by flying debris from the Ju 88, caused the engine trouble. Singleton and Haslam's three Ju 88 victories (probably all from II./KG30), which they destroyed in the space of an incredible thirteen minutes, and the loss of six other aircraft could have done little for the morale of the *Luftwaffe* raiders. They aborted the raid and no bombs fell on Hull![9] Next day, C-in-C Fighter Command, AM Sir Roderick Hill visited Coltishall. Singleton was awarded an immediate DSO, a DFC for Haslam followed, and both men were posted to HQ Fighter Command in April for special duties, which were to take a Mosquito XXX to the USA. The events of the night of 19/20 March took Singleton's score to seven aircraft destroyed and three damaged, and on 23 June, just before the trip to the USA, he destroyed a V-1. The purpose of the trip to America was threefold. They were to obtain agreement for many modifications to the SCR 720 radar, required by the RAF to be undertaken during production in the States, rather than in the UK after delivery.[10] They were also to test and assist in the development of new radars and to demonstrate the Mosquito and to liaise with the night-fighter training establishment of the USAAF, US Navy and US Marine Corps.

On 21/22 March, meanwhile, 25 Squadron Mosquitoes were on patrol again as raiders attempted another strike on London. Some ninety-five aircraft crossed the Suffolk coastline and headed towards an area southeast of Cambridge, where they were to make their turn south and head for the capital. Part of the force acted as a diversion, approaching between Great Yarmouth and Felixstowe. Two Ju 88s, flying at 23,000 ft, were intercepted by Flt Lt R.L. Davies and his navigator, Flg Off B. Bent, aloft in their NF.XVII from Coltishall. Davies shot down the first 88 into the sea thirty-five miles south-east of Lowestoft. Two of the crew parachuted out before the aircraft disintegrated and disappeared into cloud at about 7,000 ft. The second Ju 88 gave its presence away by firing a chandelier flare, and was promptly dispatched into the sea twenty-five miles south-east of Southwold.[11] Meanwhile, Fw 190s and Me 410s had taken off from bases in France and were also *en route* to London. Nos 410 RCAF and 488 RNZAF Squadrons orbited over their patrol sectors until directed by their GCI stations on intercept paths. A 410 Squadron RCAF Mosquito flown by Flg Off S.B. Huppert and Plt Off J.S. Christie shot down a Ju 88A-4 of *4./KG30* at Latchingdon, Essex, and a 456 (RAAF) Squadron Mosquito destroyed a Ju 88 off the south coast; but there was also plenty of 'trade' over Essex for the marauding Mosquitoes of 488 Squadron RNZAF at Bradwell Bay.

Flt Sgt Christian J. Vlotman and his navigator-radio operator Sgt John Wood were scrambled at 2335 hours under Trimley control. Flt Lt Parr vectored them towards the incoming raiders over the sea near Herne Bay. At about 500 ft range they spotted a Ju 188, which was the leading aircraft of the attack, dropping *Düppel* in profusion. Vlotman opened fire from dead astern and dispatched the Junkers into the sea. He was next directed to another contact heading in a westerly direction. The controller vectored him to within six miles of the aircraft, a Ju 88 of *II./KG54*, which was flying at 16,500 ft. Vlotman approached slowly, got to within 500 yards and, although he could not positively identify it, could quite clearly see that the enemy machine was dropping vast quantities of *Düppel*. Vlotman opened fire with his four cannon from 200 yards. The Ju 88 shuddered under the impact of the rounds and fell into the sea near Herne Bay. Fragments of metal and Plexiglas peppered the dome and radiator of the Mosquito and holed the starboard glycol tank. Coolant spilled away into the night, and when the glycol temperature rose to 150° Vlotman knew it was time to feather the starboard engine. He landed back at Bradwell on one engine, none the worse for wear.

Sqn Ldr Edward Bunting DFC in 488 Squadron RNZAF and his navigator, Flt Lt Phil Reed DFC, had also been scrambled from Bradwell. Bunting obtained a contact at 1¾ miles, slightly above, and immediately went below. He throttled right back and closed rapidly to 2,000 ft on a *9./KG30* Ju 88A-4 from Varelbusch flown by *Oberfeldwebel* Nikolaus Mayer dropping *Düppel*. Searchlights flicked on, and a shaft of bright white light latched onto the enemy aircraft and held it. Other beams coned Bunting's Mosquito. As Reed radioed for a 'douse', Mayer wriggled and wrestled like a caged predator in his attempt to escape the groping fingers of light, before finally eluding the Mosquito crew's attentions. The Mosquito dived onto the fleeing Junkers, which steadied into a mild, drunken weaving, and fired a burst of machine-gun fire into the bomber from 200 yards astern. It caught fire in the left wing root and engine, and flames appeared. Encouraged, Bunting again took aim and gave the Ju 88A-4 another burst from 300 yards. Bunting's camera gun recorded the image of the aircraft turning over on its back and commencing its flaming death-dive over Suffolk. What it could not capture was the resulting crash, a split second later, at Blacklands Hall, Cavendish, in Suffolk, where the bomber's fuel tanks exploded and its engines buried themselves deep into the soil. *Feldwebel* K. Maser and *Feldwebel* Karl-Heinz Elmhorst had baled out and were taken prisoner. Mayer and *Oberfeldwebel* W. Szyska died in the crash.[12]

Meanwhile, Bunting and Reed orbited the scene of their 'kill' and were then Gauntletted south-east. Reed reported 'Window', and they eventually made contact at 3¾ miles' range. Bunting closed fairly fast to 4,000 ft when searchlights suddenly illuminated him again. They obtained a 'douse', but the enemy aircraft, a Ju 188E-1 of 2./KG6 flown by *Leutnant* G. Lahl, had begun very violent evasive action. They nearly overshot beneath him, although the Mosquito was only doing 130 mph IAS. Lahl peeled off to port; Bunting turned hard left. Reed regained contact on his AI VIII at about 4,000 ft and followed him on his scope. They pursued Lahl through a hard, climbing turn to the right, and Bunting took a quick shot at 300 yards, but he could not get on enough deflection and his shots missed. The two adversaries gyrated in tight turns and another steep climb before Bunting got into the favoured astern position. Peering through his gunsight with its diffuser, he repeatedly pumped short bursts into the 188 from 250 yards. It dived, hit the ground and exploded near Butler's Farm at Shopland, Essex, shortly after 0110 hours.[13]

Another Ju 188E-1, flown by *Unteroffizier* Martin Hanf of 5./KG2, was lost on the night of 24/25 March when it was intercepted over the North Sea by an NF.XVII flown by Flt Lt V.P. Luinthune DFC and Flg Off A.B. Cumbers DFC of 25 Squadron at Coltishall. Strikes, followed by the vivid orange glow of an explosion, signalled the end of the Junkers. Hanf and his four crewmen died in a watery grave forty-five miles south-east of Lowestoft. A total of ten enemy aircraft were claimed destroyed by Mosquitoes that night. Mounting losses – Mosquitoes shot down nine enemy raiders attacking mainly London and Bristol during 23–28 March 1944 – meant that *KG2* had to operate a diversity of types, despite the fact that *Oberst* Dietrich Peltz, 'Attack Leader England', had wanted *KG2* re-equipped with Ju 88s. He disliked the Do 217, which he considered unsuitable for night raids over Britain and more suited for use as a day-bomber over the Eastern Front.

On 13/14 April, 96 Squadron shot down a German raider and on the night of 18/19 April, when the last 'Baby Blitz' raid was made on London, a further eight fell to the Mosquitoes.[14] From 20 to 30 April, Mosquitoes claimed sixteen enemy raiders as *Steinbock* raids were made on Hull, Bristol, Portsmouth and Plymouth using He 177, Ju 188 and Do 217 aircraft. Wg Cdr Edward D. Crew DFC*, CO 96 Squadron, and his navigator, WO W.R. Croysdill, who had destroyed an Me 410 over Brighton, destroyed no fewer than twenty-one V-1s during the period June to September 1944. Chasing flying-bombs was not the tame target practice that many people had thought it would be, and there were quite a few casualties. Crew and Croysdill had the nose of their Mosquito XII split open in an explosion following one attack, but the CO managed to gain enough height to get in over the top of the AA guns of the Anti-Diver belt. He held the barely manageable Mosquito in the air long enough for Croysdill to bale out. They both got down safely, landing near Worthing, although Croysdill slightly damaged his ankle.[15]

Mosquitoes shot down nine raiders on 14/15 May when more than a hundred *Luftwaffe* raiders attacked Bristol. A Ju 188 and three Ju 88s were destroyed on 22 May when Portsmouth was again the target. On 28/29 May, Neatishead GCI directed Wg Cdr Cathcart Wight-Boycott DSO, CO 25 Squadron at Coltishall, and Flt Lt D.W. Reid towards a 'bogey' over the North Sea. It was an Me 410 *Hornisse* of *KG51*, flown by *Feldwebel* Dietrich and *Unteroffizier* Schaknies, which was returning from an intruder mission in the Cambridge area. At 0239 hours Dietrich had attacked a Stirling I of 1657 OCU on approach to Shepherd's Grove. The pilot, Flg Off W.A.C. Yates, and all the crew were killed when it crashed on a dispersal, hitting and badly damaging another Stirling to such an extent that it, too, had to be written off. Dietrich and Schaknies sped off towards the coast and headed home. They did not make it. Wight-Boycott approached the Me 410 almost at sea level and fired a half-second burst into it from 700 ft. Dietrich and Schaknies fell into the sea fifty miles off Cromer. The wreckage could be seen burning on the water from twenty miles away. On 23/24 June he would add a Ju 188 destroyed to his score, and in July he shot down two V-1s. A Ju 188 followed in September 1944 when he shot it down forty miles east of Harwich, but he had to shut down an engine as it had been damaged by debris. This took his total score to seven destroyed, and shortly after this he was awarded a Bar to his DSO.

After a first tour in 219 Squadron, on Beaufighters, Tom Arden had been posted, at the end of May 1944, to 264 Squadron based at Hartford Bridge to crew temporarily with Alan Turner:

> We first flew together on 3 June, just before D-Day, and were immediately right in the thick of it, flying ten night patrols over the beachhead during June. Inevitably, we chased many bogies, which turned out to be Lancasters, Halifaxes, Thunderbolts and many Mosquitoes. On 24 June we took off at 0225 to patrol over the Seine Bay, at low level in very dark conditions under 10/10 cloud. We had four interceptions in three hours. One was a friendly Mosquito and two got away by diving low over the sea. Another we closed to visual range of about 1,000 ft, but Alan told me it looked odd and he

needed me to check recognition. It took a few seconds to dim down the AI and look out into almost full darkness. It was a Ju 188, a new modification of the 88, with longer wings and pointed tips. Unfortunately we had taken too long and suddenly he peeled off before Alan could shoot. It was unsatisfactory – we must do better.

On 28 June we did. Taking off again at 0225, we patrolled over the bay between Cherbourg and Le Havre. After an hour without any action we saw green tracer rising vertically from a German base at the mouth of the Seine. This was known to be a *Luftwaffe* navigation aid to bombers, so we turned towards it. Immediately the little cathode-ray tube of the AI set became swamped with echoes. This was Window, the first time we had encountered it, and it appeared impossible to use the set. We flew to the tracer and turned hard onto 280°, the course he would probably be taking to the shipping. The screen was still covered with echoes, which appeared to be aircraft flying towards us from about two miles ahead. Beyond that distance, the screen was clearer and it became possible to concentrate attention on one blip, which moved less than the others. It must be an echo from a plane dropping the Window to prevent it being followed by a British night-fighter. With considerable difficulty we worked our way through the Window until the target could be clearly seen, with small bundles dropping from it every few seconds and dispersing into the slipstream. It was another Junkers 188, which was destroyed by one burst from the four cannon of the Mossie.

The task went on, and a few minutes later I had another contact, which we chased and identified as a Mosquito. That was the end of our night's work. As we set course for base, dawn rose and we looked down on the hundreds of Allied ships, anchored in safety in the bay, covered by the dawn patrol of Hurricanes coming in to take our place.

In July 264 was taken off the beachhead work to try to tackle 'Divers', the name given to the V-1s at that time. London was being bombarded and the citizens were beginning to panic.[16] The day-fighters could deal with them fairly easily, but a Mossie at night was not a good weapon. We had to fly at about 8,000 ft over Kent, and when you saw the light of a Doodlebug heading for London you dived down on it, to build up an airspeed of about 480 mph. Mostly we went wrong by flying towards the light, whereas it was necessary to work out where it was going and head that way. Again and again we would all finish the dive about half a mile behind, with no chance of catching up once the dive speed had dropped off. On 21 July Alan and I judged it right for once. We came down behind the bomb at about 500 ft and 500 mph – fired – saw strikes and flipped over on our back due to a warp in the starboard wing! We knew that HK473 had a tendency to try to roll when flying fast, but this was overdoing it a bit. All the same, it was a very good aircraft and Alan and I did a lot of ops in it.[17]

Incredible as it now seems, RAF Mosquito interceptor crews were not apprised of the coming V-1 threat. Flt Lt R.W. 'Dickie' Leggett, who with Flg Off Egbert J. 'Midi' Midlane was stationed at Hurn, near Bournemouth, explains:

> It is absolutely absurd to think that here we were in a front-line squadron [418] and we hadn't been briefed about 'buzz bombs'. On the night of 18/19 June we had just done a normal routine patrol, had landed and were refuelling, when we were intercepted and told to hurry up and get off again to intercept some 'pilotless aircraft'! We were very disbelieving and said some pretty rude things to the IO. We were put on patrol by a GCI station at about 1,500–2,000 ft. It was still dark. After about forty-five minutes of absolute boredom (we were already pretty fed up after the previous two- to three-hour patrol, where nothing had happened), everything happened at once! The GCI station got a contact. At the same time this device with this great big flame came within 300 ft, going across at 90° to us. We were worried and awake. I turned the aircraft around as best I could and my navigator immediately got a contact on his radar. We were cruising at around 220 mph. I immediately put on full throttle, but of course this thing' was doing 400 mph+ and left us looking rather stupid! We took a great interest for another hour or so, but no more came along so we went back and reported what we'd seen. We were furious at not being briefed.

The first V-1 destroyed by a Mosquito was launched on 14/15 June 1944, and fell to Flt Lt Rayne Schultz DFC, who was on a freelance sortie over the sea when he was passed by a 'queer aircraft' flying in the opposite direction. Schultz, who had scored his sixth victory on 10/11 April, when he downed a Ju 188, turned and gave chase, going through the 'gate' as he did so, and shot it down. He flew straight into the debris and returned to Manston with little skin left on his Mosquito. Ben Johnson, a Fitter IIE, recalls:

> Both engines later had to be changed. Within a matter of about two weeks, every aircraft was u/s as engines were swapped for American Packard-built engines, which took about fifteen hours per 'kite'. We were sent some WAAFs to help out, but with the restrictions on what they were allowed to do, it only made for harder work to keep to our targets. Just prior to this, all Rolls-Royce engines had to have the Sun wheels in the reduction gears changed.

Schultz was posted to 54 OTU as an instructor in June, moving to 51 OTU in July.

On 25 June 1944, 85 and 157 Squadrons in 100 Group were switched to anti-Diver patrols. (By the start of 1945 85 Squadron was still using AI VIII radar sets, but at least its Mosquitoes were made more powerful, with the injection of nitrous oxide (better known as 'laughing gas') with petrol, to give the added power needed to catch the V-1s.) They operated against the 'Doodlebugs' until 20 August, when both squadrons resumed bomber support duties from Swannington. Flt Lt 'Dickie' Leggett recalls:

> The anti-Diver patrols were a free-for-all. You had to dive down on these things at an enormous rate of knots – absolutely flat-out – and do the best you could. There was no real control about it. (Our XVII didn't have the power of the Mosquitoes with injection.) Because it was a free-for-all, when we got close, to avoid collision with other night-fighter chaps going in, we were briefed to switch on our navigation lights. Colliding with another aircraft was embarrassing. However, all the Fw 190s had to do was hover around, knowing some fool would have his nav lights on. It was a fairly obvious cat-and-mouse game. Chaps didn't come back from these V-1 things – a couple of friends in particular. It is my opinion they rather stupidly put on their nav lights, lined up and got one up the backside from an Fw 190. Easy! This was all part of the anti-Diver game. I could see the other aircraft coming in with their lights on. Very useful for me to see them, but I wasn't going to put my nav lights on, and I didn't bother to tell them!

By the end of June 1944, 605 Squadron had shot down thirty-six 'Doodlebugs', and in July the squadron destroyed a further twenty-nine. One of its pilots was Flt Lt Brian 'Scruffy' Williams. On 6/7 July 1944 Williams and WO S.F. Hardy took off at 0145 hours to carry out a Diver patrol. In all, they saw eight V-1s. At 0205 hours Williams attacked and destroyed the first of three, eight miles south of Dungeness at 6,000 ft. His second 'Doodlebug' exploded after a burst from 500 yards astern, five miles north-north-west of Le Touquet, and the third exploded fifteen miles east of Dungeness. On 18 August Brian Williams sighted a group of eight 'Doodlebugs' crossing the French coast between Le Touquet and Boulogne at 2,000 ft. He attacked and shot down two. He exploded the first with a short burst from dead astern, about four miles off Dungeness, and he destroyed the second with two short bursts from astern and slightly above, about ten miles north-west of Le Touquet.

For four weeks starting on 28 June 1944, 125 Squadron and six Northrop P-61 Black Widows of the Scorton-based 422nd and 425th Night Fighter Squadrons, 9th Air Force, carried out comparative night-fighter trials from Hurn. (A further detachment also operated from Ford, starting on 15 July, against V-1s). The two P-61 squadrons, the only ones to operate in Europe during the Second World War, had arrived in England during March–June 1944, being based originally at Charmy Down. Flt Lt 'Dickie' Leggett recalls the arrival of the gloss-black aircraft and their crews, who were commanded by Col Winston W. Kratz of the 481st Night Fighter Operational Training Group:

> They were super aircraft and the Americans were great chaps, but we pulled their legs unmercifully because they'd had no luck in shooting down any enemy aircraft. They were unlucky. Personally, I believe it was because they did not have the opportunity, background or feeling for this war. It was not something that could be learned in the classroom. They were not teams like we were in the Mosquito, where a pilot and navigator were an entity.

On 5 July an NF.XVII flown by Sqn Ldr Eric Barwell DFC of 125 Squadron[18] flew a combat evaluation demonstration at Hurn against Lt Donald J. Doyle. The P-61 proved faster at 5,000 ft, 10,000ft, 15,000 ft and 20,000 ft, out-turning the Mosquito at every altitude by a big margin. The P-61 also far surpassed the Mosquito in rate of climb. The Americans concluded, 'We could go faster and slower, up or down. Faster than the pride of the British – a most enjoyable afternoon.' Flt Lt 'Dickie' Leggett, who also flew a mock combat exercise in daylight with the P-61, confirms its speed advantage:

> We started at 1,000 ft and had a formal dogfight, getting GCI to set us up about twenty miles apart. We intercepted each other using our AIs. Then we climbed at 5,000 ft intervals to gaps until we reached 30,000 ft. My navigator made notes. Although I outmanoeuvred the Black Widow, it was slightly embarrassing at our 5,000 ft gaps to find it always seemed to be waiting for me. His engines were more powerful. This gave him an extra advantage in the rate of climb, but, surprisingly, not in manoeuvrability.

On 15 July the 422nd NFS flew the first P-61 operation from England, and on the very next night scored the first 'kill' when it downed a V-1. On 5 August the 425th NFS shot down a V-1, and two days later the 422nd got its first manned aircraft. (The 425th had to wait until Christmas Eve 1944 before it got its first manned aircraft 'kill'.) 'Dickie' Leggett concludes:

> We had so many night-fighters messing about we often spent the night chasing our chums, especially if the IFF was not turned on. As there were normally about a hundred Mosquitoes and twenty Germans, the 'bogey' nearly always turned out to be a Mosquito.

Black Widow crews were keen to fire. They were so trigger-happy that it became embarrassing. Much later, I heard one 'kill' on my R/T one night. He fired, then I heard him claiming a 410. 'I've hit it! It's on fire! It's going down in flames!' Then I heard the RAF pilot's voice say, 'He missed by at least six feet! I'm not hit. I'm not going down in flames!' It was a Mosquito!

By September the Allied advance had overrun launching-sites in the Pas de Calais, but in July the *Luftwaffe* had begun mounting a new terror blitz from the skies by air-launching 'Doodlebugs' from aircraft over the North Sea. In 1943 experiments at the German research establishment at Peenemünde on the Baltic coast, where V-2 rockets were being built and tested, resulted in several He 111s being modified to H-22 standard to carry a V-1 under the wing. By the end of August 258 V-1s had been air-launched against England, about ninety of them against London. All were fired from Heinkel He 111s of *III./KG3* based at Venlo and Gilze Rijen in Holland. Normally, the Heinkels took off at night, flew low over the North Sea to evade radar and climbed to 1,475 ft before firing their missiles from approximately fifty miles offshore. In September 1944, when 177 flying bombs were air-launched on thirteen nights, the Allied advance forced *III./KG3* to abandon its bases in Holland and move to airfields in Germany.[19]

Apart from AA guns, only the radar-equipped Mosquito XIIs, XVIIs and XXXs of 125 (Newfoundland), 25, 68, 456 RAAF and 307 Squadrons[20] and Tempest V night-fighters operating in concert with ground radar stations were able to counter the new threat. At first the primary mission of 25 and 125 Squadrons was to find and destroy the Heinkel carrier aircraft, but air-launched Doodlebugs heading for England were also engaged when the opportunity presented itself. At Castle Camps, 68 Squadron's XIX crews were tasked to intercept V-1s between the launching zone and the coast. (After mid-November Mosquito crews were instructed to ignore flying-bombs and to concentrate on shooting down the Heinkel carriers). On the night of 23/24 September, when fifteen Heinkel carriers launched V-1s against England, a Doodlebug was shot down over the North Sea by Flt Lt Johnny Limbert and Flg Off H.S. Cook of 25 Squadron, but the Mosquito crew failed to return. It was raining hard and the cloud base was low the following night when sixteen Heinkels air-launched V-1s again. Over Holland Wg Cdr L.J.C. Mitchell and Flt Lt D.L. Cox of 25 Squadron at Coltishall obtained a visual sighting of a Heinkel and scored hits on the starboard wing root, but the enemy machine escaped into thick cloud at 1,000 ft. On 25/26 September the first He 111H22 to be brought down by a Mosquito occurred when WO Fitchett and Flt Sgt Hardy of 409 'Nighthawk' Squadron RCAF in 2nd TAF in a Mk XIII claimed a Heinkel over the North Sea.

On the night of 28/29 September, 25 Squadron at Coltishall was successful. An NF.XVII flown by Wg Cdr Mitchell, and Flt Lt Cox operating the AI X, took off at 0055 hours to intercept some anticipated 'trade' over the North Sea. At 3,500 ft, forty miles east of Great Yarmouth, they saw a V-1 being launched from a Heinkel. Mitchell carried out a diving turn on the enemy machine. At the same time Greyfriars control, an American-operated CHL with a superior range and GCI capacity, informed them that the Heinkel was also turning to port. Mitchell lost height to 600 ft in a turn and Cox made contact at 2½ miles' range. Mitchell closed at 200 ft above the sea and obtained a visual at 1,300 ft. Cox raised his night glasses and confirmed the 'bogey' as an He 111H22. Mitchell gave it a short burst from 400 ft dead astern. It exploded, flinging debris into the night sky and into the path of the onrushing Mosquito. Mitchell yanked the stick hard right and then turned back to see the German aircraft crash in flames into the sea, where it burned for two or three minutes before sinking beneath the dark waters.

Mitchell and Cox returned to their patrol line and saw another V-1 being launched. Losing height, Mitchell sped off after the Doodlebug, informing Greyfriars control of his bearing. They vectored him towards the source of the launch. Cox eventually obtained contact on a converging course. He waited patiently until the range closed to about one mile, and then carried out a hard turn to port, so as to close in behind the enemy machine. The Mosquito lost height to 150 ft and pounded over the waves at 220 mph as the Heinkel sailed along at a leisurely 180–190 mph, seemingly oblivious to its imminent demise. At 1,500 ft range the Mosquito crew got their visual confirmation that it was an He 111. Mitchell let loose with a short burst from 600 ft. Pieces flew off the He 111's right wing, and Mitchell added to its misery with another short burst, this time from 400 ft. The port engine burst into flames and the Heinkel crashed in flames into the sea. Mitchell searched for survivors until 0615 hours, but his action had been total.

On the night of 5/6 October, when there was broken cloud from a base of about 2,000 ft, twelve Heinkels were tasked with air-launching V-1s against England after moonset. One of them, a Heinkel 111 of *8./KG3*, which developed engine trouble, crashed in the sea about fifty miles off Great Yarmouth, and two other carriers were lost after a mid-air collision over Holland. At Coltishall seven of 25 Squadron's Mosquitoes were dispatched, and Flt Lt J.R.F. Jones and Flg Off R. Skinner returned successful. Under Greyfriars control they obtained an airborne radar contact to starboard and below them. Jones turned and closed in a stern chase, and at 800 yards the crew saw the Heinkel release a V-1. A visual sighting was obtained against a dark sky as the Heinkel He 111H-22 began weaving and losing height. Jones opened fire from 800 ft and again from 600 ft, stringing the enemy machine's fuselage and starboard wing root before he overshot the enemy at 160 mph. The Mosquito crew saw a large fire on the water at the position of last contact. The squadron added to this success with another victory on the night of 6/7 October, when Flt Lt Alfred Marshall DFC DFM and Flg Off C.A. Allen attacked another Heinkel forty miles south of Southwold and 'blew it to pieces'.[21] Flt Lt H. Humphreys and Flg Off P. Robertson of 68 Squadron brought down a V-1 by using the slipstream of their aircraft to upset the gyro control. Humphreys did the same a night later to bring down one of two V-1s they destroyed over the sea.

On the night of 14/15 October Flg Off J.H. Haskell and Plt Off J. Bentley of 68 Squadron saw two air-launched V-1s on a south-westerly course during a patrol from Castle Camps. Closing to 300 yards, Haskell fired three bursts at the first V-1, which was at 1,500 ft and 340 mph, and saw 'the light go out'. The second V-1 was coming up behind the first at 900 ft and 280 mph. Haskell fired at it head-on, but with no result. He changed direction and closed, firing from a closer range, sending the Diver down into the sea. Two nights later Wg Cdr G. Howden and Flg Off Baker of 68 Squadron witnessed a successful launch of a V-1 when they made contact with a Heinkel about fifty miles east of Lowestoft. Baker reported that the contact was ahead of them at an estimated 3,000 ft. Howden chased the contact at 1,100 ft and then gained height from astern until at 300 yards they obtained a visual sighting under a dark cloud. Still uncertain as to its identity, Howden closed to about 150 yards, whereupon a huge flash and a flame appeared, gradually, diminishing in about five or ten seconds, by which time the flying-bomb had dropped several hundred feet and proceeded normally. The He 111H-22 broke upwards to port at the moment of release. To avoid a collision with the flying-bomb, Howden turned violently to starboard and dived. Contact was not regained. Of the seven V-1s launched, only one evaded the defences.[22]

Visibility was fair, with some haze below and cloud cover above 3,000 ft, on the night of 19/20 October, when twenty-five flying-bombs were air-launched from over the North Sea. Four Mosquito crews succeeded in destroying five of them. WO D. Lauchlan and Flt Lt F. Bailey of 68 Squadron destroyed two of the Divers, and Flt Sgt A. Bullus and Flg Off L.W. Edwards and Flg Off G.T. Gibson and Sgt B.M. Lack got another two V-1s. Flt Lt 'Dickie' Leggett and Flg Off 'Midi' Midlane, now with 125 (Newfoundland) Squadron at Coltishall, got the fifth V-1. Only one of the twenty-five air-launched V-1s evaded the British ground and air defences that night. Flt Lts R.M. Carr and J.S. Saunderson of 25 Squadron saw five launches take place from low level, three of which went straight into the sea. Four nights later, when thirteen V-1s were air-launched in cloudy, slightly hazy weather, Sqn Ldr J.D. Wright and Flg Off J. McCulloch of 68 Squadron repeated Haskell's success by shooting down two of the V-1s. The AA defences shot down four more. There was patchy cloud with a base of 500 ft on the night of 25/26 October when twelve V-1s were launched. Sqn Ldr M.J. Mansfield and Flt Lt S.A. Janacek took 68 Squadron's monthly V-1 total to twelve, and an unidentified crew destroyed another air-launched V-1. Flg Offs W.A. Beadle and R.A. Pargeter of 125 Squadron destroyed a Heinkel of 2 *Staffel, KG53 Legion Kondor* piloted by *Oberfeldwebel* Othmar Hammerce.[23]

There was heavy cloud above a base of about 600 ft, and scattered rainstorms, on the night of 30/31 October when Sqn Ldr L.W.G. Gill and his navigator, Flt Lt D.A. Haigh, took off from Coltishall at 0725 hours in an NF.XVII. Hopton control vectored them at full speed towards some 'trade' reported to the east. Contact was obtained at 2½ miles' range, and Haigh instructed Gill to turn hard right. At 7,000 ft range they obtained a contact again. Gill got a fleeting glimpse of the Heinkel as it passed above them on the opposite vector. He closed rapidly to 4,000 ft and started to get fleeting sightings of the bomber as it passed through broken cloud. By now the Heinkel had released its flying-bombs and was turning left and starting to descend slightly. Gill closed range rapidly to 1,000 ft and opened fire with a long burst. Haigh and Gill saw the shells hit home around the right engine and fuselage, and pieces of debris scattered in all directions as the Heinkel dropped like a winged bird. Gill gave it another burst and saw hits strike the tail. Gill was now overshooting, so he broke away. To his chagrin, the Heinkel went down to sea level, straightened out and climbed slowly, frantically seeking cover in the cloud. It was a futile gesture; cloud was no hiding place for a searching AI X radar and its trained operator. Haigh busily operated his AI set until he regained contact with the fleeing Heinkel at 4,000 ft range. Gill closed in, determined to finish off the Heinkel once and for all. In desperation *Feldwebel* Theodore Warwas, the pilot of the 4./KG53 machine, carried out violent evasive action and climbed slightly, with one of his Jumo 211 engines smoking. Gill mercilessly pumped another long burst into its sides from 1,000 ft. This time the German aircraft floundered, caught fire and went straight down into the sea. Eleven minutes later Gill and Haigh carried out an attack on another He 111H-22. Although Gill obtained strikes before his ammunition ran out, he and his navigator were unable to confirm if it had crashed into the sea because of the 600 ft cloud base and prevailing scattered heavy rainstorms in the area. Gill and Haigh were credited with a 'damaged' to go with their earlier He 111 'kill'.

Despite the losses during October, I./KG53 (III./KG3 redesignated) was joined by II./KG53 and III./KG53 for further air-launching of V-1s. On the night of 5/6 November, in poor weather conditions, with dense cloud above 2,300 ft, twenty-seven V-1s were air-launched against England, many of them straying south of London on a strong wind. Two Heinkels failed to return, one of them the result of an accident, and the other a successful interception[24] carried out by a 68 Squadron NF.XIX fitted with AI X and piloted by Flt Sgt L.W. Neal, which took off from Coltishall to intercept incoming 'trade' over the North Sea. Flt Sgt E. Eastwood, his navigator, obtained a contact at 1½ miles' range, flying at an altitude of

1,000 ft. Cloud was 10/10ths at 2,300 ft, but Neal and Eastwood had no difficulty finding the V-1 launcher, which was travelling at 150 mph. Neal dropped to 1,000 ft, closing to 2,500 ft range, but flying at 160 mph indicated, he overshot and returned to patrol. They picked up contact again at two miles and closed to 1,000 ft, and then 500 ft, Neal lowering the undercarriage and flaps to prevent overshooting. At 1,500 ft altitude they watched the He 111 release a flying-bomb, which caused Neal to lose his night vision temporarily in the glare of the pulse jet. For twenty to thirty seconds the Heinkel flew straight and level following in the path of the V-1, before gradually losing height and turning hard to starboard. The two sergeants followed on AI and obtained a visual at about 200 yd range, 900 ft altitude. The Heinkel was silhouetted against the cloud, illuminated by the flames from the flying-bomb's pulse jet. Neal gave the enemy bomber a two-second burst at high deflection, and the aircraft dived steeply to starboard and crashed into the North Sea. A red glow was visible for fifteen miles, and the destruction was confirmed later by a fishing-boat in the area.

On the night of 8/9 November, when thirty-two V-1s were air-launched over the North Sea, Flg Off J.E. Ledwidge and WO C.A. Bonner of 68 Squadron shot down two of the missiles, many of which strayed over Kent because of 38 mph winds. On the night following, the winds were even stronger (41 mph), and eleven of the twenty-nine V-1s launched were abortive. Ten of the missiles were destroyed over the sea, Plt Offs D.J. Carter and W.J. Hutchings of 25 Squadron getting two of them. They followed this with the downing of another V-1 on the night of the 10/11th, when patchy cloud, occasional rain and a wind speed down to 23 mph were good conditions for an attack. *KG53* carried out the heaviest raid of the entire air-launched flying-bomb campaign with two separate attacks, the first beginning about two hours after sunset, at 1922 hours. In total, forty-eight flying-bombs were launched, of which fifteen aborted. AA gunners shot down twenty-five of the thirty-three V-1s that approached the coast.[25]. Mosquitoes of 68, 125 and 25 Squadrons were also successful, 125 Squadron at Coltishall dispatching a Mosquito at 1825 hours to intercept a contact over the North Sea. Flt Lt G.F. Simcock and his navigator, Flg Off N. Eric Heijne, took off in their NF.XVII, callsign Goodwill 27, and were vectored first by Neatishead GCI and then Hopton CHEL. Simcock wrote later:

> I saw what proved to be flying bombs being released, and asked Hopton if any information available. Control had no information so turned in direction of flying-bombs. We obtained a contact on target crossing from starboard to port, going east, but Hopton turned us away from this and then back towards it again. As we were turning back, I saw, slightly behind us, a Heinkel 111 by the light of its flying-bomb. Turned towards it and obtained contact at three miles

range, our height being 1,000 ft and target's about 1,500. Target did a wide turn to port and slowly lost height to 200 ft, approx. ASI 200. Followed on AI through heavy shower and closed in, getting visual at 800 ft. Target was then down to 150 ft, ASI 150. I originally intended to shadow e/a on AI hoping that he would gain height on approaching coast, but as there was more dirty weather ahead, decided to open fire at once rather than risk losing contact. Opened fire with a long burst at 600 ft, closing to 400 ft approximately. Target then at 100 ft height. Many strikes were seen on port engine and port wing root and port side of fuselage. There was a large whitish-yellow flash from the port engine and a large piece flew back from it. My observer reported seeing another flash from the port side of the fuselage, but I did not see this. E/a immediately slowed down and went into a steep port bank. I had to break away – ASI then 140 – to avoid collision. Broke to starboard and then turned back to port again and attempted to regain contact. We searched area thoroughly at about 75 ft, scanning up, but no contact obtained. The sea was very rough with 'white horses' and it was extremely dark, so consider it unlikely, as it was not on fire, that I would be able to see it hit the sea.

Although Simcock was only able to claim the Heinkel 111 as 'probably' destroyed, their victim, a Heinkel 111 of *Gruppe Stab I./KG53*,[26] was shot down. What is more, the all-out raids this night by *KG53* cost them three Heinkels.

At 0130 hours a second Heinkel[27] was shot down by Flt Lt Douglas Greaves DFC and Flg Off F. Milton Robbins DFC of 25 Squadron under Bawdsey CCI. They obtained a sighting of the enemy aircraft at 200 ft, and Greaves opened fire with a long burst from dead astern. The Mosquito crew saw strikes, which were followed by a sheet of flame about the starboard engine and wing root. Wreckage was left burning on the sea in the Thames Estuary area when the Mosquito resumed its patrol. It was the pairing's ninth victory of the war, and they had also scored a probable and one damaged.[28]

Twenty-five minutes later a second 4 *Staffel* machine[29] was shot down by Flt Sgt A.R. Brooking and Plt Off R.B. Finn of 68 Squadron. They saw four V-1s released, and Finn obtained an AI contact flying at 700 ft with a speed of 180 mph. This led to a visual sighting at 1,200 ft. Flying through patchy cloud, Brooking closed to 600 ft and opened fire. The crew saw hits, pieces flew off the starboard wing root and fuselage and a glow of burning was visible inside the fuselage. Brooking broke off the combat to avoid flying wreckage, and a few seconds later he and Finn saw the Heinkel burning on the sea.

On the night of 14/15 November *KG53* launched thirty-seven missiles during three attacks from off the coast of Lowestoft, Bawdsey and to the south of these two places. Weather conditions were poor with low cloud over the North Sea, rain, sleet and snow. In all, eleven V-1s got through the defences and eight reached London. Off Southwold the AA defences shot down a Mosquito of 25 Squadron flown by Wg Cdr W.J. Mitchell and Flt Lt D.L. Cox while they were returning short of fuel, and the aircraft crashed in a field east of Thetford Norfolk after the crew had baled out. Mitchell sprained his ankle. A second Mosquito, an NF.XVII, callsign 'Ferro 17', crewed by two US naval airmen, Lt Joseph F. Black and Lt Thomas N. Aiken, attached to 68 Squadron, took off from Coltishall. A very short time later ground controllers at Neatishead warned them of an approaching enemy aircraft. Black turned the Mosquito onto the interception course as relayed by the ground controller, and shortly afterwards Aiken made contact on his AI set with the Heinkel, which they saw release a V-1 before they could close with it. Black and Aiken ignored the enemy bomber and chased the Diver into the AA gun strip, where they too were shot down. The Diver fell harmlessly south-west of Berkhampstead in Hertfordshire. The Mosquito crashed in a field at Home Farm, Somerleyton, eighteen miles from Lowestoft, and both Americans were killed. Joe Black was due to marry his English fiancée, Nancy Annan, a WREN who had worked at Bletchley Park on the top-secret Ultra Project. Both airmen were posthumously awarded the US Air Medal and the Purple Heart.[30]

On the night of 17/18 November, 456 Squadron RAAF at Ford in Sussex flew anti-Diver patrols for the first time, sending five Mosquitoes on sorties to just off the Dutch coast. Two nights later a 456 Squadron RAAF NF.XVII flown by Flg Off D.W. Arnold and his navigator, Flg Off J.B. Stickley, chased and finally caught up with an He 111 seventy-five miles east of Lowestoft. Their quarry was a Heinkel 111H-16[31] of *5./KG53* flown by *Feldwebel* Rudolf Ripper. Arnold fired his cannon from 400 yards. Ripper's ventral gunner returned fire, hitting the Mosquito in the right propeller. Debris embedded itself in the leading edge of the right wing. As the Heinkel turned away, Arnold fired another burst and the starboard engine caught fire. He fired a third burst. Climbing suddenly to 1,200 ft, the still burning He 111 started to break up before falling over to the right in a stall turn into the Zuider Zee. The waves almost immediately snuffed out the shower of sparks and doused the flames. On the night of 22/23 November, WO J.L. Mulholland and Flg Off J.D. James of 456 Squadron RAAF chased a Heinkel, which they saw launch a V-1 from under its port wing. The Mosquito crew did not break off the chase until they were twenty miles into Holland, when bad weather finally forced them to abort and return to Ford. The night following, Mulholland and James failed to return from their patrol after chasing their quarry down to 50 ft off the sea.

Another 456 Squadron RAAF crew, Flg Off F.S. Stevens and his observer, W.A.H. Kellett, chased their quarry, a Heinkel 111 of *I./KG53*,[32] to within ten miles west of Texel in the early dawn of 25 November. They took off from Ford at 0625 hours, and the two Australians saw four bright flashes on the horizon about 1,000 ft below them. Stevens dived to 1,500 ft, and Kellett obtained two contacts at about two miles' range. They chose the nearest blip, which appeared to be taking evasive action and was flying east, back to Holland. Stevens dived the Mosquito until he was just 500 ft above the sea, then set off in pursuit. The He 111 settled onto a course for home at 500 ft, changing height every now and again and weaving continuously. Kellett's C-scope had malfunctioned, so very slowly Stevens closed the gap between them and the retreating Heinkel until they could see the enemy machine just 800 ft in the distance. All at once the Heinkel turned violently to starboard. Stevens carried out a half-orbit and contact was immediately regained. There was no cloud but it was very dark, and the two Australians had difficulty making out the fleeing bomber. There was no mistaking its return fire, though. Twice the Heinkel's gunners opened up from 800 ft, but Stevens bravely closed in still further, to 600 ft and they were able to identify it positively as an He 111. It was flying at 900 ft. Stevens opened fire with a two-second burst from his cannon, and the enemy's left engine immediately burst into flames. He closed to 150 ft, a second two-second burst going right through the fuselage, which erupted in flames, illuminating the peculiar dull light grey tailfin with its evil black swastika outlined in white. Stevens broke to starboard. The flaming torch fell, shedding a dozen or so bright green incandescent balls in its fiery wake before it hit the water about ten miles west of Texel.

The *Luftwaffe*'s air-launched Diver offensive tailed off considerably in December, and for the first two weeks of the month interceptions were non-existent. After a four-night pause *KG53* launched forty-five V-1s thirty miles off the Norfolk coast on the night of 17/18 December. It was cold with little wind and heavy cloud cover, and visibility over the North Sea was poor. In the early morning a Mosquito (callsign Goodwill 4), flown by Plt Off K.D. 'Denny' Goodyear and Plt Off J. Burrows of 125 Squadron from Coltishall, was patrolling under control from Hopton, a Chain Home Low Station on the Suffolk coast near Great Yarmouth. At 0610 hours Goodwill 4 was vectored towards three He 111H-22s at a range of 2½ to three miles. After about eight minutes one of the Heinkels broke away to starboard and Goodyear followed. In an attempt to evade the pursuing Mosquito, the Heinkel pilot began to climb and then dive, all to no avail. With daylight now on their side, the Mosquito crew visually identified the Heinkel from 1,000 ft. Closing fast, Goodyear opened fire from below and astern. He and his navigator witnessed the resulting flash from the Heinkel's starboard engine. The enemy machine dived from an altitude of 700 ft to 300 ft in a matter of seconds, and then climbed up steeply to between 5,000 and 6,000 ft with the Mosquito close on its tail. At a range of 200 yards Goodyear could see the white glow of an intense fire burning in the engine he had hit. He opened fired again, but within seconds his Mosquito went into a violent, uncontrollable spiral as the aircraft flew through the slipstream of the Heinkel, and he only managed to regain control just 200 ft above the icy waters of the North Sea. So violent was the encounter that the 'G' force had broken loose a large part of the radar equipment in the nose of his Mosquito. This in turn had rendered the electrical system to his guns useless, putting them all out of commission. It would have been futile for Goodyear and Burrows to continue the pursuit, so they returned to Coltishall and claimed one Heinkel 'probably destroyed'.

At 0550 hours on 23 December, 'Dickie' Leggett and 'Midi' Midlane, now back in Norfolk after their stint at Hurn, took off from Coltishall in their NF.XVII, callsign Goodwill 37. They knew they would soon find some 'trade' over the North Sea. Leggett explains:

> The British 'Y' Service would get information that V-1-carrying Heinkels would be taking off and we'd be told that at such and such a time they would be in place. No other op was as tidy as this. We looked at our watches and thought, 'My goodness, they'll be here in another few minutes', and sure enough, right on the button, it would all happen. It was a question of whether you'd be the lucky one, because there were lots of us. I looked at my clock and knew that at around 0230 hours there would be several Heinkels in the usual place. The enemy obviously did not know we were going to meet him. Being in a position to stab him in the back in the dark was a nice way to fight a war. One was mentally tuned to this. We felt sorry for our bomber chaps. We in the night-fighter force didn't have to drop bombs on women and children. We had to kill Germans who were trying to do things to our women and children with nasty weapons. It was a very clear and clean way to fight. Sure enough, almost on the dot we saw the flash of a V-1 being launched. At the same time ground control said they had contact. Tally-ho!
>
> There might be twelve, thirteen, fourteen of these Heinkels, all doing it at once. It was a timed op. Then they'd turn to port. I don't know why, but they always did this. Then they would go down very rapidly and head for home. Our job was to lose height quickly, go below 100 ft and pick up the Heinkel. The Mk X was a good AI, but there were a lot of sea returns and it depended on the expertise of the navigator. I had a very good one. Sure enough, the Heinkel turned left and at two to three miles we got a contact. It wasn't a good night. There was rain and 'stuff' about. The Germans only came when the weather was bad.

'Dickie' Leggett took off after the Heinkel, using his highly accurate radio altimeter to maintain position and height behind the fleeing German.

On The Defensive Again

We started to close. It was still dark and there was a lot of cloud. You knew perfectly well that on our straight and level course behind him we would get a tremendous wash from his engines. I felt it. Then for some reason, he started to turn away slightly, as if he had an indication that we were behind him. It foxed us a bit. Eventually, it settled down again. I closed in on him. It was in cloud. Guns and sights were harmonized at about 200 yards but we could not get a visual, although we could feel his slipstream. We dropped away and my navigator picked up contact again. Some people might have lowered their undercarriage at this point, but I didn't like to. I had as much flap as I dared and managed perfectly well. We waited and we waited. Off Den Helder I was getting concerned. We'd followed him for fully fifty-five minutes. We waited as patiently as one can in this situation, and eventually, as the dawn was coming up, I closed in at 300 yards' range. [The exhaust emissions at 300 ft altitude were from a Heinkel 111H-22 of *7./KG53* flown by *Unteroffizier* Robert Rosch.] I fired my cannon in his slipstream and had to put on a lot of throttle to prevent a stall. I got a number of strikes on it and that was it. The Heinkel went in very quickly. When we broke away the cloud base was only at 200 ft. It was a beautiful morning.

The Heinkel came down in Holland and four of Rosch's crew were killed, but one of the two gunners survived.

Of fifty Fi 103s that were air-launched from Heinkel He 111s against Manchester on Christmas Eve, thirty-one crossed the coast, but only one actually exploded in the city. A 68 Squadron NF.XVII, callsign Ferro 26, and crewed by Flt Sgt A. Bullus and his navigator, Flg Off T.W. Edwards, in charge of the AI X scope, pursued one of the Heinkels under Orby radar control. The Heinkel, which was flown by *Unteroffizier* Herbert Neuber of *7./KG53*, was successfully intercepted over the North Sea, and a visual sighting was obtained. Bullus fired the first of three two-second bursts of 20 mm cannon fire from 200 ft, and his shells struck the starboard wing root, fuselage and port engine. The Heinkel burst into flames, did an uncontrolled climbing turn to port and peeled off into the sea, where it was seen to be on fire for at least five minutes. A second Heinkel, which was attacked by a Mosquito of 125 Squadron over the North Sea, made it back to Holland but crashed on landing at Leck, killing one of the crew and injuring another.[33]

The air-launch Heinkels carried out their last major raid on England on the night of 3/4 January 1945, when forty-five Divers were launched. RAF night-fighter crews made no claims but three Heinkels failed to return. Two nights later a Heinkel of *7./KG53* failed to return. A Heinkel of *9.Staffel* flown by *Hauptmann* Siegfried Jessen, the *Staffel* commander and his crew, was shot down and its occupants killed near Josum airfield by a Mosquito XXX Intruder flown by Wg Cdr Russ Bannock DFC*

RCAF and Flg Off Bob Bruce DFC of 406 'Lynx' Squadron. It was his eighth victory of the war, and his second since taking command of the squadron. On 6 January WO A.R. Brooking and Plt Off R.D. Finn in a Mosquito of 68 Squadron, who failed to return, claimed the last He 111H-22 to fall to RAF guns. On the night of 12/13 January two Mosquito crews of 68 Squadron made contact with a Heinkel of *KG53* but were unable to press home the advantage. The final air-launched flying-bomb attack on England took place the following night, 13/14 January, when twenty-five Divers were launched, though only seven got through.

On 3 January 'Dickie' Leggett and 'Midi' Midlane were sent to the Fighter Interception Development Squadron at Ford to take part in Operation Vapour. Leggett recalls:

> We were pleased to learn that that the 'boffins' were planning a possible answer to the menacing Heinkels and their underslung V-1 missiles. Immediately on arrival we met other night-fighter friends and were quickly ushered into a briefing room to meet the head 'boffin', Mr E.J. Smith. He then introduced us to the captain and crew of a Coastal Command Wellington, which we had noticed on landing, but had no idea of its significance. The Wellington had been equipped as an airborne GCI station, with Mr Smith as radar controller. The Wellington would fly at 50 ft above the surface of the sea and locate 'bogeys', while we Mosquito hounds, flying at 500 ft above the 'Wimpy' at intervals of a mile, would be directed against the V-1-carrying Heinkels.
>
> After several Vapour practice patrols, on 14 January six of us flew to Manston for the first op patrol off the Dutch coast. Our navigators used a 'mother beacon' and the Alto position behind the Wellington at one-mile intervals. The whole 'shooting match' flew a fifty-mile patrol north to south, parallel to the Dutch coast. Intelligence had told us that something was going to happen. Mr Smith put us onto an unidentified aircraft, flying west at about 270° at 100 ft. It was an absolute set-up. Within a few minutes 'Midi' obtained a firm contact on his AI X and took over from Mr Smith. I was ready, excited, and thought, 'This will be easy meat.' Speed was synchronized with the target at 120 mph on a course towards Norfolk at a height of 250 ft. With my gun button set to 'Fire', we struggled through the severe downwash of slipstream from the target and quickly achieved a visual sighting while closing to about 100 yards. To our utter disappointment, the aircraft was a Warwick! In strong language I announced my frustration to Mr Smith, who replied, 'Shoot it down, as it must be hostile.' A fierce argument followed as he explained the target was not responding to IFF, so get on with it! We stupidly nudged closer and closer in an attempt to convince ourselves it was an enemy aircraft. We virtually flew in formation with it, reaffirmed

there was no V-1 missile underslung and that it was a Warwick. I wanted to tell the pilot how lucky he was that I hadn't fired! We were in the wrong position and we missed the Heinkels going out and we missed them coming back! It was the last night they came.

Altogether, about 1,200 V-1s were air-launched against Britain, although of these only 638 approached the coast. *KG53* ceased operations having lost seventy-seven Heinkels, sixteen of them claimed by Mosquitoes.

Notes

1. The *Greif* crashed at Whitmore Vale, near Hindhead, Surrey. Only the tail assembly about three feet forward of the fin survived relatively undamaged. Flg Off C.K. Nowell and Flt Sgt F. Randall of 85 Squadron claimed an He 177 of *2./KG40*.
2. MAA *The Mossie* Vol.11, August 1995.
3. HK454 crashed at Tilty, Essex. 'At the Accident Board of Enquiry I stated that in my opinion, the main spare had broken as we pulled out of the dive. The Investigators and the de Havilland representative both indignantly stated that this was not possible. They implied that Mac had undertaken unauthorized aerobatics, which I strenuously denied. Many years later I was told by a friend, who was qualified to say so, that there had been similar accidents. The cause was found to have been water seepage into the main spar which weakened it to breaking point. On 11 November 1944 with my new pilot Ted Sexsmith we took off from Amiens-Glisy on a routine patrol but soon lost an engine. We were diverted to Brussels, but Ted, making a faster than normal approach, touched down at a much higher speed than normal. We ran off the runway, along the grass for several hundred yards before slowly coming to a halt. Just as we were breathing with relief, bang, we ran into a shell hole, the nose dropped and the aircraft ground looped. We were left hanging in our straps, and when we released ourselves in the pitch darkness, we both crashed through the canopy. I suffered quite a serious gash in the head when coming into contact with a sharp fragment of perspex, which cut through my helmet. As a consequence I again found myself back in hospital for a short time.'
4. By 20/21 February 1944 Mosquito night-fighters had, since the start of 1943, claimed to have shot down just over a hundred *Luftwaffe* raiders.
5. One was a Ju 88A-4 of *8./KG6* downed by Flt Lt Reginald Clive Pargeter and Flt Lt R.L. Fell of 29 Squadron (which claimed six this night) at Withyham, Sussex. A *3./KG100 Greif* was shot down by Flt Lt Peter F.L. Hall and Flg Off R.D. Marriott of 488 Squadron, and it fell at Lamberhurst, Kent.
6. B3+CK; crew all PoW.
7. On 30 March Peter Green was posted to 96 Squadron, claiming one victory and thirteen V-1s shot down while with this unit. On 11 August 1944 he was given command of 219 Squadron in 2nd TAF's 85 Group, and here he teamed with Flt Lt Douglas 'Douggie' Oxby, as his radar

operator. Oxby has been described by Jimmy Rawnsley as ' young, slightly built, with a twinkling almost roguish eye and a keen wit that seemed always just about to bubble over. I could well imagine that in the air his commentary would come rippling over in an exuberant but unflurried stream.' Oxby had already seen service with 89 Squadron in the Mediterranean and had assisted in many successful operations. Operating over Europe the Green-Oxby team achieved considerable success. During the night of 2/3 October 1944 they claimed three Ju 87s shot down over Nijmegen, the award of a DSO for Green following in December. By the end of February 1945 he had added a further five victories, but on 1 March, while testing a Mosquito, he crashed near Amiens and was killed. At the end of the war Oxby was awarded a DSO to add to his DFC and DFM, as the RAF's top-scoring radar operator, having taken part in twenty-one successful interceptions. *Aces High: A Tribute to the Most Notable Fighter Pilots of the British and Commonwealth Forces in WWII*. Christopher Shores and Clive Williams (Grub Street, London, 1994).

8. Becker, *Unteroffiziere* G. Bartolain, A. Lange and G. Göecking and *Oberfeldwebel* H. Litschke were killed.
9. One of two Do 217s of 2./KG2 destroyed was shot down by a Mosquito of 264 Squadron and crashed at Legbourne, Lincolnshire, at 2204 hours. An He 177A-3 of 2./KGI00 was destroyed by a Mosquito of 25 Squadron and crashed into the sea off Skegness at 2146 hours. Two other Ju 88s, one from II./KG54 and a Ju 188 of 2./KG66, crashed into the sea near the Humber Lightship.
10. The AI Mk IX, a British development, was abandoned when the superior American SCR 720 became available. *Confound and Destroy*. Martin Streetly (MacDonald & Janes, 1978)
11. Two Ju 88s of II./KG54 and a Ju 88 of 7./KG6 were lost this night.
12. At around the same time Flt Lt J.A.S. Hall and Flg Off J.P.W. 'Jock' Cairns of 488 Squadron RNZAF shot down a Ju 88A-14 of 8./KG6 from Melsbroek, and it fell on Earls Colne airfield, where the aircraft and one of its 500 kg high-explosive bombs exploded, damaging three B-26 Marauders of the 323rd Bomb Group, US 9th Air Force.
13. Lahl, *Unteroffiziere* J. Fromm and R. Budrat and *Obergefreiter* Schiml were killed. *Unteroffizier* E. Kosch baled out injured and was taken prisoner. Bunting and Phil Reed were both awarded Bars to their DFCs. They destroyed a Ju 88 on 12/13 June and an Fw 190 on 16/17 June. Edward Bunting was shot down and killed by flak on 30 July 1944 while chasing a radar contact over France. Phil Reed was suffering from an attack of influenza and Flg Off E. Spedding, who flew as Bunting's radar operator-navigator, was killed also. Bunting had nine enemy aircraft confirmed destroyed.
14. A 4./KG2 Ju 188E-1 flown by *Hauptmann* Helmuth Eichbaum was shot down off Southwold by Flt Lt R.M. Carr and Flt Lt Saunderson of 25 Squadron at Coltishall. A 5./KG2 Ju 188E-1 piloted by *Feldwebel* Helmuth Richter was shot down by Wg Cdr C.M. Miller DFC, CO 85 Squadron at West Malling. Flg Off S.B Huppert of 410 Squadron RCAF at Hunsdon shot down an He 177 of 3./KG100 flown by *Feldwebel*

Heinz Reis, which fell near Saffron Walden. Two Ju 88s were destroyed by Plt Off Allen and Sqn Ldr Green DFC of 96 Squadron, and its new CO, Wg Cdr Edward D. Crew DFC* and WO W.R. Croysdill shot down an Me 410A-1 of *KG2* over Brighton. *Oberleutnant* Richard Pohl and *Feldwebel* Wilhelm Schubert were killed. Flt Lt J.A. Hall and WO R.F.D. Bourke of 488 Squadron RNZAF each claimed a Ju 88.
15. *Night Fighter*. C.F. Rawnsley & Robert Wright (Elmfield Press, 1957).
16. It had been intended that V-1 flying bombs would rain down on Britain as part of the *Steinbock* offensive, but fortunately for the civilian population of this island, problems delayed the anticipated 'rocket blitz' until 13 June 1944. On this day ten V-1s were catapult-launched at the capital from sites in north-eastern France. The *Vergeltungswaffe 1* (Revenge Weapon No. 1), or Fieseler Fi 103 *Kirschkern* (Cherry Stone), was a small pilotless aircraft with a 1,870 lb high-explosive warhead, which detonated on impact. Over the coming weeks Tempests, Spitfires and Mosquitoes chased the 300-420 mph pilotless bombs in the sky. Tempests of the Newchurch Wing destroyed 580 'Doodlebugs', as they were dubbed by the press, while Spitfire XIVs brought down a further 185. NF.XIIIs of 96 Squadron based at Ford shot down 174 and Mosquitoes of 418 Squadron, stationed at Holmsley South, Hurn and Middle Wallop, destroyed a further ninety. Ground batteries in the 'Diver Box' accounted for the rest
17. MAA *The Mossie* Vol.24, spring 2000.
18. In the spring and summer of 1940 Barwell had been a Defiant I pilot on 264 Squadron, and he and Plt Off J.E.M. Williams and Sgt Martin, his gunners, had scored six victories. Barwell added one more victory plus a probable in 1941 before flying Beaufighter IIs and then Mosquito XVIIs with 125 Squadron. Barwell and Flt Lt D.A. Haigh as radar operator destroyed two Ju 88s at night and a V-1 over the sea in 1942 while flying the Mosquito. *Aces High: A Tribute to the Most Notable Fighter Pilots of the British and Commonwealth Forces in WWII*. Christopher Shores and Clive Williams (Grub Street, London, 1994).
19. *Kampfgeschwader 53 Legion Kondor* was withdrawn from the Eastern Front for retraining as the expanded air-launch unit and *III./KG3* was incorporated into it from 15 October 1944 as its nucleus and its *I Gruppe*. Its *II Gruppe* became operational on the same day, and a *III Gruppe* began its training but did not join operations until early December. *Air-launched Doodlebugs; The Forgotten Campaign*. Peter J.C. Smith (Pen & Sword, 2006).
20. In addition the Fighter Interception Development Unit was engaged in experimental methods of interception of the Heinkel carriers, and 409 'Nighthawk' Squadron RCAF in 2nd TAF operating XIII aircraft from continental airfields was tasked with intercepting Heinkel carriers.
21. His sixteenth and final victory. Alfred Ernest Marshall from Hitchin, Hertfordshire, joined the RAF and was posted to 73 Squadron in France in May 1940 as a sergeant. He saw action during the retreat through France and in the Battle of Britain, where on 7 September his Hurricane was badly damaged, obliging him to force-land, sustaining slight injuries. In November 1940 he accompanied the unit aboard HMS *Furious* to West Africa and thence to Egypt. He saw much action during the First Libyan Campaign, his most notable day proving to be 3 January 1941. In

the morning he engaged five S-79s bombing HMS *Terror* near Bardia, claiming three shot down and a fourth damaged. That afternoon he, Flg Off Jas Storrar and the commanding officer strafed an airfield, claiming eight aircraft destroyed between them. On 23 April, however, on landing after an engagement, he was wounded during a strafing attack on his airfield. He left the unit the following month, and on 6 June 1941 was awarded a very-well-deserved DFM. Commissioned in August 1941 while on non-operational duties, he was posted to 250 Squadron in April 1942, where he quickly became a flight commander. He ended his second tour on 1 August 1942, returning to the UK and receiving a DFC in October. He served as an instructor at 51 OTU until July 1944, when he joined 25 Squadron. On 27 November 1944 he undertook a low-level 'beat-up' of his airfield on return from a sortie, but his Mosquito hit the ground and crashed, killing him and his radar operator; he was 29 at the time. *Aces High: A Tribute to the Most Notable Fighter Pilots of the British and Commonwealth Forces in WWII.* Christopher Shores and Clive Williams (Grub Street, London, 1994).
22. See *Air-launched Doodlebugs; The Forgotten Campaign.* Peter J.C. Smith (Pen & Sword, 2006).
23. See *Air-launched Doodlebugs; The Forgotten Campaign.* Peter J.C. Smith (Pen & Sword, 2006).
24. A Heinkel of *6./KG 53* piloted by *Leutnant* Heinz Redde and a *7.Staffel* machine flown by *Unteroffizier* Walter Schulz were lost.
25. Only four evaded the defences, but two of these fell in the London Civil Defence Region. One flying-bomb was shot down over the sea by Plt Off D.J. Carter and Plt Off W.J. Hutchings of 25 Squadron. *Air-launched Doodlebugs; The Forgotten Campaign.* Peter J.C. Smith (Pen & Sword, 2006).
26. A1+AB Werk Nr 162080. See *Air-launched Doodlebugs; The Forgotten Campaign.* Peter J.C. Smith (Pen & Sword, 2006).
27. A1+NM Werk Nr 161924 of *4.Staffel.*
28. Douglas Haig Greaves was born in Leeds, West Yorkshire, on 4 April 1917, working in his father's printing company before the war. He also did some private flying at the Yorkshire Aero Club, Yeadon. He married in 1939 and joined the RAF in November of that year, completing his training on Hurricanes. He was then posted to Church Fenton to train as a night-fighter, and in March 1941 joined 68 Squadron, with Sgt F. Milton Robbins as his radar operator. In September 1941 the pair were posted to 255 Squadron and late in 1942 flew to North Africa with this unit. Here they enjoyed immediate success over Bone. During the night of 16/17 December they closed on one He 111, dropping flaps and undercarriage to allow them to get very close. When fired on, the bomber exploded in a mass of flame, which they flew through, the fire burning away the fabric on ailerons and rudder and covering the windscreen with soot. They got back but had to crash-land on Bone airfield. They were both awarded DFCs early in 1943, Robbins now a WO. Their tour ended late in April and they returned to the UK, being posted to TFU, Defford. In January 1944, Greaves, now a flight lieutenant, and Robbins, a flying officer, were posted to 25 Squadron. Both were awarded Bars

to their DFC in February 1945 and were promoted again, Greaves to squadron leader and Robbins to flight lieutenant.
29. A1 + BM Werk Nr 700862.
30. See *Final Flights: Dramatic wartime incidents revealed by aviation archaeology.* Ian McLachlan (PSL, 1989). A second USN crew, Lt Sam Peebles and Ensign Dick Grinnals, were also KIA on 22 November 1944. This left only one USN crew with 68 Squadron of those sent to Coltishall to gain night-fighting experience, Lt John W. Kelly and Lt Tom Martin; both were recalled to the USA two days after the loss of Peebles and Grinnals.
31. A1 + NN.
32. A1 + BH Werk Nr 160304.
33. *Air-launched Doodlebugs; The Forgotten Campaign.* Peter J.C. Smith (Pen & Sword, 2006).

CHAPTER 6

The 'Milk Run', Markers and 'Pampas'[1]

Originally formed from 3 Group, using volunteer crews, 8 Group had started as a specialist Pathfinder Force (PFF) on 15 August 1942 under the direction of Gp Capt D.C.T. 'Don' Bennett, and was headquartered at Wyton. On 13 January 1943 the PFF became 8 (PFF) Group, and 'Don' Bennett was promoted air commodore (later air vice-marshal) to command it. 105 Squadron's few B.IX bombers, which were modified B.IVs with OBOE radar, which no one wanted, helped him achieve his objective. GEE-H (from 1944, H_2S)-equipped B.IXs of 139 Squadron and OBOE II-equipped B.IXs of 105 Squadron spearheaded the main force bombing raids. OBOE had first been used on 20 December 1942. 139 Squadron went in with the target-marking Mosquitoes of 105 Squadron, sowing bundles of the thin metal strips called 'Window', which produced a 'clutter' of blips on German radar screens to give the impression of a large bomber force. They made diversionary attacks called 'spoofs' on other targets to attract enemy night-fighters anything up to fifty miles away from the main force during the attack. Bennett's Mosquitoes were to prove so successful that ultimately, eleven Mosquito-equipped squadrons operated in 8 (PFF) Group (the other eight squadrons being equipped with Lancasters).

In addition, 1409 Long Range Meteorological Reconnaissance and Special Duties Flight[2] was established at Oakington on 22 March 1943 using Mosquitoes and crews that arrived from 521 Squadron, Coastal Command, at Bircham Newton on the 30th.[3] The flight became part of the famous Pathfinder Force of Bomber Command under the Command of Sqn Ldr D.A. Braithwaite. The unit flew its first 'Pampa' over Lorient

The 'Milk Run', Markers and 'Pampas'   119

with Mosquito DZ406 on 2 April. By the 12th, flights were being made as far afield as Genoa. Flt Lt R.B. Birchmore DFC* and Flg Off R.H.M. Vere AE recall:

> The new flight soon settled down to its routine work of gathering meteorological information of all sorts – cloud amounts, tops, bases, types, icing, position and activity of frontal systems. From then on an aircraft of the flight was invariably out ahead of any major force of Bomber Command, obtaining absolutely up-to-the-minute information of the weather over and approaching the target. This sometimes required very hurried take-offs in all sorts of weather. It became the proud boast that within twenty minutes by day, or one hour by night, of the first warning ring of the telephone, an aircraft could be airborne and on its way to obtain the weather at any place within 1,000 miles of base in any direction. As soon as equipment which could stand up to the high speed of the Mosquito had been designed, the flight developed a technique for obtaining 'Thums' at any desired point along its route. This soon proved its worth in forecasting winds and temperatures for the bombers.

Sqn Ldr Braithwaite was posted out on 2 May to 139 Squadron, and he was replaced by Sqn Ldr the Hon. P.I. Cunnliffe-Lister. The squadron soon had eight operational aircraft, and by the end of May three MR.IX Mosquitoes had arrived and were modified for meteorological use. The unit was equipped with seven MR.IX aircraft by August. Sqn Ldr Cunnlife-Lister and Plt Off A.P. Kernnan in LR502 failed to return from a 'Pampa' to Osnabrück on 28 July. Fortunately they both managed to bale out and were taken prisoner. Flt Lt Val S. Moore RNZAF took over command on 28 November.[4] The flight continued to support Bomber Command's operations throughout the remainder of the year. December was not a happy time, as the flight lost two of its crews in flying accidents in poor weather conditions.[5] On the 25th and 26th the flight was grounded, and the unit enjoyed the usual Christmas festivities in the mess. However, in the first week in January the flight was ordered to move to Wyton, and on the morning of the 8th crews flew the six Mosquitoes to the flight's new base. In the afternoon the ground personnel completed their move, thus ending the flight's nine-month stay at Oakington.

'Nuisance' raiding, meanwhile, had begun in April 1943, and was so successful that by the summer of 1943 a Light Night Striking Force (LNSF) of Mosquitoes was established within 8 Group. Mosquitoes went in up to an hour before the main attack, descended slowly and released their spoof cargoes of two 500 lb bombs, two target indicators (TIs) or 'sky markers' (parachute flares to mark a spot in the sky if it was cloudy) and bundles of Window. German fighter controllers sent up their night-fighters, so that when the 'heavies' did arrive, the *Nachtjagdgeschwader* were on the ground having to refuel. No. 139 Squadron first tried spoof raiding on the night of 18 November 1943, when flares and bombs were dropped on Frankfurt. Various plain colours with starbursts of the same or a different colour prevented the enemy from copying them.[6] On 26 November three Mosquitoes of 139 Squadron, flying ahead of the main force, scattered Window on the approaches to Berlin and returned to drop bombs.

No. 692 Squadron was formed at Graveley on 1 January 1944. In the twelve months January–December 1944 five more Mosquito squadrons joined 8 Group.[7] Bennett wanted only experienced pilots with 1,000 hours' total time for his squadrons. Gp Capt T.G. 'Hamish' Mahaddie DSO DFC AFC, SASO at Group HQ in Huntingdon, was tasked with recruiting volunteer aircrew from the main-force bomber groups. Sometimes pilots literally came knocking at his door. In June 1944 Philip Back and 'Bing' Bingham, fed up with flying Blenheims at Spittlegate and itching to fly Mosquito night-fighters, hitchhiked down the Great North Road to his office at 8 (PFF) Group HQ in Huntingdon. Back was educated at Harrow School and had joined the RAF in 1942 on a six-month university course, reading engineering at Corpus Christi College, Cambridge. He and Bingham found Castle Hill House, entered and knocked on a door marked 'Gp Capt H. Mahaddie, SASO'. Philip Back recalls:

> There sat an imposing fellow with many 'gongs'. We saluted. He looked up over his glasses and said, 'What do you want?'
> I said, 'We want a job, sir.'
> 'You'd better sit down. How many night-flying hours?' he asked.
> 'Thirty!' I said.
> 'Thirty? You mean 300, don't you?'
> I simply said, 'Yes, sir!'
> He asked us what was going on. When we had finished he said he would see what he could do. Two weeks later we were posted to 1655 Mosquito Training Unit at Warboys!

Pilots and navigators were normally put in a large room and told to pair off. Philip Back had met and crewed up with 23-year-old Plt Off Derek Tom Newell Smith DFC (who had flown a first tour on Lancasters on 61 Squadron) after both men did a dinghy drill session in the Leys Swimming School at Cambridge. Back recalls: 'On the bus back to base he said, "We're crewed up?" I looked at his "gong" and said, "You bet we are." We became an entity in the air and would fly all our ops together.'

Derek Smith did not learn until much, much later that Philip Back had only thirty hours' night-flying experience, but the navigator never had the slightest cause to doubt his pilot's ability: 'He was a natural, who handled the "Mossie" with a skill well beyond his experience and always did the right thing in our more "hairy" moments.'[8] Derek Smith adds:

> There was something special about the bomber Mosquito pilot/observer relationship. On my Lancaster tour I flew in a very close-knit crew which was all-sergeant until near the end, but I never formed any lasting relationship as close as I was to have with Phil. In the bomber 'Mossie' we sat side-by-side, almost shoulder-to-shoulder, sometimes for five or more hours, with a lot of decidedly unfriendly citizens down below for most of the time. They were no friendlier to the 'heavies', and although we relied as much on each other, we had so much more space and a little bit of the aircraft, which was ours. In the 'Mossie' every move which was made was seen by the other, so maybe it served to weld us closer together as a unit.
>
> Aircrew were a reasonably-well-educated bunch, very young, compassionate and not cruel in any way. We were all volunteers, fighting a war for the survival of the free world with knowledge of what had happened to Guernica, Warsaw, Rotterdam and then the cities nearer home. We attacked the targets we were allocated as parts of the total war we were fighting, fortunately without thought of the civilian population below until after the war had ended. We were fighting a battle for survival in the skies over Germany, often two nights out of every three, in the hope of returning to our quite comfortable messes and living-quarters. In a letter home I wrote that there were two of us to a room about the size of a large office, with two chests-of-drawers, a built-in wardrobe, two chairs, tables and reading-lamps. The food was terrific. That night for dinner we had soup, a choice of rabbit or cold meat and salad, plum pie, stewed plums, trifle or rice and plums, and cheese and biscuits. We were waited on at table and the messing was only a shilling [5p] a day.
>
> Killing was not a word in our vocabularies – we never said, 'Old Bill was killed last night.' He had either 'bought it', 'gone for a Burton', 'got the chop' or just 'had it' last night. Nearly every day on an operational squadron there were gaps not there the day before, but it was not a thing to be dwelt on. For ourselves the powers that be and Lord Nuffield acknowledged our position in particular. We had leave every seven or eight weeks, comfortable living conditions, no parades or such that others suffered, bacon and eggs on return from every operation (a luxury in wartime) and sweets, chocolate and orange juice as flying-rations, as we were often airborne for up to nine hours. I mention Lord Nuffield, as he financed a scheme under which aircrew and wives could spend leaves in first-class hotels entirely free of charge. My bride and I had a week in The Ship

Hotel at Brighton, living in comparative luxury and with all fares paid, and of course the scheme was a great boon for aircrew from the Commonwealth. All this as it was essential to keep up morale in the face of vast losses. For example, more aircrew were killed in one night to Nuremberg than pilots were lost in the whole of the Battle of Britain!

Mosquito bombers flew a series of operations to German cities in March. On some nights, including 18/19 and 22/23 March, when Frankfurt was raided by the heavies, and Berlin on 24/25 March, they acted as diversions for the main-force effort with raids on German night-fighter airfields. The night of the 30/31st fell during the moon stand-down period for the main force, but the raid on Nürnberg, destination of 795 RAF heavy bombers and thirty-eight Mosquitoes, went ahead as planned. The Met forecast indicated that there would be protective high cloud on the outward route, when the moon would be up. A 1409 (Met) Flight Mosquito from Oakington carried out a reconnaissance and reported that the protective cloud was unlikely to be present and that there could be cloud over the target, which would prevent accurate ground-marked bombing, but the raid went ahead. Mosquito spoof attacks on Cologne, Frankfurt and Kassel were identified for what they were because to the German defences they were apparently flying without H_2S. As the bomber stream was clearly recognized from the start, 246 twin- and single-engined night-fighters were sent up to engage the heavies. British jamming of the first interception of the bomber stream in the area south of Bonn was successful, but from there on in the bomber stream was hit repeatedly and the majority of the losses occurred in the Giessen-Fulda-Bamberg area. Sixty-four Lancasters and thirty-one Halifaxes (11.9 per cent of the force dispatched) were lost (*and ten bombers crash-landed in England*); it was the worst Bomber Command loss of the war.

The 1409 (Met) Flight Mosquito crews performed much valuable work during 1944. Edwin Perry and Ginger Myles, who had completed nineteen sorties with 139 Squadron were posted to Oakington, where both were commissioned mid-way through their second tour.[9] On 1409 they would complete another sixty-three sorties over occupied Europe and eighteen over the Atlantic/North Sea, to make the grand total of one hundred sorties.[10] Flg Off Perry recalls.[11]

When we went to the unit, I think, because we had become acclimatized to operating at night time, we were both rather apprehensive about being the only aircraft over enemy territory in daylight hours, which was often the case. Condensation trails (super-cooled ice crystals) emanating from the engines particularly helped the opposition locate a high-flying aircraft. However, while it was not unknown to see German planes, by frequent jinking by

Ginger and with me keeping a continuous lookout, we were able to maintain a respectable distance from any potential interceptors. Of course it was much easier to see them than at night, even with the strongest moonlight. Most of the time we used the Mosquito Mk IX, but later we received the Mark XVI, which had a superior type of cabin pressurization and different engines, but was still restricted to about 35,000 ft altitude. There was yet another Hatfield-produced Mosquito, the Mark XV, which had wings increased by an extra 5 or 6 ft. I went up to 45,000 ft in one that was loaned to the unit for a short time by Geoffrey de Havilland.

Generally the type of information sought related to amount and thickness of clouds, on occasion calling for a descent to 2,000 ft from 30,000 ft normal cruising height, strength of wind found at height flown and on rarer occasions humidity checks down to ground level. During my time with 1409 there were reports of very high winds at upper altitudes, and on one occasion I found a wind of 120 mph at 25,000 ft, which was beyond the capabilities of my mechanical hand computer. I overcame the problems by doubling angles, but it caused me quite a bit of anxiety while I worked out how to make the calculator work. Since then the presence of 'jet streams' at great heights has become well established, but I believe a number of aircraft were probably lost because the severity of these winds was not appreciated, hence they ran out of fuel before making base. Squadron Leader Mike Birkin[12] and his very good 'Spec N' navigator, John Cowan, found themselves out of GEE range and well south of Paris when their Southwold ETA fell due, which I believe confirms this view. We also saw St Elmo's fire on several occasions when the atmosphere was highly charged with electricity. This took the form of electricity discharging from the tips of the propellers, hence one felt that the engines were flying into two blue rings, rather alarming the first time seen, but not dangerous.

Apart from meteorological reconnaissances, we were occasionally called on for special jobs. Wing Commander Anderson, the Group navigation officer, detailed us on a special two-hour secret night mission on 18 March 1944. On 27 April we surveyed Essen two hours after a 'heavies' attack, adding four 500 lb bombs to the conflagration and taking photographs. On 13 May we supported the LNSF by releasing four bundles of three white flares over the west end of the Kiel Canal at Brunsbüttel from 30,000 ft. The canal lock gates were clearly seen by the bombing Mossies, who went in low for a successful attack. On 20 June during a Pampa we were told to take vertical photographs of Heligoland naval base, Pellworm Island, Nordstrand Island and Husum. During 10 September we were sent to photograph troop concentrations in the suburbs of Le Havre, taking eight runs over the city. On 12 September we dropped four 500 lb bombs on

Gelsenkirchen's Hydrierwerke Scholvern AG. We were also required to drop Window in two runs over the town between H−10 and H+10 of a heavy raid. Kiel was again visited forty minutes after a heavy attack on 16 September 1944. Photos were taken on two runs with one 500 lb high explosive bomb and a GTI photoflash released on each run. Our last Pampa and the close of our direct operations against Germany took place on 24 September 1944. The introduction of the Master Bomber to control a raid called for an additional requirement to get a Met Flight Mossie to the target area early to give an up-to-the-minute situation report to the Master Bomber by VHF before he got to the area.

Not all crews were as lucky as us. Joe Patient and Norry Gilmour had a particularly unenviable encounter: they were disabled at 27,000 ft by anti-aircraft fire when doing a 'special' Pampa carrying bombs. They went on to Berlin and released their bombs together with a brick, which Norry let out through the Window chute wrapped in the *Jewish Times*! It is doubtful whether the Germans had time to read this paper before two Fw 190 night-fighters jumped them, but the Mosquito sustained further damage. Joe turned into one of the Fws, prepared if nothing else to take it with him, while Norry sitting by his side said his thoughts were, 'Dear me, mother will never know what happened!' But at the last moment the German veered away. Joe finally broke off the engagement by going down to 200 ft and flying back to Manston. As they approached they found Manston blacked out, so the Very recognition signal was fired. When the runway lit up they had just touched down when a returning Typhoon, also making an emergency landing, skidded round and sliced the wooden Mosquito in half. Our two scrambled out and managed to extricate the fighter pilot, who was trapped and fearful that fire would develop.

The main role of the Met Flight was to ascertain the type of weather likely to affect a bombing attack, and was used to help determine whether sky or ground-target indicators should be carried by the Marking Pathfinders. Each operation was known as a Pampa. Routes were devised by Command or Group and had to take into account that the enemy might get some feel from our tracks of which cities were likely to be attacked by the main force later. Hence, if the target for the night was to be a city in the Ruhr we might be sent to the south of France, turn east to Munich and thence north to Hanover before returning to our home base. Other sorties went out into the Atlantic or up the North Sea to check positions of weather fronts, to help determine in advance when weather would be suitable for a particular operation. To give two particular examples, (1) When Winston Churchill went to Italy on 11 August, extra-long-range fuel tanks were installed and we refuelled at

Dunkeswell in Devon. Spending 6.20 hours in the air, we were able to reconnoitre the weather from south Ireland to La Corona in north-west Spain. (2) For many days prior to D-Day all flight aircraft were engaged incessantly in checking weather over the Pas de Calais and the Western Approaches. A report from one of our crews (Joe Patient) resulted in the invasion of Fortress Europe being deferred by one day.

Despite the imminent invasion of the continent, oil targets were still high on the agenda for Mosquitoes, and on 2/3 June twenty-three Mosquitoes were detailed to bomb the synthetic oil plant at Leverkusen, north of Cologne. At Little Staughton, Flt Lt Arthur C. 'Nick' Carter and his navigator, Flg Off Ernie Garrett, on 109 Pathfinder Squadron were to mark the target with green TIs from 23,000 ft. It was their 44th operation. Garratt was on his second tour, having flown the first on Hampdens and Wellingtons with 420 Squadron RCAF, followed by a ten-month stint at 19 OTU at Kinloss and Forres in Scotland. Arthur Carter recalls:[13]

Ernie Garrett and I were due to go on leave right after this night's op, and I had told my wife I would be late home. We took off on a lovely June night and I climbed the Mosquito to 35,000 ft. We were trying out a new magnetron valve in conjunction with our OBOE equipment on a target we had not hit before. We turned onto the beam, which gave us a straight and level course towards Germany, but as we approached the border, we were hit by heavy flak. The Germans were now using radar-controlled 155 mm stuff. We were expecting to find that the first Mosquito had lit up the target, but it seemed that their markers had failed, so now it was up to us to illuminate the oil plant with our green target indicators, for the following Light Night Force to drop its bombs. The port engine was not functioning properly and I had some control difficulty, but I still hoped that ML962 would get us to the target in about five minutes. Soon after, there was a huge bang and we had been hit again, but we managed to release our TIs before the Mosquito was rocked by another enormous jolt. Then almost simultaneously, all the searchlights in the vicinity were switched on and their beams criss-crossed the night sky trying to find us. This was a sure sign that we had succeeded in marking the target, which could no longer remain hidden. But this time, I was in real trouble – the port engine was on fire and the last hit had severed the aileron and elevator controls. We were doing a sort of spiral spin in the searchlights, diving earthwards, but I somehow managed to establish enough control to level out and get out of range of their beams. The engine on fire had burned itself out, but not before it had spread to part of the wing.

The side of the cockpit was too hot to touch, but Ernie managed to get it under control.

We slowly headed for Belgium, and above a thick layer of low cloud it was a beautiful moonlit night, but the cloud obscured the coastline. We guessed we had reached Calais from the coastal flak that was coming our way. Before we turned due north at Dieppe, we again encountered heavy coastal flak, with near-misses but no further damage. Thankfully, our radio equipment was still working, and after crossing the Sussex coast, we called on our emergency channel to ask for confirmation of our exact position, and we were given a course to steer. The cloud began to clear as we approached the Surrey boundary, but by this time I was having great difficulty in keeping the Mossie stable, and I knew that landing it would be impossible, especially as fire had broken out again. It was time to abandon ship through the floor hatch. Ernie was a big chap and appeared to have got stuck, so I put my foot on top of his head and he popped out like a cork from a bottle![14] I knew that once I let go of the controls it would go into a dive, but I got free in time, and the impact of the parachute opening was like being thrown against a brick wall at great speed, and it temporarily knocked the wind out of me.

I landed in a field and was soon approached by a soldier on guard duty, who, with the point of his rifle in my back, marched me to his headquarters. I soon discovered that it was a sealed unit, awaiting instructions to leave for France for the D-Day landings at short notice. I duly explained what I was doing roaming the Surrey countryside at 3 o'clock in the morning, and my squadron was informed that I was safe and well. At first, it seemed that I might have to go with them because no one was allowed to leave, but after much deliberation between the Air Ministry and the War Office, I was told that I need no longer be detained there. I'd had more than enough excitement for one night, and reflecting on the problems I'd encountered getting away from France, I was thankful not to be going there again quite so soon![15]

On D-Day, 6 June 1944, 26-year-old Plt Off (later Flt Lt) Ralph Wood RCAF, a Canadian 'second tourist' from New Brunswick, was on a train heading for 1655 MTU Warboys. As a flight sergeant navigator on his first tour in 4 Group, Bomber Command, from July 1941 to 25 June 1942, he had flown twenty-four ops on Whitley and Halifax bombers in 102 and 76 Squadrons respectively.[16] At the time Canadians were all on loan to the RAF, as the RCAF Bomber Command had not yet been established. Later, when it became active as 6 Group, some of the Canadians transferred to the Canadian squadrons. Ralph Wood and several others preferred to stay with the RAF. 'We got along fine with the Limeys and besides, we thought that where we were on loan we might get away with a little more murder and less discipline.' Ralph Wood survived a terrible crash on a training exercise on 28 June, which killed his pilot and wrote off the Halifax in which they were flying. Ralph Wood was extremely lucky to survive. He thought as he made his way to the mess for tea that it had to be a dream. He shook for two hours, as this dream became a startling reality. Then he realized that he had come 'damn close to cashing it in'. 'Twenty-four ops and we had to crap out on a lousy training trip', he thought bitterly. That night he went to the dance in Darlington, where his dead pilot had had a date with his girlfriend. He had to give her the bad news. He had never heard a girl scream before. As soon as possible, he returned to his barracks and tried to sleep. It was an experience he would never forget, ever: four crashes around their airfield, his being the fourth, played havoc with his nervous system. Ralph requested sick leave from the squadron medical officer, who was reluctant to recommend same. Instead he sent him to a Canadian medical centre in East Anglia, where he found the reception room filled with other nervous aircrew. Most of them were there to go LMF (Lack of Moral Fibre). This meant that they would be stripped of all rank and placed on general duties. They would be in disgrace but they would remain alive. Wood thought to himself, 'There but for the grace of God go I.' The most unlikely people, people like himself, could usually rise to the occasion, just as big, tough guys folded under pressure. One never knew. He was interviewed by a Jewish Canadian medical officer whose first question was, 'Do you want to quit flying?' Wood thought that he was a little surprised when he assured him that what he wanted was a little time off to get away and put things together again before continuing his tour. He was given a fortnight's sick leave, which he took in Dunoon, Scotland. The crash had affected him very deeply, and it was here that a new experience was added to his assortment of nightmares. He would wake up in the middle of the night to find himself standing on his bed and trying to push his way through the wall. He presumed that he must have been trying desperately to get out of an aircraft. Another version of this antic was to leap out of bed and find himself standing beside it, 'wondering what the hell' was going on. It was several years after the war before he was able to rid himself of what he called 'that annoying performance'.

When he returned to his base at Middleton St George, he learned why the squadron medical officer had been reluctant to allow him sick leave after the crash: all experienced aircrew were needed as most of the squadron was moved to the Middle East. Wood was now faced with the prospect of becoming a member of a novice crew. His new pilot, who on a scale of one to ten, 'rated a weak five' in his nervous estimation. Despite this, Wood had returned to ops, and he flew three more before his state of nervousness got too much for him. On 28 August he lost a Moncton school friend, Norman Ross, who was with a planeload of personnel being transported, bag and baggage, from one station to another, when it crashed soon after take-off. It appeared that some of the baggage became fouled up in the cables and controls, causing the accident. Everyone on board was killed. Ralph Wood's twenty-seventh op on 4 September, to Bremen, turned out to be a hazardous experience, magnified by his state of nervousness. On his return he said, 'This is it', and approached the CO, who agreed to retire him from ops, crediting him with a full tour. In October 1942 he was posted to instruct at OTU and was commissioned in the summer of 1943.

> As an officer I had the services of a batman, or, should I say, batwoman, as it was the WAAF who had taken over the batman's duties, freeing him for heavier duties. She would come around in the morning to 'knock you up' (awaken you) with a cup of tea. This usually got you up in a hurry, especially if you had been on the beer the night before. Besides my instructional duties, I had two other jobs during my stay at 10 OTU, Abingdon. One was to act as guard over two RAF officers who were under house arrest. They had just recently returned from the Middle East and their crime was getting caught in the station chapel, making love to a couple of WAAFs.

Canadians were supposed to do a tour of ops and a tour of instruction, and then receive a month's furlough back home in Canada. After fifteen months of instructional duties he was getting 'horribly bored' and 'very frustrated'. By March 1944 he was back in Canada and had married his fiancée Phyl, and on his return to England he asked to be posted to a Mosquito bomber squadron.

> My strategy paid off. At Warboys I ran into Andy Lockhart, an old school chum from Moncton. We had gone to school together, worked together at Eatons on Saturdays and eventually joined the RCAF about the same time. Andy was selected as pilot material, trained as such and kept in Canada as an instructor until now. While in Canada he earned the AFC for exceptional work while fulfilling his duties there. We were delighted at this chance meeting. Andy, about to do his first tour, would like to have me as his navigator because of my practical experience. I, in turn, would love to have him as my experienced pilot. Having earned the AFC sort of placed him high in my rating system. The only snag was that Andy had an RAF navigator, brought over from training in Canada. Now, Fate stepped in and this navigator was told that he would have to stay on for more training, which he hadn't received in Canada. This consisted of a course in the use of the GEE box, a navigational aid, and a bomb aimer's course. Inwardly, Andy and I were delighted at this turn

of events, and so began the saga of the *'Moncton Express'* with the team of Lockhart and Wood.

A month at 1655 MTU and we headed for our new squadron, 692, at Graveley, near Cambridge. We shared this station with 35 Pathfinder Squadron, which was flying Lancasters. A friendly rivalry existed between these two squadrons, especially when we were both frequenting the same local pub or the officers' mess. While our Mosquitoes roamed the German skies in all kinds of weather, the heavies (Lancasters and Hallybags) were more particular about when they went aloft. We took special delight in provoking the gentlemen who flew the heavies by singing our song, *We Fly Alone*, in the pubs we both frequented; it was our rewritten lyric of the jukebox favourite, *I'll Walk Alone*.

Our Mosquito was an unarmed night-bomber. We had no guns, only our speed and manoeuvrability to protect us. From Spruce to Bomber! The pilot and navigator sat side-by-side in this 'Wooden Wonder', or 'Termite's Delight', as it was sometimes called. The pilots had a steel plate under their seats to protect them. Navigators had an extra sheet of plywood. We all had a nagging fear that our jewels might be shot off. The moral seemed to be that pilots make better fathers. I wore a Mae West (an inflatable life-jacket) and a harness to which I would attach my parachute, which was kept on the floor near my feet. I sat on the dinghy, the little lifeboat all done up in a neat, square package. The rubber sucked out your piles if fear didn't. The hooks on my harness were snapped onto the dinghy clamps. If I jumped, the dinghy came with me. With the parachute on my chest and the dinghy on my ass, I wonder if I could ever have squeezed through that small escape hatch. There we were, as snug as two peas in a pod. This was no place for claustrophobia. My lapboard, charts, maps and Dalton computer completed the picture. With a 4,000-pounder aboard and the Mosquito tanked up for a 1,200-mile sortie, the worst moment for the crew was take-off. Fused or unfused, a bomb of this size might go off on heavy impact.

We were now part of the 'Light Night Striking Force', and as such flew quickly through any adverse weather to complete our task. As many as seventy Mosquitoes would each unload their 'Cookie', 4,000 lb of high explosive! And this could happen every night of the week – in all kinds of soupy weather that kept the Halifaxes and Lancasters grounded. One of the dodges the Mossies used to baffle the Nazi defence system was this: a few aircraft flew a feint at a certain target and fooled the German radar into thinking it was a raid in strength, while the main bomber force hit another city hundreds of miles away. The Light Night Striking Force of Mosquitoes raided Berlin 170 times, thirty-six of these on consecutive nights. The Mossie could carry as big a bomb-load to Berlin as the US Flying Fortress, which needed an eleven-man crew. The Mosquito flew so often to Berlin that its raids were known as the Berlin Express, and the different routes there and back as Platform One, Two and Three.

We usually slept until the last minute, then made a mad dash for the mess before the doors closed. Most of us had this timed pretty well. So well that Andy and I decided to upset the pattern by piling as many bicycles as possible on top of the latrine building. Of course, a great many missed their breakfast that morning, including the CO,[17] whose bicycle was also included. Our billets were huge tin cans, which we tried to keep heated with toy stoves and a niggardly ration of coal. These were called Nissen huts and were situated some distance from the mess.

Some nights at our debriefing my pilot and I would use up the rum ration of those who preferred their coffee without this additional fortification. This on top of our own ration had the effect of making everything seem great. The only difficulty was bicycling from the ops room to our barracks without going in the ditch. Our real treat was the flying-breakfast of bacon and eggs back at the base, and our discussions of the attack with the other crews on the raid. I used to think they used this as bait to get us to fly. Once in a while we would bicycle around the countryside, looking for farmers to sell us some eggs. We would then have the cook at our mess prepare them for a snack at night after visiting the pub. The eggs kept getting a little tougher, and eventually we realized that the farmers were passing off duck eggs on us.

Our mess parties had a habit of accelerating as the evening advanced. On one occasion an officer rode into the mess on horseback, much to the delight of the inebriated occupants. Not to be outdone, another officer jumped on his motorcycle and rode that into the mess. Then there was the night of the duel. An RAF officer who, unbeknown at the time, was suffering from appendicitis, was throwing beer mugs up in the air, breaking the chandeliers. At the same time he was telling the Canadians present that he didn't want any damn Canadians over here to fight his battles and why didn't we get the hell home? I figured that kind of talk called for a duel, and we took down the two crossed sabres hanging on the mess wall and started fencing. When I nicked him between the eyes, over his nose, our medical officer, who was black as the ace of spades (fondly referred to as old 23:59 – one minute to midnight), decided it was time to end the duel.

Every six weeks we would have seven days' leave, and London was the most interesting place to visit. Andy and I dropped into the Crackers Club and were pleased to see Ralph Nickerson's young brother there. As we talked and drank we said we hoped his brother Ralph was OK. Ralph had been shot down a short while ago and

The 'Milk Run', Markers and 'Pampas'   131

was listed as missing in action. A few hours and several beers later, who should walk into the club but Ralph Nickerson. He had escaped with the help of the French Underground. We really had cause for a super celebration that night.

Our social life in London was now being interfered with by the 'Buzz Bombs', or 'Doodlebugs', as the V-1s were called. The first Buzz Bomb fell on Britain on 13 June 1944. The V-1 was a small glider with an engine in it, and it was loaded with explosive. Jerry put enough gas in the engine to make it go to London. When the gas ran out, the bomb started its swift, random-death descent, falling down on whatever – or whoever – was underneath. It made us quite nervous when you heard the engine cut out overhead, and you waited anxiously for the bang, before continuing with your drinking and dart throwing. The V-2, or Rocket Bomb, which appeared later, was altogether different: if you heard the V-2, it would be too late. It was sleeker and climbed in a gentle arc to a height of a hundred miles before stalling and then dipping noiselessly to earth – English earth.

Our first Mosquito op was on 6 July. Andy and I took off for Gelsenkirchen, expecting anything and everything. It was an interesting trip (my twenty-eighth op of the war) and Andy's first over enemy territory. I think he thoroughly enjoyed it. On return to base we learned that we had picked up a bird on the way, and it remained there firmly lodged inside the wing, as it made a hole a foot wide on impact. We also brought back a piece of flak. Andy informed the intelligence officer at our debriefing that he had steered into some searchlights to see what effect they would have. When I regained my breath I pointed out very strongly that once caught in searchlights it was difficult to escape at high altitudes, and fighters would also have an idea as to the positioning of the Mosquito – meaning us. We went to bed, tired but happy, as the first trip – usually the worst mentally – was a success.

On 7 July we went right to the Snake's home. We were quite keyed up, too, but were not letting on to each other. A typical trip to Berlin would be a feint attack on a couple of cities on the way to our target and throwing out Window to foul up the radar. Once over Berlin we were usually caught in a huge cone of searchlights, so blinding Andy that he couldn't read the instruments. 'Are we upside-down or not?' he'd ask. I'd look down at the bombs exploding below and assure him that we were right side up. As the anti-aircraft crap seemed to surround us, Andy would throw our *Moncton Express* around the skies, trying desperately to get out of the searchlights. On three occasions we lost an engine about now, and had to limp home, as one set of searchlights passed us on to another set and so on, until they ran out of lights. When over the target, we'd bomb and get out as fast as we could. This was when I'd sit in my seat, the blood draining out of my face and my stomach in tight knots. Jesus, this could be it, I thought. And after tight moments like this I'd say, 'Andy, pass the beads.'

The trip was successful, but packed with excitement. As we did our bombing run into the centre of Berlin, our starboard engine seemed to catch fire. Andy feathered it immediately in case of the fire spreading. We finished our run, dropped our cookie and were immediately coned by a great number of searchlights. After five minutes we got out without damage. On the return journey we were coned and shot at again in the Hamburg district. Finally we reached the English coast and landed at the nearest airdrome with about twenty gallons of petrol left. We returned to base the following day after our engine was repaired. We have now been over the hottest target in Germany and feel quite good about it. One of our crews failed to return.[18]

On 10 July Andy Lockhart and Plt Off Ralph Wood RCAF were on the 'Milk Run' again – Berlin or bust. Wood recalls:

Of course, we had to get coned and shot at again over the target. As if that wasn't enough, the boys of Heligoland had a crack at us, too. The trip was exciting and a good one, but we lost a very fine crew. The pilot was our CO, a New Zealander. They think he got it near Cologne.[19] Andy and I saw a lot of action in that direction as we passed it. Andy liked the choice of names I used for the Hun when he let us have a barrage of flak. We were still keen and a bit more Berlin minded. We were coned for nine minutes there this time. On return we just made the English coast and landed with five gallons of petrol left. We were getting along fine together and our teamwork was improving. One unusual return from enemy territory, and most satisfying, included a dive beginning at the French coast, from 32,000 ft to 10,000 ft, reached at Southwold on the English coast. This eighty-eight-mile journey was completed in eleven minutes, which was fast, even for a Mosquito. With our cookie gone, our two fifty-gallon drop tanks discarded and our fuel load pretty well depleted, it wasn't too hard to accomplish this feat. Andy and I were at 25,000 ft completing our air test in preparation for the night's operation, when I happened to look up from my lap table. There was Andy, out cold and slumped over the controls. We were dropping like a lead weight – straight for the ground. My blood drained into my shoes as I managed to place my oxygen mask over his face in time for him to revive and pull the plane out of the dive. Thirty years after the war, Andy reminded me of this long-forgotten incident.

He told me that afterwards all I said was, 'Do you always take a turn that steeply?'

Hanover on 14 July was ideal for our job. The target was fairly 'warm', as were places on the way home. However, it was our turn to have a quiet night, and flak, searchlights or fighters did not bother us. In fact, we quite enjoyed ourselves. We all came back to the base without casualties. (The first operation I ever did was to this target in a Whitley in July 1941.) Berlin on 15 July, on the 'Milk Run' again, was my favorite dislike. On the way there, via the Ruhr, we managed to anger the —— and they threw up everything they had at us. After what seemed ages, we shook them off and proceeded to the target, where we were fortunate in steering dear of trouble. Coming home, we had a few more taking potshots at us, but returned to base okay. The fog at base caused us to land at our training station a few miles from base. Looking at our kite the next day we saw several flak holes: one below in front of us; one below and behind us on the bomb-bay doors; and one entered the engine covering underneath. 'A miss is a good as a mile', so here's the next trip.

On 17 July it was Berlin again – making four out of six trips to the 'Big City'. This was more than I expected. It was a satisfaction to know that they respected our raids. That might be due to the fact that we carried a cookie with us. If it didn't give them a headache, it would at least keep them awake! One lad on the way in was coned in about a hundred searchlights and was getting enough shrapnel in his direction to sink the *Queen Mary*. The poor guy stooged over Hamburg by mistake. (I'd have to watch that; it might have been us!) At the target the boys were coned here and there but no flak was shot up the beams, which indicated that enemy fighters were present. At interrogation next morning we learned that a few of the boys were chased persistently by those fighters. Joe's halo (that's mine) must have been working overtime! It was a good trip for us, though. We were on again that night and we hoped it would be a short trip this time. No luck. It was Berlin again. The trip proved quite nerve-racking, as we were both on edge all the time due to not being able to get enough sleep and working rather hard lately. We were first over the target and got coned as we waited for the markers to fall. As we let our cookie drop, the markers dropped beside our bomb burst. Andy threw the kite around in every direction to get out of the searchlights. At one time he nearly stalled her and thought we were upside-down. I told him I could still see the searchlights by looking down, so we must be right side up. On the way out we were nearly coned again over Magdeburg. Andy was a little too quick for them this time and we returned home without further trouble, definitely all in and slightly fed up. Our leave on the 21st would certainly be welcome. So far we had been to Berlin five times out of seven trips.

On the night of 20/21 July the LNSF sent twenty-six Mosquitoes to raid Hamburg. One of the crews was Ralph Wood and Andy Lockhart of 692 Squadron, but as Ralph Wood said:

Fate was against our going. Near Bremen we lost an engine, dropped our cookie and high-tailed it for home as fast as one engine would take us. We arrived back at base okay and found that our glycol had leaked out of the engine. We crossed the 'drome before landing and shot out the distress signal, which gave us priority in landing. Andy made a wizard one-engine landing (his first in a Mosquito at night). We were now ready to go on a much-needed leave as soon as we awoke.

Ralph Wood and Andy Lockhart's first op upon returning from leave was to Wanne Eickel on 5 August, but only after ops on six successive nights had been scrubbed at the last moment:

Wanne Eickel was in the centre of the Essen district, a hot spot in Germany. Our haloes were working overtime, and apart from being coned we were okay. Some of the boys caught a lot of flak. When we landed at base Andy made his approach with his wheels up. Just before we were due to touch down he opened up the throttle and went around the circuit again. (It gave me six new grey hairs.) We went to Cologne three nights later. Everything went like clockwork. The bombing was very concentrated but Andy and I managed to steer clear of most of the opposition. It meant one-fifth of our tour was now finished. It was too good to last. On 10 August we went to Berlin. However, we had a good trip and weren't tampered with. We ran short of juice on the way home so we landed near the coast, refueled and came home later. Nothing much to tell about this trip, but that is always a good sign. As usual, there were plenty of fireworks over there. The night of 12 August was a lovely change as we had a long sea crossing and not too much time over enemy territory. The target was Kiel. It was rather warm, too, as they threw up barrages of rockets, which burst too near for comfort. As they were rather demoralizing Andy kept his eyes on the instruments and I kept mine on the target indicators. We ploughed through the barrage, bombed and headed for home. We had an oil leak in one engine and a flak hole in one wing. It was a good trip and the bombing was accurate.

Our thirteenth trip on the 13th of the month was a honey. Everything worked perfectly. The target was Hanover. Our luck had been too good since our leave. It would soon be our turn to attract the searchlights, flak, rockets or fighters. We were in no hurry for it, though. We had named our kite the *Moncton Express*. I hoped it was lucky. Two nights later, Berlin was the lucky city. We paid it a short visit with our usual calling-cards of 4,000 lb bombs. It was a good trip, but we had a bit too much excitement attached to it. In short, our luck wasn't of the high standard it had been since our leave. We were coned for a hell of a long time between Hamburg and Lübeck. No flak came up, so I strained my eyes looking for the inevitable fighters while Andy concentrated on getting us out of a cone of from fifty to a hundred searchlights. As the night was black, the lights had a fine time with us. It sure made you feel naked! We were next coned over Berlin, and again when we were nearing the enemy coast on the way home. I saw a fighter, but he evidently didn't see us. When we landed at base all our petrol gauges registered zero. And so ended another trip to the 'Big City'.

On 16 August it was Berlin again. It was a good trip in spite of a lot of things going wrong. One of our compasses went unserviceable before we were airborne; then, over the North Sea we lost a carburetor stud on the port engine. Over Berlin we dropped our wing tanks along with the cookie, as the ground crew had it wired up wrong. We were coned over the 'Big City' but got out of it in four minutes with only one hunk of flak in our wing. We had an uneventful trip home and were quite tired. A feed – our rum ration – and bed, all looked pretty good to us. Our next op, on 17 August, our third night running, we have a change of targets – Mannheim – a new one to us. It was a perfect trip in all respects. We weren't tampered with a bit, but the target was fairly 'warm'. Andy and I found that little things irritated us. We were due for a night off, I guess. J for Johnnie (*Moncton Express*) was as good as her name, but another crew had it on our night off and succeeded in getting enough fighter cannon shells into it to warrant it unserviceable for some time to come. We had to borrow a kite to go to Cologne on 23 August. It was a bang-on trip with no complaints from our side. We lost one crew who crashed with their cookie after take-off, and very little remained. We missed our old kite, but we hoped we could get a new one to replace it. On the 25th we were free. One of our flight commanders became a casualty when he returned short of petrol and crashed into a house.[20]

On 26 August we went to Berlin, which turned out to be rather pleasant in spite of our being coned over the target. Everyone got home okay. We were hit by flak and we lost an engine before reaching home. Andy made another single-engine landing.

What a night our trip to Mannheim on 27 August was! One of our kites swung on take-off, caught fire and blew up. The cookie went off, but was not detonated, so it didn't cause too much damage. We saw all this as we were setting course over the airdrome. The crew got out when she caught fire and ran like merry old hell.[21] The target was quite hot. On the way in we saw a fighter and later an aircraft shot down. Over the target one of our boys bought it. The searchlights and flak followed him all the way down. Slightly demoralizing.[22] Andy and I had a smashing trip, though. The Hun was sending more fighters up after us as we were proving to be more than just nuisance raiders. According to a press report, the *Luftwaffe* now rated Mosquitoes on night attacks so high that when and if a Jerry shot down a Mosquito he was allowed to count it as two [sic]. Sometimes I wished we had some guns, too. We landed at another base because of the wreckage at our own base. A good night, but not good for the morale. Our op on 29 August to Hamburg was a good trip, too, but there was a little too much excitement to suit me. Apart from the odd piece of flak we picked up, we were untouched; but having a brush with a Jerry fighter was something different. As we left the target area a fighter got on our tail. We did tight turns and corkscrewed from 27,000 ft down to 8,000 ft. He was still right with us on his instruments. After fifteen minutes he gave up and we proceeded merrily homeward, a bit wiser from our experience. Lady Luck was certainly right beside us that night. We had flak holes in one petrol tank, wing and the body near the tail. The trip to Düsseldorf on 31 August was a good one also. The moon was the brightest of the year. It was like flying in daylight, and we could see the ground fairly well. Our ground speed was 450 mph as we had a good tailwind. After a few days of rotten weather we managed to get a trip to Hanover on 5 September. There was not much to say about it except that it was a good trip and one more to add to our total.

Philip Back and Derek Smith were posted to 692 Squadron at Graveley on 5 September, and they flew their first op that same night with a 4,000 lb bomb in the bomb-bay. Back recalls: 'The bloody plane shot up about 200 ft when we dropped it over Hanover – no one warned me!'

When ops were scrubbed too late for going to the 'flesh-pots', which was not unusual [recalls Derek Smith], homemade entertainment in the mess was the order of the day. High Cockalorum was a favourite sport, especially on two-squadron stations, as most were, and usually when sufficient anaesthetic had been consumed in the bar to deaden the pain! There were several versions, but it was usually one squadron against the other. There were various formats, but that which I remember best was where one team formed a pyramid in the corner of the anteroom with the trophy on top – sometimes a body, and at other times something considered to be of value to the opposition. The object was for the attackers to capture the trophy, and of course it resolved itself into a heaving mass of injured bodies! There were also numerous stories of motorcycles and horses being ridden around messes, which I have heard told at various stations but never actually witnessed. At Syerston, it was said that a motorcycle was ridden up the left-hand stairs, round the upper floor, down the right-hand stairs and out of the front door. It was also reported that the Padre's horse did a similar circuit, but this time, in the officers' mess. I have not the slightest doubt that these incidents happened, but when, where and how many times, I cannot be sure. What is certain, however, is that some lucky aircrew, like me, were in somewhat more danger of injury in the mess than we ever were out of it!

On 8 September Ralph Wood flew his fiftieth op of the war when he and Andy Lockhart were among the forty-five Mosquitoes that went to Nürnberg. Sardonically he wrote:

Things are looking brighter. Tonight we had a long trip to Nuremberg. We had storms all along the route, but it was a good trip. We flew across liberated France, Holland and Belgium and saw some activity along the German frontier. We had a brand-new kite tonight. It is A-for-Apple, and we're going to try and keep it. She took us to 29,000 ft with a cookie. We'll have to call her the *Moncton Express II* if we get her. Flight Lieutenant Wadsworth, a friend of mine, but a closer friend of Andy's, took off and one engine failed when he was only 500 ft up, so he landed with his wheels up, risking the great chance of being blown from here to there. One has to be over 4,000 ft up to drop a cookie or he'll get the blast, etc. The next day he was appointed flight commander, as there was a vacancy there.

On the night following, 9 September, it was another new target for the Canadian navigator:

This time it was Brunswick, which was visited by thirty-nine Mosquitoes. The name almost made me feel homesick. It was a good effort and huge fires were seen as we left the target. Our new kite lived up to its previous performance. It was now ours, and we named it *Moncton Express II*. We were nearly half-finished now. On 11 September it was the old 'Milk Run' again – Berlin [which was visited by forty-seven Mosquitoes]. We had to land away from base, as an earwig plugged the starboard jettison tank. We had more trouble at the place we landed and didn't get home until 6 p.m. the next day. At 6:30 p.m. we were having our flying supper for another trip to the 'Big City'. We were coned near Hamburg on the way in and again over the target. Another one of our crews failed to return tonight. Our trip to Berlin on the 12th was quite respectable and we got back to base without any trouble. We were coned over the 'Big City', but managed to get out of it with a little effort. We were now over the hump and on our downward journey, with twenty-four ops left to do.

Berlin at this time was the 'favourite' destination for the Mosquitoes. 'A' and 'B' Flights at 8 (PFF) Group stations were routed to the 'Big City' over towns and cities whose air raid sirens would announce their arrival overhead, although they were not the targets for the Mosquitoes' bombs. Depriving the Germans of much-needed sleep and comfort was a very effective 'nuisance' weapon, while a 4,000-pounder nestling in the bomb-bay was a more tangible calling-card. The 'night postmen' had two rounds: after take-off from Wyton, crews immediately climbed to height, departed Cromer and flew the dogleg route Heligoland–Bremen–Hamburg; the second route saw departure over Woodbridge, and went to the Ruhr–Hannover–Munich. Two Mosquito bombers that failed to return from the attack on Berlin on 13/14 September were claimed shot down south-east of the capital by *Oberfeldwebel* Egbert Jaacks of *I./NJG10* and at Braunschweig by *Leutnant* Karl Mitterdorfer of *10./JG300*.[23] Two nights later, on 15/16 September, 490 aircraft bombed Kiel for the loss of four Halifaxes and two Lancasters. Three Mosquitoes and a Stirling of 199 Squadron in 100 Group were lost on bomber support, and a Mosquito XX of 608 Squadron failed to return from a raid on Berlin.[24] *Leutnant* Kurt Welter claimed two of the Mosquitoes, one south of Berlin and the other north of Achmer, and *Feldwebel* Reichenbach of *10./JG300* one other north-west of Wittenburg.[25]

On 15 September, when twenty-seven Mosquitoes went to the 'Big City', Andy Lockhart and Ralph Wood went to Berlin for the third time running, which Wood considered was 'too much':

Our journey there and back was fine and we missed all the hot spots. The target proved quite hot and we were coned for a while. It was a horrible naked feeling, especially as there was no flak in the cone which got us. Hence, a damn good set-up for a cat's-eye fighter. It was okay, though, and we hoped for a smaller target next time.[26]

On 16 September the 'old home province' (Brunswick) was our 'target for tonight'. It wasn't a very spectacular raid because of cloud. However, it was one trip nearer Home Sweet Home. This trip was a piece of cake and we had very little trouble.[27] Berlin again on 18 September was anything but a nice trip. It was our thirteenth trip to the 'Big City'. We had the 'twitch' while waiting for take-off. Over Berlin we were coned and got caught in a huge barrage of flak. It was very unpleasant and ineffective.[28] The following afternoon we were due to start a nine-day leave, and we could certainly do it justice. Though we decided we might wait and go Wednesday morning, as we would like to have got thirty trips in before our leave, we went.'

When Andy Lockhart and Ralph Wood returned from leave they went to Karlsruhe on 29 September and started their 'last lap'. Another crew[29] had taken the *Moncton Express II* on 25/26 September, when the target was Mannheim, and had failed to return. Ralph Wood recalls:

We now had a new A-for-Apple. *Moncton Express III* seemed okay! Karlsruhe was a good trip. We could see that the target markers were well and truly placed. Our op to Hamburg on 30 September [when forty-six Mosquitoes visited the city] was another good trip, but we didn't deserve it as one of our crews left his radio on 'transmit' and talked about everything, telling when, why and how we were going to bomb Hamburg. They were waiting for us all right! Andy and I were in at the beginning and got Hell pasted at us. However, it was one trip nearer home, and that's what we wanted. We lost one crew.[30] *Moncton Express III* behaved quite well.

On 2 October it was Brunswick again, when forty-eight Mosquitoes were dispatched, and for Ralph Wood it proved to be a little 'warmer' than usual:

The full moon made you feel conspicuous. The fighters loved it. I hope we didn't have to go to the 'Big City' in this moonlight. It wouldn't have been the first time, though. It was a good raid and all returned. The next night we went to Kassel [when forty-three Mosquitoes were dispatched]. It was a poor trip all round. It brought us to two-thirds of our tour finished, so that was a help, anyway. We saw a jet-propelled enemy fighter. Our op to the Kiel Canal on 5 October was the 'Daddy' of them all! After practicing for days, we took off to mine the Kiel Canal. We dropped our vegetable from a height of 100 ft. It was wizard flying at rooftop level over the villages and farmhouses. The canal was well defended by light anti-aircraft guns and balloons. One searchlight got us and one gun opened fire at us head-on when we were about 200 ft off the deck. It was rather alarming but missed us. About a dozen [nine] were on the job and all got back, although one pilot flew back with a dead navigator beside him for company (gulp). We really enjoyed ourselves, but we certainly had the 'twitch' before reaching the target.

9 October was a bit of a change, with Wilhelmshaven our target. It was a nice easy trip and not much time over enemy territory. Our wing commander was going to try to put us on the battle order two nights running, then one off, until we finished, so we could get home

for Christmas. (Maybe!) We still had fifteen left to do. Our next one was on the 10th, and the target was Cologne. Apart from the target itself, we met with no opposition. Most of our trip was over Allied-held territory; that was nice. I could feel a string of Berlin trips coming up soon. We'd been too lucky lately. But the next, on 12 October, was a dirty-weather trip to Hamburg [when fifty-two Mosquitoes were dispatched]. The target area was clear, though, and we got heavily coned and hell shot at us. I was glad to see the last of this place. It was a good trip, though. Another one of our crews failed to return,[31] making it seven crews lost since we arrived on 6 July. It was Cologne again on 13 October. We had thirteen trips to do and it was Friday the 13th! But we fooled them and took off at 4:30 on the morning of the 14th and went to Cologne. Shocking hours, but then it was another trip, and an uneventful one at that.

On the 15th Andy took my cousin Lloyd up on the air test in the afternoon. He was an army corporal in the Intelligence Corps. I met him at the railway station and then escorted him to the officers' quarters, where we outfitted him in an RCAF officer's uniform – wings and all. We had dinner in the officers' mess, followed by a terrific party. We introduced him as my cousin in the RCAF to one and all. We all had a good chuckle over this bit of friendly deceit. Lloyd left soon afterwards by train and we took off in the evening for our target. We went to Hamburg and received the usual 'warm' welcome they handed out to us there. That was now ten trips since our last leave, and no Berlin trips yet. Our luck couldn't last much longer. Last night another crew from here failed to return.[32]

Our trip on 16 October was another short dash over the Allied front to raid Cologne again. It was a nice little trip, but we came close to some flak over the target. It was a very dark night and one of our crews [Flt Lt George D.T. Nairn and Sgt Danny Lunn] flew into the deck as he prepared to land at base. The kite was completely wrecked, but Fate brought the crew through with only minor injuries. A few trees broke their speed, enabling them to survive. We were now in the 'fast forties'. Two nights later it was Hanover and a damn good prang. We weren't touched the whole way there and back. Next day Andy and I received the immediate award of the DFC, which was for our part in the mining operation to Kiel on 5 October. The next day was a stand-down, and we were not on that night, so we had a 'do' in the mess, which was the customary treat when you got a 'gong'.

The weather had been against us of late, but we managed to get to Hamburg on the 22nd. We took off at five in the afternoon and got back at 8:30. Coming home through a violent storm we were flying up and down like a bird in a chimney. The storm pitched us all over the place. At one time there were big circles of electricity around the tips of the propellers as we made our way through the clouds. It was an eerie sight. As we left this electrical field there was a very loud explosion. I was certain we had blown up, and started looking frantically for my parachute. On our return to base we found it completely socked in with fog. Our station was equipped with FIDO, a device for burning fuel oil on either side of the runway The heat from this burning fuel would raise the fog enough for us to land in safety. We sure as hell appreciated this invention, as we had nowhere else to go. We all got down in one piece. It was a new experience for both of us. The target was unusually 'warm', but the gunners were rather clueless.

My seventieth op, on Monday 23 October, was to Berlin or bust. We had a very pleasant trip there and back, watching others get into trouble instead of ourselves. The target itself, however, proved very, very warm. It was such that we were really shaken for a few minutes. Personally, I was just waiting for a hit in a vital spot, which I expected at any moment – then to see if I could bale out. In short, the gunners below were in top form. We were over the 'Big City' at 7:30 p.m. Andy and I now had seven more to do and then it would all be over.

Others this same night were just starting their tour. On 23/24 October, 'A' and 'B' Flights in 128 Squadron at Wyton were assigned different cities: 'A' Flight commanded by Sqn Ldr Ivor Broom DFC* was given a spoof raid on Wiesbaden; 'B' Flight was allotted Berlin.[33] Flg Off Herbert 'Ed' Boulter[34] and Sgt Jim Churcher were one of the new crews assigned to 'A' Flight. Ivor Broom and his navigator Tommy Broom[35] (no relation, who was ten years older than Boulter), thought that as the new pilot looked so very young he should be called 'Bertie the Boy', and Bertie he became.[36] During the early morning of the 23rd Boulter and Churcher's names were on the battle order for that night's operations. Flg Off Boulter and Sgt Jim Churcher had mixed emotions about the coming operation before they went out to B.XXV D-Dog.[37] They were overjoyed to be part of a team at last, and they were excited and apprehensive in equal measure. They knew that the Mosquito was almost too fast to catch, and they had the cover of night and the plane had a track record of minimum casualties. Like almost every other young crew, they had that wonderful 'It won't happen to me' mentality. 'But above all else,' recalls Boulter, 'there was the determination not to let your chums down. That covered your crew, your ground crew, your flight, the squadron and above all else the other aircrews you flew with.'

Like all German cities, Wiesbaden was heavily defended by anti-aircraft guns and searchlights, and Ed Boulter and Jim Churcher returned to Wyton having been shot at by an 88 mm radar-controlled gun, but although the shell bursts were very close they had come through unscathed. They were on the battle order in the squadron office the next day when the target was Hannover, a city Boulter would visit four times in all before the end of the war. They carried four 500-pounders and no TIs in the bomb-bay, and dropped them on the target before returning to England. Wyton was shrouded in fog on their return and they were diverted to Foulsham in Norfolk, which was equipped with FIDO. Two days later they were on the battle order again, when fifty-nine Mosquitoes went to Cologne.

During October eleven Mosquitoes of the LNSF were lost on operations. New squadrons joined the force, with 142 Squadron re-forming at Gransden Lodge on 25 October and flying its first operation when its only two Mosquito B.XXVs were dispatched to Cologne. At Graveley, meanwhile, Andy Lockhart and Ralph Wood were on the last lap. Ralph Wood recalls:

> My seventy-first op was on 24 October. Three nights running and this was supposed to be the 'Big City', but it was changed at the eleventh hour and we went to Hanover instead.[38] Not a very spectacular raid, but it was one more nearer Home Sweet Home. On the way back we saw several jet-propelled enemy fighters. We did the odd bit of weaving and avoided any trouble which might have been waiting for us. We couldn't get back to base as the weather had clamped in there. We arrived back the next day at 3 p.m. Op No. 72 three days later, on 27 October, was Berlin again, but the reception committee was not on its toes that night. As a matter of fact, the whole trip was rather uneventful. Flak at the target was moderately heavy. We were briefed for the 'Big City' again on 28 October, but it was cancelled at the last minute and instead we went to Cologne, where about 700 heavies had been that afternoon. When we got there at 2030 hours it was burning merrily. The river showed up well and you could distinguish the streets by looking at the rows of burning buildings. We saw a rocket (V-2) take off and climb to 50,000 or 60,000 ft before losing height in the direction of London.
>
> It looked like we were going to finish the hard way. On 30 October it was Berlin again,[39] and my heart was really in my mouth as we lost our starboard engine and came home nearly all the way on one engine. I had visions of finishing my tour in *Stalag Luft III*, but Andy did a good job as usual and we made a one-engine landing at base. It was his third such landing. I wrote, 'Here's to an easier trip tomorrow night. (Three more.)' We got a break. It was a short trip to Cologne. We went in two hours before the heavies. I got the 'twitch' five minutes before reaching the target because I saw a jet fighter take off beside us and climb up above us. A lovely silhouette we must have been with the cloud below and the moon and fighter above. Still, we had a good trip and he didn't pick on us. The

weather on return was pretty putrid, but Andy got us back to Mother Earth in one solid piece. We saw another rocket at the same place and about the same time. Our nerves were a little on edge and it didn't take much to irritate us. We were getting very anxious to finish. Another crew failed to return. The pilot was a good friend of ours. (Nine crews had gone missing in the four months we'd been at Graveley.) Now I had got the 'twitch'! Our target on 2 November was Osnabrück, a place I always wanted to visit because they usually had a crack at us on the way home from Berlin if we came out that way. The raid wasn't brilliant, but we got there and back. We saw two jet fighters on our way home. The twitch was doing fine. We now had one more to go.

It was Berlin on 3 November [when fifty-five Mosquitoes were dispatched to Berlin], our seventeenth there, and I hoped the last; the one that I'd wanted to write about for quite a while. We took off at midnight. I'd never felt so keenly about a trip in all my life. I certainly lived every moment of it. There were numerous fighter flares and fighter contrails all the way there and back. We saw one jet fighter. The moon was rather bright, too. The raid was wizard, though. Andy and I exchanged congratulations and shook hands on it before we got out of the kite. Gosh, we were a couple of happy kids. *Moncton Express III* came through with flying colours. I could have written pages about our feelings, our 'twitch' and our relief when we got back again, but so ended my second and last tour. Our *Moncton Express* had carried us out safely and back again for our fifty trips together, to all those places on the map of Europe. For this I was grateful, and I admired Andy's skill as a pilot. Suddenly it broke through my slightly spinning head that I had now completed seventy-seven ops, and for me my war was finally over. It looked like I'd made it after all, though why, I couldn't understand. All I knew for certain was that I was very glad to be alive. I'd come very close several times to discovering all about death. Perhaps in the years ahead I might be lucky enough to find out something about life.[40]

On the night of 4/5 November 1944 Mosquito low-level visual markers marked the Dortmund–Ems Canal for 174 Lancasters of 5 Group.[41] This was one of six attacks by 5 Group in the two-month period starting 4 November 1944. There had been one previous successful attack on 23 September, which had included 617 Squadron carrying 12,000 lb 'Tallboys'. The two most vulnerable raised stretches selected for attack were on the canal near Ladbergen, between Münster and Rheine, where it briefly divides into two channels, and on the Mittelland Canal near Gravenhorst, close to its junction with the Dortmund–Ems. Both canals are in the area just north of the Ruhr, and the two canals connect this huge industrial area with Hannover, Brunswick and Berlin to the east. Maurice A. Smith DFC and Lee Page in B.XX KB401 Easy were one of the Mosquito crews who took part on 4/5 November, with the Dortmund–Ems Canal as their target. It started badly, as Smith recalls.

> Our morale was always low before take-off, mainly because we operated alone and still missed the bustle and chatter of a squadron departure and the close presence of our Lanc crew of seven. Controllers of 5 Group flew from Coningsby, which was 54 Base HQ and also housed 83 and 97 Squadrons. The Mosquito Marker force of 627 Squadron flew from nearby Woodhall Spa. The Lanc squadrons trundled off an hour or more before our solitary Mossie was due to get airborne. We would start up on the silent tarmac, using only a flashlamp to see by, check time and taxi out for our solitary take-off. At least flying control would tell the ops room we had gone. 'Easy' had been over to 627 Squadron for service and had flown back that morning. She started well and the Packard-built Rolls-Royce Merlins ran up OK. This was only a three-hour sortie, so our 100-gallon auxiliary tanks under the wings were only half full. Our load was one yellow and two red target indicators – red for marking, yellow to cancel any stray red, or German spoof marking.
>
> We lined up on the string of tiny runway lights, opened up against the brakes and started our run. Differential throttle, then rudder to check swing as the tail came up and, at 105 knots, off into the night. Almost immediately the engine notes sounded wrong and the aircraft yawed as we climbed. Check both throttles and bang pitch levers forward on their stops. Wheels up, climbing at 160 knots, height 500 ft, straight ahead. The starboard engine seemed to roar and the aircraft tried to slew to port. Perhaps the port engine had cut? No, all seemed normal there; instruments, noise, exhaust flames long and lilac blue, as they should be. Again the roar and lurch, and this time the starboard rev counter sailed up somewhere near the 3,500 mark. We had a prop trying to run away. In a few seconds of surprise and diagnosis we reached 800 ft, levelled out and throttled right back on the starboard engine. There was no question of pressing on, so we must land back. I decided not to feather the starboard airscrew. The engine was unlikely to come to more harm, and could help in emergency. A Mossie would not go round again on one engine from ground level with flaps and wheels down, so we would be committed at around 400 ft on the approach. Thought: 'When did I last practise a single-engine landing at night?'
>
> Now 627 Squadron would have a standby aircraft ready to go at Woodhall Spa. We did not have one at Coningsby. Marker Leader would be quite capable of controlling the operation if we did not show up – so long as he got there. No, let's have a go. Break radio

silence and try to sound like a training flight. Tell Woodhall you want to land and take up a spare aircraft. They will guess what is going on. They did. We landed without incident and leaped into a strange Mosquito IV, DZ418 'Baker', looked round its unfamiliar instruments, started up and taxied out. Quick engine check and away up to 10,000 ft on course. We flew at 2,850 rpm + 9 lb/sq inch, cut corners on our dog-leg course in dark cloudless sky and were near enough to see the first parachute flares fall, some minutes before the attack was due to begin. We had stuffed the nose of the Mossie down for the last ten minutes, holding about 360 knots and arriving in the Ladbergen area at 1,200 ft. Squadron Leader [Ronnie] Churcher [of 627 Squadron][42] had got things started. Visibility was good. Using their usual dive-bombing techniques, the Mossies now put their red TIs on the aiming point. A great gaggle of 170 main-force Lancs dropped their full loads of fourteen 1,000 lb GP bombs, many with long-delay fuses to add to the confusion on the ground. Some early loads fell too far east, but the error was noticed and corrected. The flares had blown away and long gone out, and even the target marking was practically obliterated.[43]

Two nights later we were briefed for a similar attack on the Mittelland Canal at Gravenhorst, only about fifteen miles north of Ladbergen. We still hadn't got our Mosquito 'Easy' back, so were using a borrowed Mk IV, DZ518 'Mike'. The weather was to be similar, but with more haze and a stronger wind. The actual marking point was not very dearly defined, and we studied the area and the buildings, memorizing any features – railway line, salt pans that might stand out. This time we flew out more sedately to flight plan, with a little more time in hand. As we turned into our last leg for run-in, we saw occasional searchlight beams fanning around to starboard. Quite suddenly, a ruddy great violet-white beam opened up bang onto us, followed at once by others. We had heard about so-called master beams, so perhaps this was one of them. But there should not have been so many lights in the gap between Rheine and Münster. We were at an effective height for predicted flak, which would probably follow. And it did – but we had moved over, luckily without the searchlights following. The time between guns firing and their shells bursting worked out as a count of one second per thousand feet. At 12,000 ft about twelve seconds from gun flash. If you dived 30 degrees to port and looked high to starboard, there was a good chance of seeing the flak burst where you would have been had you kept straight on. We were glad to be in a manoeuvrable Mossie rather than a Lanc or, Lord help us, a Stirling. A solitary aircraft was always more vulnerable, and this was one big worry for single Mosquitoes, and even more for a main-force bomber that got winged and became a straggler without even Window protection.

The first bursts had missed us and we could quickly jink out of range. But why this nasty reception over what should have been open country?

Voice from navigator, 'Should be about twelve minutes to go, Skip. I reckon that was Münster. We are a bit off course and ahead of time.' Too right, and our first hint of a Met error on wind strength.

For a final, accurate positioning beyond GEE range, the Mosquito force in particular, with their more limited space and navigational equipment, depended on a few selected Pathfinder Lancs, with all the blind aids, including H_2S radar, to drop green proximity indicators as near the aiming point as possible. Similar guidance was sometimes given for track turning points. We waited hopefully as we dived gently in the approximate direction of the target and identified with Marker Leader. No greens. No parachute flares yet.

There was an amber-tinged haze in a dark sky, and nothing could be seen below. At long last, a few flares showed ahead and left of us, and beyond, a glimpse of a green TI. A quick caustic word to the navigator, and dive hard over towards them. Faint reflections showed here and there on the ground, which could have been water or glass. As we dived lower we saw even less. A few flares backed up the dying light of the first ones. Anxious call to Marker Leader. Only about four minutes to go. He was searching. A few more scattered flares were dropping, but at 800 ft there was not a single recognizable feature below. The German blackout was faultless. I had a frightful mental picture of the main force bearing down like a great herd of elephants and even more difficult to stop. Search harder.

Tip the Mossie on edge. Marker 4 says he has found the salt pans, but practically no flares there to help. Call Flare Force Lancs and Backers-up for anything they've got left – knowing most, if not all, have already flown over. 'Marker 3, Tally Ho!'

Thank god for that Marker.[44] Where is he? Marker 2 calls for more flares. Just time to save the operation. Call up main force to delay their arrival by two minutes. Dog-leg or orbit. I could just imagine what those crews were calling us. Marker 2 is not able to back up. No longer sees the solitary TI. Marker 3 was sure he had found the spot, but the TI must have gone into the canal and been extinguished. No flares left. Four minutes after H hour. Despairing effort; full-throttle climb to 2,000 ft for a more vertical view and maybe a glimpse of a silver thread of canal. No hope. Too late. Attack should have been over by now. Dangerous to keep the main force milling around any more. Half Germany must know we are blundering around the sky north of the Ruhr. 'Abortive code sign to Codeword Force: Go home, Go home.'

There was no alternative target. In fact thirty of the Lancs, including markers, got their loads away, presumably blind, using their own H_2S. Most of the bombs had delay fuses, so we did not see them explode. Marker and Flare Force Lancs usually filled up any spare stations in their bomb-bays with 1,000-pounders.

A frightful nightmarish experience it was. What on earth could one say to the AOC – who expected a direct, personal call and first assessment, day or night, as soon as the controller landed back and found a scrambler phone in the debriefing room?

A raid assessment showed that an exceptional combination of troubles had made this attack abortive. A much stronger wind than expected blew such parachute flares as there were away to the east and scattered them. No fewer than seven of the fourteen Flare Force plus four Blind Marker Lancaster crews had suffered H_2S radar failures. The one target indicator that Mosquito Marker 3 got down in about the right place fell into the water and could not be seen or backed up by others. The green proximity markers (two in this case), which were sometimes accurate enough to serve as emergency aiming points, could not be assessed and were confused with a green route marker. Anything other than accurate bombing on such a target, out in open country, would have been useless.[45]

Unhappily, ten of the 235 aircraft were lost, for reasons not altogether clear. The relatively bright sky and good upper visibility helped enemy fighters in the target area and on the way back. The confusion and concentration of aircraft around the target would have been conducive to collisions. Landing back with a full bomb-load was no-one's idea of a picnic ...[46]

On this same night, 6/7 November, Sgt John Clark, a Scottish navigator, and his New Zealander pilot, Bill Henley, flew their first Mosquito operation since joining 571 Squadron at Oakington after crewing up at 1655 OTU at Warboys. Clark recalls:

RAF Warboys was just like so many other airfields in wartime – some Nissen huts and hangars strung together by concrete paths. There were so many aircraft flying that day it seemed as if the whole of East Anglia was one large airfield. I was told to report to an assembly hut, or briefing room, the next day. There were about twenty of us, of whom half were pilots, half navigators. For some it was their second tour of operations. For a few it was their third tour. DSOs and DFCs seemed to be commonplace among them. Not a few had what was known as an 'operational twitch'. Their eyes and heads involuntarily flicked from time to time. I stood well back in deference to all this array of talent. I was and felt a very 'sprog' sergeant.

A group captain, with so many gongs displayed on his chest that he must have been flying one wing low any time he took to the air, jumped up on a table and addressed us in no uncertain manner. We were, he said, a specially picked lot and would augment the LNSF, which was already causing the 'Hun' night-fighters a few headaches. He warned us, however, that their flak was more accurate than it had ever been. The Germans knew they were losing the war, but they were going down fighting, especially since they had been presented with unconditional surrender terms. He made the analogy of a wounded animal being more vicious when hurt. As an afterthought he tossed in the information that we would be carrying no guns whatsoever. We would have to rely on our speed to keep clear of trouble. A gasp of incredulity greeted this revelation. After a few more remarks of this nature he announced that he wanted us all crewed up within three or four days. It reminded me of those announcements in the quality newspapers: 'The engagement has been announced and a wedding will take place.' It was going to be a whirlwind courtship.

I was still standing at the back of the briefing room when a squadron leader, complete with 'operational twitch', came up to me. He had a scar, which he must have collected on one of his previous operations, across his forehead and a DSO and DFC and Bar across his chest. He looked me up and down. 'You've been saying nothing all this time, but I think you've been taking it all in. I like that. Think about it.'

I did. A cat, so legend states, has nine lives. I wondered how many he had and how many he had used up so far. Just then a little warrant officer, the only non-commissioned pilot in the room, came over to me. His shoulder flashes identified him as a New Zealander. His accent was as sharp as his profile. 'I hear you're a Scot. Will you be my navigator?'

For some reason which I could never explain, I answered, 'Yes.' We shook hands on the deal and introduced ourselves.

'I'm Bill Henley', he said. 'I've been instructing for the last eighteen months. This will be my first tour on ops.'

'Same here, only I haven't been instructing. You could say I've been like a spare one at a wedding – just hanging around. Let's have a beer and talk things over.'

We popped up to the bar in the sergeants' mess and gave each other a potted history of our service careers so far. He came from Auckland and had a brother who had been killed in the fighting in Crete in the Middle East campaign. Good God, I thought. Is no family going to be untouched by this war? I had just heard that my sister, who had become a driver in the ATS, had nearly been drowned driving a DUKW from the Ayrshire coast to the Isle of Arran.

I pulled a bit of a face. 'Too bad about your brother. Let's try to get you back to New Zealand in one piece when this war is over. Who knows, we may get our commissions and a gong to go with them.' What a load of bull, I thought. Still, it was better to look on the bright side. 'By the way, I've got to report for GEE training this afternoon. I've never used the thing before.'

He smiled. 'And I've got to familiarize myself with the Mosquito. I've never flown one before.'

A week or so later I joined Bill at Wyton, a permanent station with brick buildings and tarmac roads which seemed to ooze luxury compared with the muck and mess of Warboys. I walked round the aircraft we had been allocated to make our first familiarization flight together.

'She's got beautiful lines, hasn't she?' I observed. 'Except for this extended belly, which makes her look pregnant.'

'Yes,' Bill replied, 'pregnant with celestial fire. It's extended so that it can carry the 4,000 lb bomb. The bomb looks like an extra-large can of beans, and the casing is just about as thick as a bean can. The rest of it is all explosives. We'll have to handle it rather carefully – no belly landings – and if we drop below 4,000 ft, we're liable to get our tail blown off.'

'Are we? So now you tell me!'

I clambered up the steps after him, into the cabin of the aircraft. 'They don't give a navigator much room to navigate.' I looked at the foldaway navigation table complete with Anglepoise shaded orange light on my right, as I sat on the rather uncomfortable seat with part of the bomb-bay under it. 'I've got to get us to Germany – and back – using this', I said, pointing to the table. 'I see I'm considered more expendable than you.' At the back of his seat, armour-plating rose above his head. In my part it stopped at my waist; the rest of the space above the armour-plating was crammed with Bendix radio and LORAN. The GEE box was positioned behind the pilot's seat and was easily accessible.

The ground crew, who had been standing patiently, waiting for us to get settled, folded the telescopic ladder, stowed it away and slammed the main door shut. I in turn fitted the floor under my feet, slipping my parachute and navigation bag behind my legs. This routine was going to take some getting used to. With the aid of the ground starting 'ack', the two engines coughed into life. The ground staff waved us off the dispersal pan and in no time it seemed we were lined up, looking down the runway. Bill pushed open the throttles and the two Merlin engines took us by the seat of our pants and pulled us down the runway.

Then it happened. The aircraft swung to the right. Fortunately, our wheels were off the ground, and by a quick piece of avoiding action, we missed a hangar and pointed our nose skywards.

'Sorry about that.' It was Bill's voice over the intercom. 'It's never done that before and I'll make sure it doesn't do it again.'

I tried to be jocular. 'That's what the man said when his horse dropped dead. Anyway, why worry? We missed the hangar by about 500 yards.' What a lu-lu of a take-off! I wondered what kind of driver I had chosen – or had he chosen me? As the months rolled on, Bill was as good as his word. Our aircraft never again swung on take-off.

One morning, the whole of the OT course was summoned to present itself in the briefing room. The group captain with all the medals on his chest strode in and, without preamble, congratulated us on having completed the course. It was too bad that we had lost one crew during that time. It was unusual at an OTU. There had been no case of 'OTU-itis'. Our postings were on the notice-board outside the crew room. We were being spread among the other Mosquito squadrons in 8 Group. He left as abruptly as he had arrived. 'What on earth is "OTU-it is"?' I asked a seasoned-looking navigator.

'Well, to put it crudely, some of these intrepid bird-men like to wear a brevet,' he pointed to his wings, 'and pick up a few free beers in their "local". However, when the chips are down, they suddenly discover that they have an incurable disease which their great uncles, or some other relative in the family, had picked up fighting in the Afghan wars or somewhere else in the British Empire. They call off flying before they have to face the flak and the fighters. The powers that be treat them pretty roughly. They're stripped of their rank and brevet, then their documents are stamped "LMF" – Lack of Moral Fibre. They usually become shit-house cleaners-out."

We found that along with another crew we had been posted to 571 Squadron at Oakington, half-way between Cambridge and Huntingdon, where we would share the airfield with 7 Squadron Lancs. On 5 November we presented ourselves to the squadron adjutant of 571, Flight Lieutenant R. Stanton. Evidently our credentials had gone before us. We had been allocated to 'A' Flight, the other crew to 'B' Flight. We were introduced to the 'A' flight commander, Squadron Leader Norman A.J. Mackie DSO DFC*[47] and his Australian navigator, Flight Lieutenant Angus MacDonald RAAF DFC DFM. 'Ah yes, you're the new boys. We'll put you on ops tomorrow night.' He looked at his navigator. 'How say you, Blue?'

'Yes, the usual treatment. Blood them early. They can take the old lady L-London for their first trip.'

He sounded quite laconic about it, as if he were allocating us an ice-cream cart for a day's 'jolly' at some fairground. Didn't he realize we had waited years for this minute?

Next morning we were taken out to a dispersal pan where L-London stood. She was painted all-over black, and the flight commander's navigator hadn't exaggerated when he said she had completed over a hundred trips, if the bomb insignia stencilled on the side of the aircraft were to be believed.

'There's no practice bombing; it's been scrubbed', said the 'Chiefy' who was waiting for us. He and Bill discussed a few technical points before Bill signed the Form 700, accepting the aircraft. [Before an op a crew would complete an NFT, or Night Flying Test, in the aircraft they would fly that night.] After an impeccable take-off we headed for the Norfolk coast. I undid my waistband harness and, with a bit of difficulty, crawled underneath the dashboard on my side, to check the course-setting bombsight, which jutted out over the Perspex nose. There was also a bomb 'tit' hooked innocuously on the side of the fuselage, and the fuse-setting switches, which activated the three fuses on the 'cookie'. I glanced through the two Perspex panels set in either side of the nose. The propellers were churning the air at what seemed only a few inches from my ear holes. If one of those props detached itself and flew off, I would be like a piece of corned beef – all ground up. Rubbish! I thought. They'll fly forwards, not sideways. Anyway, they won't fly off.

'Everything OK?' asked 'Chiefy' when we got our feet on the ground again. We gave him the thumbs-up sign. 'We'll see you later', we added.

'It's your first trip, isn't it? Good luck. She'll get you back.' He nodded at the aircraft.

Bill looked at me. 'No messing – Briefing is at half-past three with take-off about half-past five. In between those times we get supper – bacon and eggs, I'm told.'

'Hmmm. It's almost worth going for that alone.'

At the appointed time we assembled in the briefing room. We immediately felt isolated from the outside world. Special policemen stood at all the entrances with revolvers hanging from their waists. On a raised platform at one end of the room, some sitting and some standing, were the CO, the flight commander, the intelligence officer and the Met officer. On the wall behind them, illuminated by strong lights, were maps of the UK, France and Germany. Superimposed on them were tapes indicating our route out and back.

'OK chaps, settle down.' It was the intelligence officer. 'Your target, as you can see, is Gelsenkirchen.'

'Where the hell's that?' I muttered. A Canadian sitting next to me leaned over and whispered, 'It's in the Ruhr – the "Happy Valley" in other words, just north of Essen. It'll be a doddle.'

Reassured on that point, I concentrated on what the intelligence officer was saying.

'We're taking you west of London, then over France to Germany. You'll attack the target from the south-west to take advantage of the winds on your leg into the target. The raid is of a diversionary nature. The "heavies" are bombing here.' His pointer jabbed at a different spot.[48] 'Because it is a diversionary attack you will Window most of the way into the target – navigators please note.'

'Jeeze,' said the Canuck out loud, 'why don't you stick a brush up our ass, then we can sweep the floor when we crawl through to the bombsight to drop our "cookie".'

The remark received a ripple of laughter, which the intelligence officer ignored. 'The target will be marked by OBOE markers, so I'll be looking for some good photographs on return.' He waffled on for some time about searchlights, flak, etc., and was followed by the Met man, who assured us that the airfield would be wide-open on our return and that the winds were in fact blowing from the south-west. Wing Commander R.J. Gosnell DSO DFC, the CO, affirmed that the 'graveyard' airfields of Woodbridge and Manston would be wide-open for any aircraft that couldn't make it back to base. 'However, I'll be waiting for each of you here. Good luck!' he wound up.[49]

As it turned out, we sat waiting for an hour-plus, looking at each other and the wall opposite, each minute seeming like an hour. Now I knew in some degree what the soldiers of the First World War must have felt like when they knew they were going 'over the top' when the whistle blew. Bill produced a shiny black pair of sheepskin flying-boots. 'I got them in New Zealand and decided I wouldn't wear them till I did my first op.' They looked pretty swep-up compared with my battered old escape-type boots, so-called because there was a single-bladed knife in a small pocket in the leg of one of them. The idea was that, should I have to bale out and resort to walking back, I could cut the leggings off and make them resemble civilian shoes.

After what seemed like aeons of time the WAAF orderly came round the rooms to tell us that the flight trucks were waiting for us. We climbed aboard, stopping at the crew room to pick up our parachutes, 'Mae Wests' and escape packs; then, crew by crew, we were dumped at our respective aircraft. I made a cursory check of the fuses on the bomb while Bill did the rest of the checks; then I followed him, navigation bag slung over my shoulder, into the cockpit. It seemed to get smaller each time I got into it, especially with the bundles of Window stacked all over the place. How we

Still taken from W/C Bob Iredale's SB-F MM412 during the precision attack on Amiens Prison on 18 February 1944, one of the most famous operations of the war, when twelve FB.VIs of 464 Squadron RAAF and 487 Squadron RNZAF breached the prison walls at Amiens Prison, which was holding 700 French prisoners. The aircraft following is SB-A MM4O2 flown by S/L W.R.C. Sugden and his navigator, F/O A.H. Bridger. *(via Jerry Scutts)*

During the attack on Amiens Prison about 400 prisoners escaped. After Arras was liberated in October 1944, 260 bodies were found buried outside the town. Among them were most of the Amiens prisoners who had deliberately stayed behind to take part in the work of mercy. They had been shot in April 1944. Here, in tribute three FB.VIs with their bomb doors open fly low over the prison after the war.

St Cyr after the attack on an airfield and signals depot by Lancasters and six Mosquitoes of 5 Group on 25 July 1944. (*IWM*)

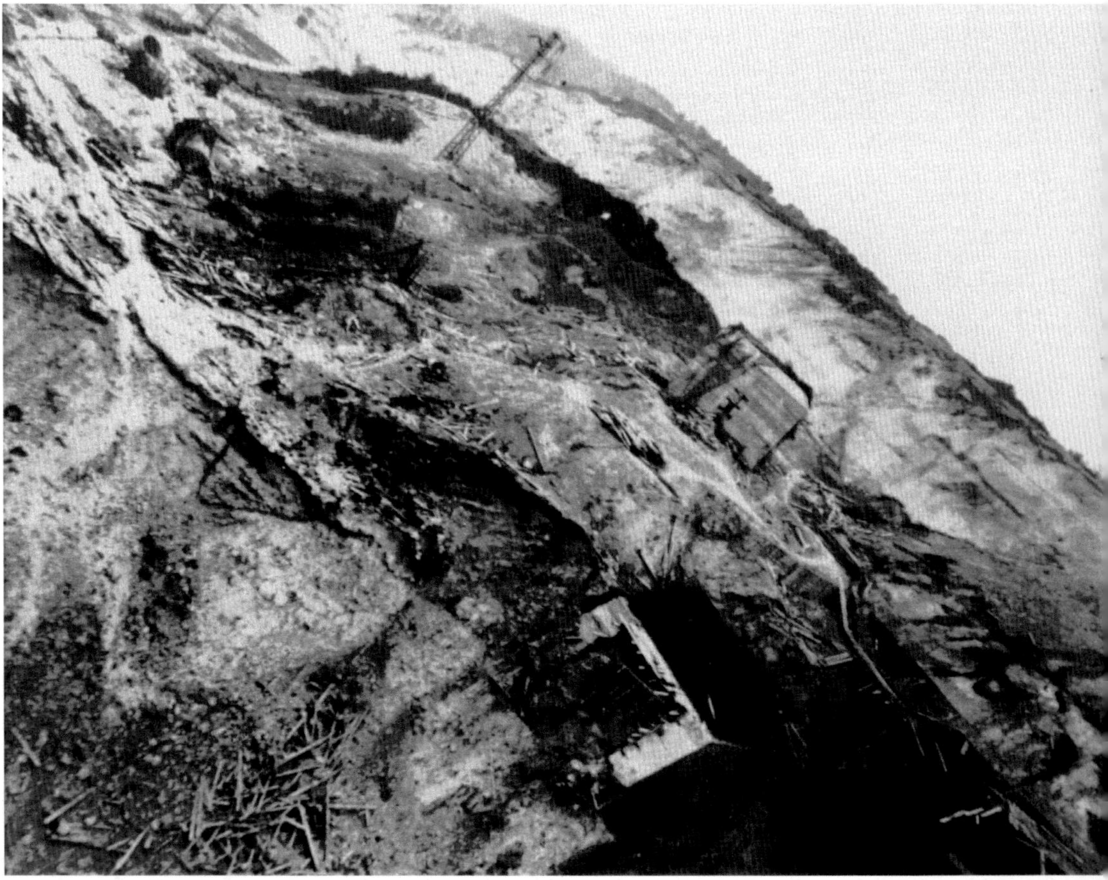

At 11.30am on 17 September 1944, 613 Squadron destroyed the old Dutch Army barracks occupied by German forces. Accuracy was essential with two rows of tightly packed housing immediately behind the barracks.

Wizernes which was put out of action by 'Tallboys' dropped by Lancasters of 617 Squadron on 17 July 1944.

On 31 October 1944 a precision attack was carried out on Aarhus University, the HQ for the *Gestapo* in the whole of Jutland, Denmark, by twenty-five FB.VIs of 21, 464 Squadron RAAF and 487 RNZAF Squadrons, each carrying 11-second delayed action bombs and led by G/C Peter Wykeham-Barnes. The operation was carried out at such a low altitude that S/L F.H. Denton of 487 Squadron hit the roof of the building, losing his tail wheel and the port half of the tail plane. Denton nursed the Mosquito across the North Sea and managed to land safely. The university and its incriminating records were destroyed.

On 31 October 1944 twenty-five FB.VIs of 21, 464 RAAF and 487 RNZAF Squadrons led by G/C Peter Wykeham-Barnes destroyed the *Gestapo* HQ at Aarhus University in Denmark with 11-second delayed action 500lb bombs. The buildings in the foreground are intact. *(IWM)*

F/O John Barry on 29 Squadron lends a hand during servicing of his NF.XIX the morning after operational flying. (*Ken Lowes*)

F/O Guy Hopkins (left), F/O John Barry (middle) and S/L Clive Kirkland standing in for the Intelligence Officer, who of course was elsewhere de-briefing other crews. Kirkland's hair parting was hurriedly altered and the Photoflood light so adjusted so that his features were in shade.
(*Ken Lowes*)

A 'Cookie' is hoisted into the bomb bay.

8 Group Mosquitoes at rest.

F/L Ed Boulter and his navigator, Chris Hart DFM on 128 Squadron in front of *B-Bertie* at Wyton. (*Ed Boulter*)

W/C 'Rod' Rodley waves off Mosquito XVI PF443/A carrying a 4,000lb cookie and piloted by Tom Empson DFC and his navigator Bert Dwerryhouse who were on their 14th trip to the 'Big City' on 128 Squadron at Wyton on 21 March 1945, the 30th successive raid on Berlin.

Bombs arrive at dispersal.

B.Mk.XVI RV297 M5-F of 128 Squadron taxies out at Wyton on B the night of 21/22 March 1945 when 142 Mosquitoes of 8 Group (PFF) made two raids on Berlin. Only one 8 Group Mosquito was lost. The LNSF of Mosquitoes raided Berlin 170 times, 36 of these on consecutive nights.

Moving a 'Cookie' into position.

HK360 was built at Leavesden as a NF.II but was flown to Marshalls at Cambridge for the fitting of SCR 720 radar and became an NF.XVII. SCR 720 (British designation AI Mk.X) was developed by the Radiation Laboratory, Massachusetts Institute of Technology and built by the Western Electric Company and the radar entered RAF service in 1943. AI Mk.X had a wavelength of 10cm with a range of 8 to 10 miles. HK360 was one of the first NF.XVIIs to enter service with 456 Squadron at Fairwood Common in January 1944, a squadron then in the forefront of Britain's night defences. On 17 April it joined the Fighter Interception Unit at Ford, which used Mosquitoes for test purposes and operational trials and eventually HK360 was SOC on 31 January 1946. HK360 is here being flown by F/Os Desmond Tull and Peter Cowgill. In the month after this photo was taken this crew shot down eight enemy aircraft over Germany and then went missing. Here HK360 accompanies captured Me 410 TF209 (10259), which was used for comparison trials with the Mosquito, crewed here by S/L Jeremy Howard-Williams and F/O F.J. MacRae. *(Jeremy Howard-Williams)*

NF.XIII HK415/KP-R of 409 Squadron RCAF which was lost in a take-off accident at Lille airfield on 18 January 1945. On 18/19 December 1944 F/Os Al Webster and Ross H. Finlayson destroyed a Ju 88 in this aircraft, which S/L A. Parker-Rees and F/L Bennett of 96 Squadron were flying when they claimed a He 177 probable over Sussex on 24/25 February 1944 and a Me 410 at sea on 13/14 April 1944. (*Ross Finlayson*)

NF.IIs of 605 Squadron. The aircraft second from left is DZ717. Leading is DZ718. (*RAF*)

NF.XXX MM695 of the Central Fighter Establishment at Tangmere in the early summer of 1945. Previously it had served on 219 Squadron at Hunsdon and ended its days as instructional airframe with 1 Radio School. The 'G' after the serial number indicated special equipment fitted, which had to be guarded while on the ground. The small 'T' antenna under the starboard wing outboard of the engine nacelle is for the radio altimeter. (*APN*)

On 21 March 1945 Mosquito fighter-bombers of 464 Squadron RAAF took part in daylight low-level precision attacks on *Gestapo* Headquarters at Copenhagen. The attack was so accurate that none of the buildings next door and behind were seriously damaged. Nearly 200 *Gestapo* men and Danish collaborators were killed and all the documents kept in the building were burnt. The first picture was taken by a member of the Danish Resistance shortly after the bombing and the second picture was taken by an Australian officer on 22 May 1945 after the liberation of Copenhagen, showing the wreckage of the headquarters building. Australians and other 2nd TAF men visited the ruins after victory and were met by Minister Morgens Fog, leader of the Danish Freedom Council, who was a prisoner in the building when it was hit, but escaped death. He congratulated the Mosquito men.

The raid on the Shellhaus in progress.

would get off the ground with 100-gallon drop tanks fixed underneath each wing and a 4,000 lb load of explosives underneath us I refused to contemplate, consoling myself with the thought that it had been done many times before. Bill, with the aid of the ground crew, started the engines, and I switched on my navigation light, spreading my charts over the navigation table. The other aircraft were 'crocodiling' their way to the end of the runway. It was comforting to see we were not alone. Their navigation lights were shining and they were being given a green flare from a caravan at the threshold of the runway. Our turn came. Bill gave the engines everything they had and trundled off.

'Come on, you son-of-a-bitch, get airborne', I heard myself muttering into my face mask as old L-London bounced once, then twice, then bounced no more. We were off the deck. I noted the time in my log. We passed over a railway line, which ran at right angles to the runway. There was a train puffing sedately along the track. We must have missed it by ten or twenty feet. I don't know if we frightened it, but it certainly frightened us.

We turned on-course, climbing steadily, listening subconsciously to the beat of the props and the throb of the engines. The blue flames of the engines spurted from the exhaust stubs in an asymmetrical pattern. While they were alarming to look at, it was very reassuring to see them. I checked our course on the climb. We were bang on track. I turned the light down on my navigation table and looked outside again. 'Here comes Eastbourne and Newhaven, and there's Brighton on our right. We'll be crossing the coast in a few minutes. I'll switch off the navigation lights.'

We levelled off at 25,000 ft. Although we were over France, heading for Germany via Belgium, I still had the feeling we were over enemy territory in spite of the fact that we were passing over places occupied by our own troops. A layer of stratus cloud covered northern France and Flanders. Probably it was best that way; so much killing and death had taken place there over the years. The cloud cleared as we approached the Ruhr valley. We seemed to be alone, with no other aircraft around, but when we turned in on our long run-up to the target, the flak and searchlights opened up on us. I gave Bill his course to fly after we had dropped the bomb, then folded away my table.

Now to get rid of this Window. I adjusted the wooden chute. Breaking open two bundles of Window, I placed them in the chute and pressed it down through the floor and through the trapdoor of the outer fuselage. Unfortunately, in my haste and the confined space, I found I had pushed the 'V'-shaped chute out into the outside air, with the 'V' scooping up the air instead of sucking it out. A 300+ mph gust of air blasted the whole cockpit with silvery metal strips of paper. I quickly remedied the situation, chucking down the remaining bundles, which slipped out of sight into the night air.

'What on earth's going on?' asked Bill. He looked like a mock-up of Santa Claus sitting in a heap of glistening metal.

'I'll clear it up after we've got rid of the bomb', I said. It would have been quite funny if we hadn't been flying in one of the most heavily defended parts of Germany. I disconnected my intercom, dived under the sea of tinsel and replugged it into a socket in the nose of the aircraft.

'How do you read me?' I asked.

'Five by five. How me?'

'Ditto. We seem to be on track. The red TIs have gone down on time. Remember to fly straight and level for half a minute after the bomb's gone – photographs, remember. I'm fusing the damned thing now.' I pushed the fuse switches. 'Bomb doors open – confirm?'

Bill parroted the phrase back to me. I watched the TIs as they came closer. I was told later that there was flak and searchlights all over the place, but I didn't notice any. My eyes were riveted on the TIs as they started to slide down the wires of the bombsight.

'Left, steady!' Bill nudged the aircraft to the left so that the TIs came back to the centre of the bombsight.

'Steady, steady, we're nearly there.' As the TIs reached the cross-wire I pressed the bomb tit.

'Bomb gone! Bomb-doors closed.' It was like reading from a prepared script. The first part of the script was totally unnecessary, as the aircraft reared up like a startled horse as the 'cookie' fell away into the night sky.

'Hold that course', I said as I waited for the camera lights to wink. There were flashes on the ground below. Which one was ours? Only the 'boffins' at base could say.

'OK, the camera's worked. Head for base.' My mouth and throat were dry and devoid of all saliva. Whether it was the tension of it all or the oxygen blowing into my mask, I didn't know, but I made a mental note to carry some chewing gum on our next trip. How totally impersonal it all seemed. I didn't really think of the German civilians who would be on the receiving end of the load of explosives I had released on them. For the first time I noticed the flak sparking around. None, as far as I could see, had hit us. My sympathies, if I had any, were for Bill, who had to sit like an automaton, viewing the whole scene and having to follow my instructions. There was no automatic pilot fitted to the aircraft. He had to fly it manually.

I scrambled back to my seat and looked ruefully at the sea of tinsel covering the cockpit. I gathered most of it up and stuck it down the chute as we flew over Holland. I reckoned I was going to have some explaining to do to the ground crew when we reached base. I turned to the GEE box. The two matchsticks, or, to be more correct, the two blips, were flickering brightly on their time bases and getting stronger the nearer we got to England. I took a fix and gave Bill an alteration of course. We were going to come in over the Cromer beacon.

I turned on the navigation lights and switched from the main tanks to the outer drop tanks. Bill always liked to keep 25–30 gallons in each outer tank, which he used for landing. I stuck my forehead against the GEE box visor again and started to home in on the two coordinates I had memorized. I was very tired, although we had been airborne for less than four hours.

Visibility was very good, and every airfield in East Anglia seemed to be flashing its green Morse-code beacons giving its identity. We joined our circuit and came in over the runway threshold onto a very nice three-pointer landing. I noted the time in my log.

At the dispersal pan the ground crew undid the catch of the outer fuselage and set the telescopic ladder in position. 'Watch out!' I yelled, as I lifted the trapdoor in the floor. They got a deluge of tinsel on their heads. It blew away in the early November breeze, which drifted across the airfield. I hurriedly explained the reason for the loose Window, which seemed to have covered everything. They took it in their stride and assured me I had not been the first navigator to make that mistake. Bill was telling the ground crew that as far as he knew we hadn't been hit by flak. I interrupted him. 'A very gentle christening, don't you think?'

'Tell that to my grandmother – you weren't sitting where I was.'

There was a moral there somewhere, I felt. Just then the crew truck drew up. We piled aboard and headed for the debriefing. A mug of coffee heavily laced with rum – a double shot for me as Bill didn't drink it – beckoned. At the debriefing the other crew who had joined the squadron at the same time as we had were having some difficulty deciding where they had dropped their bomb. The navigator had a rather glazed look in his eyes. His log sheet and charts looked as if they had been stuffed in his pockets at some point on the trip. He stated, categorically, that no TIs had gone down and that he had dropped his load 'by guess and by God' at his ETA over the target. On a replot of his navigation it was decided – and later confirmed by his photographs – that he had done some 'TNT ploughing' on the North German Plain. How he had managed it no one could understand.

I felt quite an 'operational type' after the trip. It had been pretty easy going as far as I was concerned, and I felt quite chuffed when the flight commander took us to one side and congratulated us on the photographs we had brought back.

On 6/7 November RAF Bomber Command sent out two major forces of bombers. Some 235 Lancasters of 5 Group, together with seven Mosquitoes, again attempted to cut the Mittelland Canal at Gravenhorst, but crews were confronted with a cold front of exceptional violence, and ice quickly froze on windscreens. Only thirty-one Lancasters bombed before the Master Bomber abandoned the raid due to low cloud. Ten Lancasters FTR from the Mittelland débâcle. Meanwhile 128 Lancasters of 3 Group carried out a night GEE-H raid on Koblenz. Eighteen Mosquitoes raided Hannover and eight more went to Herford, while forty-eight Mosquitoes of the LNSF carried out a spoof raid on Gelsenkirchen, to draw German night-fighters away from the two main-force raids. The Gelsenkirchen raid began as planned, five minutes ahead of the two other attacks, at 1925 hours. The city was still burning as a result of an afternoon raid that day by 738 RAF bombers. From their altitude of 25,000 ft the Mosquitoes added their red and green TIs and high explosives to the fires. A few searchlights and only very light flak greeted the crews over the devastated city. The twelve B.XXs in 608 (North Riding) Squadron began returning over Norfolk shortly before 2100 hours to Downham Market. They had to contend with cloud and icing conditions as they descended over the flat landscape. The Canadian-built Mosquito flown by Plt Off James McLean, a 26-year-old Scot from West Lothian, and his observer, 21-year-old Sgt Mervyn Tansley, from Fulham in London, began to ice up badly. McLean lost control during his descent through cloud and the Mosquito struck overhead electric power cables before crashing into Bawdeswell village church. Both whirling propellers sheered off the engine nacelles and fell into neighbouring gardens, where a tree was cut down as if hit by a chain-saw. The remains of McLean and Tansley were not recovered from the wreckage until nine days later.

After their first op, on 6/7 November, Johnnie Clark and Bill Henley had to wait four nights before they again went through the ritual of a bombing trip. This time they went to Hannover 'with a nice civilized take-off time of six o'clock'. Then followed two more trips in succession to Hannover, as Johnnie Clark recalls:

> On our third trip, on 23/24 November, we flew into a cone of searchlights quite early; Bill, who could raise or lower his seat, decided to do the latter until we had passed through them. There was no flak – an indication that fighters were on the prowl. I looked back into the night sky. We weren't making any contrails and I told him so. A few minutes later we were shrouded in darkness again, except for the dim amber light which shone on my navigation table. Bill raised his seat so he could better spot any attack which might come from a night-fighter. In doing so his oxygen tube was pulled out of his mask and fell to the floor. At first, neither of us noticed it; then the aircraft started to wallow all over the sky and went into a

steep dive. I looked up and saw that Bill's head had sunk onto his chest. He was rapidly passing out. Then I spotted the oxygen tube lying on the floor. I grabbed the control column with one hand and steadied the aircraft. With the other I ripped off his mask and my own and quickly fastened mine to his face. At the same time I switched the oxygen to emergency and stuck the tube, which was lying at his feet, into my mouth. There was nothing in the rulebook about this, I thought. What a carve-up! We readjusted our masks and attained some degree of normality. We had overshot our turning-point and were out of the main stream of bombers. I gave him a course to fly direct to the target.

The aircraft was climbing again to our bombing altitude when the first burst of tracer bullets flicked past our wings. A fighter was onto us. 'He's a bloody poor shot, whoever he is', I mumbled. 'Perhaps it's because we are climbing that he didn't give us the knockout punch.' Bill, as so often happened, didn't say anything. I stuck my nose into my charts and tried to ignore it. After all, that was Bill's department. He seemed to be tossing the Mosquito all over the sky. However, I couldn't ignore the second attack; the tracer bullets seemed to be going in one side of the wings and out the other. The engines were maintaining their steady beat, as did the propellers. I glanced at all the luminous dials on the dashboard and they were remaining steady. Then I noticed our green navigation light shining from our [starboard] wingtip. I looked past Bill's head and saw the red one shining on his side. He was busy with the evasive action.

'Hell's bells, Bill. We've got our nav lights on! No wonder the bastard is picking on us. He must think we're crazy. We must have knocked them on in that mix-up with our oxygen masks.'

I quickly switched them off and returned the oxygen supply to normal, while Bill pulled the engine throttles back through the 'gate', where he had thrust them at the first attack. After all, it was like driving a car at full speed with the choke out: it didn't do the engines any good at all.

'Do we press on or abort the trip altogether?' I asked.

'The engines seem to be OK and we aren't losing any petrol. Any sign of that fighter?' asked Bill.

'Not that I can see. Let's carry on.'

We dropped our 'egg' and came back via the Cromer beacon, as usual. On the dispersal pan I moved to the grass verge, spat out the chewing gum, which I had rolled around in my mouth since take-off, and at the same time stripped and wiped the curd which had formed on my lips. I lit a cigarette. Hell, it tasted good. Bill came over to me. He had been discussing the damage with a rigger. We had collected quite a few bullet holes in the wings, but nothing vital had been hit. 'We were lucky', I remarked.

'Yeah, we'll need a lot more luck before this tour is over. Thanks a lot for noticing the oxygen tube. I was pretty 'gaga' by that time.'

I made light of it. 'If you go – we both go; whereas if I catch a packet you can always get back to England using that little information card I give you before each trip and which you slip into the top of those shiny black flying-boots of yours.'

I had just finished lunch the next day when Bill came over to me. 'We are on the battle order for tonight, Johnnie. Briefing is at three o'clock.' At the appointed hour Bill and I presented ourselves for briefing.

'Ye Gods,' muttered Bill, 'do you see where we are due to go tonight? Berlin.' The route tapes were pinned to the map.

'So, it's the "Big City" tonight,' drawled the Canadian at my elbow, 'with spoof attacks on Hanover and Magdeburg, I wonder where the "heavies" are going tonight? Is this your first to the "Big City"?' I nodded. It was funny how everyone took the same place at briefing. Still, it was more comfortable that way.

The intelligence officer soon filled us in on where the 'heavies' were bombing that night. They were coming in on a northern route and were going to saturate Potsdam. We were going to bomb the centre of Berlin, with a view to drawing off some of the flak and searchlights from the main forces. The Germans may have had a 'busted flush', to use the Canadian's poker language, but they were still a force to be reckoned with; a fact of which the paratroopers' disastrous landing at Arnhem was but one example. Their fighters, flak and searchlights were others. That we were winning no one doubted, but it was going to take a big heave yet. The Germans were fighting for their lives with their own lives.

We were given our time on the target, which would be marked by the H_2S Mosquitoes of 139 Squadron. H_2S was airborne radar. OBOE aircraft couldn't mark as far as Berlin. Their activities were confined to the Ruhr and its environs, although their range was extending as the armies on the ground advanced. The OBOE marker was very accurate and very 'hush-hush'.

'You'll find the flak and searchlights really concentrated around the "Big City"', remarked the intelligence officer. Cold comfort for us, I thought, as the briefing progressed. When it ended I turned to the Canadian: 'You been there before?'

He nodded. 'Two or three times and as yet not a scratch to show on us.' He pointed to his pilot. 'We're hoping our luck lasts.'

We got airborne just after five o'clock, thanks to the short days at the end of November. Running up to Hannover, the GEE blips grew fainter and eventually guttered out like two spent candles. After collecting our share of flak over that city we pointed our nose towards Magdeburg. There was no need to navigate to it as the

Americans had been there during the day. The place was still burning. We turned towards the north-east and headed for the 'Big City'. The TIs went down on time and I noticed another bunch on my left. Potsdam was being marked for the main force of 'heavies'. They were operating much lower than we, the Mosquitoes, were. Then the searchlights came into play. First the bluish ones, operating singly and radar controlled, wandered haphazardly, or so it seemed. Suddenly, one of them darted sideways and caught a Lanc in its beam. The Lanc dived and wriggled left and right, but hadn't a hope as twenty or thirty other searchlights immediately lit the sky around it. It was caught in a wigwam of light. Then the sparks of flak began to burst around the aircraft. Some of the flak shells must have hit the starboard wing, for within a minute flames were rolling over the wing and the Lanc started to spin round and down ever so slowly, I thought. I heard myself yelling into the microphone which was clamped to my face, 'Bale out, you stupid bastards. You haven't a hope. Don't you know you're on fire?'

As if they had heard me, the silk parachutes began to appear in the searchlight beams. I started to count them – one, two, three – then no more. Four hadn't made it. As if to underline the whole affair which was unfolding, the aircraft seemed to disintegrate as it went down. The three parachutes hung like stationary mushrooms in the cone of light. Just then there was a flash and what looked like an explosion. Two aircraft must have collided in mid-air. There would be no parachutes coming out of that, I reckoned.

As we were running up to the target a bunch of searchlights caught us. It had been sheer good luck on their part that they did so, since all the pale blue ones were latching onto the main force on our right. I was completely blinded by the light and couldn't see the TIs, far less bomb on them. 'I've overshot the TIs – we'll have to go round again', I said into my mike, adding automatically, 'Bomb doors closed.'

'Oh, bloody hell', replied the somewhat strained voice of Bill. 'Which way do you want me to turn the damned thing?' It was the first and only time I had ever heard him swear. After a moment's thought I replied, 'Make it a wide right turn. All the others will be making a left turn after dropping their loads. We don't want to run into any of them.' Bumping into another aircraft's slipstream was no fun, either, as I had found out over Hannover when night-fighters had attacked us. Our right turn seemed to fox the searchlights. Presumably, they had anticipated we would be making a left turn, heading for home. Anyway, we lost them and were shrouded in darkness again.

I resolved to concentrate on the markers and ignore what was going on around me. This I found rather hard to do; it was difficult to tell which were bombs bursting and which were aircraft either on fire or blowing up. It seemed to me that Dante had underestimated his description of Hell. I went through the patter on our second run-in, dropped the TIs, waited for the photographs, then headed for the Cromer beacon and home. 'Sorry about the run-in to the target. I couldn't see a thing; the searchlight blinded me', I said rather lamely.

'Not to worry, Johnnie, we're still in one piece. It was a good idea of yours to make a right turn – it caught the Jerries on the wrong foot.'

I didn't explain to him that I had been thinking more of the aircraft following us than of the German defences.

We landed safely. Bill, following the laid-down instructions, opened the bomb-doors at dispersal before cutting the engines. I was doing my usual – having a pee and spitting out the wad of chewing gum which had kept my mouth moist during the trip – when an armourer of the ground staff approached me. 'I say, sergeant, come and see this. It looks a bit queer to me.'

'Nothing wrong, I hope?' We ducked into the empty bomb-bay together.

'Do you know where you collected that?' He pointed to the whole side of a flak shell embedded in one of the main spars.

'Over the "Big City", I suppose', I answered. Bill had joined us and was looking curiously at the splinter. 'I never felt a thing hit us during the whole trip. It must have gone through the bomb-doors or the fuselage. Isn't there a hole somewhere?'

'That's what's making me wonder. There's not a mark on the outer skin of the aircraft at all', replied the armourer.

I looked at Bill and found him gazing at me. 'Are you thinking what I'm thinking?'

I shrugged. 'I don't know, but I reckon we could only have collected it after I'd dropped the bomb and before you'd closed the bomb-doors – a matter of seconds.'

'That's what I thought', said Bill. 'Thank God the bomb had gone.' We turned to the armourer, who was looking as if he had seen a couple of ghosts. 'Yes, a matter of seconds – the difference between the quick and the dead.'

At the debriefing my Canadian oppo said, 'I hear you went round the target twice tonight?'

'That's right. I liked the look of the place', I answered dryly.

Notes

1. A 'Milk Run' in RAF terminology meant an operation flown on a regular basis, whereas the American term meant an easy mission.
2. Flt Lt R.B. Birchmore DFC* and Flg Off R.H.M. Vere AE, recall: 'Prior to September 1939, two flights, 1401 and 1403, stationed at Mildenhall and

Aldergrove and equipped with Gloster Gladiators, carried out a vertical temperature sounding ("Thum") of the atmosphere over base twice a day. This they did with unfailing regularity in the worst of weather. At the outbreak of war, shipping reports and continental reports disappeared under a security ban, and soon 1401 and 1403 Flights, equipped with Blenheims, were laying the foundations of the system of fixed-track, overseas meteorological reconnaissances. For this purpose 1401 moved to Bircham Newton and were given Squadron (521) status. It was soon realized that these aircraft were able to do much more than merely report the surface phenomena, as had been the case with ships, and regular "Thum" ascents and flights far out over the Atlantic and over the North Sea became the order of the day. Thus Rhombus, Bismuth, and others were established.'

3. 521 Squadron, like all other Met. reconnaissance squadrons, was in Coastal Command, and the 'Pampa' results were always required urgently upon landing by Bomber Command. After a short time, therefore, 521 Squadron was split up, and the Hudsons (which had replaced the Blenheims) and Gladiators, now augmented by high-flying Spitfires, remained in Bircham Newton, under Coastal Command. There was still one big gap in the weather map – Germany – and our bomber effort was suffering through lack of vital meteorological knowledge in the most vital places of all – over the target areas. Accordingly, it was decided to attempt to fill this gap, and arrangements were made for 521 Squadron, with long-range Spitfires, to reconnoitre targets inside enemy territory. Late in 1942 the first operation was ordered and successfully carried out. 'Pampa' was born, and soon received the acclaim of Bomber Command meteorological chiefs. Spitfires, however, were very exacting from the pilot's point of view, for he had to fly and navigate the machine, look out for enemy fighters and still take sufficient note of the weather to give a good account of it on his return to base. Consequently, it was not very long before the Spitfires were replaced by Mosquito IVs, in which a navigator could shoulder most of the pilot's load. So successful did they prove in this field, as in many others, that it remained the standard aircraft of Pampa flight.

4. After the war Val Moore joined a West African airline and was lost with all his passengers when the VC 10 of which he was captain crashed in a swamp.

5. On 3 December ML918, flown by Flt Sgt H.W. Addis and Sgt J.H. Sharpe, returning from Nürnberg, crashed half a mile short of the runway at Exeter while making a beam approach. Two days later MM238, flown by Flg Off H.M. Taylor and Plt Off Burgess, was damaged on a Pampa over France, and it crashed at Marham on return when Taylor attempted to make a an emergency single-engine landing. Nine months after its formation, 1409 Met Flight moved to Wyton, under the Command of Sqn Ldr J.M. 'Mike' Birkin. In April, 1944 Sqn Ldr, now Wg Cdr, Nigel Bicknell DSO DFC assumed command. Under his leadership the flight progressed from strength to strength, building up an enviable record of meteorological service to both Bomber Command and to the US 8th Air Force. The flight came to be relied upon, also, for a large part of the

photography, especially by night, of Bomber Command's attacks on German industry, and some outstanding results were achieved. 'Special Duties' also included Spoof raids, diversionary Window dropping and various other activities of a similar nature. On 27 June 1944, ACM Bomber Command signalled: 'Great credit is due to all concerned for the high standard of efficiency that your Flight has maintained over a long period. You are playing a vital part in increasing the effectiveness of all operations carried out by the command. Well done! Keep it up.' Towards the end of the European war, while continuing to operate to the requirements of Bomber Command, the flight received an increasing number of requests from Transport Command, which, faced with large commitments in support of the Far Eastern war, was finding it imperative to have accurate, up-to-date weather information of the routes along which it was operating. With the cessation of hostilities in Europe, Bomber Command required very few Pampa sorties, and the work of the flight became more and more under the direction of Transport Command. On 10 October 1945 the flight, then under the command of Sqn Ldr D.G. Johnson DFC AFC, was moved to Lyneham and became part of Transport Command. The flight was disbanded on 15 April 1946.
6. On 18/19 November 1943 'Bomber' Harris began his nightly offensive against Berlin. This series of raids, which were to last until the end of January 1944, brought added demands for bomb damage assessment (BDA). Flights over Germany were being made ever more difficult by enemy action, bad weather and other factors, such as smoke from still burning factories and houses – it took no fewer than thirty-one PR Spitfire and six PR Mosquito sorties before the results of the bombing of Berlin on 18/19 November were obtained. BDA became such an issue with both the RAF and USAAF bomber commands that PR aircraft were required to cover targets within hours of a raid being carried out – sometimes even before the returning bombers had landed.
7. On 7 April 1944, 571 Squadron was formed at Downham Market. A shortage of Mosquitoes meant that 571 had to operate at half-strength for a time. On the night of 13/14 April two crews from 571 and six Mosquitoes from 692 attacked Berlin for the first time, carrying two 50-gallon drop tanks and a 4,000 lb bomb. On 1 August 1944 608 Squadron at Downham Market joined LNSF. On 25 October 142 Squadron re-formed at Gransden Lodge and that same night flew its first operation when its only two B.XXVs were dispatched to Cologne. On 18 December 162 Squadron re-formed at Bourn with B.XXVs, and soon accompanied the veteran 139 Squadron on target-marking duties. No. 163 Squadron, the eleventhth and final Mosquito unit in 8 Group, re-formed at Wyton on 25 January 1945 on B.XXVs.
8. Back soloed in the Mosquito after only 55 minutes' dual in August. 'Bing' Bingham was killed on a night cross-country exercise from Wyton on 22 August when his Mosquito hit a hill.
9. 'Commissioning', recalls Perry, 'involved interviews with the CO, Mike Birkin, the station commander, Group Captain O.R. Donaldson and the AOC, Air Vice-Marshal Don Bennett, at Group HQ in Huntingdon. The great Don only asked one very elementary navigation question. He

pointed to two adjoining parallels of latitude on the wall map in his office and said, "If your aircraft is travelling at 240 knots how long to cover the distance?" On being answered "Fifteen minutes", he wished me good fortune, and the interview, taking all of three minutes, was over.'

10. Towards the end of their double tour, both Ginger Myles and Edwin Perry appeared in the *London Gazette* dated 19 September 1944, as being awarded the DFC. Unlike earlier recipients, they were not presented with them by the King but advised that they could collect them from Adastral House or have them sent through the post, which was a bit of an anticlimax! Edwin Perry eventually received a copy of the citation on 22 December 1982
11. MAA *The Mossie* Vol.13, April 1996, and Vol.14, August 1996.
12. At the end of the war J.M. 'Mike' Birkin returned to his Nottingham lace-making company, but continued as a part-time member of the Royal Auxiliary Air Force, finally becoming its Air Commodore Inspector-General and retiring to the Isle of Wight as Lord Lieutenant.
13. MAA *The Mossie* Vol. 14, August 1996.
14. Ernie Garrett landed on the roof of the town hall at Caterham. He recalls, 'Fortunately my 'chute snagged a chimney, which saved me from a dangerous fall to the ground. I called out, hoping that someone might be around, but at 3 o'clock in the morning, whoever heard me must have thought that I was a rowdy reveller returning home with the milk, and I was told in no uncertain terms to "shut up". I had no idea what sort of building I had landed on, and having failed to summon assistance, I broke in through a window and made my way to the ground floor, where I could see a chink of light under one of the doors. Inside were some Fire Watchers on night duty, playing cards, and with their help I was able to phone the squadron to advise them of the situation, although I didn't know at the time whether Nick had landed safely. Transport was provided to take me to nearby RAF Kenley, and during the late afternoon of 3 June we were picked up by a Lancaster and flown back to Little Staughton. We went on leave immediately following this event, and so missed an active participation in the D-Day operations. Nick and I flew another nineteen trips together, and completed a tour of ops in mid-August 1944. Nick and I flew together for nearly a year, but off duty we did not socialize very much – our friendship was that of amiable flying partners. He was married and lived off the base with his family, and we did not keep in touch after I was repatriated to Canada in September 1944. I remained in the RCAF after the war, finally retiring in 1964.
15. ML92 crashed on a house in Ridgemount Avenue, Coulsdon, killing an 18-month-old baby boy and injuring his parents. Four other children, who were in a back bedroom, were unhurt. The blazing petrol tank fell through the roof of a house in Woodlands Grove adjoining Ridgemount Avenue. See *'Mayday...Calling Mayday*. Joyce Smith.
16. See *Flying Into the Flames of Hell*. Martin W. Bowman (Pen & Sword, 2006).
17. Wg Cdr 'Joe' Northrop DSO DFC AFC.
18. Flg Off F.N. Plumb tried to put down at Weston airfield in Somerset on the return, but bounced back into the air. He opened up to go around

again, but the starboard engine failed and a wing dropped. The aircraft was wrecked and Plumb and his navigator were injured.
19. *Major* Hans Karlowski of 2./NJG1 shot down PF380 flown by Wg Cdr S.D. Watts DSO DFC MiD and Plt Off A.A. Matheson DFM RNZAF off Terschelling, and the crew were lost without trace.
20. Sqn Ldr W.D.W. Bird and Sgt F.W. Hudson were killed when they crashed at Park Farm, Old Warden, near Bedford. It was believed that the pilot misread his altimeter.
21. Flt Lt T.H. Galloway DFM and Sgt J. Murrell ran to safety.
22. Flg Off S.G.A. Warner and Flg Off W.K. McGregor RCAF were shot down and killed.
23. Sqn Ldr C.R. Barrett DFC and Flg Off E.S. Fogden of 608 Squadron (KIA) and Plt Off G.R. Thomas and Flg Off J.H. Rosbottom of 692 Squadron (KIA) both crashed near Nauen.
24. Flt Lt B.H. Smith RCAF and Sgt L.F. Pegg KIA.
25. One of Welter's victims was a 515 Squadron FB.VI in 100 Group flown by Sqn Ldr C. Best DFC and Flt Sgt H. Dickinson (KIA). Sqn Ldr J.H. McK. Chisholm and Flt Lt E.L. Wilde of 157 Squadron disappeared without trace. Reichenbach's victim was an FB.VI of 239 Squadron, 2nd TAF, flown by Flg Off E.W. Osborne and Plt Off G.V. Acheson (KIA). Welter claimed another Mosquito north of Wittenberg on 18/19 September (B.XV DZ635 of 627 Squadron, which crashed at Schiffdorf in the eastern outskirts of Bremerhaven. Flt Lt N.B. Rutherford AFC and Plt Off F.H. Stanbury KIA when one Mosquito FTR from a heavy raid on Bremerhaven.
26. One Mosquito FTR from the raid on Berlin.
27. Twenty-nine Mosquitoes visited Brunswick and one FTR.
28. 33 Mosquitoes went to Berlin and all returned without loss.
29. Flg Off L.J. Brennan RNZAF and Flg Off T.J. Bolger RAAF (both KIA).
30. The Mosquito flown by Flg Off J.P. McKenzie (injured) and Sgt H. Welch was wrecked after crashing in a ditch while trying to land at Warboys.
31. Flg Off N.H. Hornby and Sgt W.D. Crail were lost without trace.
32. *Unteroffizier* Hans Durscheidt of I./NJG10 in an Fw 190 claimed a Mosquito, which failed to return from the raid on Berlin and crashed north of Duisburg. XVI MM184 of 692 Squadron. Flg Off F.H. Dell (Evd) and Flg Off R.A. Naiff (KIA).
33. On the night of 23/24 October Bomber Command dispatched 1,055 aircraft to Essen to bomb the Krupp works. This was the heaviest raid on the already devastated German city so far in the war, and the number of aircraft – 561 Lancasters, 463 Halifaxes and thirty-one Mosquitoes – was also the greatest to any target since the war began. Altogether the force dropped 4,538 tons of bombs, including 509 4,000-pounders on Essen. More than ninety per cent of the tonnage carried was high explosive, because intelligence estimated that most of Essen's housing and buildings had been destroyed in fire raids in 1943. Five Lancasters and three Halifaxes FTR from the raid.
34. His parents had emigrated to Theodore, Saskatchewan, Canada, in late 1918, and Herbert Edward Boulter was born there on 15 April 1923. On 14 February 1937 his father died, and in 1938 Bertie and his mother sailed

for England and took residence in Norwich, where his mother had originated. On 15 April 1941, on his 18th birthday, Bertie enlisted in the RAF. See *Mosquito To Berlin; The Story of Ed 'Bertie' Boulter DFC, One of Bennett's Pathfinders*. Peter Bodle FRAeS and Bertie Boulter DFC (Pen & Sword, 2007).

35. On 25 August 1942 Flt Lt Tommy J. Broom and his pilot, Flt Lt Edgar. A. Costello-Bowen were one of three 105 Squadron Mosquito crews detailed to raid two electric power stations and a switching station at Brauweiler, near Cologne. Their Mosquito hit an 80 ft electricity pylon and crashed at about 240 mph in Paaltjesdreef Wood at Westmalle in the Belgian hamlet of Blauwhoeve. Incredibly, both men survived, and they were eventually able to escape to Spain, thanks to the French Underground. On 6 October they arrived in Scotland by ship from Gibraltar. Costello-Bowen was killed in August 1943 while CFI at 1655 MTU, when he was a passenger in a Ventura. After a rest as chief ground instructor 1655 MTU, Tommy Broom resumed operations with Flt Lt Ivor Broom on 571 Squadron, 128 Squadron and then 163 Squadron; Ivor as a wing commander and Tommy as a squadron leader. They completed fifty-eight operations (twenty-one to Berlin). See *The Men Who Flew The Mosquito*. Martin W. Bowman (Pen & Sword, 2003).

36. Air Marshal Sir Ivor Broom KCB CBE DSO DFC** AFC was born in Cardiff in 1920. He joined the RAF in 1940 and within eleven months was posted to 2 Group, 114 Squadron, on Blenheims as a sergeant pilot at West Raynham. In 1941 he joined 105 Squadron and then 107 Squadron in Malta, still on Blenheims. Aircraft and crew losses were very great, and soon all the commissioned officers were killed. Ivor was granted an immediate commission, and led daylight raids on such targets as Argostoli, narrowly missing the hills behind the target, which was a tanker and which was blown sky high. Ivor became a legend in Malta, and was awarded the DFC in 1942. Forty-three of his operations out of forty-five were daylight raids in Blenheims. In May 1944, back in England and posted to Oakington, he joined 571 Squadron on Mosquitoes. His observer was Flt Lt Tommy Broom DFC**. After thirty-three operations with 571 Squadron, they were posted to 128 Squadron in September.

37. No. 128 Squadron was equipped with B.XVIs and B.XXVs. All 8 (PFF) Group airmen had to undergo decompression tests, but although the XVI was pressurized, crews never used it on operations. Boulter notes, 'You couldn't drop Window, and we were afraid to use pressurization in case we were holed. We could still fly at 30,000 ft and above on oxygen.'

38. On the night of 24/25 October there was no main-force activity. Sixty-seven Mosquito bombers visited Hannover and other cities, while twenty-five Lancasters and nine Halifaxes again sowed mines in the Kattegat and off Oslo.

39. When sixty-two Mosquitoes were dispatched, and one – Flt Lt Shackman AFC and Sgt A.B. McGlynn of 692 Squadron, FTR.

40. 'I have a certain pride in what I did, but I don't expect others to share it. I hope my eighteen visits to Berlin accomplished something. On our return trip we faced the terrors of murderous flak concentrations and the new formidable adversary in the form of the first jet fighters rising into

the skies over Germany. As I think of all the fine men who lost their lives, I almost feel guilty at being alive. Most airmen who made it through a tour of thirty operations were grounded and glad of it. I managed to survive seventy-seven operations, flouting the law of probabilities – among 40,000 Canadians killed in WWII, fully 10,000 were in bombers. Andy and I were to attend an Investiture at Buckingham Palace on 12 December 1944 to receive the DFC from His Majesty. However, we were both very anxious to return to Canada and our families. We therefore forfeited this honour and boarded the *Queen Elizabeth* in Liverpool for New York. About the time the investiture was being held, I was meeting Phyl in Montreal for the continuation of our honeymoon.'

41. Another forty-three Mosquitoes went to Hannover, and six visited Herford. Twenty-nine Mosquitoes also took part in the raid on Bochum by 749 aircraft.
42. Sqn Ldr Ron Churcher DFC* RAFVR had completed a tour of operations with 106 Squadron at Coningsby flying Hampdens, Manchesters and Lancasters. His second tour was with 619 Squadron at Woodhall Spa, and this was completed in January 1944. Soon afterwards he was posted to the operations staff at 5 Group HQ, Morton Hall, near Swinderby. In July 1944 he had joined 627 Squadron. His last trip was to Oslo Fjord on 13 December 1944. He was awarded the DSO on 13 April 1945. See *At First Sight; A Factual and anecdotal account of No. 627 Squadron RAF.* Researched and compiled by Alan B. Webb, 1991.
43. The attack had been short and concentrated: 930 tons of bombs fell, all but 5% dropped in a circle of 530 yards' radius about the MPI. This worked out at about twenty-five 1,000 lb bombs per acre, the best concentration achieved by the group to date. PRU photos would show the extent of damage and success. Three Lancasters had been lost, two to fighters after leaving the target area; and two enemy fighters were claimed shot down.
44. Flt Lt Leo 'Pop' Devigne DFC and his navigator, Australian Sqn Ldr Frank W. Boyle DFC* RAAF of 627 Squadron.
45. In all, 235 Lancasters of 5 Group, together with six Mosquitoes of 627 Squadron, which attempted to cut the Mittelland Canal at its junction with the Dortmund–Ems Canal at Gravenhorst, but crews were confronted with a cold front of exceptional violence, and ice quickly froze on windscreens. Only thirty-one Lancasters bombed before the Master Bomber abandoned the raid due to low cloud.
46. 'No. 5 Group went back to Mittelland Canal a couple of weeks later and, with only slight opposition, found and emptied it properly.' (On 21/22 November,138 Lancasters and six Mosquitoes of 627 Squadron successfully attacked the canal banks of the Mittelland Canal near Gravenhorst, and 123 Lancasters and five more Mosquitoes of 627 Squadron attacked the Dortmund–Ems Canal near Ladbergen, and a breach was made in the only branch of the aqueduct that had been repaired since the last raid.) 'Then, a month later, when frantic work on the part of the Germans had just finished patching it up for use again, it took an even bigger pounding, this time in daylight. At the same time, the Dortmund–Ems was also successfully attacked and emptied. Traffic through Munster Locks was reduced from a 1944 monthly average of 844,000 tons to north

and east and 535,000 tons from north and east to 14,000 tons and 11,000 tons respectively in January 1945. Extracts from official reports speak of 5 Group's second attack on Ladbergen. It "breached the canal at the same place, but this time the breach on the western by-pass was much wider. The eastern by-pass was also hit and two lengths of the embankment totalling about 1,500 ft were destroyed. Two bombs pierced the viaduct over the River Glane ... the water, carrying barges with it, flowing into the surrounding countryside ... the Mittelland Canal was also drained for the first 18 miles because a safety gate had been left open."'

47. Plt Off Norman Mackie began his first tour with 83 Squadron at Scampton in May 1941, flying a total of twenty-three operations on Hampdens before converting to the Manchester and finally completing his tour of 200 hours in March 1942. The award of the DFC was gazetted in May 1942 while he was 'on rest', instructing at 29 OTU. Mackie rejoined 83 Squadron for a second tour in November 1942. In the meantime his squadron had been incorporated into the Pathfinder Force, flying Lancasters from Wyton. Acting Sqn Ldr Mackie was shot down on his twentieth Lancaster sortie on 11/12 March 1943 by *Feldwebel* Gerhard Rase of 6./NJG4 at Signy-en-l'Angle (Marne), as the first of his four-night *Abschüsse* (victories), and his radar operator, *Unteroffizier* Rolf Langhoff, in a Bf 110 night-fighter from St Dizier. Norman Mackie was captured by a *Wehrmacht* patrol on the second night after baling-out, and was imprisoned in a room in their command port with his flying-boots removed. He managed to force a boarded-up window and to escape without raising the alarm. With the help of French Resistance groups he reached Switzerland in early April. At first he was imprisoned in the Prison de St Antoine, Geneva, but he was later released and classed as an internee. During the second half of 1943 he worked for the British Air Attaché before making a clandestine departure from Switzerland on 6 December 1943. He and his fellow escaper made it to Spain on 20 December. A short spell of imprisonment followed in Figueras, but eventually Mackie was released and he reached England via Gibraltar on 17 January 1944. On return to the UK he briefly served as a Lancaster flying instructor at PFF NTU before he was appointed as squadron leader flight commander to form 571 Squadron in 8 Group on 23 April 1944. He went on to complete another forty ops, being awarded the DSO before he was finally rested in December 1944. *Night Airwar: Personal Recollections of the conflict over Europe, 1939-45.* Theo Boiten (Crowood, 1999).
48. A total of 235 Lancasters and seven Mosquitoes of 5 Group would be bombing the Mittelland Canal, and 128 Lancasters of 3 Group would be bombing Koblenz.
49. During the afternoon of 6 November a large heavy daylight attack was made on the Nordstern synthetic oil plant at Gelsenkirchen. In all, 707 heavies were dispatched, supported by thirty-one Mosquitoes and a fighter escort; 514 bombers caused widespread damage to the plant, and a second raid was planned for the evening with forty-eight Mosquitoes, one of which was L-London and the Henley-Clark crew. The first aircraft, flown by Wg Cdr Jerry Gosnell and Flt Sgt Stan Emmett, would take off at 1738 hours.

CHAPTER 7

'Nuisance' Raiders

By late November 1944 Bertie Boulter had got used to life on 128 Squadron at Wyton. Every raid was different in some way or other. Sometimes it seemed to be very busy all the time, other times it was much easier, though all the time he was acutely aware that every German city was ringed with anti-aircraft guns and searchlights. Crews were told at briefing if they were on the main raid or a spoof. If they were the first wave of the main raid then they knew that the heavies would have taken off before them, so that they would arrive over the target a few minutes after them to bomb on the TIs. As they were at different heights it was not unusual to see no one going out or on the return. That was how Boulter and the other Mosquito crews liked it:

> When we did see someone else it was usually time to take avoiding action. Unless it was a bright moonlit night, the first indication that you were close to another aircraft was the turbulence created by the props. Then you knew it was close. You immediately pushed on the stick, throttled back and hopefully swept underneath him. It was only then that you saw the blue flames from his exhausts, and certainly the underside of the aircraft or the silhouette against the sky, if the night was clear.

On 18 November a three-and-a-half-hour round trip took Boulter and Churcher to the huge synthetic oil plant at Wanne-Eickel, only ten minutes past the Dutch border near Venlo, with a bomb-load of four 500-pounders. The raid was carried out by 285 Lancasters and twenty-four Mosquitoes of 1 and 8 Groups, and one Lancaster was lost. Large explosions seemed to erupt in the plant, and post-raid reconnaissance showed that some further damage was caused. Their next operation, to the Sterkrade synthetic oil refinery on 21/22 November, when 270 aircraft, including twenty Mosquitoes, took part, was very similar. But on 25/26 November, when 128 Squadron at Wyton formed part of a force of sixty-eight Mosquitoes that attacked Nürnberg, things were very different.

One of the aircraft that took part was D-Dog flown by Ed Boulter and Jim Churcher. In the bomb-bay was a 4,000 lb bomb, which they released from 25,000 ft. Boulter recalls:[1]

> Suddenly, an unseen German night-fighter put several shells into the Mosquito. The starboard engine began to run rough. We lost coolant and the engine began to register high temperature and low oil pressure. I feathered the prop. It was all quite 'light-hearted' at this point because the Mosquito could perform marvellously on one engine. However, twenty minutes passed and the port engine began to behave in the same way! Things were getting a bit hectic! I swapped engines all the way back, feathering one to cool down the engine and then switching to the other when it got hot. Near the coast of France we were talking to Manston Emergency and they tried to persuade us to fly 'the ten miles remaining'. (We actually had twenty-five to thirty miles to go). It was 4 a.m., 7,000 ft over Dunkirk and both engines were trailing forty-foot-long flames. A 'Mossie' does not glide too well! I throttled back and we baled out. We came home on an MTB on the 27th.[2]

On 30 November the LNSF mounted the second major daylight raid of the month when five Mosquitoes from 128 Squadron were part of a force of twenty Mosquitoes from their unit and 571, 608 and 692 Squadrons, dispatched to the *Gessellschaft Teerverwertung* in Meiderich, a suburb of Duisburg. 'Sky markers' defeated the solid cloud cover, and smoke seen rising to 10,000 ft was testimony to their bombing accuracy.

On the night of 9/10 December, *Feldwebel* Reichenbach of 4./NJG11 claimed a Mosquito near Berlin, but the sixty Mosquitoes that attacked the 'Big City' returned without loss. Two nights later, when eighty-nine Mosquitoes went to various city targets, one of the aircraft that failed to return from the raid on Hamburg was claimed by *Oberleutnant* Kurt Welter of II./NJG11.[3] *Unteroffizier* Scherl of 8./NJG1 claimed a Mosquito east of Hagen on the night of 12/13 December when 540 aircraft attacked Essen, but though six Lancasters were lost, all twenty-eight Mosquitoes that attacked Essen and forty-nine others that raided Osnabrück returned safely.[4] Another daylight raid was dispatched on 11 December, when two waves drawn from 128 Squadron raided Hamborn. When the 13th day of December broke it was under a very heavy frost, and towards mid-morning thick fog enveloped stations in Norfolk and operations were scrubbed very early. That night fifty-two Lancasters and seven Mosquitoes of 5 Group flew to Norway to attack the German cruiser *Köln*, but by the time they reached Oslo Fiord, the ship had sailed, so instead other ships were bombed. On 15/16 December, 327 Lancasters and Mosquitoes of 1, 6 and 8 Groups raided Ludwigshafen for one Lancaster lost.

Being on a squadron [recalled Johnnie Clark] was to be quite remote from the rest of the world. Time passed quickly, except for that gap between briefing and take-off, which seemed an eternity. Bill, thanks to his magpie instincts, had a gramophone and a large pile of records. At first he and I sat on our beds listening to the records. Then one or more crews engaged in flying on the same trip would slip into our room and listen to Bing Crosby, Vera Lynn, the Ink Spots *et al*. Singing the sentimental songs in vogue at that particular time took our minds off the trip that lay ahead. Usually, one of the tunes swung around in our heads subconsciously while we were airborne. To get the wrong tune didn't help when you were waiting to be pounced on over Germany. Once Bill remarked, 'I've never heard a nightingale since I came over to the "Old Country".' Ann Shelton had just warbled out about the one that sang in Berkeley Square. 'There's still time', I answered. Someone else joined the conversation. 'Can anyone tell me why we are doing formation flying on our night-flying tests? It frightens me fartless, all this tucking up to one another. At least at night I can't see you lot. This formation lark puts you too close to me.'

We found out pretty soon. Seemingly, the CO hadn't gone batchy, as we had thought. We had done a trip to Hagen and another to Berlin and were waiting to take off again to the 'Big City' when we were summoned to the briefing room on the morning of 11 December. We were told that we were going to take part in a bombing raid on a distillation and coking plant at Duisburg.[5] It was going to be marked by OBOE aircraft. The idea was that we were going to form in pairs behind the markers, then, when they opened their bomb-doors, we would open ours, and when we saw their bomb drop, we'd press the bomb tit and release ours. That meant that upward of two dozen 4,000 lb bombs would hit the coking plant together. In order that those following would see when the marker bomb was released, the formation would step down 50 or 100 ft behind the aircraft in front. It also kept the following aircraft out of the slipstream of those ahead. It worked like a charm, except that the likes of us, who were in the middle of the formation, found ourselves flying through a cascade of 4,000 lb bombs. Those, allied to the numerous flak bursts, combined to make us long for the cloak of darkness. No wonder the daylight boys reported heavy flak. To our knowledge, the idea was never repeated. What the effect of it was we never found out – Berlin was a 'piece of duff' by comparison.[6]

I decided one thing after the trip, and discussed it with Bill: 'Do you think you could wind the aircraft up 1,000 ft above our flight-planned level on our next op?' Bill looked at me and I explained my reasoning.

'That sounds like good common sense', said Bill. 'I think I can. It'll keep us out of the others' paths.'

'Good. I'll speak to the photographic section about our change of altitude, then they can adjust the camera for the extra 1,000 ft.' Apparently, I hadn't been the first to think of the idea. The corporal winked and smiled. 'You've decided to join the other clever buggers up top. I don't blame you.'

The next night [12/13 December, when forty-nine Mosquitoes were dispatched] we flew to Osnabrück, bringing our tally of ops into double figures. We completed the trip and we went on the beer with the boys the next night. The day following, the flight commander wanted us in his office. We laid on all the bullshit we had ever been taught – marching in, saluting and banging our feet in the approved manner.

'What in God's name are you playing at? Sit down', came the laconic request from the flight commander. His Aussie navigator had his ample bulk parked on the seat in the corner of the office. 'By the look of them they must think they're going to be put on a fizzer', he said. 'Park your asses on these chairs.' A burnt matchstick protruded from the corner of his mouth. We sat on the edge of our chairs, not quite knowing what was coming.

'You've been posted', said the flight commander.

We looked rather crestfallen. 'Cheer up. I've been asked to supply two crews for 162 Squadron which is starting up at Bourn.'[7] He doodled with a pencil on the blotting-pad in front of him. 'It's being reconstituted as a Pathfinder Mosquito squadron. I was warned that they didn't want any rubbish, so it's quite a compliment to you both.'

'Yeah,' added his navigator, 'they don't want kangaroos that can't jump. You're good "press on" types with lots of ops left in you.'

'It's a bit of a shoestring airfield compared with here,' broke in the flight commander, 'but you'll get used to it. By the way, I've recommended you both for commissions.'

They wanted their pound of flesh, however, and a week before Christmas 1944 [on 17 December, when forty-four Mosquitoes took part in a spoof raid] we were detailed for a trip to Hanau. We took off, in heavy fog, dropped our 'cookie' on the target and returned with some degree of apprehension gnawing at us. We needn't have worried, for a wind had picked up, blown the fog away and substituted snow and sleet instead. We landed safely. We left the next day, 18 December. The Canadian navigator and his pilot were the other crew who were posted. After a lot of asking and swearing we found the adjutant's office. He was in a complete muddle. I noticed he was wearing wings above his breast pocket, which I found reassuring. I reckoned if he could have jumped into an aircraft and got the hell out of the place, he would have been a happy man.

'What a shambles the whole thing is', he said. 'It's a silly question, I know,' remarked Bill, 'but there are aircraft here for us to fly, I suppose?'

The adjutant looked up from his jumble of papers. 'Yes, that is one thing that is not in a muddle. There are a lot of brand-new Mk XXV "Mossies" in the hangars or on dispersals waiting for you. We've got to get operational in a couple of days. That's an order from God himself.' He jerked his thumb in the vague direction of Huntingdon. We presumed he was referring to our intrepid AOC.

'By the way, there's a meeting of all you members of the squadron in the briefing room at six o'clock tonight, so don't get ideas of going out on the piss to Cambridge or the Caxton Gibbet. See you then.'

We nodded, left him to untangle his knickers, climbed aboard the 30 cwt truck and directed the driver. The billets were warm, even if they were a bit rudimentary. NCOs and officers mucked in together, at least as far as living accommodation was concerned, and we were all on 'Bill and Ben' terms within the hour.

The CO [Wg Cdr C.J.D. Bolton DFC] looked as if he had just left the Upper Sixth. His display of 'gongs' disproved that. Our flight commander, on the other hand, wouldn't have looked out of place in a comfortable chair by the fireside, wearing a pair of slippers. He must have seen 30–35 summers – aged by our standards. The rest of the bunch seemed to be a cross-section of the Commonwealth and the Colonies. Besides members from every county in Great Britain, there were Australians, Canadians, New Zealanders, a South African, 'Ossie', who was a Scots tea planter from Ceylon, and a sugar planter from Jamaica. There was even a Czech. How he arrived in the squadron only he knew. We were going to meld into a new squadron. All of us had flown on ops before. It was satisfying to know that Bill and I were no longer 'sprogs' but had several trips under our belts.

We were operational in two days, but without night-flying tests on our aircraft. The foggy weather precluded that. We were called to briefing on the afternoon of 21 December. We had to do a spoof raid on the important marshalling yards at Cologne/Nippes. The heavies were going to bomb it again an hour or two later, the idea being to help cut the jugular vein feeding the Ardennes offensive.[8] Apparently, it was far more ferocious than had been anticipated at first, and had caught the Allies on the wrong foot. When the intelligence officer said we would drop Window on our way into the target, Bill smiled at me and asked if I was going to make a Father Christmas of him again.

Just after six o'clock we groped our way onto the runway and got airborne safely. The fog had been swirling across the field in banks; sometimes it was clear, sometimes it cloaked everybody and everything. It had been an on-off trip from the start. The Met men could give no assurance about the fog, either on take-off or return. The heavy boys were going to follow us after an interval, so that each time our trip was delayed, the main forces had to fall back in time. The weather over the target was pretty bloody. Snow showers drifted across the Cologne area and it seemed as if the defences hadn't much heart for putting up a barrage. It must have been cold and bleak on their gunsights that night. I threw the Window out on the run-up to the target, making sure the chute was positioned correctly, and dropped four 500 lb bombs on the TIs which had been put down by the OBOE markers; then headed for base. Before we crossed the coast at Cromer we heard over the R/T that all was not well. All the fields were out owing to fog, although some aircraft had got into Wyton, which was still producing some holes in the fog. But many were running around East Anglia like scalded cats. I used this expression to Bill. He glanced in my direction: 'Have you ever landed at an airfield using FIDO?'

'No, have you?' Woodbridge and Manston had it. Flicking through the sheets of flimsies I was reading, I said, 'There's one at Foulsham.' FIDO [Fog Investigation and Dispersal Operation] consisted of two raised pipes running either side of the runway and well back from it. There was a crossbar at either end, and the theory was that oil was injected into the pipes, which had holes in them, at various intervals. The oil was then set on fire and the resultant heat lifted the temperature and with it the fog that blanketed the runway. It was a dangerous and expensive way of getting aircraft down in foggy weather. I glanced at the petrol gauges. We still had plenty of juice left. If the worst should happen and we couldn't get into Foulsham, we could always head south. 'Let's have a stab at Foulsham.'

We crossed the coast and I didn't have to give Bill a course to steer as we could see the red glow of the burning oil that showed we were on track for Foulsham. From the chatter on the R/T it was evident we were not the only ones with the idea. We joined the queue circling the airfield, being tossed around by the turbulence of the upcurrents from FIDO. At least, we hoped it was the upcurrents and not the slipstream from some other aircraft, which had forgotten to switch its navigation lights on. At last our turn came, and Bill pointed the aircraft's nose at what seemed to be a raging inferno. He kept the gyro compass lined up on the main runway. It was no easy task, as the nearer we got to the flames the more the turbulence tossed us around. When we had almost given up hope of getting down, we burst through the fog and saw the runway ahead of us. Bill had more nerve than I would ever have had. I would have overshot and abandoned the landing. He pulled back on the steering-column and we thumped onto the tarmac. The flames from FIDO were licking up on both sides of us but, although dazed by the experience, we obeyed the R/T injunction from the control tower to clear the runway as quickly as possible, as there were other aircraft following on behind us. With the aid of a 'Follow Me' van and the torches wielded by ground crew, we got to an overcrowded dispersal pan and cut the engines. We found that our aircraft and the ground crew were covered in thick oily flecks of soot.

'It sticks like shit to a blanket', said one of the distraught ground crew, whose face looked as if he had been made up for a Black and White Minstrel Show. Bill phoned base to say we were safely down, and we slept where we could find a place on the mess floor. Next morning, in gin-clear conditions, we flew over to Bourn. As we rumbled down the runway at Foulsham, we caught a glimpse of a Fortress lying across the FIDO installation. He hadn't quite made it.

Two nights later, when forty Mosquitoes visited Siegburg and fifty-two Mosquitoes were dispatched to the Limburg railway yards, the weather was still very poor. At Bourn 162 Squadron contributed six Mosquitoes for the raid on Limburg. One of the pilots was John Whitworth DFC, who had flown a tour in 1942 on Wellington ICs with 37 Squadron in the Middle East before joining 142 Squadron, and then 162 Squadron in the winter of 1944/5, where he flew fifty ops with his superb navigator, Bill Tulloch DFC. Whitworth recalls:[9]

Our job in the LNSF was to wake up Germany, especially Berlin, every night if possible, in almost any weather circumstance. Bomb-loads were small. Routes to Berlin were always skirting Bremen, Hamburg, Hanover, Magdeburg, etc. Only severe snow and icing conditions caused cancellations at the last moment. In all my eighty-seven ops the one which stood out was on 23 December 1944. It wasn't good on take-off, but on return from Limburg cloud was down to about 350 ft. The first aircraft got down on SBA (Standard Beam Approach) OK, but just in front of me Bill Lucas came in too fast (who didn't in nasty conditions!) and went through the end of the runway. Immediately the rest of us, struggling with the dots and dashes of SBA, were diverted to Graveley, a base which had FIDO. What a wonderful sight Graveley was. There in the middle of all the low cloud and fog was this great hole of flames and clear air, with the runway lights down the middle! The tension went, and despite the much-talked-about 'uplift' on approach (which was nothing), we were all four rapidly down safely. FIDO was a great invention, which not only saved many lives and aircraft, but also relieved so much tension among crews at a time when we were all at our most fearful – bad conditions at the end of an op.

After returning from Edinburgh on Christmas leave, Johnnie Clark had met up with his pilot Bill Henley and had flown the 'long slog' to Berlin. The Scottish navigator had hitch-hiked to Peterborough and then stood in the corridor of a crowded, dirty train all the way to Edinburgh, where he had the usual wartime Scots New Year. His sisters and his father guessed he was flying on operations, but had not mentioned it to his mother. At the end of his leave he caught the Colchester night train from Waverley Station, which was looking even dirtier than on those occasions earlier in the war. He knew he'd be flying that night and would need his wits about him. He got a cup of tea from the engine driver of the train, which connected with the Colchester one, and he arrived back at base about midday. Bill Henley, who had spent his leave with some distant relatives of his in Kent, told him that he had done the night-flying test without him and that they were due in the briefing room at three o'clock. They were airborne just before 1800 hours. Clark tried to ignore the searchlights and box barrage flak over Big B, concentrating on his charts, illuminated by the small navigation light that stretched over them. They dropped their bombs, got their photographs and headed for home. Clark turned the oxygen up and found that it perked him up quite a bit. While they were emptying their bladders at the edge of the dispersal pan after landing, Henley had told him that it was their thirteenth trip. 'Oh, was it? Superstitious, are you?' Clark had asked. 'No,' said Bill Henley, 'I just thought you'd like to know.'

Clark spent New Year's Eve drinking beer in the Caxton Gibbet with the rest of the squadron who were not on ops. Bill Henley, ever diligent, told him that they were on the battle order next day and they had to report to briefing at six o'clock that night. News that their fourteenth op [on 1/2 January] would be Hannover met with the usual comments. 'Christ, not that bloody place again. It's been burning for days', said the Canadian out of the corner of his mouth.

Clark continues:

At 2045 hours we got airborne and climbed to our cruising altitude via the Cromer beacon. There were quite a few snow clouds around, but the steady beat of the engines and the propellers was reassuring. I switched the taps from the 100-gallon drop tanks to the main fuel supply. The changeover went smoothly, and after crossing Holland we saw Hannover burning long before we got there. We knew it was no spoof fire, as the Germans needed every bit of fuel they could get their hands on for domestic use and for armaments. I moved the wad of chewing gum to the other side of my mouth as I pointed out the blaze to Bill. 'There's the target. Seems as if we're only going to stoke up the blaze and turn over the rubble. I'll get up to the nose and prime the bombs. You OK?'

'Yes. Just awaiting your directions. They may have lost their night-fighters, but their flak looks pretty hot.'

I glanced around. The sparks from the 'ack-ack' peppered the sky. What was it some cynic had said? 'The flak was so thick I cut my feet walking on it.' Hell knows what the Yanks thought, looking at all the black powder-puffs of smoke that those sparks left in the sky. Still, that was their pigeon. We did not attract any searchlights, and in the anonymity of darkness we dropped our bombs on the target, then headed for base.

I don't know how long it was after we left the burning city that it happened. It may have been two minutes, it may have been ten. The aircraft gave a lurch and the engines began to splutter. I quickly raised my eyes from the navigation table and looked at Bill, who was scanning the dials on the dashboard in front of him. 'What the hell's the trouble?'

'Quick, switch on to the drop tanks again.'

I switched the levers over and the engines coughed a bit and then resumed their steady beat. 'No fuel starvation there', I muttered. The fuel in the 'drops' we worked out at between 55 and 60 gallons. Not enough to get us back to England. 'Just in case, make the heading 250°. We don't want to ditch in the North Sea in this weather. That heading should take us towards Holland and Belgium.'

I tried the port engine's main tank again, but the engine spluttered and died almost at once. Bill had put the aircraft into a nose-down attitude to keep up the speed and prevent it from stalling while we switched tanks.

'Let's have it on the "drop" again', said Bill.

When the port had picked up we tried the starboard one, with the same result. Bill sucked in his breath. 'I'll keep it on the starboard engine until it dies on us, then go on the port one. I'll keep the speed up by losing height.'

We were down to about 18,000 ft from our original 26,000 ft. Although outwardly calm, we knew that when the petrol in each of the drop tanks had gone we had to go as well. It was galling to us to know that although we were sitting on plenty of 'juice', we couldn't get to it. The flak had seen to that; it must have cut the pipes from the main tanks, as the gauge showed that we still had plenty of fuel in them. We settled on the starboard engine only until it packed up, our reasoning being that we wouldn't be chopped to pieces by a whirling propeller when we baled out, as the escape hatch was situated on the starboard side under my feet. We sat and waited for it to die on us. Each minute took us nearer the Allied lines and away from Germany. Their citizens, so we had been told, were not averse to hanging any aircrew from the nearest tree or lamppost, if aircrew dropped among them.

The port engine was purring away by now. We would have to get out soon. Neither of us showed any panic, even though we felt it. It was the waiting that was the worst aspect of the whole thing. If we could have jumped and got it over with we would gladly have done so, but every minute we stayed in the air meant we got nearer to safety and freedom. We were caught between instant action and playing the waiting game. We knew we were going to 'hit the silk', as the Yanks said, eventually.

I started to get ready to jump, clipping on my chest parachute. I realized I hadn't had it checked since I drew it from the Parachute Section at Wyton several months previously. I hoped it would open when I pulled the D-ring. Then I smashed my elbow through the GEE box radar tube, realizing after I had done it how stupid a thing it was to do. After all, if the aircraft were going to crash, the GEE box would be mangled up with the rest of it.

Bill made one transmission on the R/T, giving our callsign and saying we would be baling out in the next few minutes. Bloody hell, was this really happening to us? I turned and bent down to lift the floorboard under my feet so that I could get to the outer door. It had a pedal attachment to it. One press of the foot on the pedal and the whole door was supposed to jettison. Nothing happened. I pressed again, then realized the door was jammed. In leaning forward to reach the handle to release one side of it, I caught my parachute D-ring in the edge of my folded-up navigation table. The result took me by surprise. A small spring or something forced out the pilot 'chute, and the main canopy spilled out in front of me. I gathered up the folds of the 'chute in one arm, edged round the hole where the floor had been and faced the tail of the aircraft. I didn't want to break my back when I dropped out. Then I told Bill about the outer door having jammed. 'I'll have to unhook it and let it swing in the wind. What height are we now?'

'Bill grunted. '10,000 ft and all the needles are knocking on the stop.'

'I'd better go now and leave you some time to get out.' I pushed the lever holding one side of the door. It swung open. I looked at the dark void under my feet. I noticed flames flickering from the starboard engine. 'Hell – we're on fire! I'm on my way now. Good luck. See you back at base.' Sheer bravado on my part, as I didn't think either of us would make it.

'Hey!' Bill shouted. 'You've got your oxygen tube and intercom flex caught between yourself and your parachute!'

I raised my thumb in acknowledgement, unhooked one side of my 'chute with one hand and tore off my helmet and oxygen tube. My other hand was clutching my spilled 'chute. I stuck my legs into the black void under me and slipped off the edge of the floor into the night.

After landing, I gathered my parachute and dusted the snow off my battledress. I was in Holland. Almost at once, two British soldiers approached me and ordered me to put up my hands. Apparently, I'd landed in a minefield and they didn't believe I could have come from this direction! I suppose the frozen ground kept the mines inert!

Eventually, I was flown to Alconbury and thence returned to the squadron at Bourn. I removed the symbolic axe from my pillow, put there by the other crews. After all, I hadn't got the 'chop' yet. My back was acting up a bit and my testicles felt as if they had been thumped by a truncheon. I was told Bill was in hospital in Belgium with frostbite in both feet. His flying-boots came off when his 'chute opened and he had to walk quite a way through the snow in his stockinged feet before he met up with the 2nd Army. Consequently, he lost the skin off both his feet. I remembered the pride and joy Bill had for his shiny black boots he had brought all the way from New Zealand. The adjutant had offered to fix me to fly with another pilot till Bill came back, but I said, 'Like hell you will.' The thought appalled me. 'I'll wait for Bill to get out of the "boneyard".'

Bill arrived a week or so after me. He seemed more perturbed about losing his flying-boots than by the frostbite. We compared notes. He gave me the impression that he was highly delighted that I had insisted on waiting for him to return. I brushed his remarks aside by mangling part of the marriage ceremony by saying, 'Till death us do part.'

By 5 January 1945 Flg Offs Philip Back and Derek Smith in 692 Squadron at Graveley had flown over thirty ops together. The start of January was hectic for them. Derek Smith wrote to his sister, 'We've done three trips in the last three nights to Berlin, Hannover and Nürnberg. It's a nice way of spending New Year's Eve, going to Berlin. Still, there was a party in the mess when we got back so we had a slap-up meal and a good time.' Phil Back and Derek Smith had set off for Berlin in T-Tommy. Back wrote:

We had feathered one engine over Holland due to lack of power and lost some height. At about 27,000 ft the other engine stopped. We discussed baling out but it looked such a bloody long way down and we were over the sea, we decided to try and get down. We could see the lights of Woodbridge. We crossed the coast at about 18,000 ft and requested permission to land.

'What is your trouble, T-Tommy?'

'We have lost both engines.' – long pause – 'Land, T-Tommy.'

We got into the circuit about 12,000 ft on the upwind cross-leg – lost all the rest of our height to cross the boundary high and very fast, wheels down and a bit of flap. God knows what our speed was. I know it was over the limits for the aircraft. The next morning I got a bollocking from the engineering officer, for they had found nothing wrong. We were collected on 6 January in the Oxford and the next day I flew back to Woodbridge and flew T-Tommy home to Graveley. A day or two later I got another bollocking from Wing Commander Joe Northrop. I was expecting a Green endorsement in my logbook and was somewhat miffed at completing a dead-stick landing, in a 'Mossie', at night, losing about 15,000 ft in one enormous circuit and getting the wheels down – and getting my balls chewed up for doing so!

Derek Smith adds, 'It was a remarkable bit of flying and really deserved a medal. I can only think our otherwise amiable Wing CO guessed we had been a little too high!'[10]

During January–May 1945, LNSF Mosquitoes made almost 4,000 sorties over the dwindling *Reich* for the loss of fifty-seven 'Mossies' shot down or written off. The LNSF bombed Berlin on sixty-one consecutive nights. When, on 14/15 January, eighty-three Mosquitoes raided Berlin and Ed Boulter of 128 Squadron piloted BXVI MM204 to the 'Big City', a new navigator, Sgt Chris Hart from Derby, was in the right-hand seat. Boulter recalls:

Weather predictions were so bad the main-force heavies didn't go on ops that night. It was decided that six Mosquitoes from each of the six squadrons would go to Berlin so it could be reported, 'Last night our aircraft bombed Berlin.' The wind velocity predicted was 120 knots from the west. This was wrong. It was considerably more. So we all arrived at Berlin sooner than expected and I overshot the city. At this time I was surprised to see two searchlights pointing up. They then descended pointing westward to Berlin. This happened twice. Then the penny dropped. I can only assume that the searchlights belonged to the Russians. They pointed up, down, twice, to Berlin. We had to go back now that the PFF markers were down. Right speed, right heading, height, 4,000 lb bomb.

Over Woodbridge the cloud base was 1,100 ft. I must have heard it on the radio. The weather had changed to heavy drizzle and fog. I did three approaches on the SBA and didn't on any approach see a light. By this time battling the headwind left us very short of fuel. I think I heard on the Wyton circuit two Mosquitoes crash, both out of fuel. It was fair bedlam on the radio. I thought things were getting a bit serious. I was just commencing a climb away from Wyton when the voice of my flight commander came on the radio, 'Bertie, this is Ivor Broom. This is not a request, this is an order. You are to climb to a safe height and bale out.' He repeated this to any other aircraft airborne. (I found out later that the lights had been lit on the short runway – the wrong runway. Ivor and Tommy had landed and Ivor went into the tower and chucked out the wing commander CO).

I'd run every tank dry except the inner tanks. I throttled back near Thurleigh and prepared to bale out. Chris Hart went out. I remembered that you should never bale out of a Mosquito without getting hold of the D-ring first. My solution was to hang onto some bit of the navigator's seat, my right hand on the D-ring, with legs bent, and jam my back to the door. To leave the aircraft I just had to straighten my legs and the slipstream pulled me out. It took the skin off my shins. I landed and walked down to a farmhouse and knocked on the door. A first-floor window opened. I explained that I'd baled out of a Mosquito returning from Berlin. I asked if I could use the telephone. In a clear voice he said, 'There's a phone box down the road a hundred yards on the right!' And the window slammed shut!

I had no money. As I walked along the road I was approached from the rear by a US staff car leading a track and searchlight followed by an ambulance. The Americans put me out of my misery and took me to Thurleigh and the warm. They didn't find my navigator until the next day. He had wrapped himself in his 'chute, and locals found him next morning, still asleep![11]

On 25 January 1945 163 Squadron re-formed at Wyton on B.XXVs under the command of Wg Cdr Broom DFC**.[12] Ed Boulter was among those posted to the new unit, as he recalls:

Ivor was Ivor. You couldn't have a better CO. Ivor told us all individually. I was chuffed and very pleased to be asked because I was going with Ivor and Tommy Broom, who was promoted to squadron leader. Ivor took the nucleus from 128 Squadron but he couldn't take all the best guys. He had to take some of the dross as well! He had to have new crews from 1655 or other squadrons. After it happened it was quite incredible. We never separated completely. We still felt part of 128 – they almost melded from a social point of view into one. There was no rivalry whatsoever. All the high jinks were on 128. I can't remember even changing rooms.

Wg Cdr Broom had instructions from AVM Bennett for 163 Squadron to become operational immediately, and 163 Squadron flew its first operation on the night of 28/29 January, when four B.XXVs dropped Window at Mainz (a spoof raid for the attacks by 602 aircraft on Stuttgart). In February the LNSF flew 1,662 sorties. The 1/2 February attack on Berlin was the largest Mosquito bombing attack on the *Reich* capital since the formation of the LNSF. Some 122 aircraft were dispatched in two waves to bomb Berlin. No aircraft were lost. On the night of 2/3 February, while two other forces bombed Wiesbaden and Wanne-Eickel, 250 Lancasters and eleven Mosquitoes of 5 Group attempted to bomb Karlsruhe. Cloud cover over the target caused the raid to be a complete failure, and the Mosquito marker aircraft that dived over the city failed to establish the position of the target. To make matters worse, fourteen Lancasters were lost on the raid. German cities were continually bombed early in the month, and all were marked by Mosquitoes of 8 and 5 Groups. On 5/6 February sixty-three Mosquitoes attacked Berlin. By way of a change, on 7/8 February 177 Lancasters and eleven Mosquitoes of 5 Group attacked a section of the Dortmund–Ems Canal near Ladbergen with delayed-action bombs, but all missed their target. Meanwhile, thirty-eight Mosquitoes attacked Magdeburg, sixteen bombed Mainz and forty-one others attacked five different targets. On 8/9 February Mosquitoes of 5 and 8 Groups marked Pölitz oil refineries for 472 Lancasters, twelve of which were lost. The first wave's objective was marked by the 5 Group method, and the Pathfinder Mosquitoes of 8 Group marked the second. The weather was clear and the bombing was extremely accurate, and severe damage was caused. On 10/11 February eighty-two Mosquitoes bombed Hannover and another eleven raided Essen. The night following, 12/13 February, seventy-two Mosquitoes attacked Stuttgart and fifteen others hit Misburg and Würzburg.

Bill Henley and Johnnie Clark did not get off the ground until the middle of February, although they did a couple of air tests combined with practice bombing, just to break them in. When they finally presented themselves at briefing, they found that the usual place had been left for them. Some faces were missing and they would never see them again. 'Hi'ya, flight sergeant,' Clark said to the Canadian, 'it's an honour to have you sitting next to me, sir.'

'Spherical objects to you', came the reply.

'My, you've improved your language, too!'

'Like hell I have. Look at where we're going tonight [14/15 February] – Dessau. That's south-west of Berlin – it's like an elephant's foreskin: a bloody long haul.'

We kept the idle banter going while the various bigwigs had their say. As we climbed from the runway, Bill switched on his microphone. 'Nervous?' he asked.

'No more than usual'. I replied. 'It's a pity we didn't land a short trip, though, to break the ice. How are you?'

'I'll have to get used to these boots I've been issued with – otherwise I'm OK.'

We chattered on much more than usual until it came to changing the fuel intake from the outer drop tanks to the main supply. We were both listening to the throb of the engines and the beat of the propellers. Everything went according to the textbook. By the time we had crossed the Dutch coast we were behaving like an experienced crew and not like a couple of scared rabbits.

We dropped our bombs on time and headed for base. We had encountered flak over the target and were skirting Hannover and the flak barrage that rose so accurately from there when our starboard engine started vibrating, sending shudders through the aircraft. 'Curse that damned place Hannover', I thought.

'I think it's the prop that's copped it', said Bill. 'The engine revs seem to be all right. I'm going to feather it.' He pressed the button. The engine went dead and the prop rigid. The aircraft stopped vibrating and Bill started slowly to lose some height and to keep the forward speed up.

'Shall we head for home or what?' he asked.

'I don't think we should head for base, as the Met men said there was a cold front line squall stretching across the North Sea. We would have to go through it. That would be no fun with both engines, but on one – well, it's anyone's guess.' I had hoped we would fly over the top of it.

'Where to, then?' His voice was as sharp as a pin.

'Manston in Kent. That way we'll fringe the south end of it, I hope.'

'St Elmo's fire was flickering its blue veins across our Perspex windscreens when we dipped into the cloud. We were tossed around like a bottle on a surf-pounded beach. Lightning hit the cabin repeatedly, followed by thunder almost immediately. How the aircraft stuck together only God and the manufacturers knew. We bounced out of the storm as quickly as we had gone in. We landed on our one engine. The starboard prop had a jagged hole in one of its blades and was twisted like a badly broken leg. The fact that it and the lightning storm hadn't broken up the aircraft was a tribute to the people who had built it as much as to Bill, who had kept the thing in the air until we reached this graveyard called Manston. We could find no other damage.

I turned to Bill. 'I'm going to report sick. My ears are all bunged up and I have a bad cold. At least, that's my story. It will get us off flying for a week or so.'

'You do that, Johnnie. I'll back you up if necessary.' We were both rattled and twitching a bit, and we knew it. There was nothing wrong with my ears. Strange, I reflected; had anyone suggested three or four months before that I would be contemplating doing such a thing, they would have received a rather dusty answer in reply. However, once I had stepped into the Clearance Centre I felt ashamed. Aircrew were lying on stretchers. They had burns, flak wounds, arms bandaged and legs in splints. I felt a complete fraud. I said to Bill, 'Come on, let's go to the mess.'

Back at Bourn, a 'Wing Ding' had been laid on in the mess. What started off as a civilized party developed into a real 'thrash'. 'Ossie', the Scots tea planter from Ceylon, climbed onto the bar counter.

'Right!' he bellowed. 'I think we all need a bit of practice at landing on FIDO. I'll be the controller.' Newspapers and magazines were confiscated from the lounge, rolled up and placed in almost parallel lines on the highly polished mess bar floor. Tins of Ronseal were sprayed on the papers. 'Let's make it realistic,' said someone, 'get the feather cushions from the lounge and we'll have 10/10ths feather visibility.'

The idea was to slide down the polished line between the burning papers and have the air full of feathers at the same time. 'Ossie' bellowed out the time-honoured phrase, 'Come in Number One, your time is up!' Whereupon the CO whipped down the burning line of newspapers on his bottom and crashed into the stove at the other end. The atmosphere of the burning papers plus the clouds of feathers made the bar almost untenable.

It could have been worse. They could have burned the place down. At one party a bunch of aircrew from another squadron had found a pile of bricks, sand and cement. Contractors were building an extension to the mess. The chaps used the lot and bricked up the CO's car, which was parked outside. The contractors had been reported as saying that they hoped they were better flyers than they were bricklayers.

At briefing the following afternoon on 19 February, my Canadian oppo flopped into the seat beside me. 'Jeeze! Look where we're going tonight – way down south', he said. I followed the tapes on the Master Plan. It looked a little place south-west of Berlin called Erfurt. Why it was going to receive the heat treatment from us was explained by the intelligence officer. It was a centre for light engineering, and in order that we hit it fair and square we were going to go in at 7,000 ft, abnormally low for us. No flak or opposition was expected. We duly bombed Erfurt and left it blazing. I saw what I took to be a church steeple tumble into the flames and secretly hoped that the few faithful left in that town were tucked up in their shelters and didn't suffer the indignity of dying in the House of God.

On the way back, over Holland, we spotted what we thought was a jet aircraft boring its way through the atmosphere. It was heading straight for us. It rose level with us and continued on upward, arching north-west on its sightless way towards England. It was a V-2. I quickly spotted the place from which it had been launched. I was not the only navigator to do so, and I understood the place was located the next day and bombed out of existence.

We were full of coffee and rum when 'Ossie' and his navigator arrived at the debriefing, having bombed the town by themselves, as they had been about an hour behind us. They, like us, reported no opposition. 'By God,' 'Ossie' said in his blunt way, 'I can't see that town contributing much to the Nazi war effort now. It was burning beautifully when we attacked.' He gave a graphic description of the carnage we had created. The powers that be hadn't thought so, however and we did two more trips to Erfurt, with similar results. Each load we dumped on the place contained one long-delay bomb, which must have disturbed the residents for many hours after the raid. We puzzled over our trips there, as it stretched our flying endurance quite a bit. It wasn't until after the war that I saw films of the gas ovens in the concentration camps, with the trade plates on them stating that they had been built in Erfurt.

Seventy-seven Mosquitoes went to Berlin on 21/22 February. No aircraft were lost. On the following night, seventy-three Mosquitoes went to the 'Big City' without loss, although one of four Mosquitoes was lost on a raid on Erfurt. In March 163 Squadron alone visited Berlin twenty-four times. On 6 March forty-eight Mosquitoes led by OBOE-equipped Mosquitoes of 109 Squadron to provide marking, bombed Wesel, which was believed to contain many German troops and vehicles. One of the most dramatic marking operations of the war occurred on 14 March when a Mosquito of 5 Group and eight OBOE Mosquitoes of 105 and 109 Squadrons set out to mark for 5 Group Lancasters in attacks on the Bielefeld and Arnsburg viaducts. Four Mosquitoes attempting to mark the Arnsburg viaduct for 9 Squadron failed in the attempt, with no damage to the viaduct. Three of the OBOE Mosquitoes were unable to mark the Bielefeld viaduct for 617 Squadron, but B.XVI MM191, flown by Flg Off G.W. Edwards of 105 Squadron, succeeded in getting its markers on target, and more than a hundred yards of the Bielefeld viaduct collapsed under the explosions.[13] The largest operation ever on Berlin occurred on the night of 21/22 March when 138 Mosquitoes attacked in two waves. Only one aircraft was lost. On 27/28 March three Mosquitoes of the Light Night Striking Force were missing from a raid on Berlin,[14] and a 627 Squadron Mosquito was lost during a 5 Group minelaying operation in the River Elbe. One of the Berlin losses was a Mosquito of

692 Squadron, which was lost without trace, and the other two were involved in a collision.

Returning from leave, Bill Henley and Johnnie Clark congratulated each other on winning their 'gongs' [DFCs]. Clark recalls:

> Bill's commission had come through a week or two beforehand, so we were feeling pretty much on top of the world. We were preparing to get our heads down knowing we would be flying the next night, probably to Berlin. We'd done fifteen trips to the 'Big City' so far. The Air Council seemed bent on sending Mosquitoes to Berlin every night, and we were told, when we turned up for briefing the next day, that our target was the usual. We were to go over the target on our tod. Ten past three in the morning was our time.
>
> That night was a night to remember. As we flew over north Germany, heading for what had been Hamburg, and before we turned and pointed our nose at Berlin, we could see the whole of Heligoland, Denmark and south Norway, with the moon reflecting off the North Sea, which looked like polished steel against the dark ground. The searchlights caught us, followed by the flak. We ran the gauntlet. I dropped our bombs and we emerged unscathed.
>
> On landing back at base we had our routine pee. The pee tube in the aircraft froze up if we used it. We were then driven to an Intelligence hut, where a group descended on us. They were tired and jaded, unlike us. We had been flying on oxygen for 4½ hours, then jacked-up with coffee heavily laced with rum. That and the knowledge that another op was behind us made us feel like spring lambs, which was more than could be said of the Intelligence mob. We dictated our report and headed for the billet. We crept into our beds and went out like lights.
>
> Life went on as if the war was going to last for ever. Things were changing a bit, however. At each briefing to the 'Big City' (where else?), we were issued with a plastic label which we hung around our necks. It was imprinted with a Union Jack and stated in Russian that we were Englishmen. We were told that if we were shot down and didn't finish up a mangled heap, we were to raise our hands above our heads. What would happen if we landed among a bunch of fanatical Germans was never mentioned. As most of the Russians, so the story went, couldn't read, it was a case of heads you win, tails I lose – and a lump of lead was waiting for us wherever we landed. When I strung one of these labels, complete with white tape, around my neck, I felt like an evacuee from the 1940 era.
>
> The Allies had crossed the Rhine and had fanned out over Germany. The 'Huns' were still fighting, albeit in their own Fatherland. We did get a break and bombed Nürnberg one night. Strange to think it was in that city that the Nazis' evil dream which turned

the world upside down had all started. Then we bombed Berlin again. It was our last trip there, and we discarded our plastic labels with the Union Jack and switched our efforts to Munich, with just one break in Kiel. Why Kiel, no one knew; not even the intelligence officer. We were sent back to Munich as a farewell punch. Perhaps we were helping the Yanks. We didn't know.

Bill and I compared notes. We had completed forty trips; eighteen of them had been to Berlin during the non-stop bombing of that city by Mosquitoes. We were told that Mosquitoes had visited the 'Big City' nearly forty nights on the trot. We had grown older, if not wiser, during that time. Any other target offered to us had become quite a novelty.

One night, after a late trip to Munich at the end of April, we were walking back to our billets with bed very much in our thoughts. 'Listen,' I said, and held my finger to my lips, 'you said you had never heard a nightingale when we played that record of the one that sang in Berkeley Square. Well, you're hearing one now.' Through the stillness of the morning one was singing as if there were no tomorrow. 'Now you can tell your folks back home that you have heard one.' We stopped and listened. All thought of sleep had left us.

The last attack on the 'Big City' by Mosquitoes took place on the night of 20/21 April when seventy-six Mosquitoes made six separate attacks on the German capital. Flg Offs A.C. Austin and P. Moorhead flying Mosquito XVI ML929 claimed the last bombs dropped on the 'Big City' when they released four 500-pounders at 2.14 a.m. GMT. All the aircraft returned safely. Two Mosquitoes were lost on 21/22 April when 107 Mosquitoes bombed Kiel. Another attack was flown against Kiel on 23/24 April by sixty Mosquitoes, which returned without loss.

On 25/26 April twelve Mosquitoes dropped leaflets over PoW camps in Germany telling Allied prisoners the war was almost over. It was feared that the enemy might stage a last stand in Norway when ships laden with troops began assembling at Kiel. Therefore, on the night of 2/3 May three final raids by 142 Mosquitoes from eight squadrons in 8 Group (and thirty-seven Mosquitoes of 100 Group) were organized. In the first raid, a record 126 aircraft from 100 Group, led by sixteen OBOE Mosquitoes, attacked airfields in the Kiel area with Napalm and incendiaries. In the second and third attacks, one hour apart, 126 Mosquitoes of 8 Group bombed through thick cloud using H2X (the US development of H_2S) and OBOE. That same night Ed Boulter (who had flown nineteen operations to Berlin), flew his fiftieth operations when they took part in the raids. It was the last Bomber Command raid of the war.

In the period January–May 1945, LNSF Mosquitoes had flown almost 4,000 sorties. Altogether, 8 Group's Mosquito squadrons flew 28,215 sorties, yet they had the lowest losses in Bomber Command – just 108 (about one per 2,800 sorties) – while eighty-eight more were written off on their return because of battle damage. This is an incredible achievement, even more remarkable when one considers that well over two-thirds of operations were flown on nights when the heavies were not operating. The greater proportion of Bomber Command airmen who failed to return – 38,462 – were RAF. Next highest loss was the Royal Canadian Air Force with 9,919 personnel. On every night of every operation, wives and girlfriends, friends and family prayed that it was not their loved one that had 'bought it' or 'gone for a Burton' or 'got the chop', as death was termed in the idiom of the day.

Virginia 'Peggy' Scott had met Roy Dow, her Canadian husband, on Saturday 2 September 1939, at the Maison de Dance in Stockton-on-Tees, when Roy, from Fort William, Ontario, was on a navigation course nearby. In the heady war-charged atmosphere of the time, Thomas Roy Asquith Dow and Peggy Scott enjoyed a whirlwind courtship, and despite little money (Roy was paid just £21 a month) and with death around every corner, they got married on 9 November. Roy whisked Peggy off in his Morgan Four-Four, painted British Racing Green, for a lightning fifty-six-hour honeymoon in her home town of Newcastle before rejoining his squadron at Thorney Island, Hampshire. He would fly forty-nine ops on Beauforts of Coastal Command and turn down a group captain post in Canada before finally being granted his greatest wish; he wanted to fly the Mosquito. On 23 October 1944 the 139 (Jamaica) Squadron pilot received the coveted gilt Pathfinder eagle. By spring 1945 Roy Dow was a squadron leader DFC with almost ninety ops in his logbook. 'Peggy' waved her husband off from their house close to RAF Upwood on a sunny morning, 3 April 1945. The popular Canadian's red hair was groomed neatly under his RAF cap and his PFF badge shone proudly beneath his RAF wings on his best blue uniform. The one with the faded wings, which he wore on ops, hung, unwanted, in his wardrobe because he was not scheduled to fly that night. Before mounting his bicycle for the short ride to the base, he said, 'I'll be in for dinner, Peggy. Be a good girl!'

Later that day, Peggy heard four Mosquitoes take off and thunder over the house on their nightly operation. They were Berlin-bound. Peggy had heard the sound of the Merlins hundreds of times before. On eighty-nine occasions, Roy had come back safely, and anyway, hadn't he said he wasn't on ops that night? She only began to worry much later. Lying in bed, she heard three Mosquitoes return. One was missing. She had a premonition that something was wrong. A key turned in the front door and she heard footsteps on the stairs. The bedroom door handle turned. She called out, 'Roy!' He didn't come in. She knew then that her Canadian pilot was dead.

On the night of 3/4 April, ninety-five Mosquitoes went to Berlin and eight to Plauen, and one of the five Mosquitoes that went to Magdeburg was flown by Sqn Ldr Roy Dow DFC on his ninetieth op. He and his 28-year-old navigator, Flt Lt J.S. Endersby, were shot down and killed by an Me 262 of *10./NJG11*. Theirs was the only loss of the night.

Peggy was distraught. Next morning she ran outside into the back garden, a 4 lb hammer and a chisel in her hand, and destroyed the Anderson shelter Roy and her father had built while on leave. Roy and J.S. Endersby were laid to rest in the Olympische Strasse British Cemetery in the Russian Zone in Berlin, after the Russians had given permission for their bodies to be interred there. Endersby left a young, pregnant widow, Margaret. Years later, Peggy found these words, penned by Roy, tucked away in her household recipe book:

> *'I'll gird tighter my armour and advance in the fight with a brave heart.*
> *And bravely I'll battle for right.*
> *I'll blanch at no danger and quail at*
> *no might – If you will pray for me.'*

Notes

1. See *Mosquito To Berlin; The Story of Ed 'Bertie' Boulter DFC, One of Bennett's Pathfinders*. Peter Bodle FRAeS and Bertie Boulter DFC (Pen & Sword, 2007).
2. Ed Boulter adds: 'After Nuremberg if anything was going to happen it felt like it was going to happen to me. On 16 December ops were cancelled after we took off and we had to jettison the 4,000 lb bomb in the North Sea. On 18 December I hit some H/T cables after take-off because I didn't climb enough and chopped off part of the Plexiglas nose. Again we jettisoned the 4,000 lb bomb in the North Sea before landing at Woodbridge. After a hairy take-off on 5 March 1945 Jim Churcher decided he'd had enough. He was entitled to call it a day, and did so. That night when we went out to the aircraft there was snow on the ground and the fitters were working on the starboard engine with a canvas windshield and torches. I contacted the squadron CO and asked what I should do, because it looked like the aircraft would be another half an hour. He said, "Don't worry, you are to go to Berlin." On take-off the starboard engine was misfiring and the aircraft was trying to roll to the right. Luckily, it kept running. We climbed away and dropped our cookie in the North Sea. I accepted Jim quitting. He felt that "someone was trying to tell us something", and after twenty-one trips, decided enough was enough. I sympathized with him. Being the pilot, I had the benefit of not flying with an idiot flyer like me! I couldn't quit.'
3. XVI MM190 of 128 Squadron. Flt Lt R.C. Onley and Flg Off G.B. Collins RAAF KIA.
4. The only Mosquito lost was a 306 Squadron NF.XXX that was hit by a V-2 in mid-air during an Intruder patrol!

5. Forty-eight Mosquitoes of 8 Group were to bomb the coking plant and thirty-two the Meidrich benzol plant, 571 Squadron dispatching six Mosquitoes to each of the targets. Sgt John Clark and his pilot, WO Bill Henley, were one of the crews attacking the benzol plant.
6. Next day an analysis of the photo recce photographs showed that at least seventy per cent of crews had hit the target and that considerable damage had been done to the distillation plant. No aircraft were lost.
7. On 18 December the LNSF, or Fast Night Striking Force (FNSF), as it had become known at Bennett's insistence, was increased when 162 Squadron re-formed at Bourn with B.25s. Soon it was accompanying 139 Squadron on target-marking duties. Bennett thought we should be called the Fast Night Strike Force because his Mosquitoes carried a 4,000 lb bomb load to the target – fast, unlike the American B-17s and B-24s.
8. A total of 136 aircraft – sixty-seven Lancasters, fifty-four Halifaxes and fifteen Mosquitoes – of 4, 6 and 8 Groups were dispatched on the night of 21/22 December, and no aircraft were lost. the target was cloud covered and only a few bombs hit the railway yards, but forty wagons, a repair workshop and several railway lines were destroyed.
9. MAA *The Mossie* No. 34, September 2003.
10. On 12 March 1945 Derek Smith completed his tour of fifty ops as a navigator on Mosquitoes, and he was awarded a Bar to his DFC. On 14 March Philip Back and Alex 'Sandy' Galbraith RNZAF, Joe Northrop's navigator, were posted to 139 Squadron. Philip Back flew his fifty-first op on 25 March, and flew nine more before the war's end.
11. Five Mosquitoes from the Berlin raid crashed in England and three crashed in Belgium.
12. AVM Don Bennett dispatched Ivor Broom to Wyton to form and take command of 163 Squadron, the 11th and final Mosquito unit in 8 Group, re-formed at Wyton on 25 January 1945. The squadron flew its first LNSF operation just four days later, when four Mosquitoes dropped Window at Mainz ahead of the PFF force. In all, Wg Cdr Broom completed 103 operations, fifty-eight of them on Mosquitoes, being awarded an immediate Bar to his DFC in 1944 for a low-level moonlight raid, mining the Dortmund–Ems Canal, and a second Bar to the DFC for an Ardennes daylight tunnel raid on 1 January 1945, while with 128 Squadron. Finally he was awarded the DSO for outstanding leadership and devotion to duty.
13. Twenty-eight of the thirty-two Lancasters dispatched carried Tallboy bombs, and one from 617 Squadron dropped the first 22,000 lb Grand Slam bomb.
14. An unusually high loss percentage, as the average losses usually only amounted to 0.99 per cent of the fast Berlin raiders.

CHAPTER 8

The Enemy Within

From 1943 to 1945, Mosquito FB.VI and later NF.XII and NF.XIII squadrons in 2nd Tactical Air Force also intruded over the *Reich*, bombing and strafing German lines of communication and *Luftwaffe* airfields. One of the main proponents of Day Ranger operations over France and the Low Countries was 418 (City of Edmonton) Squadron RCAF at Holmsley South, which had re-equipped with FB.VIs in March 1943 and had flown Flower Intruder operations out of RAF Ford, Sussex, using AI Mk IV and Mk VIII. The squadron would have the distinction of destroying more enemy aircraft both in the air and on the ground than any other Canadian squadron, in both night and daylight operations. Flg Off Bernard Job, Flg Off Jack Phillips's navigator, recalls:

> Being one of the pioneers in Intruder operations, the squadron worked at perfecting techniques aimed at surprising and intercepting enemy aircraft over their own airfields at night and generally disrupting airfield activity. Given opportunity, ground targets were strafed. The absence of AI equipment in the aircraft plainly made the task of interception much more challenging, but as results showed, hardly impossible, given the acute observation and perseverance demonstrated by crews. What made this type of offensive operation so different from many others was that, having been assigned designated patrol areas, often a group of airfields in France or Germany, crews were then free to plan their own routes to and from these areas. Intruder aircraft almost always flew at low altitude, firstly in order to avoid unwanted enemy radar detection, but also to arrive on target at something like aerodrome circuit height. There were, of course, variations on the theme of Night Intruder patrols.

One of these was that of a Ranger, whereby a single Mosquito penetrated freelance deep into enemy territory, even as far as Poland and southern Bavaria. Later, Day Rangers took place, usually by pairs of aircraft surprising and destroying enemy aircraft both in the air and on the ground, far afield. The Baltic States became a favourite run, thereby exploiting the Mosquito's long endurance at low speed.

No. 418 Squadron had flown its first FB.VI operation on 7 May 1943. A month later, on 24 June, Plt Off John Todd Caine, who was 23 years old and came from Edmonton, Alberta, graduated at 12 (P) AFU at Spitalgate, training on Blenheim Is, gaining an 'above average' rating. A few months earlier, on 30 December 1942, at No. 11 SFTS at Yorkton, Saskatchewan, he had graduated with wings, with an assessment of 'an above average pilot who shows good airmanship'. After a month of indoctrination flying, John Caine made his first 'Intruder' to the Rennes district on 9 November 1943. His first victory came during a Night Intruder on 21 December. After a fruitless patrol of Speyer and Karlsruhe airfields, he proceeded to Delune airfield near Metz and spotted an aircraft in the circuit beaming navigation lights. He attacked the aircraft on approach and it crashed short of the airfield.

On 27 January 1944 Caine and his navigator, Plt Off Earl W. Boal, were off on their first Day Ranger, with Flt Lt James Robert Frier 'Ted' Johnson and Flg Off N.J. 'Jimmy' Gibbons leading, to Clermont airfield. On arrival they spotted a Ju W34 liaison aircraft in the circuit. Both aircraft attacked and destroyed the aircraft ten miles south-east of Bruges. Caine then destroyed a Ju 88 flying west of the airfield. Johnson, who was 27 years old and came from Omemee, Ontario, also destroyed a Ju 88, and they jointly destroyed another Ju W34. Johnson also damaged a Ju 86. One month later, on 26 February, during a Night Intruder to the Munich area, Caine saw an aircraft land with landing-lights on and continue taxiing. He attacked and set the Bf 110 on fire. On 12 March he and Boal were off on another Day Ranger, Flg Off Jasper and Flt Lt Marten leading, to Toulouse airfield in southern France. There was no activity at Toulouse so they set course for Clermont-Ferrand. On arrival they spotted an Fw 190 circling the airfield. Caine first attacked the aircraft on the ground and set on fire a Ju 52 and a Ju 86P, both confirmed by Jasper. He then heard Jasper shout, 'Bandit on my tail.' Caine immediately turned toward the 190, which pulled up and vanished.

Ted Johnson was awarded the DFC in March, and he returned to Canada in April. On 15 April John Caine received a telegram from the C-in-C, ADGB, that he was awarded a DFC. The previous day he had flown another Day Ranger, to the Copenhagen area, with Sqn Ldr Robert Allan Kipp, who was 24 years old and came from Kamloopa, British Columbia, and his navigator, Flt Lt Peter Huletsky, leading. On reaching the Kattegat they sighted three Ju 52/3m minesweepers fitted with degaussing rings flying in formation at sea level. Caine also spotted a fourth Ju 52/3m. All were apparently on mine-detonating operations. After the three aircraft were shot down, the fourth ditched. Each pilot claimed two aircraft destroyed. Then they attacked Copenhagen Kastrup airfield. Caine blew up an He 111 and then attacked a row of Dornier Do 217s. One aircraft caught fire. They then made a further attack, setting another Do 217 on fire and damaging another Do 217 and a Ju 52. The latter two obviously had no fuel on board. *En route* home, as they passed Grove airfield, two Fw 190s attacked them. Kipp dropped his long-range tanks and pulled away.[1] Caine forgot the tanks until one Fw 190 opened fire, fortunately missing. He then dropped the tanks and pulled away. In his logbook he states, 'I then extracted the digit!'

On 8/9 May Caine made a Night Ranger to the Baltic Coast. At Putnitz he found three flying-boats burning navigation lights in Saaler Bay. There was a lighted patrol path along the water. There were five more flying-boats lined up just south of Putnitz. After two attacks, he left a Do 18 and a Bv 138 burning on the water, and claimed two Do 18s damaged. He was out of ammunition. This took his score to twelve aircraft destroyed on the ground or water, with five more damaged on the ground or water. On 21 May Caine was awarded a Bar to his DFC. On leaving 418 Squadron on 27 May, he was assessed, 'Exceptional, with very fine fighting qualities'. After a well-earned holiday back in Canada, Caine then did his rest tour as an instructor at No. 7 Mosquito OTU at Debert, Nova Scotia.[2]

April/May had been the high point of the Canadian squadron's rich harvest of victories on Day and Night Rangers, when they shot down thirty aircraft in the air and destroyed thirty-eight on the ground, and by May they had claimed a hundred victories. On 21 March American 1st Lt James F. 'Lou' Luma[3] and Flg Off John Finlayson and Flt Lt Donald Aikins MacFadyen and 'Pinky' Wright had flown a long-range Ranger over France. Luma attacked Luxeuil airfield, where he shot down a Ju W34 and a Ju 52/3m transport, and damaged two Gotha Go 242 glider transports and two Bf 109s on the ground. MacFadyen, a 23-year-old from Montreal, shot down a Blohm und Voss Bv 141, which was coming in to land. Moving on to Hagenau airfield, he proceeded to destroy nine Gotha Go 242 twin-boomed troop transports and a Do 217 on the ground.[4] Luma finished his tour in April and was awarded both a British and a US DFC. Flt Lt Stanley H.R. 'Stan' Cotterill DFC and 'Pop' McKenna destroyed four in a night sortie. In three months, 27 January to 16 May 1944, Flt Lt Charlie Scherf DFC RAAF, who was 27 years old and was from Emmaville, New South Wales, racked up twenty-three destroyed, thirteen of them in the air. Scherf had worked as a grazier on the family sheep ranch before joining the RAAF in September 1941. He was promoted squadron leader at the start of May, and received a Bar to his DFC, with a DSO following in June. A month later he left the UK via the United States for his native Australia, where he instructed at 5 OTU Williamstown, near Newcastle NSW, still on Mosquitoes.[5]

On the night of 19/20 May, when RAF Bomber Command carried out raids by 900 aircraft on five separate rail targets in France, Wg Cdr Norman John 'Jack' Starr DFC and Plt Off J. Irvine of 605 Squadron in an FB.VI flew a successful Intruder sortie over France.[6] Starr and Irvine took off from Manston at 0100 hours for their patrol, and headed for the vicinity of Florennes, where landing-lights were obligingly switched on, as a twin-engined aircraft prepared to land. Starr and Irvine, whose Mosquito was at 2,000 ft, were assisted further when a searchlight on the north-west side of the airfield was switched on and began sweeping the area before it was switched off, the operators presumably satisfied that there were no Intruders following the landing aircraft. Starr dived to attack, while his prey, oblivious to the Mosquito's presence, blinked its landing-light on and off sufficiently for Starr to estimate his position on the runway. Just as he was about to open fire the German aircraft switched on its landing-light again and appeared to be travelling at about 20 mph. Starr gave the aircraft a 1 ½-second burst of cannon only, and strikes were seen in front of the machine and then all over the aircraft. (Starr and Irvine were unable to identify their victim.) By this time the Mosquito was very close to the ground in the dive, and Starr had to pull out very sharply. As he pulled out, Starr and Irvine saw the German machine catch fire and all the airfield lights were switched off. They orbitted the airfield and saw a motor vehicle with powerful headlights dash up to the now blazing aircraft. The fire crew took about twelve minutes to extinguish the flames.[7]

Early in 1944, 85 (Base) Group was formed for the purpose of providing fighter cover over the continent leading up to, and after, D-Day by the transfer from Fighter Command to 2nd TAF of 29, 264, 409 'Nighthawk' RCAF, 410 'Cougar' RCAF, 488 RNZAF and 604 Squadrons. In January 1944 the first to transfer to 85 Group was 264 Squadron, which went to 141 Wing. (The last, 219 Squadron, would transfer from Fighter Command to 147 Wing on 26 August.) As part of the new-found offensive, the main work for the FB.VIs of 138 and 140 Wings was Day and Night Ranger operations and Intruder sorties from England.

One of the Mosquito Intruder pilots at this time was American 1st Lt James Forrest 'Lou' Luma of 418 Squadron RCAF stationed at Ford, Sussex. Luma recalls:

> Ford was located on the beautiful south coast of England. Like many RAF aerodromes, it consisted of two paved runways at right angles to each other. Circling the perimeter of the aerodrome was a paved taxiway. The aircraft were parked in blast bays located outside this perimeter. Blast bays were 'U'-shaped revetments that protected the aircraft from all but a direct hit by a bomb. The blast bays were in

clusters with a taxiway leading from each cluster to the perimeter taxiway. The taxiways and runways were lighted at night, but only when aircraft were using them. Life at Ford was good. We had a comfortable officers' mess and were billeted in private homes that had been taken over by the government. We had our own rooms and were awakened and brought tea in the morning by a batman, who was an RAF enlisted man.

No. 418 Squadron consisted of 'A' Flight and 'B' Flight, which alternated duty. Fin and I were posted to 'A' Flight. The squadron's Mosquitoes had the paintings of Al Capp's 'Li'l Abner' characters on them; each aircraft had a different character from Dogpatch. The aircraft that was assigned to Fin and me – D for Dog – had a painting of Moonbeam McSwine on it.

Sometimes when we were on standby, we would conduct a night-flying test. Fin and I would fly the airplane for thirty minutes or so to determine its mechanical fitness. Sometimes we would also practice air-to-air gunnery, using a camera gun. At other times we would do an in-flight compass swing. After landing we would leave our parachutes and helmets in the seats in order to save time in case of a scramble. The 'erks' (ground crew) would correct any mechanical problems we might have experienced and would top off the fuel tanks. The erks were a hard-working, dedicated, loyal part of the team, and they did not receive the recognition they deserved. At least not from me. I was too young and egotistical to think that anyone other than myself was contributing to any success that I might achieve.

After we had finished our night-flying test, we would have supper at the officers' mess before reporting in at the ops room for the night's duty. The ops room was a medium-size room with reasonably comfortable chairs to lounge in while we were on standby. It had planning tables for the navigators and the walls were plastered with silhouettes of German aircraft for boning up on aircraft recognition. We killed time by reading, talking and listening to the radio. Sometimes we would listen to the English-speaking 'Lord Haw Haw', who broadcast Nazi propaganda from Germany. The music on his station was usually better than what the BBC offered.

Usually we were given our targets as soon as we arrived at the ops room, and would plan our flight accordingly. At other times, we reported to the ready room and remained there on standby, waiting for a scramble. We were dressed and ready to go. Pilots had flying-gloves made of thin chamois that fit tightly to the hands. The preferred style of flying-boots had a dress shoe on the foot with fleece-lined uppers. In the event you baled out over occupied territory, you would cut off the uppers after you were on the ground by using a small knife carried in a pocket in the boots. This left you with black, low-cut dress shoes that could pass as part of your civilian attire when being helped by the Underground to get out of the country. Each crew member carried a packet containing the currency of the country they would be flying over (usually French francs) and a map printed on cloth.

Luma carried out his most memorable flight on the night of 21/22 January, when 648 bombers attacked Magdeburg. (Berlin was also bombed in a diversionary raid by Lancasters and Mosquitoes, and flying-bomb sites were also hit.) Luma's seventeenth operation was the one that entitled him and his navigator to have their first swastika painted on the side of their Mosquito FB.VI, as he recalls:

> My navigator, Fin [Colin Finlayson] was sick, so another navigator, Flight Lieutenant Al Eckert, was assigned to my plane. We took off from Ford at 2215 hours on a Flower to Hildesheim, Germany, near Hanover. By now ops were pretty much routine for me. On each of my early flights I fully expected that I would see an enemy aircraft, but it didn't happen. Now I was pretty much resigned to the fact that I might put in a whole tour without ever seeing an enemy aircraft. It was possible; some of our crews did come up scoreless. When Al and I took off, there was no reason to believe that this wouldn't be just another uneventful op. The weather was sour, with a lot of low cloud and haze, which made navigation difficult. We reached an airfield that was lighted with perimeter lights. After orbiting the airfield we found a pin-point that fixed the airfield as Wunstorf. Shortly after that we saw two bright lights on the other side of the airfield. We came in to meet them very nearly head-on. They proved to be on an aircraft that had just taken off from the base. We were at 1,500 ft and the enemy aircraft passed over us at 2,000 ft. As he passed over us we identified him as a twin-engine aircraft with one white light just under the nose and one under the tail.
>
> We did a quick orbit to port, coming in behind him, and chased him for fifteen to twenty miles. As we closed, he was climbing through about 4,000 ft. In my excitement at seeing my first enemy aircraft, I very possibly came close to losing the opportunity to chalk up my first kill. I had overestimated our closing speed, and overshot him. As I threw down the landing-gear to slow us down, the thought that my buck fever was going to cost me the chance of destroying my first enemy aircraft left me with a sick feeling in the pit of my stomach. With the gear down, the Mossie rapidly slowed, but we were still not in a position to shoot at him. We were directly below him. By now the nervous excitement had disappeared. I did a quick turn to port, followed by one to starboard. This brought us under his tail – about 500 ft below and 250–100 yards behind. I was calm and

I knew we had him in the bag. We were in position. I pulled back on the stick, placed the centre of the gunsight slightly forward of, and midway between, the points where the exhaust flames emerged from the engines. Then I fired all my cannon and machine-guns. Strikes on the fuselage were followed by a big ball of fire, which enabled us to identify the aircraft as an Me 210. A large piece broke off to the left and he went down. Al Eckert saw him go in, explode and burn on the ground. After our return to base, the erks found two pieces of plywood from the enemy aircraft embedded in the leading edge of the Mosquito's starboard wing.

Not long after destroying the Me 210, there was an article in the Air Ministry Weekly Intelligence Summary about a *Luftwaffe* ace by the name of *Major* Prinz Heinrich zu Sayn-Wittgenstein, a highly decorated *Luftwaffe* night-fighter pilot who was killed in air combat on the night of 21/22 January 1944. The Intelligence Summary went on to say that he had shot down eighty-three aircraft. It also said he had shot down five RAF aircraft within a few hours of meeting his death. I found it interesting that I was the only RAF/RCAF pilot who had shot down an enemy over the continent that night.

On the night of 5/6 June, on the eve of D-Day, all six Mosquito fighter squadrons in 2nd TAF carried out defensive operations over the invasion coast. Fewer than fifty enemy aircraft plots were made on 5/6 June.[8] Then things hotted up. No. 264 Squadron flew jamming patrols before they went looking for enemy fighters. There was also another role for the Mosquitoes, as Bernard Job of 418 Squadron recalls:

> The squadron was stationed at Holmsley South near Bournemouth, and six aircrews were detailed to act as 'flak bait' to cover the paratroop and glider drops in the Cherbourg Peninsula, by drawing searchlights and flak away from these more vulnerable aircraft. So successful was this that two of the six were hit, one so badly that it crash-landed near base and burnt up. The crew ran![9]

On the night of 9/10 June Sqn Ldr Robert Barson 'Bob' Cowper, who was 21 years old and came from Broken Hill, New South Wales, and Flt Lt Bill Watson, his radar operator, destroyed an He 177 and a Do 217 while covering the Normandy beaches. Before the war Cowper had worked for three years as a draughtsman before joining the RAAF in December 1940. His brace of victories over the Normandy invasion area were his third and fourth victories of the war. While flying Beaufighters from Malta in July 1943, he had destroyed two Ju 88s over Sicily. He and his observer were four days behind enemy lines before reaching safety. On the night of his first victory, a bomb or a mine apparently jettisoned by the Ju 88 exploded and damaged their Beaufighter, forcing them to bale out into the sea, where they were eventually rescued by a hospital ship. After his tour ended, and after a rest, he had been posted to 456 Squadron RAAF in May, where he was a flight commander. On the night of 14/15 June Bob Cowper and Bill Watson destroyed a Ju 88 over the sea, and on 4/5 July they downed an He 177 thirty miles south of Selsey Bill. It took Cowper's score to six, and to this should be added a V-1 destroyed. He was awarded a Bar to his DFC in February 1945, and Watson was awarded the DFC.

It was on 14/15 June also that 2nd TAF Mosquitoes destroyed eight enemy aircraft over the continent. One of them fell victim to Sqn Ldr Russ Bannock RCAF and Flg Off Bob Bruce, their first victory since joining 418 Squadron a few days earlier.[10] Bruce recalls:

> We wasted no time, and after practice trips on the first three days set off on our first Intruder, a two-hour patrol off Bourges-Avord airfield. Luck was with us, and after some time we spotted the exhaust of a night-fighter as it passed overhead. We picked it up as it turned on final approach, but had to break off to the south due to heavy anti-aircraft fire. Fortunately for us the pilot switched on his landing-lights. We attacked in a shallow dive and fired a burst of cannon and machine-guns. As it exploded and caught fire we recognized it as an Me 110. We were subjected to a barrage of AA fire from the north side of the airfield, and we turned sharply to the left to avoid this wall of fire, but Russ was reefing so hard on the elevator that we did a high-speed stall just as we almost turned 180 degrees ... We exited to the west of the field, still carrying two bombs under the wings, and by the time we reached Holmsley South our fuel reserves were getting low. It was a memorable first trip.

On 24/25 June 1944, 488 Squadron RNZAF crew Flt Lt George Esmond 'Jamie' Jameson DFC RNZAF and Flg Off A. Norman Crookes, his navigator from Derbyshire, were on patrol from Zeals in NF.XIII[11] R for Robert over France, covering the advance of the Army near Lisieux. Crookes picked up a stray contact twenty miles south-west of Bayeux, and, closing in quickly, Jameson shot down an Me 410.[12] Four nights later, on 28/29 June, Jameson and Crookes destroyed a Ju 88 ten miles north-east of Caen as it was about to bomb British forces landing at Arromanches. Crookes's DFC was announced for his share in three of Jameson's victories. In June, 488 Squadron was credited with nine victories over the beachhead area. At the end of July the New Zealand squadron moved to Colerne near Bath, where Jameson was devastated to learn that both his brothers had been killed. His elder brother was serving with the New Zealand Army in Tunisia, and his younger brother died in a Beaufighter during training at East Fortune. Tragically a cable from New Zealand informed Jamie that his father had died on hearing the news of the death of two of his sons. Jameson's mother immediately appealed to the New Zealand government to allow Jamie to return home and take over the family farm of nearly 2,000 acres in Rotherham, near Canterbury. The High Commissioner, Mr (later Sir William) Jordan, visited 488 Squadron and told Jamie that he had done more than his duty and that he should return to his mother. Jamie was persuaded to apply for a passage on the next ship repatriating time-expired New Zealanders and Australians via the USA and Panama. However, before Jameson departed he was determined to avenge the untimely deaths of his brothers.[13] On the night of 29/30 July the Kiwi and his faithful navigator Crookes took off in R for Robert to patrol the Coutance-St Lô area. They returned having claimed three Junkers 88s and a Dornier Do 217 destroyed. Their second victim was confirmed destroyed by a navigator of 410 Squadron RCAF, who saw the Ju 88 hit the ground five to six miles south of Caen, explode and burst into flames. Jameson fired 320 20 mm shells to destroy all four aircraft in the space of just twenty minutes, a feat that took the New Zealander's score to nine e/a destroyed.[14]

In the run up to D-Day, 29 Squadron of the ADGB had been the first Mosquito unit equipped with the superior AI Mk VIII radar to be released for intruding over the continent. While still equipped with Beaufighter VIFs, the unit had had its first taste of offensive night operations in spring 1943, when it began Night Rangers over airfields in German-occupied France. After converting to the Mosquito in the summer, 29 Squadron reverted to defensive operations in the ADGB, finally mounting its first Intruders over France on the night of 14 May 1944. Flg Off R.G. 'Bob' Stainton, a 34-year-old navigator in 29 Squadron at Hunsdon, has vivid memories of a narrow escape he and his pilot, Flt Lt George E. Allison, had during a Night Intruder on the night of 5/6 July 1944 in Mosquito NF.XIII MM553:

> We night-prowlers liked the 'blanket of the dark' better than any romantic moonlight, and this night we were to visit the Coulommiers district again – Bretigny, Melun, Orly. There was a full moon. It was like daylight, as it had been on the night of the Nuremberg raid. The moon shone on French villages, woods and roads a thousand feet below us; for we had decided that at this height a 'cat's eye' Fw 190 had less chance of spotting us, although light flak had more, and we were still not low enough to escape German radar detection. No aerodromes seemed to be lit – ominous inactivity amid the luminous tones of a countryside so peaceful and still. The Seine was a bent silver ribbon, but we saw one aerial beacon flashing. This was awkward, as was the fact that Bill Provan[15] had already been a nuisance, shooting at trains and stirring up wasp nests. It was our choice of height, however, that directly led to trouble. We failed to

pin-point an important small lake, and shortly afterwards narrowly missed the Melun wireless masts. At least we now knew exactly where we were.

Suddenly, near Bretigny, we were lit by a searchlight, and tracer shells passed behind the tail. 'What's the time, Bob?' It was 0242, and we were both wishing the clock would go faster, when there was a series of explosions under us. We felt the shock and shudder of their impact. Other tracers wove light-tracks behind and above, and as suddenly stopped. The Mosquito was shuddering (us with it). It even seemed to me that the fuel cocks were hot. I got my parachute on as George, without speaking, though I could hear him snort, dived almost to the ground. For a second I wasn't sure that he had control, and began feathering the port propeller. There was no further attack. We managed to make a little height, 1,800 ft, and in spite of a spasmodic shaking at the tail-end of the fuselage the aeroplane seemed to be holding her own. To lighten the load we dropped the wing-tanks and fired our cannon with empty bravado over that tranquil landscape. Headway was slow at 170 IAS (with the wind from port and against us, our ground-speed was about 145 mph), but it gave me time to double-check our course and track and ETA at the coast. We prayed for accuracy and that no part of the ship would fall off. I kept my parachute on, hoping that no predator would creep up behind us, for we could not have taken evasive action. And how that black hole in the propeller-blade eyed us! We decided that if we met flak at the coast we would bale out. 'We'll paddle round to the beachhead in the dinghy.' Mild laughter. To our relief, neither event occurred.

The crossing seemed age-long, and George asked every few minutes exactly how far we had to go. However, we did not quarrel. At last we could see the flashing 'K' of the Friston beacon west of Birling Gap. 'May Day! May Day!' There was no reply. We reached Ford to my wry satisfaction exactly as calculated, and from 1,800 ft went straight in to land at 170 knots. High speed is vital when you have only one engine, and too slow a turn becomes an immediate and fatal stall. The wheels were down but we used no flaps. Half-way along the runway the wheels still had not touched nor had the speed dropped. We both lifted the undercarriage lever. She dug her nose in like the 'wheels' in a wheel-barrow race, hit something, threw her tail up and turned an exact somersault amid a splintering of wood and Perspex. Something cold and sharp closed on my left hand, twisting it behind me. We were stuck fast, upside-down. Metal creaked, petrol escaped with an overpowering stench. There followed the long drawn-out waiting for the gas to burst into flames as it touched hot metal. I remember only one thought: 'At least you had your cricket.'[16] No? No fire? An age of waiting followed while

I struggled in vain to free my left arm and the sweat dripped from my face.

Forty-five minutes later the blood-wagon and crash crew arrived and began trying to hack us free. It was some time before they realized that if the aeroplane was upside-down they were trying to cut their way through the guns. Someone had an attack of good sense and broke open the escape-hatch. It was the doctor. He also stuck a needle into my elevated bottom. They freed my arm. We were both very wide awake when they pulled us clear, and I remember lying on the stretcher in a delicious twilight of sensation, comfortable and still conscious enough to appreciate this unbelievable freedom. Only later did I discover that the crash crew had stolen my torch, commando knife and the box of escape equipment we always carried.[17]

On 25/26 July, when 412 Lancasters and 138 Halifaxes returned to Stuttgart and other large forces bombed Wanne-Eickel and flying-bomb sites in France, two 2nd TAF Mosquito Intruder crews were successful over the continent. On 26/27 July, Sqn Ldr R.S. Jephson and Flg Off J.M. Roberts of 409 Squadron RCAF destroyed a Ju 88 over Caen, but their NF.XIII was brought down by the flying debris and both men were killed in the crash. The only other Mosquito claim was a Ju 188 at Melun by Flg Off Frank E. Pringle and Flg Off Wain Eaton of 29 Squadron.

In August seventy-seven enemy aircraft were destroyed in the air by the seven night-fighter and fighter-bomber squadrons of 2nd TAF. On 1/2 August Sqn Ldr James D. Somerville and Flg Off G.D. Robinson of 410 Squadron RCAF in NF.XIII MM477/'U' equipped with AI VIII, shot down of a Ju 88 north-east of Tessy at 0100 hours. Somerville reported:

We took off from Colerne at 2310 hours and went to Pool 2. Handed over to Robust and given vector of 100 degrees, then over to Circular and later to Radox GCI. We intercepted a Stirling on southerly vector and then told to vector 190 degrees, 140 degrees and finally 230 degrees from the Seine estuary. Control told us they had a Stirling. In the meantime, having crossed inland we pulled over to starboard of the Stirling and was immediately given patrol vector of 280 degrees. After flying on this course for two to three minutes, chandelier flares were seen north-west of us. Immediately Radox told us to vector 320 degrees, as my 'turkey was gobbling' and they could not help us much. While still on 320 degrees contact was obtained three miles range 5 o'clock 40 degrees. Closed in to 2,000 ft, when visual was obtained on an a/c weaving thirty degrees on either side of 320 degrees. A straight course was flown on visual when a/c cut across in front of Mosquito on one of the jinks, range dropped to 600 ft. A/c now identified as Ju 188. The enemy crew evidently saw us at approximately the same time, and did a violent peel off to starboard, but luckily peeled off directly into the chandelier flares, and visual was maintained during the dive. E/a pulled up into steep climbing port turn. We turned a little harder than e/a, and the range dropped to approx. 900 ft, where I opened fire, allowing one ring deflection. After what appeared a short burst, the port wing of the e/a disintegrated outward of engine nacelle. The e/a flicked over into a steep half spiral to starboard and dived vertically into the ground approx. ten miles north-east of Tessy. There a violent explosion followed. No return fire experienced. Landed back at Colerne 0500 hours.

The night following, 2/3 August 1944, Sqn Ldr Frederick John Allison Chase and Flg Off A.F. Watson of 264 Squadron got their fifth enemy aircraft since D-Day when they destroyed a Ju 188 (or 88) ten miles west of Argentan. Sqn Ldr James Somerville and Flg Off G.D. Robinson of 410 Squadron RCAF in MM477/U scored their third victory when they shot down a Do 217 six miles north-west of Pontorson at 2255 hours. Somerville wrote:

I was first given vector of 190 degrees after a group of bogies, then vectored 170 degrees and finally on 150 degrees from twenty miles north-east of Avranches. Contact obtained three miles range 50 degrees off and to starboard height 7,000 ft ASI 220 mph. Target was doing a gentle weave. I closed to 1,000 ft and identified as a Do 217 by pulling off to starboard and getting a silhouette against a bright northern sky. I pulled back into line astern and opened fire at approximately 800 ft. It appeared that e/a must have seen me at the exact split second that I opened fire, as it started a fairly hard starboard turn. On the first burst, half of the e/a port tailplane and the port rudder flew off, and evidently I must have holed his oil tank, because my windscreen and a/c became smothered in oil. I experienced great difficulty in maintaining a visual through the film of oil. E/a then started doing a steady starboard orbit and losing height rapidly, as if the pilot had been killed or was having difficulty in controlling his a/c. After the first burst the combat developed into a dogfight, as return fire was experienced from the dorsal and ventral guns of the e/a. No hits appeared to register, although the fire appeared to be uncomfortably close. I reopened fire every time I got close enough to see the e/a through oil, which was gradually clearing due to the slipstream, at the same time e/a kept firing back at me. It appeared that the e/a dived vertically into the ground from 3,000 ft at the precise moment when I had used all my ammunition. I orbited port and saw the e/a strike the ground and burn furiously. (Position approx. six miles north-west of Pontorson.) No parachutes were seen to leave the e/a. But my navigator on the last burst told me he saw the other half of the tailplane leave the e/a. Intermittent flak was experienced throughout, and on returning to base found that my main plane had been hit by a 13 mm shell inboard of the port engine nacelle.

Flt Lt 'Jamie' Jameson DFC's tenth victory on 488 Squadron RNZAF came on the night of 3/4 August when he shot down a Ju 88 that was about to dive-bomb British Army troops near St Lô. He fired just sixty 20 mm cannon shells to down the Junkers. Next day came news of his sailing date for New Zealand. On 6 August Jameson and Norman Crookes took off on their last sortie together in R-Robert. The controller informed them that 'bandits' were making for the front line. Jameson gave a 'Tallyho' (enemy sighted) over his R/T, and he claimed a Ju 88 damaged five miles west of the Vire before notching his eleventh victory, a Ju 88 fifteen miles east of Avranches. R for Robert landed back at Colerne to a rapturous welcome. Jameson returned to New Zealand, and the award of a DSO followed. Crookes, who after the war became a teacher in Kent, received a Bar to his DFC. Jamie's score made him the highest-scoring New Zealand fighter pilot of the war.[18]

On the night of 5/6 August, Flt Lt John A.M. Haddon and his navigator, Flg Off Ralph J. McIlvenny, flying XIII MM514, took off on a night patrol. Haddon wrote:

> McIlvenny and I had taken off from A8 at 2200 hours on our first night sortie from the American beachhead, and ground control was using us to calibrate some new radar on the British beachhead. Our patrol line lay about fifty kilometres south of Caen at about 5,000 ft. Unknown to us, a Junkers 188 was on a westerly course, fairly well east of the British Sector. An 88/188 would follow him some twenty minutes later. Both could have been aiming at targets anywhere in the American Sector. Patton had just made his breakout of the beachhead towards Rennes in the extreme west, but the Canadian and British forces were still being held fast somewhere south of Bayeux and Caen. Falaise was still in enemy hands. We could see ground artillery fire from that sector. It was a brilliant moonlit night, a little before midnight. Control told us there was trade coming up flying much higher than we were, and gave us several southerly courses to steer. Because we had been unusually low and had to climb as we tried to reach our target, we found ourselves having difficulty catching up with it, but it made things easier by gradually turning from west to north-north-west towards the general direction of our own airfield. We were pretty sure we were after a fellow Mosquito and that our interception would be no classic encounter –

just another tail chase. Controllers who put you in such a position weren't high on aircrew popularity lists.

Mac had the bogey on radar for some minutes before I saw a tiny speck ahead in the sky at a distance of 3,500 ft. At 2,000 ft Mac voiced the opinion that it could be a Ju 88. He was using night glasses. Pilots seldom believed that navigators could tell a Lancaster from a Lysander, but as Mac was much above average, discretion became the better part of valour. We slid well to one side and below so that we weren't silhouetted against the moon as we had been, which also gave us a chance to see the aircraft from the best angle. As we closed, it was clear that our target was a 188 and that he didn't know we were there, a very desirable situation. Keeping it that way, I got in to 800 ft and checked for the tenth time that the guns were set to fire, the props were in near fine pitch and the gunsight dim enough to see through. I then pulled up behind him and opened up. I first hit his port engine, then the fuselage, and we ducked when something left the aircraft. It was on fire on the way down, then its pyrotechnics blew up and finally it went in near somewhere called Domfront.

Before we had time for the usual mutual admiration to begin, we got a call from Ops to turn south-east again because there was more trade at twenty-five miles and below us. I put the nose hard down and eventually Mac got a number of contacts. I ended up overshooting and needing more help from Ops and Mac. It was clear that this was no sitting-duck. He knew we were there and what he had to do about it. After several visuals on an 88 that was all over the sky, doing steep turns, climbing and diving, I finally managed to hold him visually and fly as in a day combat. Now night aerobatics are not to be recommended because you topple your major instruments and lose them when you need them most. It is also very easy to lose speed and spin-in. However, Mac and I had developed a drill for such circumstances, and he called height and airspeed to me every few seconds so that we would not fly into the ground. As I tried to turn inside the 88 to get my gunsight on him, I found him flying in a very tight turn, much too low for comfort. Suddenly he went on his back and dived, perhaps having stalled. Shortly afterwards there was a great flash from the ground, and both Ops and Mac lost contact. Later the French Underground confirmed time and place near Antrain where it had gone in.

On the night of 6/7 August, Wg Cdr J.D. Somerville DFC RCAF and Flg Off G.D. Robinson of 410 Squadron RCAF in NF.XIII MM566/'R' equipped with AI VIII shot down a Ju 88 at St Hilaire to take their personal victory score to four. Somerville wrote:

Took off from Colerne at 0050 hours/landed back at 0325 hours. I was put on patrol east–west (south of St Malo). I was given a vector of 060 degrees, and after being on this vector for a short time Tailcoat told us to vector 280 degrees, as he had something for us. I did several one-off vectors until finally on 240 degrees contact was obtained at two miles range, 30–35 degrees above, 12 o'clock. My observer told me to climb hard as e/a was considerably above us. Our height was 4,000 ft. My starboard engine was missing badly but we managed to climb to about 5,500 ft, where a visual was obtained about 1,000 ft above, dead ahead. Flak was starting to emanate ahead of e/a, which seemed to frighten him somewhat, and he did a turn to port and started to let down slowly, which suited us as the starboard engine was giving considerable difficulty. When I saw him start to turn I cut across the inside of his turn and pulled in to about 900 ft, slightly below, where I recognized him as a Ju 88. Pulled in a little close and saw two large bombs carried externally inboard motors. Pulled up and opened fire at approximately 700 ft. A few strikes were seen on the starboard engine, which caught fire. E/a did a wide sweeping spiral to port from 3,000 ft and struck the ground with an extremely violent explosion, scattering debris over a large area. Tailcoat fixed us at 180 degrees beacon FM fifty-five miles (St Hilaire du H. area). No return fire or evasive action experienced. I claim one Ju 88 destroyed.

On 6 August, 604 (County of Middlesex) Squadron at Zeals, which had joined 141 Wing, 2nd TAF, in April, transferring to 147 Wing 85 (Base) Group, on 3 May, became the first Mosquito fighter squadron to move to France, when it transferred to A-8 at Picauville on the Cherbourg Peninsula. On 7/8 August Flt Lt Davidson and Flg Off Willmott of 264 Squadron had to fly through the explosion of their Ju 88, which blacked the entire aircraft and burnt off the rudder fabric. Nothing daunted, they landed their Mosquito safely on a strip just behind the beachhead. On 11 August, 264 Squadron joined 604 (County of Middlesex) Squadron at Picauville on the Cherbourg Peninsula. Flt Lt John A.M. Haddon of 604 Squadron recollects:

> By the time 2nd TAF came into existence, the Allies had had four years of night-warfare experience to devise airfield systems that could function well at night as well as protect aircraft on the ground from attack, largely using wide dispersal, aircraft blast sheltering and minimal visibility from the air as defensive systems. As aircraft became heavier, grass-surfaced fields fell out of use. By D-Day engineers had perfected systems of construction that could carry entire airfields overseas, not too different in facilities from any modern field of that time. One invasion airfield, A-8 at Picauville,

west of St Mere Eglise in the American Sector, was built in about forty-eight hours, including runway, dispersals, taxi paths, control and refuelling, using a base of sand covered with tar paper. Designed to last thirty days, it lasted fifty-five or so, and was home to three American day fighter-bomber squadrons and two RAF night squadrons. The RAF was doing night cover from A-8 because someone, quite wrongly, had convinced the planners that the US night-fighters were inadequate. I heard that the A-8 designer was a Canadian. Again by 2nd TAF time, aircraft carrying heavy radar and equipped with cannon firing 2,400 rounds of 20 mm ammunition a minute could be operated out of such fields in all-but-total darkness. As far as I know there was only one fatal crash in the fifty-five days of A-8's existence.

Like most wartime flying operations, the longer a night-fighter crew had survived, the longer it would continue to survive. Crews of 604 and 264, the first night squadrons on the beachhead, had no less than one full tour of duty each behind them. As I recollect it, 604 shot down some fifty to sixty hostiles for the loss of two or three crews from D-Day to VE-Day. Life for aircrew wasn't all that bad in Normandy. There were so many experienced crews available and food was so much easier to furnish in the UK than on the beachhead, that for one period we got ten days' home leave every three weeks. As usual, staff seemed to get better quarters than fighting forces. At A-8 the staff lived in the former German Army Commander's HQ, known as the 'Château', while aircrew were put into a centuries-old, partly burned-out, insect-ridden farmhouse known to us as the 'Shiteau'. We eventually rebelled and moved into tents.

Although fast scrambles had been additional ways of getting night-fighters airborne, the usual procedure was to have aircraft constantly on patrol at about Angels 10, positioned to intrude into hostile air space when required, with minimum loss of time. The speed difference between a Ju 88 and a Mosquito was sufficiently slight that the long stern chases of earlier years were out of the question. Security considerations had prevented the very latest airborne radar from being operated from bases so close to enemy lines, so the squadrons operating from Normandy had to use a radar that could only see in a cone (like an ice-cream cone) looking forward, which limited their interception capabilities. I now forget the maximum range of that radar, but probably it was two or three miles.

A time-saving manoeuvre, if a ground controller had been good enough to put you onto a bandit on a closing angle, was to wait for your RO to get radar contact and assess the target's course and speed as it came towards you, then at the critical moment determined by the RO, turn hard across the face of the bandit and continue turning until hopefully it reappeared in the radar cone in front of you. If you turned too soon, you got in front of him, not a good thing if he was also a night-fighter; if you turned too late it meant a long stern chase. It was the RO's skill and the crew's total integration that determined success or failure. Most crews had spent years perfecting their techniques.

On a good moonlight night a normal night-fighter pilot could (visually) see an aircraft as a dot at about 4,000 ft; on a black night 1,500–2,000 ft was pretty good. The RO's job was to get his pilot to that range, nicely positioned for the kill. Under the operating conditions of normal static warfare, ground control could reasonably assure a crew whether or not a target was hostile. Under invasion conditions such as Sicily or Normandy, the chances of a target being hostile were perhaps ten or twenty to one against. I was told that when we were airborne at H-hour-6 of D-Day, and over a beachhead and sea area some thirty miles long by twenty miles deep, there were up to twenty other TAF night-fighters, as well as Dakotas towing gliders, the odd bomber and quite a few Fighter Command aircraft trying to get into the act. My logbook shows much the same to be true for the next two weeks as we covered the fleet and invasion area. Sorting things out wasn't easy.

Experienced night crews knew that it was vital to treat any interception as a technical exercise and make full identification, rather than go blustering in and shooting down some unfortunate Allied crew while the adrenaline was flowing. The only exception to this identification-first principle came from US anti-aircraft gun crews on the beachhead, who generally fired at anything within range, especially before they got used to having night-fighters based in their midst.

On the night of 6/7 August, Mosquitoes of 2nd TAF claimed nine enemy aircraft over France. Among the missing was *Hauptmann* Helmut Bergmann, a *Ritterkreuzträger* and *St.Kpt* of *8./NJG4* with thirty-seven kills, during a sortie in the Invasion Front area of Avranches-Mortain. No trace was ever found of his Bf 110G-4 or his crew. On the night of 7/8 August, when 1,019 heavy bombers blasted the Normandy battle area, Mosquitoes of 2nd TAF claimed ten more victories, almost one for each bomber lost. On 8/9 August, 2nd TAF Mosquito crews scored another three victories, as 170 Lancasters and ten Mosquitoes of 1, 3 and 8 Groups attacked oil depots and storage facilities at Aire-sur-Lys and the Forêt de Lucheux in France for one Lancaster lost.

On the night of 14/15 August, Sqn Ldr Somerville and Flg Off G.D. Robinson of 410 Squadron RCAF in NF.XIII MM477/'U' equipped with AI VIII went in search of their fifth victory. Fifteen miles due west of Le Havre they picked up a contact, as Somerville relates:

> I pulled in behind the e/a, range about 1½ miles, and started to close. E/a at this time began to climb and do about a rate half turn to starboard. We maintained contact on the AI, closing the range till finally the e/a levelled off at approximately 10,500 ft after turning a complete 360 degrees. At this time I was very well shrouded. The range at this time was about 1,800 ft, almost directly above. I started to pull up, and on decreasing the angle off the exhausts disappeared, visual being lost. However, the visual was regained at approximately 800 ft range 20 degrees, off. I pulled in to 600 ft and recognized e/a as a Ju 88. During this period my navigator was getting his Ross night glasses, and from directly underneath the e/a he confirmed my recognition. At this range I noticed two heavy-calibre bombs slung externally inboard of the engines. I dropped back to 450 ft, pulled up to dead astern and opened fire at this range. The fuselage of the e/a burst with a violent explosion and disintegrated into the air. No return fire was experienced. The majority of the debris fell off to port. I pulled up in a very steep climb and broke to starboard. I asked control for a fix and was given fifteen miles due west of Le Havre. Time 2325 hours. I claim this e/a destroyed.[19]

On 26 August, 219 Squadron joined 147 Wing, 85 (Base) Group, 2nd TAF, and on 3 September 264 Squadron made a move to Caen/Carpiquet with the first patrols flown over the Paris area, and later over Brussels. The only real excitement was when Flt Lt Moncur and Flg Off Woodruffe did not return from a low-flying exercise on the afternoon of the 19th. They did come back a week later, having been shot down in the St Nazaire area. On the 14th, 264 Squadron flew back to Predannack – ostensibly to re-equip, but anyway by then the war had got too far out of sight. Victories in September and October did not match those scored in June and July, but the night-fighters nevertheless maintained a credible response. During September they destroyed twenty-eight enemy aircraft of many types, and in October a further fifteen were destroyed. On 25/26 August, 138 Wing took part in all-out attacks on troop concentrations and vehicles in the Rouen area who were attempting to retreat across the Seine. Attacks continued on the night of 30 August against railways in the Saarbourg and Strasbourg areas.

Though V-1 patrols had occupied most of 418 Squadron's time in July and August, they were interspersed with other types of activity, 418 reverting, in September, to Rangers and abortive Big Ben patrols (trying to 'jam' V-2 rockets). No. 418 finished the war with the distinction of destroying more enemy aircraft both in the air and on the ground, than any other Canadian squadron, in both night and daylight operations, as Bob Bruce, Russ Bannock's navigator, recalls:

> We did Flowers harassing enemy bases in support of the invasion or of bombers and Day Rangers hunting in pairs. These were carried out at low level and ideally with cloud cover at 1,000 ft or more, to facilitate evasion if attacked. Our first of these was on 28 June 1944, led by Flight Lieutenant C.M. Jasper (Long Beach, Ca.) and his navigator, Archie Martin. Jas was one of several American pilots who joined the RCAF. Crossing Denmark at treetop height, we found a Ju 88 crossing the Baltic, close to a fair-sized vessel. Jasper destroyed the Junkers in the air, but was caught by the ship's fire. I vividly recall his blazing tailfin above the seemingly static ship. The damage was limited and he flew home successfully. Night Rangers and Flowers gave similar opportunity, if we were lucky enough to detect enemy aircraft. For a higher success rate AI was needed, with which 406 Squadron was equipped. But we were lucky sometimes, and Russ's shooting was deadly. Sometimes bad weather intervened. On 15 August *en route* for Avignon we met such thunder and up-draught over the Massif Central that we had to pull out and return. We had gained 4,000 ft over the mountains in a few seconds; we might equally have lost them. Russ compared the stresses he encountered there with the worst ever in his subsequent career as a test pilot. (On another trip to Breslau in October we flew 5.25 hours without a pin-point and of course no result. Good DR depends upon accurate flying).
>
> We did two other Day Rangers, one to Copenhagen with Sid Seid (another Californian) and Dave McIntosh, with gratifying results, the other alone arriving at Parow, on the Baltic coast, at sunrise. We found an OTU in full operation. After destroying two Me 108s in the circuit, we were attacked by another, older-type Me 109. We broke off at treetop height but our port engine caught fire (due to debris holing the radiator). We feathered and returned on one engine, landing back at Hunsdon after 7 hours 15 mins. No. 418 had established a high success rate in Day Rangers during the first six months of 1944.[20]

Life for Dave McIntosh was never dull flying with Sid Seid. McIntosh recalls:

> Shortly after dawn on 15 October 1944, Sid and I were flying in a Mosquito fighter over our target, Stargard, a German airfield northeast of Berlin. We were a long way from home (Hunsdon, an airfield thirty miles north of London), and still had farther east and north to go to a second target, Kolberg, another German aerodrome, before

we could head back to England. 'Heading back' were the sweetest two words I knew during the war, apart from 'arrival Hunsdon' (or any other friendly base). We were in the process of attacking *Luftwaffe* planes on the ground – we had seen none in the air, thank heaven – and there was a whole array of them for our picking: Messerschmitt fighters, Junkers night-fighters, Stuka dive-bombers and Focke-Wulf fighters. We had flown low (treetop) level, pulling up over power lines, and had so completely caught the Jerries by surprise that a hundred of them were drawn up for what we surmised was a Sunday morning (which was what it was) church parade. I say surmise because neither Sid nor I ever went to church (in his case, synagogue) except, perhaps, to give the squadron padre a lift occasionally when he was particularly down in the mouth because of heavy non-attendance at his services in gymnasium, hangar or open air. Fear of death in war might have driven some flyers to God, but it didn't drive them to church.

Sid dived at one group of planes, aiming at the wing roots where the fuel were located, and blazed away with our 20 mm cannon. He blew up a Messerschmitt with a one-second burst on our first run. We got turned around for another run at the field and Sid fired a two-second burst at three planes, one exploding. As he finished the salvo, he spotted two more planes, one a Stuka, on the south side of the field. He got in a quick burst and the Stuka exploded just as we started going over on our port side. We were only 20 ft off the deck, and when Sid tried to correct our roll we stalled and the stick flew out of his hands.

We should have been dead right there and then, spread in little pink and red pieces all over Stargard airfield. If the Germans could find anything at all to pick up, the two of us would have fitted easily into one shoe or cigar box. But the Mosquito in an unexplained flick righted itself, and we were flying straight and level at a height of ten feet. The explanation for this baffling Mosquito self-manoeuvre didn't interest me; only the result did. Later, I wondered vaguely whether our plane's callsign, Credo 29, had anything to do with our survival: belief, resulting in a perfect cribbage hand. When my nerves steadied (as much as they ever did – a controlled jangle) a few minutes later as we raced over the sunlit autumn leaves toward Kolberg, I said to myself, 'Boy, the rest of your life is pure gravy. Every minute after flicking out of the lethal stall is an unearned bonus.'

On 2 October 1944, Flg Off Roy Emile Lelong of 605 Squadron took off from his forward base at St Dizier, and went looking over the Baltic to add to his score of three victories. It proved a very fruitful sortie for the 27-year-old New Zealand carpenter from Auckland and his navigator,

Plt Off J.A. McLaren DFC, who sighted enemy seaplanes in Jasmunder Bay. Lelong claimed five Dornier Do 24s destroyed and two damaged, and a Blohm und Voss Bv 138 damaged in the air. Lelong returned to base on one engine, where his camera gun film revealed that he had shot down the Bv 138 and that five Do 24s had been destroyed, one probably and five damaged on the water.[21]

At this stage of the war the *Luftwaffe* had become increasingly wary in its use of its dwindling aircraft resources. Consequently, the Allied air forces had to employ imaginative tactics to find and destroy them. Since the *Luftwaffe* was doing less and less flying, Flt Lt F.A. 'Ted' Johnson DFC RCAF and his navigator, Flt Lt N.J. 'Jimmy' Gibbons, of 418 Squadron had speculated that it should be possible to catch them on the ground at night. After some experimentation they had established that on nights when there was a full moon there was sufficient light to carry out an air-to-ground strafing attack in a shallow dive from about 1,500 ft above ground level. Any higher and it was difficult to see objects on the ground, while any lower would give insufficient time to aim the Mosquito's guns, fire a burst and pull out from the dive before striking the ground. Best visibility was obtained by positioning for the attack with the moon on the opposite side of the target. The Mosquito crew had studied intelligence reports of *Luftwaffe* flying activity, and had noticed that in recent weeks there had been several indications of aircraft flying in the vicinity of Erding airfield. It was deep within Germany on the far side of Munich, at the limit of the Mosquito's range. But they had calculated that if they pre-positioned their aircraft from their operational base at Hunsdon to Ford airfield in Sussex, and refuelled and launched from there with full tanks, they could make the round trip. So at the next full moon phase they rechecked all factors, obtained authorization for the operation on the night of 2 October 1944, moved their Mosquito to Ford in the late afternoon, refuelled, then took off at 2015 into a hazy autumn night. The moon had not yet risen, but it would be up in an hour and the Met forecast had said that although there was a weather front over Germany it should be well east of their target by the time they arrived, and the skies should be clear.

The Met man was wrong. After flying for three hours at 500 ft AGL in the hope of avoiding being picked up by German radar, Johnson and Gibbons arrived in the area to find the sky completely obscured by thick, low-hanging clouds. There would be no help from the moon. Determined not to return without trying to attack their target, they flew north of the enemy airfield to a predetermined sharp bend in the Isar river, which could be seen even on this moonless night, and using an accurate course heading, airspeed and time made their first abortive pass. The Germans did not react as they overflew the airfield, so Johnson and Gibbons speculated that no radar alert had been given to the defences, and indeed, they might still be uncertain if this was a hostile aircraft or one of their own with radio communications problems. As their Mosquito streaked close to 300 mph through the night sky a few miles east of Munich, searchlights flicked on to the south-east at Erding airfield and nervously probed the dark clouds above. Johnson said, 'Jim, turn our navigation lights on and off a few times. The natives are getting restless.' A few flashes of the nav lights, and the German crews doused their searchlights and waited and wondered.

Again they reached their pin-point over the river bend and carefully turned so that when they recrossed in a southerly direction they would be on the desired course at exactly the selected height and airspeed. The Mosquito passed over the river – precision was essential to success under these adverse visibility conditions. Gibbons clicked his stopwatch and breathed into the microphone mounted in his oxygen mask. '2 minutes 28 seconds to go.'

Ted Johnson grunted acknowledgement and rechecked that the safety guards were off on both the cannon and the machine-guns. He tweaked the dimmer control lower on the reflector gunsight to reduce the dim glow of the circle of light with its central dot on the windscreen that was his aiming guide. He needed the gunsight as dim as possible to maximize his chances of seeing something on the ground in the target area. Dim outlines sped under the Mosquito as the two Merlin 25s growled their power across the night sky. Wispy cloud flicked by. Tension in the dimly lit cockpit mounted as the crew strained forward in their safety harnesses, striving to see objects on the ground. The airfield ahead remained totally blacked out. There was no sign of hostility. Johnson rechecked speed, course and altitude. Gibbons glanced at his stopwatch and said, '30 seconds', then began a countdown at ten-second intervals. As he called out, '10 seconds', Johnson replied, 'Airfield in sight!' and eased forward slightly on the control column, anticipating the need to initiate a quick dive as soon as a target was seen. His right thumb and forefinger tensed over the button and the trigger on the control column that would fire the cannon and machine-guns. Suddenly the vague outline of a single-engine aircraft sitting on the airfield swept under the Mosquito's nose and the pilot made a spasmodic movement to start a dive but in the same second knew it was too late. 'Damn!' was all he said as the airfield continued to race away beneath and the indistinct outlines of hangars on the southern boundary were left behind. Still no reaction from the airfield defences.

The Mosquito made a wide sweeping turn westwards and continued around onto a northerly heading. Gibbons spoke. 'What kind of aircraft was that?'

Johnson replied, 'I'm not sure. Could have been an Me 108, an advanced trainer. I couldn't see in time. Let's have one more go.' A green Aldis-type hand-held signal light directed a series of dots and dashes toward them from the airfield control tower. The Mossie crew was unable to decipher the message since, whatever it was, it was in German. 'Jimmy,' said Johnson, 'I think they believe we want to land. Give them a few more flashes on the nav lights, then leave them on steady.' Then, as an afterthought, he added, 'Make damn sure you switch them off the instant I fire the guns!'

Over the kink in the river they commenced their third run. Johnson eased the Mossie down 100 ft hoping to improve the ability to see objects on the ground, and concentrated on holding the air speed and heading. He turned the ultra-violet cockpit instrument lighting a notch dimmer and eased forward on the hard dinghy pack that was numbing his buttocks after three hours. The airfield ahead remained in total darkness. A trickle of sweat itched its way down the pilot's back. His open mike picked up the navigator's rapid breathing. '20 seconds to go', said Gibbons tensely. A moment later Johnson saw the blurred outline of a tree on the airfield perimeter and realized that he had seen it on their second pass. The parked aircraft had to be just ahead! Without waiting to actually see his target, he pushed the Mossie's nose down into a shallow dive and at the same moment saw the shadowy outline of the German aircraft. Rapidly he brought the central 'bead' of his reflector gunsight onto it and squeezed both triggers.

The cockpit floor vibrated under their feet from the thunderous bellow of the four 20 mm cannon, each spewing rounds at the rate of 600 a minute. Simultaneously the four 0.303 mm machine-guns chattered their deadly hail. Streams of glowing tracers lashed forward from the Mosquito's nose, and immediately a pattern of strikes from the mixture of ball, incendiary and explosive shells were seen to envelop the German aircraft. The stench of cordite fumes filled the Mossie's cockpit.

On the ground the suspicious anti-aircraft crews were tracking the mysterious Intruder in their sights, and instantly the Mosquito fired they loosed a barrage at it. Yellow, white and red fiery streams venomously arced through the darkness, clawing to destroy the attacker. As they pulled from the dive, the Mosquito crew heard a loud bang. Their aircraft shuddered. They had been hit! Johnson concentrated on controlling his aircraft and keeping as low as he dared without running into the hangars on the edge of the field. The German flak continued to hose up at them from all sides, but he knew that they could not fire too low lest they strike their own buildings. The volume of incendiary bullets slashing the sky actually provided enough light to see the oncoming hangars well enough to pass over them with minimum clearance. Rapidly they swept away from the hostile area and the ground fire ceased. It was only then that Johnson glanced out toward the left wingtip and exclaimed, 'My God, Jimmy, you forgot to turn the nav lights out!' The Mosquito was vibrating badly. The rudder pedals were tramping back and forth so furiously that the pilot could not hold them, and he finally withdrew his feet from the battering. Slowing the aircraft reduced the severity of the vibrations somewhat, but did not stop them. Anxiously the navigator peered toward the tail of the Mosquito, but was unable to see the extent of the damage. Johnson set course to pass south of the heavy defences around Munich, then turned for England while watching the engine temperature gauges for any sign of overheating and the fuel gauges for loss of fuel. At the reduced speed it would take over three hours to reach home base. Would the Mosquito hold together that long?

Knowing that they had thoroughly stirred up the enemy defences, they kept as low as they dared and maintained a watchful eye over their tail for German night-fighters. It was a long flight home. The official maximum endurance of this version of the Mosquito was 6¼ hours. They landed back at Hunsdon after 6 hours 15 minutes! The fuel gauges all read nearly zero. Upon wearily clambering down from the cockpit, Johnson and Gibbons were able to see by the aid of their ground crew's flashlights the damage to their beloved Mosquito. The tailplane and elevators were sieved with shrapnel holes, there was a ragged one-foot hole in the starboard tailplane and the rudder was only a skeleton of ribs, but it had brought them home. As they trudged towards the operations room for debriefing by the intelligence officer, they heard one of the ground crew remark, 'They sure build these Mosquitoes tough!'

In all, Johnson flew forty-three operations as a pilot with 418 Squadron, but none were as eventful as this.

Fellow Canadian, Flt Lt Rayne Schultz DFC, who had returned to 410 Squadron in December 1944 and teamed up with Flg Off J.S. Christie as his radar navigator, scored three victories in mid-April 1945 to take his score to eight aircraft destroyed. He received a Bar to his DFC on 6 July and was posted home to Canada in August. In April also, another Canadian pilot, John Caine, who had flown with 418 Squadron in 1944 before enjoying home leave and promotion to flying officer, was back in the UK, posted to 406 RCAF Intruder Squadron at Manston, flying the NF.XXX Mosquito and with AI Mk X radar. He crewed up with Flg Off 'Spud' Tindall, a navigator-radio operator. Caine was eager to start Night Intruders with the help of AI. His first op was a Night Intruder to the Munich area, but 'no joy'. On 24 April Caine refuelled in the afternoon at Juvincourt and teamed up with Sqn Ldr Don McFadyen and Flt Lt Sail in another Mosquito on a night FEF flare dropper at Eferding airfield, arriving at 0300 hours. Caine managed to set a Ju 88 on fire and sprayed two Fw 190s on the ground. He was hit by AA, badly damaging his tail, but he limped home. On 2 May he was off on another flare-dropping venture – 'Verdict 22' to Copenhagen-Marrebaek. The 'Verdict 22' aircraft never showed, so he dropped flares, revealing some mine-detonating Ju 52/3ms. In one attack he was able to set two of them on fire. At the end of May he was awarded a second Bar to his DFC. That was the end of the war for Caine. He was credited with twenty aircraft destroyed and a number damaged. He stayed with the squadron, which had been moved to Predannack, until it was disbanded in September. In June he married Jane Ford, whom he had met as a corporal WAAF in the signals office at Ford airfield. While John hailed from Edmonton, Alberta, Jane came from the Edmonton district of North London.[22]

In 1944/5, the 2nd TAF's main work remained Day and Night Ranger operations and Intruder sorties over the *Reich*. In 1944 and early 1945 also, FB.VIs in 140 Wing and 138 Wing continued to make history. In daylight they carried out legendary low-level raids on Nazi buildings in the occupied countries where key Resistance members were held captive, and equally daring raids were made on enemy headquarters in France, Holland and Denmark, which held hostage political prisoners and incriminating records. Not for nothing would 140 and 138 Wings become known, as the '*Gestapo* Hunters'. The first in this series of low-level pin-point raids took place on a bleak winter day, 18 February 1944, when heavy snow blanketed airfields in England and the French countryside from Brittany to Picardy.

Notes

1. Kipp had joined the RCAF in June 1940 and was commissioned on completion of training. He served as an instructor until 1943 when he departed for the UK. Finally, in November he joined 418 Squadron and was awarded the DFC in May 1944 and a DSO in July, while Huletsky was awarded the DFC and Bar. By 14 June they had scored ten aircraft and one shared destroyed, one shared probable and one damaged plus seven destroyed on the ground and eight damaged on the ground. At the end of June 1944 they were posted to ADGB HQ and were later posted to the Fighter Experimental Flight at Ford, where they remained until July 1945, seeing more action during March–July that year and scoring several ground victories. Kipp returned to Canada and was released in October 1945. He rejoined the RCAF a year later but was killed in a flying accident in a DH Vampire at St Hubert on 25 July 1949. *Aces High: A Tribute to the Most Notable Fighter Pilots of the British and Commonwealth Forces in WWII*. Christopher Shores and Clive Williams (Grub Street, London, 1994).
2. Boal was awarded the DFC in June. A second Bar to Caine's DFC was gazetted in October.
3. Luma was born in Helena, Montana, on 27 August 1922. After joining the RCAF he was posted to England in January 1943, where after a sorting-out process, through some sort of error or mix-up, Luma received an exceptionally high grade in a night-vision test. As a result, he was assigned to Night Intruders, though at the time he had no idea what a Night Intruder was. At 60 OTU he learned to fly the Mosquito and practised air-to-air gunnery and air-to-ground gunnery. After several weeks at OUT, Intruder trainees were instructed to informally pair off into crews. Colin Finlayson, a Canadian from British Columbia, and

Luma agreed to crew up together. While at OTU Luma decided to transfer to the US Army Air Forces. The official policy at the time, agreed to by the Americans and British, was that a crew would not be broken up, so after he was sworn in as a 1st lieutenant he was permitted to return to the RCAF to finish his tour of operations before returning to the USAAF. Luma was a USAAF pilot on detached duty with the RCAF. After finishing OUT, Luma and Fin were assigned to 418 Squadron RCAF.

4. MacFadyen had joined the RCAF in May 1940. His first score came while flying FB.VIs with 418 Squadron, when he was awarded a 'probable' on 22/23 December 1943 against a UEA. He followed this in early 1944 with the destruction of an Me 410, a Ju 52/3m and five V-1s. Promoted to squadron leader, MacFadyen joined 406 'Lynx' Squadron in November 1944, where he flew the NF.XXX on Night Intruders. He was awarded a DFC and Bar, an American DFC and the DSO during his two tours, and he finished the war with a tally of seven aircraft and five V-1s destroyed in the air and five aircraft destroyed, one probable and seventeen damaged on the ground.

5. Scherf left the service in April 1945 to return to the family ranch, but he found it difficult to settle back to civilian life, starting to drink heavily. He was killed in a car accident on 13 July 1949. *Aces High: A Tribute to the Most Notable Fighter Pilots of the British and Commonwealth Forces in WWII.* Christopher Shores and Clive Williams (Grub Street, London, 1994).

6. Starr had taken command of the squadron on 11 April after a successful career with 23 Squadron in the Mediterranean, where he had destroyed two Ju 88s and damaged two other aircraft. On 6/7 May he scored his first victory for the 'County of Warwick' Squadron by destroying a Bf 110 at St Dizier airfield for this third kill overall.

7. Starr destroyed an Me 410 and a UEA in 1944 to take his final score to six destroyed, one probable, two damaged, two destroyed on the ground + one V-1 destroyed. Starr was killed early in January 1945 when he was flying as a passenger aboard an Avro Anson, which crashed near Dunkirk, killing everyone on board. He was *en route* to get married at the time.

8. Flg Off Pearce and Flg Off Moore in a 409 Squadron NF.XIII claimed a 'probable', while the only Mosquito kill was by Flg Off R.E. Lelong RNZAF and Plt Off J.A. McLaren of 605 Squadron in a FB.VI, who destroyed an Me 410 seven miles south-east of Evreux airfield.

9. The FB.VIs of 21, 464 and 487 Squadrons in 140 Wing, 2nd TAF, were to remain at Thorney Island until December 1944, when the Australian and New Zealand squadrons both sent advance detachments to Rosières-en-Santerre, France. At Lasham, meanwhile, 2nd TAF's other Mosquito fighter-bomber wing – 138 – comprised 107, 305 (Polish) and 613 Squadrons, which late the previous year had re-equipped with FB.VIs after flying Bostons, Mitchell IIs and Mustangs respectively. It was planned to transfer 138 Wing to airfields in France when the outbreak from the Normandy beachhead came. The 2nd TAF was further strengthened early in 1944, when 85 (Base) Group was formed for the purpose of providing fighter cover over the continent leading up to and after D-Day. No. 85 Group was created by the transfer from Fighter Command of

29, 264, 409 'Nighthawk' Squadron RCAF, 410 'Cougar' Squadron RCAF, 488 Squadron RNZAF and 604 Squadron. The first Mosquito fighter squadron to transfer to 85 Group was 264 Squadron, in January 1944, which went to 141 Wing. (The last, 219 Squadron, would transfer from Fighter Command to 147 Wing on 28 August.) As part of the new-found offensive, the main work for the NF.XIIs and NF.XIIIs of 85 Group and the FB.VIs of 138 and 140 Wings was Day and Night Ranger operations and Intruder sorties from England.

10. Bannock was a pre-war civilian pilot, and he had been an instructor and ferry pilot until finally getting a posting to England in February 1944. After completing a Mosquito OTU course at High Ercall and Greenwood, Nova Scotia, he joined 418 Squadron at Holmsley South in May. No. 418 Squadron had been engaged in Night Intruding against enemy airfields, as well as conducting low level Day Rangers against airfields when operating in pairs. While at Greenwood he teamed up with navigator Robert Bruce, who recalls, 'In 1939 I was a graduate of Edinburgh University with a first in Music, a brilliant outlook and no money. Deeply influenced by the poetry of Wilfred Owen, who was KIA in November 1918, I joined the Friends' Ambulance Unit (as gallant a bunch as any military). But after 2½ years I knew the war was ruinous and I must be part of the ruin. I was accepted for aircrew training. I was almost 28. Russ on the other hand was young in years – 23 – and old in flying experience and leadership. I arrived at Holmsley South about 10 June, Russ a few days earlier.' Bannock and Bruce went on to destroy eight more e/a and eighteen and one shared V-1s.
11. MM466.
12. Jamie had flown Beaufighter IIs and VIs in 125 Squadron and had his first combat during night raids on Cardiff and Swansea in the summer of 1942. After a Heinkel 111 had bombed his own airfield, Jamie pursued the enemy aircraft and shot it down into the Bristol Channel. He landed to find that the bombs had killed the WAAF fiancée of his squadron friend. In August Jamie destroyed another He 111, and while on detachment in the Shetlands he claimed a Ju 88 as 'damaged', although later information indicated that the bomber had crashed on landing at Stavanger. He was credited with the destruction of a Do 217 on 11/12 February 1943, and he then went on 'rest', becoming a gunnery instructor. In January 1944 he joined 488 Squadron, which lost nine crews in flying accidents for just two enemy aircraft destroyed. Morale was very low, and although Jameson and Crookes patrolled night after night along the east coast, very little activity had come their way.
13. In July the six Mosquito fighter squadrons in 2nd TAF shot down fifty-five enemy aircraft and claimed two probables. In August seventy-seven enemy aircraft were destroyed in the air by the seven night-fighter and fighter-bomber squadrons. On 1/2 August Canadians Sqn Ldr James D. Somerville and Flg Off G.D. Robinson of 410 Squadron shot down of a Ju 88 north-east of Tessy. Somerville and Robinson scored their third victory when they shot down a Do 217 six miles north-west of Pontorson. On the night of 6/7 August Somerville and Robinson shot down a Ju 88 at St Hilaire to take their personal victory score to four. On the night of

14/15 August Sqn Ldr Somerville DFC and Flg Off G.D. Robinson DFC of 410 Squadron RCAF got their fifth victory, a Ju 88, fifteen miles west of Le Havre. Somerville was promoted to wing commander and given command of 409 Squadron RCAF.
14. The 2nd TAF and ADGB destroyed at least 230 aircraft at night over the Channel, France, the Low Countries and Germany, June 1944 to April 1945.
15. Flg Off William Wright Provan, another 29 Squadron pilot.
16. In 1938 Bob Stainton had been a brilliant captain of the Sussex cricket team.
17. George Allison was killed on 22 July on the squadron's first Day Ranger. His navigator, Sub Lt (A) C.W. Porter FAA, also died.
18. 'Jamie' Jameson died aged 76 in a bulldozer accident in 1998.
19. Somerville and Robinson's five victories in August earned them the DFC, which they both received on 20 October, at which time Somerville was promoted to wing commander and given command of 409 Squadron RCAF.
20. On the night of 29/30 August, Russ Bannock and Bob Bruce, paired with Flg Off Sid Seid, a Californian, and Dave McIntosh, blew up a Ju 88 on the ground at Copenhagen-Kastrup and a Bf 110 at Vaerose airfield. Seid, who scored hits on a line of three aircraft, observed a mechanic working around the tail section of the Bf 110 as they approached. 'After one look at us,' Seid recalled, 'the "Erk" broke all speed records during a sprint in an easterly direction. During my attack, another "Erk" was observed descending a high ladder near the roof of a hangar. Upon seeing us, the speed of his descent was suddenly and forcibly increased by a backward fall from near the top of the ladder. I claim this "Erk" as "probably destroyed".'
21. Five days later, on 7 October, two Mosquitoes of 605 Squadron destroyed ten enemy aircraft near Vienna and damaged six more. Roy Lelong finished the war with seven confirmed victories, one probable, three damaged and three V-1s destroyed. After the war he joined the RAF and in 1952 he went on exchange to the US 5th Air Force in Korea. He then flew Hunters with 43 Squadron and in 1955 took command of 257 Squadron.
22. After settling in Edmonton, they had three children – Judy, Todd and Jill. John Caine rejoined 418, an Auxiliary Reserve Squadron in Edmonton, flying B-25 Mitchells, where he was promoted to squadron leader. He retired in 1951. Although he was offered a permanent commission in the RCAF and had offers from the two national airlines, he chose to join his father's fur farm. MAA *The Mossie* No. 36, September 2004, by Russ Bannock.

CHAPTER 9

Jericho

Inside Amiens prison on the deserted Route d'Albert, 24-year-old André Leroy awaited his fate. Amiens was the chief city in the Somme department, its famous Gothic cathedral the largest church in France. In 1940 the surrounding area had been put to use for airfield construction. It was natural that the people of Picardy despised the Germans, who had caused so much slaughter on the battlefields of the Somme in 1914–18. Occupation was harsh, and disobedience could result in deportation to Germany or death. Those who could joined the resistance. An accident at an early age had left Leroy, who was born at Daours, near Albert, on 24 May 1919, with one leg shorter than the other, so he was not accepted for military service and he soon joined the Underground. From February to December 1941 he took part in sabotage actions with a group leader called 'Michel'. From January 1942 to February 1943 André worked with the Intelligence Service, supplying information about the Germans. He then spent five months distributing clandestine papers in addition to forging sixty-two identity cards and hiding twenty saboteurs. During the second half of 1943 he had been a railway saboteur, with twenty-two acts to his credit, including in July the railway at Thiaumont-Grandcourt. In November he had been about to sabotage the aeroplane factory at Meaulte when the *Gestapo* arrested him at his parents' home. After lengthy interrogation and torture, André had been condemned to death. The sentence was to be carried out on 19 February 1944.

Dr Antonin Mans, Public Health Officer and Defence Chief of the Somme Department, was under sentence of death, too. But news of a rescue attempt had been smuggled in to him by Monsieur Dominique Ponchardier, the dark-haired, dark-skinned leader of the whole of Occupied France of a group called the 'Sosies' under the guise of a message from his wife. Ponchardier had requested an urgent air strike to break open the 22 ft high and 3 ft thick walls surrounding the three-storey building, which rose to 66 ft and was built in the shape of a cross. There would be casualties, but better to die from RAF bombs than be shot by a German firing squad. Eleven members of the local *Frances Tireurs et Partisans Français* (FTPF) had been shot in the jail in December 1943. More prisoners, perhaps twenty, fifty or even a hundred, were due to be executed on 19 February. Mans had been in Amiens jail since 12 November 1943, caught with almost the entire Amiens group after the treachery of an unknown member. Only one or two whom Madame Mans had been able to warn had managed to escape. The doctor stared at the massive lock in the heavy oak door, which shut him so securely in his ground-floor cell. He could not see how a rescue attempt was to be achieved.[1]

In January information had been received in London that 196 loyal Frenchmen were being held in captivity in Amiens prison, many under sentence of death. The most important Frenchman in the jail, which held 700 French men and women, of whom about 250 were political prisoners, was Monsieur Raymond Vivant, a key Resistance leader and *sous-préfet* at Abbeville. Only four days previously still in charge of the coastal sector of Somme province, he was now awaiting a trial whose outcome was certain. There were Captain André Tempez, regional Resistance leader, Jean Beaurin, the 20-year-old deputy leader of the FTPF, Maurice Holleville, another leading FTPF man, and Monsieur Henri Moisan, a member of the *Organisation Civile et Militaire*. Moisan was immured with three other Resistance men in a tiny cell twelve feet by seven on the second floor. Arrested by the *Gestapo* in August 1942 for suspected complicity in an act of sabotage, he had subsequently been allowed to return to his home in Boulevard Jules Verne, Amiens – the house where the famous writer had died in 1905. But on 26 January 1944 he had been rearrested, and he was now awaiting the inevitable result of a long and bitter interrogation. There was Monsieur Gruel, another member of the Amiens group, now occupying a cell on the first floor formerly occupied by Dr Mans. All day on 16 and 17 February Mans listened for the sound of aircraft engines, but none came. In two days he and his fellow Resistance operatives were to be executed.

At noon on 16 and 17 February Dominique Ponchardier and a small band of faithful followers patrolled the fields near the jail, keeping hidden as far as possible, seeing without being seen. Ponchardier's main fear now was that news of the proposed attack might leak out. It had been no use keeping the secret to himself – he had had to tell a small army of Resistance men in order to have help ready for the escaping prisoners. It would be pointless to expose them to the hazards of bombing and then leave them to be recaptured. Altogether he thought he must have told over a hundred people. It only needed one informer, or one careless contact, to wreck the whole plan. The Germans would bring the executions forward and the RAF would arrive too late. But Amiens jail was silent, cloaked in snow. There was no evidence that the Germans were any more on their guard than usual. And there was no sign, either, of the RAF. They were cutting it fine. On the morning of the 18th, Ponchardier decided that if they did not come that day they would not come at all. He thought it quite probable that for political reasons the attack had been called off. He had built his hopes so much on the RAF that he dreaded the passage of time up to midday, fearing the mortal blow to the Resistance if the RAF did not come. The morning evaporated, and the last minutes up to midday galloped by. At twelve o'clock all Ponchardier's men were in their places, the doubts born of delay written clearly on their faces. The conviction was growing that they had been abandoned. In the next three minutes they would know.[2] A formation of nineteen Mosquitoes had taken off from Hunsdon at 1055 hours with snow falling and were headed for Amiens prison. Crews were delighted to get airborne after snowstorms and thick cloud had led to several postponements in the previous few days.

The plan was to breach the 140 yd long and 110 yd wide rectangular wall surrounding the prison in two places by Mosquitoes of 140 Wing, 2nd TAF,[3] using eleven-second bombs. These would be dropped from 10–15 ft by five FB.VIs of 464 RAAF led by Wg Cdr R.W. 'Bob' Iredale and six of 487 Squadron RNZAF, led by Wg Cdr Irving S. 'Black' Smith. The concussion from the bomb explosions should open the cell doors to give most of the prisoners a chance to escape. Wg Cdr 'Black' Smith recalled, 'After four years of war just doing everything possible to destroy life, here we were going to use our skill to save it. It was a grand feeling, and everybody left the briefing room prepared to fly into the walls rather than fail to breach them.' If the first two waves of Mosquitoes failed, six FB.VIs of 21 Squadron led by 38-year-old Wg Cdr I.G. 'Daddy' Dale had orders to flatten the prison complex. AVM Basil Embry, AOC 2 Group, had been forbidden to go on the raid because of his previous exploits in France. Gp Capt Percy C. Pickard DSO DFC, CO 140 Wing, was in overall command of the raid.

'Pick' Pickard had joined the RAF in 1936, and in 1940, as a flight lieutenant, he had achieved an unwanted fame through his clipped, natural playing of the pilot of Wellington F-Freddie in the film *Target for Tonight*. After completing a bombing tour he commanded 161 Squadron at Tempsford, assisting directly in the dangerous work of subversion and sabotage in France. On 27/28 February 1942, as a wing commander, he led the force of a dozen 51 Squadron Whitley aircraft carrying British paratroops in the raid on Bruneval that resulted in the capture of vital German radar secrets.

Pickard and his navigator, Flt Lt J.A. 'Peter' Broadley DSO DFC DFM, flew in F-Freddie,[4] a 487 Squadron Mosquito, with the 464 Squadron formation. Flt Lt Tony Wickham, in a specially equipped Film Photographic Unit Mosquito IV,[5] with a cameraman, Plt Off Leigh Howard, was to film the bombing operation. 'Tony' Wickham had been one of the three pilots in 105 Squadron who on 30 January 1943 had helped disrupt *Reichsmarschall* Hermann Göring's speech in Berlin. That night Wickham had treated British listeners to the BBC's 9 o'clock news to an account of the action. Flt Sgt Leigh Howard had been the Film Unit cameraman on the 27 May 1943 Mosquito daylight raid on the Zeiss Optical factory at Jena.

The Mosquitoes rendezvoused with Typhoon IBs of 245 (Northern Rhodesia) Squadron over Littlehampton, but 174 (Mauritius) Squadron failed to make the rendezvous. Over the Channel the weather improved, but by then two Mosquitoes were forced to return.[6] About ten miles from the target, Flt Lt B.D. 'Titch' Hanafin and Plt Off C.F. Redgrave of 487 Squadron RNZAF were forced to abort because of an engine fire. The remaining Mosquitoes descended to 100 ft, and they pressed on at no higher than treetop level, avoiding power lines and known flak batteries. The formation swept around to the south of Albert, and the crews picked up the long, straight tree-lined road to Amiens. Descending to 10 ft, their propellers swirled wispy snow clouds in their wake. The poplars on the road ended abruptly, and a mile in the distance the prison stood out in fresh snow. The Mosquitoes split up and attacked in four waves from two directions at 1201 hours precisely, as the guards were eating their lunch.

The first bombs were dropped on the outer walls on the east and north sides of the prison by the four 487 Squadron FB.VIs led by Wg Cdr 'Black' Smith. Their bombs shot straight through or over the eastern wall and careered across the courtyard before crashing into the western wall on the far side. One of the bombs struck the main prison building. The two Mosquitoes attacking the northern wall from the north aimed for the right-hand end and hit the junction of the northern and western wall. The five FB.VIs of 464 Squadron and Pickard's Mosquito closely followed them. Their target was the main building and the guards' quarters at the east and west ends of the prison. Wg Cdr 'Bob' Iredale pin-pointed the guards' quarters, let go his bombs so that they would skid right into the annex, with the sloping roof of the prison inches from the belly of his Mosquito, as he climbed over it. Eight Typhoons of 174 Squadron provided escort over the target, while six Typhoons of 245 Squadron covered Wg Cdr 'Daddy' Dale's four remaining 21 Squadron Mosquitoes, which orbited ten miles to the north, ready if needed. The first bombs blew in almost all of the doors, and the wall was breached. At the insistence of his cameraman, Flt Lt Tony Wickham made three slow passes over the ruined jail, which was now disgorging smoke and flame and fleeing men, and Plt Off Leigh Howard shot cine film of the flight of the prisoners. Wickham turned away in a tight left-hand circuit and called to Howard: 'Can we go now?'

'Let's have just one more.'

'Here we go, then.'

This time they discovered how to distinguish the prisoners from the guards. As they flew over the prison, the guards flung themselves flat on their faces. The prisoners kept on running.[7]

Among them was André Leroy, who seized the chance to escape. After recovering from his injuries he returned to the Resistance.

On the second floor, Henri Moisan was lying on his bunk reading and awaiting the midday distribution of soup. He jumped up at the sound of aircraft engines, and through the high cell window saw a khaki-camouflaged Mosquito flash by at rooftop level. In the same instant the first explosion blew in all the windows throughout the prison. Moisan and the other occupants of his cell shrank back towards the door. Several more violent explosions followed, and Moisan sensed that he was falling, and with him a great quantity of masonry and prison fittings. His fall ended on the floor below, where he lay badly injured but still conscious, completely buried by debris and overwhelmed with shock. He was rescued by another prisoner, Louis Sellier, who abandoned his own chance of escape to save Moisan.[8]

On the first floor, Jean Beaurin of the FTPF, together with the three other men in his cell, was thrown to the floor again and again by successive explosions. The four men kicked open the half-unhinged cell door and emerged onto the landing to survey a scene of frightful devastation. Beaurin's brother had been killed and his mother wounded, but he could not find them. He was joined by his comrade Maurice Holleville, and together they made a dash for the breached wall. Monsieur Gruel of the Amiens group, like many others, had been killed in his cell – the cell occupied until recently by Dr Mans. Dr Mans, on the ground floor, was one of the first to get clear of the prison building. Stunned by the explosions, he found that his desire to escape had gone. All that remained was the vague knowledge that it was his duty to do so if he could. He staggered through the wrecked hall and out into the courtyard. Almost at once he heard someone calling his name.

'Dr Mans!'

It was Captain Tempez, calling to him from his first-floor cell. He went back into the building, found a key in the smashed *Gestapo* offices and clambered up the twisted iron staircase. He opened the door of Tempez's cell. Other prisoners whose cell doors had not been blown open were clamouring to be released, and someone grabbed the key from his hand and rushed on down the corridor.

Behind the shouts of those still imprisoned lay the muted groans of the wounded, the maimed and the dying. Still following his instinct, Dr

Mans closed his mind to these heart-rending cries. He slid down the iron supports of the mangled staircase and emerged into the courtyard.

On the ground in front of him lay a woman, her legs severed at the thigh. Her husband was on the ground beside her, cushioning her head. Dr Mans was compelled to stop in front of them.

It was his duty to escape. It was his duty to the Resistance; it was his duty to France. It wasn't just a question of saving his own life. The whole Resistance organization would collapse if the leaders failed to escape. Only by regaining their freedom and consulting together could they ever hope to uncover the informer and fight back. But wasn't there another duty, a duty to one's fellow men? Was it a mistake to think that this was a wider duty, the duty to humanity, without which all resistance to evil was meaningless?

He knelt down beside the woman. There was little he could do for her. He heard Tempez calling behind him.

'What are you going to do, Dr Mans?'

'I'm staying. I shall do what I can for the injured.'

'Then I shall stay with you.'

Several other Frenchmen under sentence of death joined Mans and Tempez in the rescue work. Helpers from outside pleaded with them to go, but they refused. The work of mercy was not halted by racial barriers. Many of the guards had been wounded and they too were treated by Dr Mans and his party.[9]

Ponchardier and his followers, and the people of the village, stayed within the prison walls until 12.15, by which time about 400 had escaped. Then they dispersed as quickly and quietly as possible. The Germans did not arrive in strength for some time.[10]

Pickard was the last over the prison, and after dropping his bombs he circled the area at 500 ft to assess the results. Satisfied that the Mosquitoes had done their work, the success signal *RED-RED-RED* was radioed to 'Daddy' Dale so that they could return home. Almost immediately, Fw 190s of II./JG26 attacked the Mosquitoes and took on the Typhoons. *Feldwebel* Wilhelm Mayer[11] singled out F-Freddie and sent it crashing in flames near Albert, and Pickard and Broadley were killed. *Leutnant* Waldemar 'Waldi' Radener of 7./JG26 shot down a Typhoon flown by Flg Off J.E. Renaud north of Amiens, and the pilot was taken prisoner. Sqn Ldr Ian McRitchie and Flt Lt R.W. 'Sammy' Sampson's Mosquito in 464 Squadron RAAF was downed by flak. The Australian second flight leader was wounded in twenty-six places and he crash-landed at over 200 mph near Poix. McRitchie survived and was taken prisoner, but Sampson was dead. He was one of two brothers, both over normal aircrew age, who had sold their farm in New Zealand at the outbreak of war to join the RAF. Both were killed in action.[12] Hanafin, meanwhile, was limping home on one engine. He was again hit by flak, which paralysed one side of his body. He was met and escorted home by 'Black'

Smith, and he made a perfect landing at a forward airfield in England. Foul weather over the Channel claimed another Typhoon, flown by Flt Sgt H.S. Brown.

In March 1944 Dominique Ponchardier sent the following message to London:

> I thank you in the name of our comrades for the bombardment of the prison, we were not able to save all. Thanks to the admirable precision of the attack the first bomb blew in nearly all the doors and 150 prisoners escaped with the help of the civilian population. Of these, twelve were to have been shot on February 19. In addition, thirty-seven prisoners were killed, some of them by German machine guns, and fifty Germans were also killed.[13]

More low-level pin-point daylight raids, for which 140 and 138 Wings[14] would become legendary, took place in 1944. On Tuesday 11 April, six Mosquitoes of 613 Squadron led by the CO, Wg Cdr R.N. 'Bob' Bateson DFC, successfully bombed the *Gestapo* headquarters in The Hague. All six Mosquitoes got back safely, without a shot being fired at them. Five weeks later a report reached the RAF that the operation had been highly satisfactory. For his leadership of this operation, Bateson was awarded the DSO and received the Dutch Flying Cross from Prince Bernhard of the Netherlands. An Air Ministry bulletin later described the raid as 'probably the most brilliant feat of low-level precision bombing of the war'. On 14 July, Bastille Day, eighteen Mosquito crews of 21, 464 and 487 Squadrons, led by Gp Capt Peter Wykeham-Barnes DSO DFC* and Flg Off Chaplin, destroyed a German barracks at Bonneuil Matours, near Poitiers.[15] On 31 October, twenty-five FB.VIs of 21, 464 and 487 Squadrons, each carrying eleven-second delayed-action bombs made another daring low-level raid, this time on Aarhus University, the HQ for the *Gestapo* in the whole of Jutland in Denmark.[16] In 1945 140 Wing flew two more pin-point bombing operations, to Denmark. They bombed the *Gestapo* HQ in the *Shellhaus* building in Copenhagen on 20 March, and carried out an equally audacious daylight strike on a school building on the outskirts of Odense, which was being used by the *Gestapo* as an HQ, on 17 April. Both raids were successful.[17]

There were other tasks for 2nd TAF Mosquito fighter-bombers in the build-up to D-Day, as R.W. Smith, an FB.VI pilot in 613 'City of Manchester' Squadron, recalls:

> Sometime before D-Day, the squadron was asked to provide two aircraft to fly on a mission which, except for the aircrew concerned, was kept completely secret. One aircraft had a pilot and navigator and the other a pilot and a visiting passenger in the shape of an Australian wing commander. Subsequently, after D-Day, we learned

that the passenger was General Browning, in fact, and that the mission had been to fly over the airborne and parachute dropping-grounds in Normandy. On the night of the D-Day landings and for many nights afterwards, the squadron's chief role was patrolling over and behind enemy lines, attacking troop movements and anything in the way of enemy activity on the ground. Our mode of entry and exit was via the sea corridor between Alderney and the Cherbourg Peninsula, entering France at Granville and then making our way to the 'Tennis Court', which was our patrol area. It did not always work out according to plan. On our first patrol, which was in the Caen and Vire area, we found ourselves in solid cloud between 2,000 and 3,000 ft as soon as we crossed the coast. We could not get below the cloud because in places the ground rises to almost 2,000 ft. The GEE was being jammed so badly that the screen was covered with 'grass', and John [Flg Off Jack Hepworth] was unable to verify our position. After stooging around our patrol area for the required time and seeing nothing, it was time to return home. We decided to fly so many minutes due west to bring us over the sea, then fly north for home. This we did, and after turning north we broke cloud into a lovely clear night, immediately to be caught in a cone of searchlights when flying at a height of 4,000 ft. At the same time all hell seemed to be let loose, with tracer coming up from all sides. Instead of being over sea, we were approaching Cherbourg. We just put the nose down and went weaving and skidding in a dive, passing over the breakwater of Cherbourg at about 400 ft. We landed at Lasham unscathed.

During the period 5 June to 11 July, John and I completed seventeen operational sorties – all at night. In June these sorties were all in the Normandy area, attacking roads, bridges, marshalling yards and any lights or movements seen. Sometimes we would rendezvous with Mitchells dropping flares for us to operate under in certain conditions. My chief recollections are of the fires, which seemed to be burning night after night at Caen and Vire. Lasham airfield is several hundred feet above sea level and, unless the cloud base was on the deck, we usually tried to return to base rather than to divert to Hartford Bridge. If we were diverted, we got less sleep and still had to get back to Lasham next morning. So, with low cloud over England, we tried to fly back under it, and in so doing sometimes encountered the Navy. The Navy was quick on the draw and didn't seem to recognize the colours of the day. We would quickly disappear into cloud and settle for Hartford Bridge. From 6 July onwards we went further afield, to places south of Paris, Châteauroux, Orléans, Nantes, La Rochelle, Le Mans, Tours, Rouen, Evreux and Dreux, still on the hunt for bridges, railways, trains and transport.

No. 138 Wing received incoming reports on 25/26 August of a concentration of troops and vehicles in the Rouen area and of attempts to retreat across the Seine. This now seemed to be a critical area and could well be a pivot to the successful advance of Allied troops into Belgium and Germany. An all-out attack in this zone was set for the night of the 26/27th. One of the crews that took part was Flt Lt Eric 'Tommy' Atkins DFC* KW* (*Krzyz Walecznych*, the Polish Cross of Valour) and his navigator, Flt Lt Jurek Majer, in 305 Polish Squadron at Lasham. They were at this time veterans of twenty-five Night Intruder operations. The night before, they had been searching the railways between Belgium and Germany for trains carrying V-1s or V-2s, and had attacked one in the darkness but could not determine the extent of the damage. As they were searching the scene, a German aircraft suddenly attacked them. Luckily, their attacker missed and Atkins was able to do a tight turn and give a burst of gunfire in return, before returning to Lasham 'in a state of some excitement'. Atkins recalls:

> Being small and light, the Mosquito could fall foul of bad weather conditions. On the other hand, in emergency conditions when caught in flak, searchlights or being attacked by enemy aircraft, it could be flung around the sky in almost impossible manoeuvres that a pilot might think twice about in daylight. The Mosquito responded to the controls like a thoroughbred racehorse, with speed, precision and a sixth sense of judgement linked to that of the pilot. I have also known the Mosquito to turn in such a tight circle at night to get away from searchlights and flak beamed onto it that it virtually 'disappeared up its own orifice'. A Mosquito could fly well on one engine, providing you had the speed and height to gain a level flight over a long distance. Many a Mosquito pilot flew from Germany on one engine, but the landing could be tricky and you never knew whether the other engine would overheat and pack up! A Mosquito would also do a safe belly landing, providing you remembered to come in without any undercarriage and flaps – then it would probably turn over. I landed at night on a grass 'drome at Epinoy, France, with no undercarriage, no flaps and a bomb aboard! The only annoying thing was that the ambulance and MC took over half an hour to reach us. They were waiting to see whether the bomb went off! The aircraft had only minor damage and was soon returned to service again. Other Mosquitoes landed with half a wing missing. Despite its wooden construction, the Mosquito had strength and endurance and was easier to repair. You simply spliced another wing on! The speed of the Mosquito also meant that the operational time was less (unless you were Ranging).

We were told on returning to Lasham and our tent that we would be needed again that night, 26/27 August, for the all-out attack at

Rouen. We tried to get some sleep during the day, but we were pretty tense still after the NFT of our aircraft, and as we entered the briefing tent in the late afternoon. The briefing was fairly simple – we had to tour the Rouen–Gisors–Dieppe area and bomb and strafe anything that moved, and in particular, the mass of vehicles trying to retreat across the Seine. A second operation that night was also expected of us! It was a good night for flying, not much cloud, and with our 'cat's eyes' we could pick out shapes on the ground. We flew quite low, at 800 ft in the darkness, and picked out roads and railways. We had flares and cannon and we had been told that there might also be illumination from pathfinders, but not to depend on it as the battle looked like being prolonged. My worry was that with so many Mosquitoes in the same area we had the further concern of avoiding each other! We soon picked out the convoy, and some of the vehicles were already on fire. We bombed by the light of our flares and then turned around to gun the area again – the smoke rising up seemed to fill the cockpit and warned us that we were too low in the darkness. Our deed done, we turned for home. At that moment, a dark shape dived in front of us, missing us by inches. 'Another damned Mosquito!' said Jurek.

When we got back to Lasham the ground crew was standing ready to reload tanks, guns, etc., proud to be taking their part in the operation. We were quickly debriefed, and then into our Mosquito and away again. This time we attacked a road junction clogged full of enemy transport, just outside Rouen. They were a 'sitting target', although the light flak coming up at us did hinder a straight bombing run, and we had to come round again. We scored some serious hits, and once again our ammunition and bombs were expended and we started for Lasham and our cold, dank tents.

On the ground Jurek looked at me and, grinning, said, 'What about doing what you English call a "hat trick"?' I said it was OK by me if we could get turned around in time. The ground crew were magnificent, and it was almost like a professional 'pit stop'. This time there were many aircraft in the area. We decided to bomb a goods train, which we found in the Rouen–Rheims–Givet area. We obtained a 'near-miss', but damage had been done and on our way back we expended all our remaining ammunition on the conflagration around Rouen and the Seine. It was, indeed, the 'Rout of Rouen'. We congratulated the ground crew and ourselves, and after debriefing, flung ourselves on our bunk beds in the tent and slept and slept! Our next operation was to be on the railways at night around Saarbourg and Strasbourg on 30 August, which indicated how successful our Army advance had become and our far from unsuccessful efforts to support them!

The 2nd TAF received the highest possible commendation for these attacks, and this support continued. At 5 a.m. on 31 August 1944, pilot Sqn Ldr Stanislaw Grodzicki and Flt Lt Adam Szajdzicki, navigator, in 305 (Polish) Squadron, had just landed back at Lasham after a four-hour patrol over north-east France when they were one of six Mosquito crews put on the battle order for the day's operation.

I had got up late from bed,' remembers Adam, 'and was in rather a hurry to get to the mess for lunch. I collected my bicycle from behind the tent.

'Adam,' I heard the voice of Sqn Ldr Grodzicki, my pilot, say, 'where are you going?'

'To lunch', I said.

'Forget it. Take your things and come quickly for the briefing. We are flying with five Mosquitoes. Orlinski is leading.' Wg Cdr B. Orlinski was our CO at the time.

'Hard luck,' I said, 'there goes my lunch.'

But the news excited me because it could be an interesting operation. I went back and collected my bag, which was lying under my bed where I had left it earlier in the morning. The ops tent was not very far away, and arriving there I found that some of our crews were already there and others were arriving. Everybody was asking the same question: 'Where? What?'

The map on the wall was marked with a red thread for our track. The route out was over Portland Bill, Guernsey, Arromanches, then south of Auxerre, north of Langre, ending just north of Epinol. A US flag was pinned in Auxerre, indicating that there were American forces. The flight plan was already written on the board for us to copy. To the briefing came the group captain, our CO and two assistant officers. One of them I knew from previous briefings. The other, a 'new face', held a big roll of papers under his arm.

Wing Commander Orlinski called the briefing to order and began: 'Gentlemen, our destination is Nomexy, where there are reservoirs estimated to hold more than three million gallons of German petrol, which must be destroyed. We will fly six aircraft, and not five as stated in the order.

He named the sixth pilot, Flight Lieutenant Smith. Smith had only recently joined our squadron and was known among us as Matilda because he used to sing or whistle the song, which had a Central American rhythm — 'Matilda, Matilda, took your money and went to Venezuela'. He was the only Bahamian crew member among us. He appeared, beaming with pleasure. It was his second or third operation.

Orlinski said that we were flying in pairs stacked to the rear, but before the last checkpoint we would separate and increase the distance between the aircraft to four miles apart because we would be attacking our target from low level, one by one, and our bombs were fitted with eleven-second delay fuses. He added, 'I don't want any of you getting blown up by our own bombs. The navigation to the target will be done by my navigator and I will tell you about the start later.'

Now the 'new face' stepped forward. 'Well, gentlemen, here is your target.'

With those words he opened the papers. These were the photographs of our destination. He passed them around, saying, 'Please have a good look at them and memorize them well to make sure that you will find your target.' After a while he continued: 'The photos were taken on the same track as you will be heading for the target. There is also a photo of the last checkpoint. That is the photo with four large buildings beside the loop in the river bend. Now from that checkpoint, which we will call zero point, you will have to take a course of 022 for four minutes, then – Bang! – you will be over your target. I am afraid that the target will not be too visible from the zero point.' He was finished.

The zero point was very good indeed, and could not be mistaken. I tried to memorize the details that were not shown on the map. The three big petrol reservoirs stood on the eastern side of a railway line running north from Epinol to Nancy on an azimuth of about 35–170 degrees. Beyond was the river lined with high trees. I was impressed with the preparations that had been made for this raid. Drawing our track through the target, I thought that it had been well chosen. On that approach we probably would not see the light between the tanks, and it would present a more certain target for our bombs. The navigation officer gave us the exact run-in time from the zero point, and Orlinski assigned each crew a position in the formation. We were No. 2.

He continued, 'At 1500 hours proceed to your aircraft, start engines on my signal. We will start rolling right away to avoid overheating the engines, as it is very hot today. The start will be in pairs, with the second pair accelerating when the first is at the end of the runway. After take-off, turn left. Remember to empty the drop tanks as soon as possible. In the bomb-bay are two bombs with eleven-second delay fuses. Remember you will be dropping them from low level, so don't get too close behind one another. Over the UK and the Channel we will fly at 2,000 ft, and later over France we will come down to 200 ft. At this time we have had no reports of German fighter activity along our route, but you never know – so watch it! Keep total radio silence. Only break it in an emergency. Any questions?' 'Oh yes,' he added, 'there will be the usual man with the Aldis lamp at your dispersal point. Signal him when you are ready and obey his signals.' For the benefit of the CO and Matilda, the briefing had been conducted in English.

'We are ready, sir', said Orlinski, saluting the CO.

The CO returned the salute and said to us, 'Good luck, boys. Let's go to our aircraft.'

I checked the contents of my navigation bag, collected the flares of the day and put one of them into the top of my left boot. I stuffed my pistol into the top of the right boot. Then, from the box, I collected a 'chute and the harness with the dinghy attached to it and the bag. This made a very heavy load, and it was not easy to carry it the hundred or so yards across the clearing, where our aircraft was standing. Just before leaving the briefing tent, I snatched up the photo of the target and pushed it inside my battledress blouse.

At Z-Zebra the ground crew were waiting and reported that the aircraft was OK. Stan, my pilot, went to check the aircraft logbook, and I dropped my gear on the ground and went to check the suspension of the bombs. I gave them a friendly tap and wished them a good journey and a good landing.

Stan and Adam went through their take-off checks and finally, at 1535, taxied out to the runway. Adam looked back at the 'wonderful line of Mosquitoes', and one by one they took off.

It was quieter in the cockpit now as the aircraft climbed in a wide left turn. There was only the noise of the wind outside and the hiss of the fresh air in the ventilators. After one circuit, No. 1 waggled his wings and we set course for Winchester, levelling off at Angels Two [2,000 ft]. Then we changed course south for Portland Bill and Portsmouth, full of all sorts of shipping, slipped by on the port side. Craft of all sorts were heading to and from Normandy, some of them towing barrage balloons.

We followed No. 1 to Arromanches. I spotted three Dakotas heading north-west, probably flying home the wounded. I watched the sky for bandits and noted the course and height changes in my log. Dropping to 300 ft and increasing speed, we passed Auxerre on the port beam, and the ground whistled by. We were keeping well clear of the built-up areas because the Germans could still be there, even though the briefing map showed that the Americans had captured the area. We also knew that our own ack-ack chaps were a bit 'trigger-happy'.

I pushed the safety switch to arm the bombs, logged the time and shouted to Stan to tell him. The loop in the River Maine came in sight, and Chaumont was visible on the port beam. Up to now everything was going fine and quietly – we were two minutes early.

The ground sped by beneath us as I searched the sky for bandits – thank God none were visible. I pulled out the photograph of the target and tried to sort out the details in my mind. This was my last chance to do it. We just had to find the bloody target! I kept repeating this over and over again. I checked my watch again – in three minutes we should be at the zero point. Ahead appeared the four buildings, then the bend in the river, just as the photo showed.

'We are coming to point zero, dead ahead. Can you see it?' I said to Stan.

'OK', he said, steering the aircraft slightly to the right and increasing the distance from No. 1 to make sure that we were making 022 degrees over the zero point.

'OK', said Stan again. 'On course.'

I opened the bomb-doors as we flew over the zero point, and noted the time. But we could not see the target ahead. Instead there was a hill. Orlinski changed course to about 060 degrees and headed towards Epinal on our starboard. Stan spotted him and shouted, 'Where is No. 1 going? Are you sure we are on the right track?'

'Check that you are on 022 degrees', I replied. I gave a quick glance at the photo and saw that there were vineyards on the slope of the hill between the zero point and the target. I saw vineyards on the hill in front of us. I suddenly realized that French farmers, logically, had probably planted the vineyard on the south slopes of the hill facing the sun.

'Another one and a half minutes to go', I said. 'The target must be over the hill.'

'Are you sure?' asked Stan.

'That's the course they told us to steer. One and a half minutes to go. There is some flak on the far right.'

I had a feeling that soon our Mosquito would start chopping up the vines, we were flying so low. We were going parallel to the slope of the hill.

'Forty-five seconds to go', I called.

Stan pulled up the Mossie over the top of the hill. 'Oh Santa Madonna! What a sight!'

Straight ahead and below were the reservoirs, standing at an angle to our course, just like the photo. Stan pushed the stick sharply forward and I shot out of my seat, my head hitting the canopy.

'Bombs gone!' called Stan, putting the starboard wing down and pulling the aircraft up. I spotted the bombs. The right one was slightly ahead of the others and seemed to be going for a break between the tanks. Damn! The second one was heading directly into the middle tank. I held my breath. Is it going to be a direct hit? Oh no! God! It's gone over the tank. Damn! I realized that when we were over the hill and climbing that we had not enough time and distance to put the aircraft into a steeper dive; therefore the bombs had been released too high. One had exploded in the river, one in a field behind it. I was absolutely disgusted. All that way for nothing!

'They missed the tanks', I told Stan.

'Look out for our Mosquitoes and their whereabouts', requested Stan, pulling the aircraft up into a very tight left turn. The G-force was pushing me into my seat. I felt a pain in my bottom; the dinghy was not very comfortable as a seat cushion. I wanted to stand up to have a better look around. I was worried about our starboard side because aircraft could be coming from that quarter. Looking over the port wing I saw the river approaching and through the canopy I saw the burning tanks. We passed over the river, then over the railway and at that moment a Mosquito passed right under us. Bombs were bursting in the railway yard as we climbed, always in that sharp turn. We flew over the town's houses, then some trees and a hill, while another Mosquito was pulling away from the yard.

The tanks were coming up at 10 o'clock. The G-forces became less tormenting. Stan put the Mossie into a dive and the turn became gentler but steeper. The tanks were at 12 o'clock when Stan opened fire with the cannon. Suddenly the aircraft started to shake and the airspeed dropped by 40 mph. Tracers hit the ground in front of the tanks on the far left and slowly rose until they pierced the tanks. A red tongue of fire burst from the lower part of the tank, and as the aircraft slid further to the right the tracer hit the central tank. This also burst into flames, as did the third tank, which blew up, sending a great cloud of black smoke into the air. We were heading straight for it.

Oh God! That smoke will cover us.

The Mosquito stopped shaking, and the next instant we ran into the dark cloud. The cockpit became dark and smelly for a few seconds before we came out into the clean fresh air beyond. The smell persisted as we made a wide left circle, while happily admiring the fire and looking to see if there was anything else that we could destroy. At that moment a Mosquito passed over the yard.

'Hey, Blue chaps,' came a voice on the radio, 'there is smoke towards the north.'

Before we had finished the circle I spotted another Mosquito passing along the yard. In turn we came in line with the rail line. Stan pushed the stick forward and started diving toward the freight cars standing on the rails, opening fire on them. I noted some flashes on the cars, but this time we did not manage to start new fires. Stan was preparing himself for the third run when on the radio came Orlinski's voice.

'Blue, Blue, return to formation over point zero.'

Stan immediately set course south. Suddenly, on the radio came the song, 'Matilda, Matilda, took your petrol and went to Venezuela. Ha ha!'

I counted six Mosquitoes making formation as we set course for home, along the same route as we had taken on the way in. The return flight went quietly and we landed at base at 1955.

At the debriefing Flight Lieutenant Leimiesozonek, Orlinski's navigator, explained that they had turned eastward after the zero point because he could not see the target ahead. He had turned towards what he thought was a camouflaged target. We found out that the second pair had followed No. 1, thinking that we were wrong. The third pair did not follow us over the hill because they couldn't see the target, so they went around the hill to look for it; these were the Mosquitoes I spotted flying over the rail lines. For his efforts Stan was awarded the *Virtuti Militari* decoration, and I was awarded the *Krzyz Walecznych* (Cross of Valour).[18]

On 17 September Operation Market Garden took place. Thirty-two FB.VIs of 107 and 613 Squadrons in 138 Wing were detailed to attack a German barracks at Arnhem, while 21 Squadron at Thorney Island bombed three school buildings in the centre of Nijmegen, which were being used by the German garrison. Both raids were to eliminate the opposition before the airborne forces went in later that day. Flg Off Nigel L. Gilson, a navigator in 107 Squadron, had been spending a day's leave in Winchester and was all set for an enjoyable evening to round it off at a dance-hall in Basingstoke. However, a friend gave him the news that he had to return to Lasham immediately, as the squadron was confined to barracks overnight:

> We were met by the usual expectant rumours, but could still learn nothing definite except that we were to be up for briefing at 0530. Ours was a quiet mess that night, only admin officers were drinking more than lemonade, and all aircrews were in bed by about 10 – most unusual for us! Rising before midday was a bit of a strain, but 0530 on Sunday found us all milling around the briefing room with an exceptional complement of 'braid and scrambled egg' among us. The tense gaiety and laconic humour of briefing are something one remembers but can't adequately describe. I can recall only two things: the CO's description of the purpose of the Arnhem landing (for that was the cause of the trouble) – 'If this one comes off the war will be over in 14 days'; and his description of the anticipated reception of the paratroops – 'They expect to slide down stocks of 40 millimetre.' A minor flap broke out while navigators struggled with maps, rulers, protractors and computers, working out tracks, courses, winds and other essentials to the successful combat of

hostile gremlins, until at last there was a welcome break for a hasty bacon and egg breakfast. It was a hectic and hilarious meal, then we were back for a final route check and squadron briefing on formation and tactics.

Time for take-off was altered twice, but at last we went to our aircraft, where tired ground crews, who'd been working half the night, were just finishing bombing and arming up. Flg Off Phil Slayden, my pilot, and I sat on the grass waiting for the signal to get into our aircraft. In the peace of a brilliant Sunday morning war seemed very far away. Only Dougie, who'd come to the squadron the day before, remarked on the incongruity of it all; the strains of *Abide With Me* from a nearby hangar service sounded too ominous to his unaccustomed ear to pass unnoticed! The ground crew gave us the usual strict orders to do a good job with their aeroplane and wished us a brief but sincere 'Good luck', and we taxied out. We took off into a clear sky already filling with squadrons of ungainly gliders and tugs, took up formation and set course. Soon the English draught-board gave place to a sea of rippled blue and finally to the deeply cut green flats of Holland.

Arnhem identified itself for us – the natives, or their uninvited guests, were distinctly hostile – but we rejoiced in our speed and ploughed in. At first one could watch things quite objectively; one gun team was firing explosive shells, with tantalizing persistency, right on our track, and I wondered absent-mindedly by how much they would miss us. Then we dived to attack. I bent to switch on the camera, began to rise, then instinctively ducked again, only to be conscious of an explosion and a shower of Perspex splinters. I jerked up, looking anxiously at Phil, and heaved a sigh of relief when I saw that he was OK and that we were climbing again. At least, I think we were climbing – neither of us was quite sure what happened in those thirty seconds. A glance showed that the gun team had been robbed of their prey by the dive, and the shell had burst above us, merely shattering our cockpit cover.

Suddenly Phil called, 'Hey, the bomb-doors are shut, we couldn't have dropped the bombs!'

I jammed them open and he pressed the tit to drop the bombs; we looked behind for the flash, but there was none, and then we remembered that we'd opened the doors before the dive and must have closed them instinctively during the attack. But the look behind had shown us one thing – an aircraft with our markings suddenly catching fire in the starboard petrol tank. The flames spread rapidly to port, covering the cockpit; the aircraft lost height and finally hit a house and overturned into the river. We shall not forget that quickly. Woody and Mac were in that mass of flame.

It was only a matter of minutes before we were over the Zuider Zee again, flying below formations of gliders and tugs. We felt sorry for them – they hadn't our speed, they had to fly straight though the flak, and their occupants had to go down on 'chutes or without engines or guns – no future in that.

The CO called up to check formation. As we called 'Here' to our own callsign, we waited anxiously to hear who was missing. Two failed to reply – two out of fourteen. Woody and Mac, Ted and Griff had bought it – tough luck; we should miss them.

On 18 September the Germans counter-attacked and forestalled an American attempt to capture the bridge at Nijmegen. Market-Garden has been described in an official report as 'by far the biggest and most ambitious airborne operation ever carried out by any nation or nations'.[19]

Altogether, nine Mosquito bomber squadrons now equipped 2nd TAF. In September 1944, following the outbreak from the Normandy beachhead, plans were in progress to move them to airfields in France. By November 107, 305 (Polish) and 613 Squadrons of 138 Wing finally arrived in France, to be based at Epinoy near Cambrai, France. By this stage of the war the *Panzers* and other German troops were being given no respite in the daylight raids by Mitchells and Bostons and the nightly visits by Mosquitoes. Flt Lt Eric Atkins DFC* KW*, on 305 (Polish) Squadron, recalls:

> Prisoners captured complained, 'We are attacked all day and then the Mosquitoes harass and bomb us at night. We cannot *"ein Schläfchen machen"* (take a nap) or *"eine Scheisse machen"* (have a crap) – we are caught with our pants down!' Nowhere was this more apparent than when we attacked the *Panzer* billets on the night of 6/7 December 1944 in the village of Wassenberg, just south of München-Gladbach, on the edge of the Ruhr itself. The attack on the billets would be my seventy-eighth operation, the twenty-sixth in my third tour. My navigator was Flt Lt Jurek Majer, a Pole who spoke little English. There was talk that I would be stood down after this operation, and this made the raid even more significant. As all aircrew know, it can be a superstitious moment when you wonder whether you will 'get the chop' on the last one.
>
> However, there was no time to worry about the consequences to me of the operation – there was much to do! The Met officer warned us that although the weather was set fair for the night, snow was on the way. (December's weather was the worst of an already bad three months. On some nights we operated when visibility at the base was less than 800 yards.) Our route to the target took us near Brussels. It was a very dark night, but the radar kept us on the track. There seemed to be a lot of activity about. I was probably more finely

tuned than normal on this trip, and thought I saw enemy aircraft on our beam, but Jurek just grunted and got on with his navigation. There was not normally a lot of conversation in our Mosquito – we both had our jobs to do and we reserved speech for when action was needed – no idle chatter!

My thoughts drifted to three operations ago, 29 November, when we had attacked Hamm, in the east Ruhr area. The weather had been appalling and the flak over the target was heavy. After bombing, something had gone wrong with our aircraft, the electrics and hydraulics were amiss and I had to 'belly-flop' at night at our new base at Epinoy near Cambrai, France, a grass aerodrome on a slight hill. Without flaps we floated almost off the top of the hill before I forced it down. I hoped nothing like that would happen to us tonight!

Jurek said that we were approaching the German border, and now we saw much more activity – searchlights and tracer fire. We were flying at about 3,000 ft.

'Look out for flares and a river', said Jurek. We had HE and incendiary loads, flares, cannon and machine-guns. We were not the only ones attacking this target, and it should have been well lit up. However, we were among the first in. I came down much lower, soon picked up the Roer river and then saw the target. There were no flares at the time, but there was a glow, and Jurek confirmed that it was Wassenberg. We could see the fires starting as we did our first run. In the light of the flares we dropped we came round again and bombed and strafed the target. All hell seemed to be let loose below, and heavy flak was coming up just south of us. There was some rain about and I remember thinking that it might put the fires out!

We did another run strafing with cannon fire. 'That's enough,' said Jurek, 'save some for the others!'

A black shape zoomed up and passed our nose. 'What the hell's that?' I cried, then realized that it was probably another Mosquito going in to attack.

We had overstayed our welcome. Flying straight and level in the darkness, heading for base, we checked our instruments, oil pressure and engine temperatures. I had flung the Mossie around rather a lot and sometimes engines overheat, then you have to shut one down. However, everything seemed all right and Jurek grunted the course back to base. It had been a very successful operation. The *Panzers* had been caught 'with their pants down'!

After we had landed and been debriefed, the station commander told me that it had been my last operation. They were standing me down on my seventy-eighth – 'enough was enough!' I was very disappointed, however, to lose Jurek – he had to carry on with another pilot to finish his second tour.

On 21 November, 136 Wing was created within 2nd TAF by the arrival, from Fighter Command, of 418 and 605 Squadrons, which transferred to Hartford Bridge. That month fourteen enemy aircraft fell to the guns of the 2nd TAF Mosquito night predators. The signs in December 1944 were that the weather and other factors would limit Mosquito nightfighter activity over the *Reich*.[20] Only three Ju 88s and two Bf 110s were destroyed between 4 and 18/19 December. On the last named, Flt Lt Charles E. Edinger RCAF and Flg Off C.C. Vaessen of 410 Squadron in NF.XXX MV527 shot down a Ju 88 south of Bonninghardt for his fifth victory. His sixth, a Stuka, would follow on Christmas Eve. Wg Cdr James D. Somerville DFC, now in command of 409 Squadron, scored his sixth confirmed victory, flying NF.XIII MM456 with Flg Off G.D. Robinson DFC, when they dispatched a Ju 88 in the Kaiserworth area. Somerville wrote:

> While patrolling at Angels 10 under 15119 Control (Squadron Leader Allen), we were vectored south as the Hun was reported to be active in the American Sector. We were then advised of trade, and after receiving initial vectors of 130 and 280, we were vectored 190. Controller advised us that he was keeping us on a slightly converging course to bring us in behind the target beyond the 'Hot Spot' at the same time, instructing to reduce to Angels 7. We started down, but as the control then advised that the target had started to climb, we levelled out at Angels 9. AI contact was obtained at a range of five miles, and closing rapidly I obtained a visual at 1,600 ft. Closing to 800 ft below and directly beneath, both my navigator and I recognized the target as a Ju 88, flying at approximately 160 mph indicated, which necessitated my lowering my undercarriage to prevent overshooting. At this juncture, the e/a turned west and started to dive. I followed and overtook the e/a with an indicated speed of 270 mph. I closed to 600 ft and pulled up, but did not fire as I momentarily lost visual owing to a dark cloud in the background. I closed to within 300 ft and opened fire. I observed strikes on the fuselage but no flames. I attempted to reopen fire but my guns had jammed, so I continued to follow the aircraft down, which by this time was doing hard evasive – making hard peel-offs to starboard and port, until it finally dived in from 1,500 ft. My navigator and I both saw it hit the ground and explode with a brilliant flash, but it did not appear to burn on the ground.

The *Luftwaffe* was powerless to stop the inexorable advance westwards, but there was one last attempt to try to halt the Allies. Since 20 December 1944 many *Jagdgeschwader* had been transferred to airfields in the west for Operation *Bodenplatte*, when approximately 850 *Luftwaffe* fighters took off at 0745 hours on Sunday morning 1 January 1945 to attack twenty-seven airfields in northern France, Belgium and southern Holland. The four-hour operation succeeded in destroying about a hundred Allied aircraft, but it cost the *Luftwaffe* 300 aircraft, most of which were shot down by Allied anti-aircraft guns deployed primarily against the V-1s.

Sgt John Walsh, a Liverpudlian and a navigator in 487 Squadron, and his pilot, Flying Officer John Patterson, flew their first operation, a three-hour round trip from Thorney Island to Arsbeck, on 21 January 1945. Walsh had trained at Greenwood, Nova Scotia, and training losses had been high, many of the Canadian-built Mosquitoes ending up in the Bay of Fundis. However, the 21-year-old 'Scouser' was 'desperately keen' to fly the 'fast weapon'. Losses climaxed near the end of his training, and he had been one of only four to volunteer for Mosquitoes. Leeds-born 'Pat' Patterson had been an instructor in Canada, where he had met and married a delightful Canadian girl. Both men had teamed up at High Ercall. 'Ginger' Walsh recalls:

> North-west Germany was divided into three, one for each Mossie wing, then into three again, one for each squadron. The 2nd TAF Spitfires and Mustangs, which attacked the German Army on the ground during the day, returned with details of troop concentrations and targets, which we then bombed by night. Our main target was anything that moved, especially trains and transport, but you were bloody lucky to find a moving target at night! Trains were a high priority, but they were blacked out and we were lucky to see them. On the Arsbeck op we flew at about 1,000 ft through low cloud to the target. I navigated all the way using maps 'illuminated' by a tiny pin-prick of light from my torch filled with three layers of paper in the bottom to retain our night vision and prevent us from being seen from the air or the ground. (GEE could not be used too far into Germany before it got interfered with and 'railings' confused the two–three 'spikes'. I had to take the best signal, the best 'cut'.) Moonlight was a bastard. You could count the rivets. Over Germany on moonlit nights I felt that I had no clothes on. Our mates in the squadron had been to Arsbeck earlier and had started fires. We would bomb on the GEE-set co-ordinates. I selected the four bombs, fused them, and Pat pressed the 'tit' on his spectacle control-column.
>
> On the way home Pat saw a train for what was the only time. The first I knew was that the Mosquito was suddenly standing on one wing! We had been told that if we saw a train we were to go straight in – no messing! Pat circled (he was following his instincts) for the best position, then adopted a shallow dive and went in, all four 0.303 and four cannon blazing. By now I was 'climbing out of the roof'. The sky filled with 40 mm flak. I soon learned that German ack-ack gunners were mustard! In the cockpit cordite fumes and dust filled

the air. Pat broke off immediately, and on my advice flew to the west! On reflection it had done us good. It was thought provoking.

It was a terrible night. Ron Batch, a fellow navigator I'd been with at navigational school and had known for eighteen months, who had already flown two ops, failed to return. He and his pilot had 'got the chop'. Forty-eight hours later, Ron's father, a Metropolitan Police inspector, came to see me. He wanted to know what area of Germany Ron had been flying over and any other details; Ron was his only child. I could tell him nothing. It really carved me up.

We got shot up ourselves one night. We got back and landed and the props had barely stopped when our two faithful ground crew opened the door (we never bothered with the ladder). They asked if we'd hit anything. They were always so thrilled, so keen, that we should be successful. They asked, 'Were you fired at?'

I said, 'Yes, I think it was the British Army!'

'Were you hit?'

I said, 'No.'

Then they pointed to a hole beneath the wing! I looked and was thrilled. It was strangely exciting! However, next day they could see that the hole had been caused by oil dripping from the guns – our Mossie was a clapped-out machine and had flown many ops.

During January 1945, 2nd TAF Mosquito night-fighters shot down seventeen enemy aircraft, including, on 23/24 January, two Junkers, which were dispatched by 409 ('Nighthawk') Squadron NF.XIIIs. At this time Ju 88S-3s of *1./KG66* and *Lehrgeschwader 1* were carrying out bombing and mining operations against river traffic in the Scheldt estuary in an attempt to stem the flow of supplies to Antwerp. Plt Off M.G. Kent and Plt Off Simpson in NF.XIII MM466 shot down a Ju 88 of *LG 1* over the mouth of the Scheldt.[21] While there is some doubt about which was Kent and Simpson's victim, there is no question which Ju 188E-l was shot down three miles west of Dienst by the CO, Wg Cdr James D. Somerville DFC and Plt Off A.C. Hardy.[22] The Ju 188E-l[23] flown by *Obergefreiter* Heinz Hauck was on a clandestine mission for KG200's *Kommando Olga*. Hauck took off from Rhein-Main and he successfully dropped two agents near Gilze Rijn in the liberated part of Holland before heavy AA bursts and searchlights gave away their position to the Nighthawk crew, who were returning from patrol at 8,000 ft. Somerville and Hardy were directed by 'Rejoice', a GCI station, towards the bogey, now six miles distant at 4,000 ft. Somerville reduced height and Hardy was further assisted by 'Bricktile' and then 'Laundry' GCI stations, until they came upon the Ju 188E-1, which was now flying at 3,000 ft. Hardy had difficulty keeping their quarry out of the ground clutter on his AI Mk VIII scope at their height of 2,500 ft until finally he got a contact at two miles. Somerville closed to 1,500 ft for a positive identification. Satisfied, he closed still further and opened fire with his cannon at 200 ft. His first burst set fire to Hauck's port engine and the 20 mm shells caused a brilliant explosion that forced the Mosquito pilot, momentarily blinded, to break away. Somerville came in again for a second burst as Hauck desperately dived and stall-turned in a vain attempt to extinguish the flames. Somerville's second burst missed, but his third ripped the Ju 188's port wingtip off and the enemy aircraft dived steeply into the ground. It was Somerville's seventh and final victory of the war.[24]

In December 1944, 464 RAAF and 487 RNZAF Squadrons had sent advance detachments to Amiens and Rosières-en-Santerre, France. On 6 February 1945, 21 Squadron, also of 140 Wing, left southern England and joined them. Their arrival coincided with the first anniversary of the Amiens raid by 140 Wing Mosquitoes on 18 February 1944, when 'the walls of Jericho' had come tumbling down. Pickard's widow was flown out especially from England to visit her husband's grave and for the mass in Amiens Cathedral. 'Ginger' Walsh was among the personnel who attended, and afterwards he visited the wall, now patched, through which the French Resistance had escaped:

> The bulk of our squadron was billeted in Amiens. At first I slept at Meharicourt, near the bomb dump in what had been the *Luftwaffe* hospital site at the airfield. *Wehrmacht* and *Luftwaffe* personnel too badly wounded to be evacuated were still there. Later the local village butcher adopted a friend, Bob Belcher, and me, and we were billeted at his elderly mother's small château. Near our base was a huge First World War cemetery filled with thousands of white crosses. We buried Flg Off Joe Coe and his fellow New Zealander squadron leader pilot there after they crashed on take-off one day and their bombs and fuel load exploded. Joe had already lost his fingers and been badly burned in a Wellington crash earlier in the war. At their funeral a group of French schoolchildren sang 'God Save the King'.

One of the crews in 305 Squadron at Epinoy at this time was pilot Flt Lt Reg Everson, an ex-railway policeman, and his navigator, Flt Lt Tony Rudd, a university graduate. They had crewed up at 2 Group GSU at Swanton Morley in September 1944. Everson recalls:

> At Epinoy our enthusiasm was somewhat dampened when we found the airfield covered with six feet of snow and we spent most of the daylight hours using shovels to help clear the runways. Eventually flying was possible, taking off along runways with snow piled high on either side. It did, however, concentrate the mind and made the pilots even more careful than ever to avoid a swing

on take-off. Night patrols were carried out most nights, incurring a number of casualties, attacking enemy road and rail transport when possible, and bombing rail junctions on GEE when bad weather prevented visual sightings. One night we returned from patrol to find 10/10ths cloud at 200 ft over the base. As our GEE set had gone 'on the blink', I declined the offer of a diversion to Brussels (I learned better later) and received permission to land at base. This proved somewhat 'hairy', but landing was completed without damage. No operations were carried out for the next few nights, diverted aircraft having to return to base, and the weather remained such that even the birds were walking. Normal service was resumed until 13 February, when the squadron had a break from operations to practise for a daylight formation operation – Clarion. As it was to be a twelve-aircraft formation, some crews (including us) were not involved. However, on the day of the operation, 22 February, it was decided to increase it to maximum effort, and all crews and serviceable aircraft were to be involved. Without the benefit of practice we had an unenviable position, eighteenth in an eighteen-plane formation.

Wilf Jessop, Wg Cdr Jack Wickett's navigator in 418 Squadron, recalls:

After testing the aircraft for night-flying, and with fine weather, we expected to do our usual night patrol. However, operations were cancelled and bad weather was given as the excuse, but navigators were instructed to report at 0630 hours the next morning with long-range maps. We were cautioned about security. AVM Basil Embry, Officer Commanding 2 Group, appeared next morning and explained our part in Operation Clarion, which was to attack road junctions, railways, transport and buildings in north-western Germany, aiming in twenty-four hours to annihilate German ground transport. Nine thousand Allied aircraft were to take part in the operation.[25]

Clarion was intended to be the *coup de grâce* for the German transport system, with 9,000 Allied aircraft taking part in attacks on enemy railway stations, trains and engines, cross-roads, bridges, ships and barges on canals and rivers, stores and other targets. It was to be the last time that the Mosquitoes operated in daylight in such numbers. For half an hour the Mosquitoes of 305 Squadron wreaked havoc in the Bremen–Hamburg–Kiel region. Wg Cdr S. Grodzicki DFC led 305 Squadron, and Sqn Ldr P. Hanburg led the British flight. The German ground defences were strong. Ten aircraft suffered damage and one with a British crew was lost; the pilot was killed and the navigator taken prisoner. Reg Everson recalls:

We flew in close formation at 4,000 ft until we crossed the enemy lines, when we encountered some light flak bursting at that height. We took evasive action and rejoined the formation as soon as we were clear of danger. When we arrived at the area Stade, River Elbe, we broke into pairs. I was No. 2 to WO Smith. Our main targets were barges and shipping, secondary targets being warehouses, trains and road transport. During our patrol we attacked railway trucks. The eighteen aircraft did considerable damage, and eight of them were damaged by ground fire. We then set course for base, formating on WO Smith at low level. Shortly after leaving the patrol area we passed over a machine-gun post, and Smith's aircraft was hit and caught fire; we saw it make a crash-landing. Not being sure of our exact position, and as we had used up all our machine-gun ammunition and cannon shells, I climbed to a safer height of 4,000 ft, at which we could get an accurate GEE fix. We soon found out where we were! The guns of Bremerhaven opened up and the air was filled with black puffs of exploding shells. A sharp diving turn to port down to nought feet followed, for a reassessment of the situation. Bremen was to our south, so a course was set for Zwoller on the River Yssel, which was the 'bomb line' for the day. Once we felt safer from immediate danger, we made a tentative climb to 4,000 ft to enable us to use GEE to keep away from further 'hot spots'. Shortly after we reached this height, an American Mustang formated on our starboard wing. A cigar-chewing pilot waved a friendly greeting before peeling off to go about his own business. As we approached Zwoller I opened the throttles to maximum boost, put the nose down to get maximum speed and crossed the River Yssel as quickly as possible. The rest of the trip was uneventful.

P.D. Morris, pilot of a Mosquito FB.VI fighter-bomber in 613 (City of Manchester) Squadron at Epinoy near Cambrai, France, on 22 February, recalls:

My navigator, Ron Parfitt, and I had flown together on every operation since arriving in France on 19 November 1944. Six days after arriving at Epinoy we did our first night operation – the first of forty. However, on 22 February we were briefed for our first Day Ranger sortie against the enemy. All the squadrons were to take part, and the area given to Ron and me to patrol was the very north of Germany up in Schleswig-Holstein, near the Danish border. Our job was to patrol a large area and attack with bomb, machine-gun and cannon any enemy transport or personnel we spotted. After being able to cause a little havoc on various targets, the time came for us to make our way home. To do so, we were to go directly west until we reached the North Sea and to fly back to friendly territory before crossing to land back again. We were flying fairly low, roughly at about ten to fifteen feet, as it was safer. As we crossed over very-low-lying fields that were separated by dykes, which were about the same height as that at which we were flying. I was looking well ahead when I suddenly saw a German soldier 300 yards in front who was having the audacity to be firing from the top of the dyke directly at us. This I thought was not good enough, so I armed first my four machine-guns and then my four cannon. After that I took a very careful bead on this presumptuous fellow. When about one hundred yards from him I pulled both triggers, but all that emerged from my guns was complete silence! However, I was determined at least to frighten him badly, so I passed over him a few feet over his head and saw him fall flat on his face. I feel after that he must have headed for the nearest schnapps! When we got out over the sea I decided to try out the guns again, so having armed them I pulled the two triggers and both guns fired perfectly. Until that moment my aircraft had not been known as any particular friend of the Germans! This soldier, if still alive must be among the luckiest imaginable!

Doug Mault and his navigator, John Bulmer of 613 (City of Manchester) Squadron, were instructed to 'attack anything that moved'. Mault recalls:

We flew out in squadron formation (a new experience) at low level across Belgium and Holland, which was still occupied, into the North Sea, and then turned east to our patrol area. We carried long-range tanks under each wing, and these we dropped, which put all our bomb-dropping tackle out of order. We were carrying two 500 lb bombs in the bomb-bay, and these would not budge. Fortunately, the guns were still operative, and we put them to good use against a railway engine and some road transport, which turned out to be a horse and cart. We hit the road behind it; the horse bolted and the driver fell back into his load! Was it a farmer with a load of manure? We shall never know. After attacking the engine we flew, by mistake of course, directly over a light flak battery, which opened fire. We were travelling very fast and very low and were fairly safe because of this, but it is always frightening to see tracer, especially when you remember that tracer only represents a small proportion of the stuff flying around. The journey back was due west over the sea towards Norfolk, and then south, still over the sea, to cross the French coast near Calais, and then to base. The fuel gauges were getting down towards zero when we landed after 4¾ hours, approaching maximum range and, of course, still carrying two bombs and one wing tank. An electrical fault was diagnosed later, so we were forgiven because we really had tried everything to dislodge them.[26]

At 1117 hours Wilf Jessop and his pilot, Wg Cdr Jack Wickett, led 418 Squadron's twenty aircraft in formation at a height of about 1,000 ft from Hartford Bridge to Aldburgh, and then over the North Sea to Holland at fifty feet above the waves.

While over the sea we sent three aircraft back home. One was hit by birds and damaged. Two collided due to ballooning drop tanks during the tricky and dangerous manoeuvre of skidding out of formation during the drop and skidding back in. We climbed just before reaching the Dutch coast, then dropped down to fifty feet again to avoid German radar. When the formation reached the east coast of the Zuider Zee, Wickett ordered the seventeen aircraft remaining to split up and go for their individual targets. We cruised along at 240 mph, 50–100 ft above the ground. At about 1230 hours our aircraft was hit by light flak near the Dortmund–Ems Canal south-east of Osnabrück, before reaching our target. The aircraft was on fire, and as the wheels and flaps were hanging our hydraulics had probably been damaged. My pilot broke radio silence to say we had been badly shot up and would try to land in a marshy area. I had given him a course of 270° magnetic for home, but he could not keep the aircraft in the air, and made, in the circumstances, a marvellous landing alongside the canal. The whole of my side of the cockpit caved in, and with our cannon shells and machine-gun bullets exploding, I got out rather sharpish, not having a parachute hanging on my backside to hinder me. My pilot, sitting on, and fastened to, his parachute, was having difficulty getting out.

I have a faint recollection of helping him, knowing we were sitting on top of two 500 lb bombs ready to explode. Out we both ran like the clappers away from the aircraft – the direction did not matter! We got about sixty yards away when the bombs went off. We were glad of the eleven-second delay fuses on them. Armed Germans quickly picked us up, and it was then that I found I had only one boot on. We were taken to a barge on the canal, where my pilot was briefly questioned. Most of the Germans on the barge were quite young, about 15, and manning an anti-aircraft gun. Towards late afternoon we were marched off in the direction of the remains of our aircraft, and I had visions of us being disposed of near it. I mentioned this to my pilot, but we decided to hang on a bit. We arrived at a factory, which was shut, and our guards could not get in, so they took us back to the barge. I think they thought they could hand us over to someone else. Some of them lost a bit of sleep that night guarding us. I found out much later that this operation turned out to be the costliest to date for 418 Squadron – four aircraft failed to return to base.

No. 21 Squadron was one of the lucky ones that day, losing only one aircraft, flown by Fielding-Johnson and Harbord.[27] No. 464 lost two, and 487 took a hammering and lost five, principally because they chose to take the long route around the coast and got caught by flak and fighters as a result. No. 2 Group lost twenty-one Mosquitoes on Clarion, with forty damaged. The Mosquito was not, after all, invulnerable. But Mosquito night-fighters were still more than a match in a straight fight with German night-fighters.

On the night of 24/25 March, 604, 605 and 410 Squadron crews shot down four more enemy aircraft. On the night of 25/26 March, crews in 409 and 264 dispatched two Bf 110s and a Ju 88, plus one 'probable'. There was a great deal of activity on 26/27 March, with raids concentrated on the Rhine bridgehead at Emmerich, and as a result the *Luftwaffe* was forced up into the night sky, but with disastrous results. Flt Lt Al Gabitas of 488 RNZAF Squadron recalls:

> At this stage of the war the Germans were feeling the effects of the Allied bombing on their synthetic petrol plants, and were obviously trying to conserve fuel. This meant that their night-flying activity tended to be concentrated onto particular nights, with long intervals of inactivity. The night of 26/27 March was to be a busy one, with raids against the Rhine bridgehead at Emmerich. Flight Lieutenant Johnny Hall DFC, an Englishman on the squadron, and his navigator, Pilot Officer Taylor, contacted a Junkers 88 and brought it down twenty miles north of Emmerich after several bursts of cannon fire. But the Mosquito itself was damaged by flying debris and burst into flames as it landed on its belly at Gilze Rijn in Holland. Fortunately the top hatch slid back easily and the crew escaped unhurt.

Chunky Stewart and Bill Brumby were also on patrol over the bridgehead, in NF.XXX NT263. About eight miles north-west of Bocholt they intercepted a Bf 110, which, after a short burst, hit the ground with a brilliant explosion. Their radar set then became partially useless, but even so, Brumby managed to pick up a contact, which turned out to be an He 111. Stewart gave the Heinkel a quick couple of bursts and it went into a steep dive. At the same time Stewart realized that he was being chased by a German night-fighter, and he had to break off the engagement.

Flt Lt Al Gabitas adds:

> Following these successes there were many hours of patient patrolling and sky searching, and it was well into April [the night of 7/8] before Chunky and Bill were directed to a 'Bogey' over the Ruhr. In the long chase that followed the rear gunner on the Me 110 opened fire on the Mosquito several times, but Chunky was not able

to get his sights onto the enemy or fire his guns. Presently a small fire started in the tail of the Messerschmitt, and then grew larger, until it dived into the ground and exploded. Although their guns were not fired, Chunky and Bill were credited with one enemy aircraft destroyed. The enemy had shot off his own tail. Thus Chunky, in a comparatively short time, had brought his score up to five enemy aircraft destroyed and one damaged. Recognition of this achievement was to come with the award of DFCs to both Chunky and Bill. Unfortunately the paperwork for the awards was rather slow, and they were not announced until after the squadron had been disbanded and had left the continent. I did not see Chunky again until 1949, by which time he was a full partner in his legal firm in Dunedin, and making a name for himself in the profession. Sadly, he lived for only a few short years after the war, and died suddenly in his home town from a massive coronary. All those who knew him were profoundly shocked at the death in times of peace of one so apparently fit and comparatively young.

Meanwhile, 264 Squadron had moved back to France, to 148 Wing at Lille/Vendeville. Its move had coincided with a snowstorm, and the squadron had had to endure the weather with very little heating or comfort until the snow cleared early in February. Both January and February were complete operational blanks, as the *Luftwaffe* was not keen to show itself at night at all, but near the end of February four pilots left for Gilse/Rijen to carry out Operation Blackmail. This was intensely secret at the time, but it entailed carrying Dutchmen, Air Force and Army, and one woman over occupied Holland by day and night to maintain wireless communications with agents of their Underground movement. This task was performed well and was particularly useful, although it had been refused by 2 Group, which considered it to be too dangerous. March saw plenty of patrols being flown from both Lille and Gilse, but it was not until the 25th that any success was achieved, a Ju 88 destroyed and another damaged, the first combat since 10 August. March in fact saw a heavy toll of German aircraft by 2nd TAF Mosquito night-fighters. On 5/6 March Flt Lt Don MacFadyen DFC RCAF in 406 Squadron, flying NF.XXX NT325, destroyed a Ju 88G at Gerolzhofen.

When, on 21 April, 'Ginger' Walsh and 'Pat' Patterson in 487 Squadron in France flew an op to Emden, everything that could go wrong went wrong. Walsh remembers the event:

We took off and landed at Melsbroek first, before coming to the Rhine. We had a funnel only about two miles wide. A Mossie that had aborted flew back past us at a closing speed of more than 600 mph and narrowly missed us! Crossing the Rhine we almost hit a barrage balloon that our boys were flying from a barge. We ended up at 1,000–1,500 ft in the middle of a German airfield. I compressed myself into a small space, but nothing happened. We turned west and came back towards Hamburg. Finally, we dropped our bombs on a German town. 'Pat' threw the aircraft around, but nothing happened. Back at Amiens our NZ squadron leader, who was acting CO, berated 'Pat' for bringing his ammo back.

'Pat' must have taken it to heart, because four days later, on 25 April, when we were coming back from Emden, he lowered the nose and began firing. I told him three times that we were nearing our lines! His target could have been a haystack or it could have been Hitler. 'Pat' continued firing off our ammo. We got light flak; the tracer was utterly fascinating and missed us, but I had to do something. I reached up and fired off the red and yellow colours of the day from the Very pistol mounted in the roof of the cockpit. It did the trick! The cockpit filled with cordite and there was a big flash.

'Pat' exclaimed, 'What the —— was that?'

I giggled and told him that I'd fired the Very pistol. You never gave away the colours of the day, but it was of no consequence to me! The firing stopped. I had visions of a German down below looking at his flimsy [his 'colours of the day', which could be easily destroyed when no longer needed].

It was on this operation that Flight Lieutenant Johnny Evans and his navigator, Flying Officer Ifor Jenkins, were lost. Johnny had lost two pilot brothers killed in the war. I'd spent time in Montreal with Ifor. They put out a Mayday call:

'I'm on fire and losing height!' They'd got him.

Another voice said, 'You'll be all right.' Evans replied caustically, 'It's all right for you.' That was it – they were dead.

With the end of the war in sight, Mosquito crews still went out at night to the furthermost reaches of the diminishing *Reich*, and there were more losses. On the night of 26/27 April, Flt Lt Reginald Arthur 'Dusty' Miller DFC*, and his navigator, Flg Off William Barclay, of the Night Fighter Development Unit at Ford, were to attack Wels and Horshling airfields in northern Austria, about fifteen miles apart, strafing them with cannon and machine-guns. 'Dusty' Miller's long and distinguished career had begun in 1941 and was punctuated with a series of adventures, during which he downed seven *Luftwaffe* and Italian aircraft and probably destroyed one other.[28] Miller and Barclay were told that two 'Mossies' from another squadron were going with them, and that they would meet them in France. Bill Barclay recalls:

> The plan for the night of 26/27 April was for our aircraft to carry parachute flares, go in first, drop the flares and so light up the target.

Then all three aircraft were to 'have a go' at any planes that were parked on the 'drome. In the afternoon we flew across to France to refuel and meet the other crews to talk things over. We arranged a rendezvous above a lake at a set time, about thirty miles from the first target at Wels, then, on receiving a codeword on the R/T, we would all set course together for the target. The first crew took off, but they had to land immediately with engine trouble, which left two of us. The other crew got off OK and we followed. I remember before taking off, debating with myself whether or not to keep my Mae West on – they are really bulky things, and there is very little room in a Mossie cockpit. I decided to keep it on as it made my parachute harness fit better, a very necessary precaution, as a slack-fitting harness can give one a serious injury.

We set course at 10.30 p.m. It was a perfect night, a clear sky and a full moon, making navigation fairly easy. Soon we were into Germany, having a look at the fighting down below. We reached the rendezvous dead on time, 12.45 a.m., and gave the codeword, but the other plane was late, so we flew around for a few minutes, gave it again, got the answer and off we went.

Down low, about 1,000 ft above the ground and with 270 mph on the clock, we soon arrived at the target, then up to 3,000 ft – open bomb-doors and down went two flares, a steep turn around and there lay the enemy 'drome before us. It was like daylight beneath the flares, but not a sign of any aircraft – it was completely empty. Cursing our luck, we set off for the other 'drome at Horshing, reached it in a few minutes, and flew across at 3,000 ft, dropping our last two flares. This time when we came around we could see twenty or more aircraft standing around the 'drome.

The other plane was making its first attack, and the reception it was given was definitely not friendly – light tracer and plenty of flak. Naturally the ack-ack gunners had seen our flares go down at Wels, and they were waiting for us. Down we went to make our contribution, cannon and machine-guns belting away, their flak doing likewise. The sky seemed full of red fingers pointing at us, but we knew they were not fingers. We got one Jerry Ju 188, set it on fire, then we came round again for 'just one more go'.

The same welcome, and this time we damaged two planes, then just as we were finishing the run we were hit. I felt as though someone had given me a terrible blow on the right side of my body, and for a moment I was stunned. When I pulled myself together a few minutes later, Dusty was getting the plane under control and getting some altitude, so I had a look around to see what was what.

We had been hit on the starboard side between the engine and the fuselage. I had been hit by a piece of shrapnel, and my right arm was dead useless and bleeding very badly. The floor and side of the fuselage were riddled with holes and our maps were scattered all over the place, there were no lights, a large chunk was missing from the wing and the starboard engine was on fire.

Dusty was uninjured, so he stopped the starboard engine and helped me clip my 'chute on, called the other plane and told them we were on one engine and would try to make it back to base. I said a silent prayer to myself. After a few seconds the port engine began to overheat, it must have been hit in the cooling-system, the temperature gauge was going up and up. I jettisoned the door, our exit, ready to bale out. Dusty realized that we could not make it, as the engine would soon be going, and he told me to bale out.

We said 'So long' to each other, and I started wriggling through the door, which is quite small, got half-way out and stuck. My arm handicapped me, but Dusty soon cleared me. He put his foot on my back and pushed. I pulled the ripcord, but for a moment nothing happened. 'I've had it', I thought, then the 'chute opened and stopped me with a terrific jerk.

We would be about 2,000–3,000 ft high when I got out, and as I was coming down I could still the plane but no sign of Dusty coming out, and suddenly the port engine blew up and the plane went down with Dusty still in it. It must have only been about twenty seconds after I cleared, the plane crashed, exploded and burst into flames. I knew then that there was no hope of Dusty being alive.

Then I realized the ground was rushing up to me, so I relaxed according to instructions and made my landing. Luckily I just missed a wood and fell on some grassland, rolled over a few times, stopped, then stood up and thanked my lucky stars I was in one piece. There was a cottage about a hundred yards away, so I quickly got rid of the 'chute and Mae West and left the spot, heading east towards the Russian front. I looked at my watch and found that it had stopped at 1.08 a.m. It had stopped a piece of shrapnel, too.

I felt lonely as I walked on through the night, and the bright moonlight made me feel as if anyone could spot me. I kept to the edge of the woods and fields for safety, but there seemed an awful lot of farms, and each one meant a detour. I once stumbled upon a gang of German army lorries, parked in a wood. I stopped, waiting for someone to challenge me, but everything was quiet and I went on. Eventually I came to a small river. There were the remains of a bridge which must have been bombed. I walked alongside the river for a while and found a narrow part where I crossed it the 'wet way'.

After that I felt decidedly cold and miserable, and my wounds were certainly making themselves felt. My right foot and leg were giving me trouble, although I had not thought I had been hit there. On I went until 4.30 a.m., when I came to a village and decided to have a look at it and see if there was a doctor's house around, for I had no desire to let my wounds become septic. The war was almost over, and I knew I wouldn't be a PoW for long. Luck was with me. I found a building with a light and a red cross on the door. I knocked and out came a Jerry, sleepy-eyed and wanting to know what I wanted. Then he saw who I was and took me inside. It was a barrack room. There were dozens of Jerry soldiers in their bunks. I found out later that it was a rest home for the troops from the Russian front. The Jerry took me upstairs to the medical quarters, woke up the chap on duty and then proceeded to pull bits of shrapnel out of my arm, bathed it and wrapped it up. I was then given a drink and lay down on a form, wondering what would happen next.

Came the dawn, and just like a British barracks I heard 'Wakey, wakey' or its equivalent in German, the troops crawled out of bed and I became the centre of attraction. The soldier who took me in turned out to be the sergeant major; they gave me something to eat and told me that I would see the medical officer when he came on duty. One of the soldiers could speak English, for he'd worked in Liverpool for some years. Then came the officers and lots of questions, and, of course, lots of wonderful lies from me.

Finally I saw the doctor, and he said I would be going to the hospital that day. 'OK by me', I thought. The soldiers treated me quite well and didn't even search me. They told me they were Austrians, that I was in good hands and that I was fortunate not to have met up with any civilians, or I would have been beaten up. In the afternoon, transport arrived to take me to hospital, a large flat cart with a chair on it (for me), two horses, a driver and a guard. They must have been short of petrol, I thought, and off we went.

The hospital was a beautiful place on the edge of a lake, where we had made our rendezvous the previous night. They put me on a stretcher and then X-rayed me and put my foot in plaster, bandaged me up and so to bed. All very good treatment, I thought. I lay there, the doctor visiting me now and then. The local *Gestapo* came and questioned me. They told me they had found the plane and the body of Dusty. I lay there for two weeks until the Americans came, and then back to England, so concluding my most vivid war experience.

Notes

1. Dominique Ponchardier's *Sosies* group, which undertook sabotage and escape activities as well as espionage, had ruled out a combined *Maquis* operation to break into the jail, overpower the guards and release the prisoners, after a similar operation in the adjacent province of Aisne against a jail at St Quentin in January had resulted in disastrous failure. At once the guards at all the prisons in Occupied France were strengthened,

and many more arrests had been made. *Strike Hard, Strike Sure*. Ralph Barker (Pen & Sword Military Classics, 2003).
2. *Strike Hard, Strike Sure*. Ralph Barker (Pen & Sword Military Classics, 2003).
3. No. 2 Group had been transferred to 2nd TAF on 1 June 1943. AVM Basil Embry replaced AVM d'Albiac at HQ, Bylaugh Hall, with the task of preparing 2 Group for invasion support in the run-up to Operation Overlord, the invasion of France. Embry was an excellent choice for the new-found role. He successfully fought off an attempt to re-equip 2 Group with Vultee Vengeance dive-bombers, and saw to it that his Lockheed Ventura-equipped squadrons were re-equipped with the Mosquito FB.VI, which was armed with four cannon for Night Intruder operations. Re-equipment began in August 1943 with 140 Wing at Sculthorpe, when 464 RAAF and 487 RNZAF Squadrons exchanged their obsolete Lockheed machines. No. 21 Squadron closely followed them, in September, all three squadrons moving to Hunsdon in December 1943.
4. HX922.
5. DZ414/O.
6. Flt Lt E.E. Hogan and Flt Sgt D.A.S. Crowfoot, and Flt Sgt A. Steadman and Plt Off E.J. Reynolds, in 21 Squadron. Two Typhoons in 245 Squadron aborted with fuel problems.
7. *Strike Hard, Strike Sure*. Ralph Barker (Pen & Sword Military Classics, 2003).
8. Moisan was covered in bloodstains and dust, and with his clothes torn to shreds he was taken for dead by the Germans, but his friend Sellier got him on a stretcher and the *Défense Passive* took him away in an ambulance. He recovered and was eventually liberated by the advancing British armies.
9. After Arras was liberated in October 1944, 260 bodies were found buried outside the town. Among them were most of the Amiens prisoners who had deliberately stayed behind to take part in the work of mercy. Captain Tempez was among them. They had been shot in April 1944. Dr Mans survived and was eventually deported to Germany, where he spent the winter of 1944/5 in the labour camp at Fallersleben. *Strike Hard, Strike Sure*. Ralph Barker (Pen & Sword Military Classics, 2003).
10. *Strike Hard, Strike Sure*. Ralph Barker (Pen & Sword Military Classics, 2003).
11. KIA 4.1.45.
12. *Strike Hard, Strike Sure*. Ralph Barker (Pen & Sword Military Classics, 2003).
13. After the Liberation it was found that of the 400-odd escapers, only about 250 had retained their freedom; 102 prisoners had been killed in the attack and seventy-four wounded, some of them by small-arms fire from the guards. Within two or three days of the raid it was learned that M. Raymond Vivant and twelve Resistance leaders who would otherwise have been shot within forty-eight hours were among the escapers. *Strike Hard, Strike Sure*. Ralph Barker (Pen & Sword Military Classics, 2003).
14. On 15 October 1943, 138 Wing at Lasham began operating FB.VIs when 613 (City of Manchester) Squadron joined 2 Group. In December 305

(Polish) Squadron converted from the Mitchell and in February 1944 107 Squadron converted from the Douglas Boston. As planned, 138 Wing transferred to airfields in France when the outbreak from the Normandy beachhead came.

15. This was followed by another daylight attack on the Caserne des Dunes barracks at Poitiers by twenty-four FB.VIs of 487 and 21 Squadrons escorted by Mustangs on 1 August. The Château de Fou, an *SS* police HQ south of Chattelerault and Château Maulny, a saboteur school, was attacked by twenty-three FB.VIs of 107 and 305 Squadrons on Sunday 2 August. That same day, 613 Squadron attacked a château in Normandy, which was used as a rest home for German submariners. See *Mosquitopanik!* Martin W. Bowman (Pen & Sword, 2004).

16. The operation was carried out at such a low altitude that Sqn Ldr F.H. Denton of 487 Squadron hit the roof of the building, losing his tailwheel and the port half of the tailplane. Denton nursed the Mosquito across the North Sea and managed to land safely. The university and its incriminating records were destroyed. Among the 110–175 Germans killed in the raid was *Kriminalrat* Schwitzgiebel, head of the *Gestapo* in Jutland, and *SS Obersturmführer* Lonechun, head of the Security Services. See *Mosquitopanik!* Martin W. Bowman (Pen & Sword, 2004).

17. Four Mosquitoes and two Mustangs FTR from the raid on the *Shellhaus* for the loss of nine aircrew. Of twenty-six prisoners on the sixth floor, eighteen escaped. The remaining prisoners died in the building. The *Jeanne D' Arc School* was bombed by mistake during the raid, and eighty-six children were killed and sixty-seven wounded; sixteen adults also lost their lives, with thirty-five more injured. Several other people were killed elsewhere as a direct result of the attack. See See *Mosquitopanik!* Martin W. Bowman (Pen & Sword, 2004), and *Mosquitoes Menacing The Reich*. Martin W. Bowman (Pen & Sword, 2008).

18. The huge petrol dump at Nomency near Nancy was destroyed. Twelve FB.VIs of 464 Squadron attacked a dozen petrol trains near Chagney from between 20 and 200 ft, and caused widespread destruction.

19. Of over 10,200 British airborne troops landed in the Arnhem area, 1,440 were killed or died of their wounds. Some 3,000 were wounded and taken prisoner and 400 medical personnel and chaplains remained behind with the wounded; about 2,500 uninjured troops also became PoWs. There were also 225 prisoners from the 4th Battalion, the Dorsetshire Regiment. About 450 Dutch civilians were killed. The operation also cost 160 RAF and Dominions aircrew, and twenty-seven USAAF aircrew and seventy-nine Royal Army Service Corps dispatchers were killed and 127 taken prisoner. A total of fifty-five Albemarle, Stirling, Halifax and Dakota aircraft of 38 and 46 Groups failed to return, and a further 320 were damaged by flak and seven by fighters, while 105 Allied fighter aircraft were lost.

20. Altogether, 2nd TAF NF.XXX and NF.XIII crews knocked down ten enemy aircraft on 23/24 December. On Christmas Eve 1944, eighteen German aircraft were shot down, five of them by four Mosquito crews of 100 Group. The rest were shot down by Mosquitoes of 2nd TAF,

which dispatched 139 Mosquitoes on that night to targets in south-west Germany.
21. *LG1* lost three Ju 88s this night, including one flown by the *Gruppe Kommandeur*, *Hauptmann* Hecking (301348 L1+GK) and one flown by *Oberleutnant* Huber, *Staffelführer 6./LG1*, in 331294 L1+NP. On 3/4 February, Kent and Simpson added to their score by downing a Ju 88. Flt Lt B.E. Plumer DFC and Flt Lt Hargrove of 410 Squadron, in an NF.XXX, dispatched an He 219 *Uhu*.
22. In NF.XIII MM456.
23. 260542 A3+QD.
24. Hauck, his observer, *Gefreiter* Kurt Wuttge, *bordfunker*, *Unteroffizier* Max Grossman and *Feldwebel* Heinrich Hoppe, the dispatcher, baled out and were taken prisoner.
25. On the night of 21/22 February and east of Stormede airfield, Flt Lt Don A. MacFadyen DFC RCAF of 406 Squadron, in NF.XXX NT325, destroyed a Bf 110. Flt Lt K.W. 'Chunky' Stewart and Flg Off Bill Brumby of 488 Squadron RNZAF were patrolling over Holland when they were warned by ground control that they were being followed by a strange aircraft. Flt Lt Al Gabitas, a fellow NZ pilot on the squadron, recalls: 'A sort of dogfight ensued in complete darkness between the two night-fighters, guided entirely by their own radar. With a great deal of weaving about Chunky managed to get behind the other aircraft. After brief visual contact it was identified as a Junkers 88G night-fighter. Following a quick burst of cannon fire on a fairly wide deflection, it blew up in mid-air. This was a duel to the death between evenly matched opponents in which the outcome was determined by superior flying and gunnery skills, and more than a slight edge on the technology.' The enemy machine exploded near Groenlo. Three more victories were recorded on the night of the 21/22nd, which went to 2nd TAF Mosquito crews.
26. 'My Private War' by Doug Mault. MSS *The Mossie* No. 30, January 2002.
27. Hugh Henry Fielding Johnson had joined 21 Squadron in March 1944, and he flew his first operation on 26 March with his navigator, Flg Off L.C. Harbord. Fielding Johnson was known on the squadron as 'Fee-Gee' (or 'Fiji'), and he sported a typical RAF moustache. 'Fee-Gee' also wore a navigator's or an air gunner's brevet above his right breast pocket, perhaps out of respect for his illustrious father, Sqn Ldr W.S. Fielding Johnson, who was also a pilot and a qualified air gunner. At 52, Sqn Ldr Fielding Johnson was the oldest air gunner on operations in the RAF, serving as gunnery leader of a 2nd TAF Mitchell squadron taking part in an attack at Venlo in Holland. His aircraft was severely hit by flak over the target. The captain gave orders to jump. Johnson climbed down from his upper turret and, at 8,000 ft, jumped. As he said later, 'This was the thing I have always wanted to do. As soon as I had pulled the cord I found the sensation quite splendid.'
28. Miller, of Sully, Glamorgan, trained as a night-fighter pilot in 1941, being posted out to the Middle East as a sergeant, where he joined 89 Squadron. On 7 March 1942 he went with the first detachment of Beaufighters to be sent by the unit to operate on Malta with 1435 Flight, with Sgt Francis J. Tearle as his radar operator. The night of their arrival, they claimed the

unit's first victory over the island, shooting down a Ju 88C night-fighter flown by one of the leading pilots of *I./NJG2*. By June they had claimed four victories, and during the night of 27/28 May had also strafed a number of E-Boats, seeing explosions on three of these. Commissioned in June 1942, both were to be awarded DFCs. Returning to Egypt, Miller was dispatched to the UK via the Cape of Good Hope aboard the *Laconia* with a number of other night-fighter crews. On 2 September the vessel was torpedoed and sunk off the West African coast. After several days in a lifeboat, he was picked up by a Vichy French cruiser and interned in North Africa. After the Allied invasion later in the year, he was released and returned to the UK, where he was posted to 54 OTU as an instructor. In 1944 he commenced a second tour as a flying officer with 604 Squadron, flying with Flt Lt S.H.J. Elliott, a one-legged radar operator, or Plt Off P. Catchpole; most of his successes appear to have been with the latter. He claimed a further three victories with this unit and received a Bar to his DFC in October, Catchpole being awarded a DFC at the same time. Miller was then posted to the FIU at Ford, which later became the FIDS with CFE at Wittering and then Tangmere. *Aces High: A Tribute to the Most Notable Fighter Pilots of the British and Commonwealth Forces in WWII.* Christopher Shores and Clive Williams (Grub Street, London, 1994).

CHAPTER 10

'Jane'

VE-Day on 8 May, with all its victory bonfires, street parties and merry-making, was a party of mixed emotions. There were those who were just relieved it was all over, and many others who were overwhelmed by an awful sadness. In London crowds gathered early, encouraged by the warm sunshine. Bells pealed; flags flew from all the buildings. Shop windows were filled with red, white and blue clothes, flowers and materials. Aircraft flew overhead, and streamers, ticker tape and paper poured out of every window and balcony. Hermione, Countess of Ranfurly, on the fourth floor at the Air Ministry in Adastral House, Kingsway, thought that it was 'a brilliant time' to throw some of AM Slessor's 'more boring papers' out. She peeled the canvas off one window and emptied the contents of five waste-paper baskets onto Kingsway. She eased her way into the Strand and progressed at 'snail's pace' towards Trafalgar Square: 'It was a good-natured multitude, and except for the sounds of feet and voices there was a silence over London – a silence loaded with emotion. A few people were crying and a few were laughing, but the majority trudged forward silently.' In Trafalgar Square the steps, lions and lamp-posts were 'coated with people'. Whitehall appeared to be 'paved with heads'. A *Daily Mirror* reporter wrote:

> This is it – and we are all going nuts. There are thousands of us in Piccadilly Circus. The police say more than 10,000 – and that's a conservative estimate. We are dancing the Conga and the jig and *Knees Up Mother Brown,* and we are singing and whistling and blowing paper trumpets. The idea is to make a noise. We are. Even above the roar of the motors of low-flying bombers 'shooting-up' the city ... We are dancing around Eros in the blackout but there is a

glow from a bonfire up Shaftesbury Avenue and a newsreel cinema has lit its canopy lights for the first time in getting on for six years. A huge V-sign glares down over Leicester Square. And gangs of girls and soldiers are waving rattles and shouting and climbing lamp-posts and swarming over cars that have become bogged down in this struggling, swirling mass of celebrating Londoners.

Though Allied servicemen were glad that the 'whole dirty business was over', many were in limbo. The war had lasted so long that many could hardly believe it was over. They could not remember very clearly what it was like to live without a war; it seemed so long ago. When RAF Transport Command required a fast Air Delivery Letter Service (ADLS) for the Middle East and Europe, the Mosquito was considered most suited for the carriage of diplomatic and urgent service mail. It was also considered essential that the most experienced aircrews available should be employed. In late May 1945, 162 Squadron at Bourn exchanged its Pathfinder eagle for the greyhound of King's Messenger, and moved from 8 Group, Bomber Command, to 46 Group, Transport Command, at RAF Blackbushe. 'B' Flight, which comprised eight Mosquito Mk XXV aircraft, was selected. Wg Cdr Peter McDermott DFC DFM, the 'B' Flight commander, who had joined 162 Squadron on 26 December 1944, flying on its last raid of the war against Pasing Power Station (Munich) on 24 April, was appointed detachment commander. He recalls:

> After a motor-cycle reconnaissance, I led the formation to Blackbushe on 7 June, flying low over the airfield before breaking into a stream landing. When I went to the tower to apologize for this brash behaviour, the SATCO – a burnt-faced veteran – passed it off with 'I didn't notice – we're far too busy here.' One up to him, and an appropriate welcome – and we were given every assistance from then on. We were temporarily based at the south-east end of the airfield, but shortly moved to a group of hard standings and buildings a bit further to the west, to the south of the A30 and backing on to the sharp bend of the Minley Road to Fleet. There were gates on the A30 to the east at the junction with the Fleet–Eversley Road. When the short runways were in use, the gates were closed and all traffic was diverted to the south (around what is now signposted as a detour. When the road was open, we still had to cross it to and from the in-use runway and our dispersals – not marshalled, but there was a sign at the barriers warning vehicles that they had to give way to aircraft. A large whirling propeller disc was a bit of an inducement to allow precedence! We had an unofficial competition on how many vehicles we could hold up while effecting the crossing. The low density of the road traffic may be judged by the high jubilation if we made a five!

Flt Lt John E.L. John Gover DFC*was detailed to go to Copenhagen very soon after he had arrived at Blackbushe and before he had time to study the layout of the airfield and its taxi tracks, as he recalls:[1]

> I gathered that the crew who should have gone were not available. Realizing I would have to return in the dark, I went into the control tower before taking off and explained that on my return I should need help to find my way to my dispersal in the shape of a vehicle with an illuminated 'Follow Me' sign on it. 'Don't worry, old boy, we'll look after you', I was told. So off I went. I duly came back in the dark, and after landing, called the control tower for the promised assistance. However, instead of sending a vehicle as I had requested, the control officer on duty gave me directions from the tower, which I'm sure I followed. The result was I got hopelessly lost and ended up facing car headlights! In a fury I called the control tower and said I was switching off the engines before I killed somebody. My unfortunate navigator and I abandoned the aircraft in the middle of the road and walked to the mess. I was supposed to report to Customs, but did not bother about that formality. I happened to see the customs officer in the mess, and told him where the aircraft was if he wanted to inspect its contents. He smiled weakly as if I'd made a joke he didn't quite understand. However, I was not in a joking mood.
>
> I imagine the aircraft was towed away, but nobody reprimanded me. What happened to the control officer concerned I've no idea, nor did I care; I was so angry. I felt I'd done everything I could to get to my dispersal but had merely wasted my time. I reckon I held up a lot of vehicles on the road.

Wg Cdr Peter McDermott continues:

> The operational task was to deliver any urgent mail or packages to British locations throughout Europe. (This excluded the extensive requirements of the Nuremberg War Crimes Trials, November 1945 until August 1946, which were serviced by a special flight of Ansons at Croydon.)
>
> Frank Roberts, who flew twenty-six Mosquito sorties with 571 Squadron at Oakington in 1945 and later with 98 Squadron, made four visits to the court hearings during the trials, and was present when Goering and Hess were sentenced. His job at the time was to deliver Foreign Office mail from the courthouse. He obtained by some means a press pass, and saw these war criminals at close hand. 'It was unbelievable to see the perpetrators of these crimes sitting only 25–30 ft away from me. To sit so close to Hermann Goering and Rudolf Hess, who were both members of the Nazi hierarchy, is

something that I would never forget. The language translations were almost simultaneous over our headsets. I heard Goering speak – he was bombastic.' Frank had no idea what was in the mail he was handling, as the security procedures were so tight. 'The mail would be loaded in the bomb compartment of the Mosquito, and once we got to our destination we opened the bomb-doors and someone else collected it. We never saw the post at all.' The Nürnberg trials lasted ten months and ended with twelve death sentences being passed down, including on Goering, who managed to cheat the hangman at the last moment by taking poison. Three others received life sentences, four long terms, in prison and the rest were acquitted.

In August, the operational task was extended to include delivery of British newspapers to UK forces in north-west Europe on the day of issue. Codenamed 'Jane', presumably a reference to the *Daily Mirror* cartoon character who tended to drop all her clothes at frequent intervals, this was a welfare service dreamed up by a padre somewhere 'up the line'. Unfortunately, he had quite forgotten the financial implications – the cost of the papers and their delivery to Camberley railway station – and eventually a vast bill arrived at the squadron. It was passed to 46 Group and, one hopes, was eventually settled. The service was required to operate with regularity regardless of weather conditions. This was no worry, as before being accepted for the LNSF, pilots were required to have at least one full tour of night-bombing operations under their belt, or else 1,200 hours of instrumental flying with 200 hours' documented instrument-flying. To ensure co-operation *en route*, each pilot carried a card signed by an AVM at SACEUR (Supreme Allied Command Europe), instructing authorities throughout Europe to assist us and stating that the pilot was entirely responsible for authorizing his own flights, whatever the weather conditions. This was heady stuff for young men. But there were only two crashes, both fatal and both due to engine failure on take-off.[2]

Nevertheless, the system was found hard to bear by many station commanders until they discovered from on high that it really meant what it said. I even had brushes (understandably, I suppose) with the Blackbushe station commander on the point. Once, I instructed the SATCO to put FIDO in action to land one of my aircraft. 'What the hell do you mean by ...' was his welcome when I was summoned to the presence to explain my enthusiastic action! The card was waved.

Again, when one of my pilots (a Norwegian in the RAF) did a spectacular steep-turned circuit at 'deck' level under very low cloud, I was summoned to his office – I seemed to spend most of my time being summoned thus for the first few weeks. 'I don't care about all the cards in the world – I won't have split-arsed young pilots showing off their inexperience around my airfield.' 'Sir, he was an airline pilot before Norway was invaded and has about 7,000 hours in his logbook.' The group captain was a bit speechless. Perhaps the last straw was when I did an SBA approach in somewhat less than marginal conditions one afternoon. Fortunately, the AOC was in the tower at the time, and before the station commander could say anything, he seized the mike and said, 'Well done, pilot of V for Victor.' Despite the trouble we caused him, he was very kind to me.

The card failed only once – at Melsbroek (Brussels). President Truman was passing through on his way back from the Potsdam Conference, and without warning or permission the US Army had swept onto the airfield and a gun-toting GI stopped me entering my aircraft. Furious, I went to the control tower and demanded to know who was controlling the airfield, the RAF or the Americans. A shirt-sleeved figure sitting on the steps of the dais looked up at me and said, 'Don't ask me. I'm only the station commander and I'm marooned here.' It was only one of the 'notorious' Atcherly brothers, 'Batchy' I think.

All the routes and many of the procedures were experimental, so I naturally flew as many of them as possible first time to arrange local facilities and so forth. The first route flight on 15 June was to Brussels–Wiesbaden–Wunsdorf. The grass airfield at Wunsdorf was rather short for the Mosquito, and despite warnings to the contrary, many of my pilots made use of the undershoot area. This practice abruptly stopped when a farm labourer, complete with horse and cart, was blown up by an unplotted land-mine where they had been touching down! The second route flight on 17 June was to Gordemoen, north of Oslo (Oslo Fornebu was far too small for the Mosquito). We went via East Fortune (north-east Scotland) to top up with fuel. During the short time we flew this route, we tried to deliver the odd barrel of beer to the British Forces there. But this stopped after one barrel blew up when the (unpressurized) aircraft was forced to fly high to avoid the weather. The barrel was in the nose of the aircraft, and the escaping beer had a deleterious effect on the electrics!

By the end of July we were air-dropping newspapers instead of landing to off-load, so this route was changed to Hamburg–Scheswigland (drop)–Fornebu (drop)–Kastrup (Copenhagen), where we landed and handed over to another crew for the return flight. The newspapers were picked up at Camberley station just before midnight and sorted into destination loads before being packed into metal drums, which had a bomb-lug welded on. Take-off time was 0430Z (GMT) and the first drops were made from 100 ft in the dark on the target of goose-neck flares. On 31 July I flew the first flight (logged as five hours.). The drop at Schleswigland on grass was successful, but at Fornebu, approaching from the north over the hill, disaster struck as some of the drums burst on the hard surface. Hundreds of newspapers were carried south by a very high wind, and and as I later reported, we found ourselves flying QBI down Oslo Fiord through newspapers! A simple solution was rapidly evolved. The newspapers were packed in (flexible) airmen's kit-bags with the bomb-lug on a wooden batten strapped to each bag. No more bursts! Naively, the bags were marked, 'Return to RAF Blackbushe by the fastest route' – most of them in fact came back.

The southern route for 'Jane' dropped at St Denis Westram (Ghent), Evere (Brussels), Gutersloh, Detmold, Buckeburg, Celle and Valkenburg (Holland), returning to Blackbushe without landing.[3] We also dropped or landed at Wunstorf. Other regular routes with mail took in Berlin, Vienna (Schwechat), Naples (Pommigliano), Rome (Ciampino), Istres, near Marseilles, Athens (Hassini), Undine and Prague (Ruzeyn). There were a few hairy tussles with the Mistral around Istres. For both routes take-off was at 0430Z, and after summer the early loads were dropped from 100 ft onto a target of goose-neck flares.

The tasks grew, and the remainder of the squadron, including the CO, Wing Commander M. Sewell, and the 'A' Flight commander, Squadron Leader W.E.M. Eddy, joined in in August 1945. Regular destinations in addition to the above were Vienna, Naples, Rome, Marseilles, Athens, Prague and Wunstorf. Specials took in other destinations, of course.

By 15 August 1945, VJ-Day, 1,032 Mosquitoes had been built in Canada. One of the Mosquito men who had double cause to celebrate the night in some style was Philip Back, who, on 25 May 1945, with his navigator, Sandy Galbraith, had been posted from 139 Squadron to Woodhall Spa to join 627 Squadron, part of the 'Tiger Force' earmarked for the invasion of Japan. On 28 July 1945 Philip had married his fiancée, June Debenham, a nurse at King's College Hospital, London, whom he had met in September 1944 when she attended the University Air Squadron Passing-Out Parade, accompanied by her father, Professor Frank Debenham. In 1910–12, the professor had been the geologist on the ill-fated Scott Expedition to the Antarctic. More recently, he had been one of the lecturers who had taught Philip during his RAF Short Course at Corpus Christi College, Cambridge.

June and Philip motored home from their honeymoon in Dorset in their 1937 black Ford, stopping off at Blackbushe to find that his old 139 Squadron friend, Wg Cdr Mike K. Sewell, was in command of 162 Squadron. Philip Back asked for a 'job'. Sewell granted his wish. Elated, the Backs set off again, but they only got as far as Stevenage. It was VJ-Night, so they turned around and drove to London to join in the wild celebrations, but their black Ford got only as far as Oxford Street, which was blocked by thousands of delirious, flag-waving and cheering crowds. Their car was picked up bodily by an enthusiastic throng and carried through Oxford Street, until they were lowered gently onto the road. They made their way, with the rest of the milling crowds, to Buckingham Palace, where Philip and June climbed onto the Queen Victoria Memorial amid the gathered news cameramen to witness the grand sight of HM King George VI, Queen Elizabeth, the Princesses and Winston Churchill wave to the massed crowds.

Philip Back DFC motored back to Woodhall Spa, and a few days later drove down to Blackbushe again to take up flying duties with 162 Squadron. He was crewed with Tim Baron. As well as delivering documents and diplomatic mail to many European capitals, 162 Squadron was also tasked with making regular deliveries of daily newspapers to these capitals, and to certain RAF bases in Germany and Holland.

Only some of 162 Squadron had continued with their unit – the bulk were brought in from tour-expired aircrews selected from the other 8 (PFF) Group Mosquito squadrons. After their fortieth op, John Clark and Bill Henley, who had flown fifty-one ops together in 571 and 162 Squadrons up until 25 April 1945, had gone on leave, only to return to Bourn to discover that the airfield was deserted. Crews had either been pensioned off or posted to a holding unit. Ground crews had been offered 'Cook's Tours' over bombed-out German cities, although some had refused to go, claiming the trips were too dangerous! For Clark and Henley there would be no more flak, no more fighters, no more searchlights and no more night-fighters. There would be no more passing the cemetery the Americans were making at Madingley, either. Their war might have been over, but their days flying the Mosquito had not ended, for they, too, joined the 'élite' at Blackbushe. Henley could have returned to his native New Zealand if he had wanted, but he said to Clark, 'I've been thinking about it and I've decided it would be stupid not to see Europe and elsewhere at the Air Force's expense, before heading back home. I might even find my brother's grave in Crete. From what the Adj said, we'll be swanning around all the capital cities and seeing a bit of the world we've never seen before.'

John Clark was delighted. They had been a team, the two of them, and he would have felt 'pretty lost' without him. But Bill Henley had made the wrong decision when he decided to see Europe and the Middle East. John Clark explains:

A month or so after our arrival in Blackbushe, I was detailed by the CO to navigate a wing commander from the Air Ministry to Cairo. We spent a week there. Meanwhile, Bill had been crewed up with another navigator and detailed to ferry a Mosquito to Malta. He and the navigator were returning in a Dakota transport. The pilot was flying serenely through a layer of cloud embedded in the stratus layer; a death's head if ever there was one! The aircraft was torn to pieces. The passengers and crew were flung out and scattered over the countryside. I learned about it on my return from Cairo. I felt almost guilty when I heard the news. It was the only time Bill and I had not flown together. Better that he had returned to New Zealand and tried to teach the Kiwi birds there how to fly.

Philip Back and Tim Baron also had a close shave. The flight on 23 December 1945 to Kastrop in Denmark with a consignment of diplomatic mail went well enough, and they returned late on Christmas Eve with a radiogram, Christmas turkey, cutlery and Copenhagen china secreted in the bomb-bay. As Philip approached Blackbushe in the dark, half-way down the runway the chap in the tower turned off the perimeter lights. Philip had yet to cross the A30 road, which bisected the end of the landing strip!

All I could do was run-up my engines and flash my landing-lights on to warn the cars on the road to stop while I crossed in front of them! Fortunately, they did and I crossed to my dispersal without further incident. I arrived at my in-laws' home at Camberley laden with presents from Denmark like Santa Claus.

Michael Carreck DFC and his pilot, Peter Rowland, made a flight to Rome, as Carreck recalls:[4]

Pete unstuck us from the Blackbushe runway early one dark morning with every square inch of the Mosquito's cockpit, the glass nose up front and the space behind the radio packed with tins of cocoa. Unrationed cocoa might have been in short supply, but our local grocers knew that we 162 crews were now a mass market. They laid in huge supplies and we bought it by the hundredweight.

Pete checked the Cocoa Express in at Ciampino Airport and off went the cocoa to Italian kitchens. Lira in heaps awaited our pleasure. We got out into the streets of Rome, where likeable traders retailed goods that fell off the backs of lorries. They offered us bargains, 'Because you are my friend', after thirty seconds' acquaintance. We stocked up on wristwatches by the dozen.

A day or two of luxurious living in Rome, and then we lifted off for Athens and lobbed in at Hassani Airport. There was a 'Knock, knock' at our door once again, and shrill squeaks greeted the first sniff of tobacco. Cigarettes were the hard currency of Europe. Folding money was just paper. Put it away, anything could happen to it. 'Real' money was cigarettes. For them a man would sell the family farm, treasured heirlooms and, if pushed, his darling daughter.

Sadly, what with the sign, 'No Cigarettes', Pete and I could only gather a hundred or two at a time, even from our carefully wooed tobacconists, small change for us 'Blackbushe Barons'. Greece, however, harvested its own tobacco. Our beaming clients departed, ticking loudly, as Pete and I began stuffing cigarettes by the thousand into canvas kitbags. And so back to Rome – lira like you wouldn't believe. Out to the shops and then Blackbushe.

On one flight back from Rome we ran into dirty weather – no chance of reaching home. We pondered where to land. Avignon, I suggested. Fortunately, on the circuit we happened to notice a P-51 Mustang nose on runway, tail in the air. Whereupon Pete mentioned he'd never seen the Leaning Tower. Then, horror, as we touched down at the USAAF airfield at Pisa a throttle link snapped. Our undercart buckled, our props bent back, we slid along like a flat-out Ferrari, steel strips of runway rearing up behind us like twisted Meccano until we screeched to a shuddering halt, inches this side of an alarmingly deep ditch. In moments we were surrounded by the United States Army Air Force. 'A screwdriver, a screwdriver!' cried Pete. 'Guy's in shock, Homer', said a 'lootenant' to a nearby sergeant. 'Go fetch a sonovabitch screwdriver.' But Pete wasn't in shock. He was unscrewing the wing panels of what was left of our Mosquito, and tossing out parcels, featherweight parcels – the morning's shopping in Rome.

Nylons! Nylons! For a pair of which a girl might well surrender her virginity to an American GI. Nylons for stocking-deprived girls in Britain who were crayoning make-believe seams down the backs of their legs. 'Nylons! Oh, darling, however can I thank you?'

Alf Rogers and his pilot, Flt Lt McEwan, flew a Pampa over Denmark and northern Germany on 24 May 1946, just a few weeks before demob. Rogers recalls:[5]

We took off at 0520 into 10/10ths low cloud and rain. These conditions persisted until we were about thirty miles out over the North Sea, when we suddenly ran into clear skies and bright morning sunshine. This was going to be a pleasure trip. A weather flight with no weather to report. So we sat back and admired the view. On the homeward leg we noticed that for some reason the fuel consumption rate was somewhat greater than usual. A quick bit of mental arithmetic confirmed that we would have enough fuel to get back home, but not much to spare. As we approached the bad weather we had left behind some three hours earlier, Mac called up base to enquire about conditions there. They assured us that though the weather was not good it should not be a problem, so there was no need to divert. So we carried on to base. There we found cloud base about 500 feet, raining heavily and very limited visibility. By now we had not enough fuel left to divert – we were committed to landing at base. We began to orbit base preparatory to landing, but visibility was so restricted that after a couple of circuits we lost sight of the aerodrome. I immediately thought of Lincoln Cathedral up on a hill a few miles to the south of base. So I told Mac to head north for a couple of minutes and I would guide him back using GEE. By now the fuel situation was critical – we had to get down – soon!

As we approached base using GEE, Mac caught sight of a runway. It was not the runway in use, but we were in no position to bother about such niceties. He selected wheels and flaps down and called control to say we were coming in cross-wind. He told me to watch the undercarriage lights while he concentrated on what was going to be a difficult low-level approach. When we reached the point of touch-down I said, 'Wheels not down yet.' Mac said, 'Oh Dear', – or words to that effect! As he began to open the throttles to go round again the undercarriage lights came on and I called out, 'Wheels down!' He cut the throttles and we hit the runway somewhat harder than usual. We veered off the runway onto the wet grass and skidded and slithered our way to the perimeter track. We taxied round to dispersal with the fuel gauges uncomfortably near to 'empty'. After parking we climbed out commenting, 'It's a bit too near demob for this kind of thing!'

In September 1949 the Mosquitoes flew in the Battle of Britain flypast over Buckingham Palace, the last time they were to do so. Iain R. Dick, a pilot on 4 Squadron at Wahn, just south of Cologne, recalls:

No. 4 Squadron was detailed to fly to West Malling for our Mossie Mk VIs to fly in the Battle of Britain flypast. On return we were to relocate at Celle. Because the squadron only had seven aircraft, the eighth having been purloined by the station commander as his own personal hack, we were forced to 'borrow' a machine from our sister squadron, No. 11 – which, quite naturally, leant us the tattiest one that it had, to make up the flight. After the flypast, we entertained the crowds at West Malling Open Day with some formation and dives and low-level bombing on the airfield. I flew 'jockey' with the flight commander, Flight Lieutenant Jimmy Gill, the last time he ever flew as a pilot, having to transfer to the Equipment Branch owing to high-tone deafness. I was to do the R/T. (Jimmy eventually retired as an air vice-marshal and donator of the Gill Sword.)

On our return to BAFO after the show, on the Sunday, I was detailed to fly the 11 Squadron heap of timber back. I lined up on the runway after our lovely, immaculate seven aircraft had left

(I suppose so that my heap didn't disgrace them!) and 'led with the port trigger'. However, as the throttles reached the end of their travel, so I thought, I edged the starboard lever that extra fraction. Unfortunately, being a poor old heap of a machine, I was not aware that the wire across the 'gate' was not there, so the starboard engine went into overdrive! As I slewed off the runway onto the grass, I was horrified to see in front of me the West Malling Gliding Club in full operation. By locking the brakes and slewing around a bit I managed to miss them, apologized profusely to the tower, taxied back to the starting-point and tried again, this time using only ¾ throttle – and with a VERY red face. We made it okay the second time ...

Sadly, not all the Mosquito men made it to de-mob. Flg Off Richard A. Sargeant, a 22-year-old navigator born in Wandsworth, who before the war had been an apprentice electrician at Harrods, had begun his RAF training in 1941. After completing training in Canada in 1943 Dick Sargeant began Mosquito training at the end of January 1945, and afterwards joined 162 Squadron. On 8 May 1945 he and his fiancée Betty celebrated the end of the war in Europe. They thought they were now safe, and intended to marry in 1947. Meanwhile, he and his pilot, Flg Off Roy T. Philip RAFVR, had begun flying newspapers and mail to the continent. On Saturday 18 August Betty received a telephone call to say that Dick was missing. A few days later she received a telegram. What she dreaded became a sad truth. On the morning of 16 August Philip and Sargeant's Mosquito had hit a hill near Berlebeck, south of Detmold. There were no survivors. Part of Betty died with him the first time, of loss, but eventually she promised herself not to die a second death, of forgetting him.

He continued to live on in her memory as the young man of 21 whom she adored, always in his springtime, while Betty moved into autumn and winter.[6] In all, 55,573 Bomber Command crew did not return during the war. To paraphrase a famous poem:

> *They are not dead – but only flying higher.*
> *Higher than they've flown before.*

Notes

1. MAA *The Mossie* Vol.15, January 1997. John Gover flew thirteen operations to Berlin in 1944. On the night of 4/5 June he crashed returning from a raid on Cologne, and his navigator, Flg Off Edward Talbot DFC, was killed. See *Mosquito Menacing The Reich*. Martin W. Bowman (Pen & Sword, 2008).
2. MAA *The Mossie* Vol. 13, April 1996.

3. They were, in fact, all known by their military code numbers: B61, B56, Y99, R14, B151, Bl18, and B93 respectively.
4. MAA *The Mossie* Vol. 34, September 2003. On 25 September 1942 Plt Off Pete W.T. Rowland had been one of the four 105 Squadron pilots who took part in the raid on the *Gestapo* HQ in Oslo. Carreck had been an observer on Blenheims at 17 OTU Upwood, 2 Group's finishing school, before being posted to 105 Squadron at Swanton Morley in late 1941. He took part in many Mosquito operations, finishing with the 6 December 1942 raid by ninety-three light bombers on the Philips works. His tour over, he was posted to 17 OTU 'on rest' as an instructor. See *Mosquito Menacing The Reich*. Martin W. Bowman (Pen & Sword, 2008).
5. MAA The Mossie Vol. 26, late summer 2000.
6. MAA *The Mossie* Vol.18, January 1999.

Index

Aachen 23, 27, 30, 32
Aalborg 69
Aarhus raid 224
Acklington 39, 64, 71
Addison AVM E B 72
Allison F/L George E 198–200
Amiens prison raid 218–224
Amiens 31–32, 240
Anti-*Diver* patrols 100, 108
Apeldoorn 64
Arden Tom 97–99
Arnhem 233, 252
Arnsburg viaduct 184
Atkins, F/L Eric 'Tommy' DFC* KW* 226–227, 235–236
Aulnoye 31

Back Philip 120–121, 136–137, 178–179, 189, 261–262
Bailey, F/O R K 73–78
Bannock W/C Russ DFC* 111–112, 197, 208, 216–217
Barclay F/O William 'Bill' 247–250
Barwell S/L Eric DFC 101
Bath 197
Bawdsey 107
Beckett F/O J R RAAF 44–45

Bedford 38
Bennett AVM Don 17, 118, 181, 189
Benson S/L James G DFC 68
Berggren S/L J V 9
Berlin 8–9, 22, 26–27, 132–133, 135, 138–139, 141–143, 158–159, 169, 178, 181, 184–188, 195
Bielefeld viaduct 184
Bircham newton 161
Birchmore F/L R B DFC* 119
Blackbushe 257, 261
Blessing S/L Bill 18
Bochum 24, 26–27
Bodenplatte Operation 237–238
Bonn 26
Boothby Graffoe 39
Boulter F/O Herbert 'Ed' DFC 141–142, 168–169, 179–181, 188
Bourn 174, 183
Bradel Major Walter 66–67, 81
Bradwell Bay 44
Braithwaite, S/L Dennis 20–21, 119
Brandon F/L Lewis DSO DFC 68
Bray F/L Robert W 22

Broadley F/L J A 'Peter' DSO DFC DFM 220, 223
Bromley 45
Broom, AM Sir Ivor 19, 141, 165, 180–181, 189
Broom, Tommy DFC** 19, 165
Browning General 225
Bruce F/O Bob 197–198, 208, 217
Brumby Bill 245–246
Brunswick 137, 139
Bufton W/C 'Hal' E DFC AFC 17
Bunting F/L Edward 48, 87, 95–96
Burbridge S/L Branse 53, 61
Burmeister & Wain 8

Caesar-Gordon P/O Angus DFM 25, 35
Caine P/O John Todd 191–192, 213–214, 217, 262
Cambrai 235
Cambridge 51, 94, 120
Carl Zeiss instrument Works 10–11
Carreck Mike DFC 262–263, 266
Carter F/L Arthur C 'Nick' 125–126
Caserne-les-Dunes 252
Castle Camps 37, 63, 69, 91
Chelmsford 45, 91
Chemondiston 50
Clacton 45
Clarion Operation 241–242
Clark Sgt John 147–160, 170–178, 181–186, 261–262
Clayton F/L Sid DFC DFM 7, 9–10, 12
Clerke S/L Rupert F H 38, 54
Clermont-Ferrand 191
Colchester 175
Coleby Grange 49
Colerne 65, 197, 200–201
Cologne 18, 24, 26, 140, 264
Cologne/Nippes 172
Coltishall RAF 24, 44, 88–89, 94, 96, 103–106, 109–110

Conches 29
Coningsby 144
Copenhagen 8, 191, 224
Courtrai 31
Crew S/L Edward DFC* 43, 57
Cromer 65, 91, 173, 175
Crookes F/O A Norman 197–198
Cundall W/C Henry John 'Butch' AFC 22–23, 31, 33
Cunliffe-Lister S/L the Hon P I 119
Cunningham W/C John 'Cats Eyes' DSO* DFC* 39, 42–43, 47, 55–56, 59, 61
Cybulski P/O A M 15, 70

D-Day 193, 196
Dedelsdorf 69
Deelen 29, 33, 68
Delune 191
Dessau 181
Detling 48
Dick, Iain R 264–265
Dieppe 38
Dortmund 65
Dortmund-Ems canal 143–147, 181, 189
Dow, S/L Roy DFC 187–188
Downham Market 162
Duisburg 24, 27–28, 31, 169
Dunkeswell 125
Düsseldorf 24, 26–29

Eastbourne 45
Eaton F/O Grenville 30–32, 35
Edinburgh 175
Edwards, W/C Hughie 8, 12–13
Eindhoven 65, 68
Elberfeld 29
Ely 34
Embry AVM Sir Basil 37
Endersby, F/L J S 188
Epinoy 235, 240, 242
Erding 210
Erfurt 184

Index

Essen 21, 24, 26, 28, 134
Everson F/L Reg 240–242

FIDO 173–174
Fisher, Lt 'Bud' 22–23
Ford 67, 190, 193
Forêt-de-Mormal 23
Forres 125
Foulsham 173–174
Fox W/O J E 'Jack' 30–32, 35
Frankfurt 33, 120, 122

Gabitas F/L Al 245–246
Gallacher S/L J F C 18, 21–22
Garrett Ernie 163
Gelsenkirchen 18, 131
Genoa 21
Gibbons F/L N J 'Jimmy' 210–213
Gill S/L L W G 105
Gilling-Lax Sgt Graham 45, 47–48
Gilson F/O Nigel L 233–235
Gilze Rijen 29, 68, 102, 246
Gordon F/L John 'Flash' DFC 24
Gover F/L E L John DFC* 257, 265
Gransden Lodge 142
Graveley 35, 120, 143
Gravenhorst 143, 145
Great Leighs 91
Great Yarmouth 109
Greaves F/L Douglas 107, 116
Green S/L Peter 46
Grimstone F/Sgt A R 'Grimmy' 46, 58
Grodzicki S/L Stanislaw 228–233, 241

Haddon F/L John A M 202–206
Hagen 23
Hague The 224
Hamburg 21, 24, 134, 185
Hannover 24, 142, 156, 158, 175, 181
Harris ACM Sir Arthur 38, 162
Hartford Bridge 97, 237, 244

Hay P/O 7, 19
Hayes F/O Gamble DFM 24
Hengelo 5–6, 8
Henley Bill 147–160, 170–178, 181–186, 261–262
Hildenborough 91
Hoare W/C Bertie Rex O'Bryen DSO DFC* 63–64, 69
Holmsley South 190, 197
Honily 52
Hopton 105–106, 109
Howitt S/L Geoff DFC 45–46, 49, 52, 56
Hunsdon 43, 45, 47, 53, 210, 213
Huntingdon 120
Hurn 99, 101, 110

Irving F/O George 'Red' 45–46
Isfield 47

Jameson F/L George Esmond 'Jamie' DFC RNZAF 197–198, 216
Jena 11
Jericho Operation 218–224, 240, 250–251
Jessop Wilf 241, 244
Job F/O Bernard 190–191, 196
Johnson Ben 99–100
Johnson F/L F A 'Ted' DFC RCAF 191, 210–213
Jones F/O W D 47, 52–53, 60
Juliandorp 33

Karlsruhe 139, 181, 191
Kiel 186
King's Lynn 38
Kinloss 125
Kipp Robert 191, 214
Knapsack 24, 26–27
Krefeld 28

Ladbergen 181
Laon 31
Lasham 215, 226, 233

Le Havre 98
Le Mans 31–32
Leeuwarden 29, 33, 73
Leggett F/L R W 99–102, 104, 110–113
Leipzig 27
Leverkusen 26
Lille/Vendeville 246
Limburg 174
Lincoln 39
Lintott F/O J P M 45, 47–48
Little Snoring 72
Little Staughton 125
Lockhart Andy 128–143
London 51, 85, 88, 131
Lowestoft 95–96, 107
Lübeck 36
Ludwigshafen 26
Luma 1st Lt Lou 192–196, 214–215

Mackie P/O Norman 167
Magdeburg 181
Maguire F/L Bill 47, 51–52, 60
Mahaddie G/C T G 'Hamish' DSO DFC AFC 120
Majer F/L Jurek 226–227, 235–236
Malan, G/C 'Sailor' DSO* DFC* 46, 58–59
Malta 3, 261
Manchester 111
Mannheim 135, 139
Manston RAF 28, 55, 173, 182, 193
Marham 17–18, 22–23, 28, 34
Market-Garden Operation 233–235, 252
Maulny Chateau 252
Mault Doug 243–244
McDermott W/C Peter DFC DFM 256–260
McIlvenny F/O Ralph J 202–203
McIntosh Dave 208–209
McRae F/O Basil 78–79
Meulan-les-Mureaux 31
Middle wallop 43, 51, 65
Middleton St. George 127

Midlane F/O Egbert J 'Midi' 99–100, 104
Miller F/L Reginald Arthur 'Dusty' DFC* 247–250
Misburg 181
Mitchell P/O T M 7
Mittelland Canal 143, 145
Moore F/L Val S RNZAF 119
Morris P D 242–243
Muirhead F/O G K 18
Munich 213
Myles F/Sgt V J C 'Ginger' 18–21, 122

Nantes 9
Neatishead 93, 108
Nijmegen 233, 235
Nixon Sgt W 'Nick' Nixon MiD 38–39, 86–87
Nomency 252
Norway 9
Norwegian airmen 50–51
Norwich 36, 43–44, 51, 65–66
Noseda W/O Arthur 8
Nuremburg War Crimes Trial 257
Nuremburg 137

Oakington 21, 118–119, 122, 147, 150
Orléans 10
Osnabrück 143, 169
Oslo 1, 4–6

Paderborn 9
Parry S/L D A G 'George' 4–6
Patterson F/O John 238–239, 246–247
Perry F/Sgt Edwin R 18–21, 122–125
Philip F/O Roy T 265
Philips factory, Eindhoven 6
Phillips F/O Jack 190–191
Pickard G/C Percy C. DSO DFC 220, 223
Pölitz 181

Ponchardier Dominique 224
Portsmouth 49
Predannack 67, 79, 207

Ralston S/L J R G DSO DFM 7–8, 10, 12
Ranfurly, Countess of 255
Raphael Gordon 55
Rawnsley F/L C F 'Jimmy' DFC DFM* 40–42, 47, 53, 56
Reynolds S/L Reginald DFC 8–9, 13
Rheinhausen 28
Robinson F/O G D 200–204, 206–207, 217, 237
Rogers Alf 72–73, 263–264
Rosieres-en-Santerre 240
Rouen 227
Rudd F/L Tony 240–242

Saarbourg 227
Sanders, Bruce 1–10
Sargeant F/O Richard A 265
Saunders AVM H W L 'Dingbat' 46
Schleswig/Jegel 68–69
Schott glassworks 10–11
Schultz P/O Rayne D DFC 69, 87, 99–100, 213
Scorton 39, 45
Seid Sid 208–209
Shand W/C W P DFC 7, 9
Shellhaus raid 224, 252
Shoeburyness 91
Simcock F/L G F 106–107
Singleton F/L Joe 88–89, 92–94
Sismore F/O E D 'Ted' DFC 11, 13
Skelton Bill 53, 61
Slade W/C Gordon 37–38
Smith Maurice A DFC 144–147
Smith P/O Derek T N DFC 120–122, 136–137, 178–179, 189
Smith R W 224–226
Smith W/C I S 'Black' DFC 36–37, 221

Solingen 28
Somerleyton 108
Somerville S/L James D 200–204, 206–207, 217, 237
Speyer 191
Spittalgate 120
St Dizier 69
St Trond 29, 33
Stainton F/O R G 'Bob' 198–200
Steinbock Operation 84–97, 115
Stevens F/L 18
Stewart 'Chunky' 245–246
Strachan F/O R A 'Dick' 25
Strasbourg 227
Stuttgart 181, 333
Swaffham 26
Szajdzicki F/L Adam 228–233

Texel 109
Thorney Island 215, 233, 238
Tilley-le-Haut 27
Tilty 113
Toulouse 191
Trappes 31–32
Trenchard, Lord 26
Trier 10
Trimley Heath 44, 85, 95
Truscott P/O Philip 37–38
Tulloch Bill DFC 174
Turin 21
Twente 29

Upwood 187

Vapour Operation 112
Varies-sur-Marne 31
VE Day 255
Venlo 29–30, 33, 68, 168
Vere F/O R H M AE 119
Volkel 33

Wahn 264
Walsh Sgt John 'Ginger' 238–240, 246–247
Wanne-Eickel 134, 181

Warboys 34, 120, 126, 147
Ware 38
West Malling 45–46, 264
West Raynham 73
Wheeler S/L Brian DFC 6
Whitworth John DFC 174–175
Wickett W/C Jack 241, 244
Wiesbaden 141, 181
Wight-Boycott W/C Cathcart M 70–72, 97
Williams F/O Brian 'Scruffy' 66–67, 81, 100
Witten 23, 28
Wittering 36
Wolstenholme F/O Kenneth 21–22, 28, 31
Wood F/L Ralph RCAF 126–143
Woodbridge 173, 179
Woodhall Spa 261
Woodman S/L 'Tim' 64
Wooldridge W/C John de L DFC* 15, 110
Wrotham 47
Würzburg 181
Wyton 17, 19, 173, 180, 169, 189

Young, W/C R H AFC 6
Yoxford 89

Zeals 197, 204